The Eisenhower Court and Civil Liberties

The Eisenhower Court and Civil Liberties

Theodore M. Vestal

Westport, Connecticut
London

Library of Congress Cataloging-in-Publication Data

Vestal, Theodore M.
   The Eisenhower court and civil liberties / Theodore M. Vestal.
      p. cm.
   Includes bibliographical references and index.
   ISBN 0–275–97284–4 (alk. paper)
   1. United States. Supreme Court—History—20th century.   2. Civil
rights—United States—History—20th century.   3. United States—
Politics and government—1953–1961.   I. Title.
   KF8742.V47   2002
   342.73'085—dc21   2001051175

British Library Cataloguing in Publication Data is available.

Library of Congress Catalog Card Number: 2001051175
ISBN: 0–275–97284–4

First published in 2002

Praeger Publishers, 88 Post Road West, Westport, CT 06881
An imprint of Greenwood Publishing Group, Inc.
www.praeger.com

Printed in the United States of America

The paper used in this book complies with the
Permanent Paper Standard issued by the National
Information Standards Organization (Z39.48–1984).

10 9 8 7 6 5 4 3 2 1

For Pat, Suzanne, Edward, and Charles, my Supremes

Contents

   An unnumbered photo section follows page 159.

Tables

Preface

For many people the Supreme Court of the United States is the most fascinating of our government's institutions. The nine, mainly anonymous, justices referee disputes between different branches of government as well as between states and the national government and protect individuals from constitutionally unauthorized government action. Their decisions affect the lives of all Americans. In interpreting the language of the Constitution and balancing the interests of the conflicting parties, the justices give meaning and application to our individual and group rights and liberties. In the process the Court, as the potent and omnipresent teacher, articulates contemporary American political theory. People who study the Court are thus concerned with the meaning of America.

"America" would mean much less if there had been no Warren Court. From 1952 to 1969, the Supreme Court under the Chief Justiceship of Earl Warren redefined the meaning of civil liberties and civil rights. The Court, among other things, put an end to government-sanctioned racial apartheid, nationalized the Bill of Rights in a due process revolution, started an equal protection revolution, required more representative legislative bodies, broke down puritanical restraints on artistic expression, and proclaimed a right of privacy. The Court achieved many of its activist-libertarian successes during the 1962–1968 terms, but several of its most significant achievements were accomplished by a more judicially restrained Court that operated principally during the Eisenhower administration and had, for a few years, a majority of justices appointed by Ike. That "Eisenhower Court" operated during troubled times when America was simultaneously coming to grips with ending racial segregation in the South and confronting the threat of communism at home and abroad. The Eisenhower Court justices disposed of many of the judicial "loose ends" left by its predecessor, the Vinson Court, and provided the framework for the crowning achievements of the later Warren Court. The way the Court operated at that time in achieving a generally more libertarian position in civil liberties is a lesson that should not be forgotten. Unfortunately the Eisenhower Court has been underrated by historians and is increasingly neglected as a subject of study. Many of the Court's decisions that garnered national attention at the time have been all but forgotten in the new century. This book attempts to remedy that situation by providing analysis of the principal decisions of the Eisenhower Court and looking at its justices and their work together to reach compromises in judicial decision-making. In describing the Court's labors, I have relied heavily upon the work of observers who were writing in the 1950s and early 1960s.

So many talented people assisted me in my intolerable wrestle with words and meaning and numbers that it would be a daunting task to list them here. Primarily I have learned much about constitutional law from my students. Study of the Supreme Court is a lifetime endeavor or, perhaps more correctly, a habit. As a student, I was told, "the law is a jealous mistress, demanding great attention but giving great pleasure." In passing on the wisdom of that declaration to present-day students with consciousness-raised expectations regarding gender, the best I can come up with is "the law is a handsome hunk"—a statement that doesn't convey the same eloquence, but the students get the point. The few, the precious few, university students who take the time to study the Supreme Court gain an informed knowledge about the real meaning of their individual rights. Such students usually are "hooked" on the subject and continue the tradition of constitutional law aficionados, following the Court as well as the elections returns—when the two are distinguishable—long after they leave the academy. These lifetime students come to appreciate the elements of liberal learning involved in the study of law, the courts, and civil liberties. Their interaction with me has been invaluable in my learning.

Among my teachers, colleagues, and friends who were especially encouraging to my endeavors were Sam B. McAlister, Fred Rodell, Robert Rutland, Donald Kommers, and Michael Tolley. Robert A. Horn, Arnold Rogow, and Don E. Fehrenbacher read an early version of this work and offered suggestions for its improvement. William Adsit, my student research assistant, did yeoman's service in helping prepare tables based on the Supreme Court Data Base. Grants from Oklahoma State University's Political Science Department, the Dean of Arts and Sciences Office, and the Vice President for Research facilitated this study, as did the assistance of Bill Elliott and James Lackey of OSU's Computing and Information Services. No work of this magnitude would be possible without the help of skilled librarians, and I symbolically tip my cap to the helpful folk at the Library of Congress, Manuscripts Division; the Yale Law School Library; the Firestone Library and Seeley G. Mudd Library at Princeton University; the Library of the State of California, the Stanford University Library; the Southern Methodist University Law Library; the University of Tulsa McFarlin Library and the College of Law Library; and the Library of OSU, especially the Patent and Trademark Library.

Introduction

No matter whether th' constitution follows th' flag or not, th' supreme court follows th' iliction returns.
Finley Peter Dunne, "The Supreme Court's Decisions" in *Mr. Dooley's Opinions*

Most of the time, the Supreme Court of the United States flits through the American psyche as part of a subconscious civics lesson. People are aware of its presence as an institution heading one of the three branches in the governing scheme of separated powers in the national government. But unless the Court hands down landmark decisions having far-reaching effects on government and society, the judiciary exists as background noise to "politics as usual" in the minds of many. Compared to the publicity-seeking, self-horn-tooting elected officials in Congress and the executive branch, the justices of the Supreme Court are an anonymous group about whom the public knows and cares little—until the Court shatters the complacency by interpreting the Constitution in ways that focus citizens' attention. That was exactly what happened when the Court not only "followed" the presidential elections of 2000 but actually determined their outcome. Suddenly the Court again was on center stage in the American political drama, and the media scurried to attempt to understand what the justices had done and to inform the public. For a fleeting moment the national spotlight focused on the low-profile Rehnquist Court whose election opinions would place it in the pantheon of historically significant Courts. Then it was back to business as usual—out of the limelight.

In contrast to the restrained Rehnquist Court that for the most part stayed out of the headlines at the turn of the twenty-first century, the Warren Court, the most important modern Supreme Court, continually drew public attention during its sixteen-year existence from 1953 through 1969. Under the leadership of Chief Justice Earl Warren, the Court seemed constantly assailed and defended for its acts and its failure to act. The Warren Court's revolutionary significance in cases dealing with civil rights and civil liberties, due process, equal protection, First Amendment freedoms, and privacy is well documented.[1] The fruits of this judicially inspired and led revolution profoundly changed the way Americans viewed politics, equality, and the protection of individual rights. Most of the accolades of the Warren Court are ascribed to what the Court accomplished after justices appointed by President John Kennedy joined the Chief Justice and Justices Black, Douglas, and Brennan to form a solid majority of libertarians who usually upheld civil liberties claims against the government. This consolidation of the libertarian bloc occurred before the beginning of the 1962 term of the Court. Scholars cite that term as the time when "the Court the public currently identifies as 'the Warren Court' came into being."[2] Historian Kermit Hall writes of two Warren Courts, the first existing from 1953 through 1962.[3] Mark Tushnet contends that "the Court's actions between 1954 and 1962 do not, on the whole and with the large exception of *Brown v. Board of Education*, play a major role in the public or historical perception of the Warren Court."[4] The nine terms of the Court headed by Warren before 1962 have been described as "beginnings," "stalemate," and "the early years." None of the titles are satisfactory and tend to downplay important work of the Court during that era.

If the "real" Warren Court did not come into being until 1962, what should one call the Court in the years from Warren's appointment in 1953 until the retirement of Justices Frankfurter and Whittaker? I suggest "the Eisenhower Court" as an appropriate title. There are several reasons to justify using the president's name to identify the pre-Warren Court. First, there is the precedent of the appellation of "the Roosevelt Court" for the Court during FDR's administration. Secondly, the period covered, 1953–1962, was primarily during the administration of President Dwight Eisenhower (with little more than a year overlapping with the Kennedy presidency), a time when "moderate Republicans" dominated government and probably reflected the prevalent views of society—as opposed to the liberal Democrats who were to come to power in 1961. Third, during this time, Eisenhower appointed the Chief Justice and all new associate justices, and the Eisenhower appointees constituted a five-justice majority on the Court from 1958–1962. Their accomplishments were significant in their own right and also set the stage for what the Warren Court subsequently was to do. This book will describe the work of the Eisenhower Court and its impact on the nation as reported by analysts of that time and pay retrospective homage to a Court that has not received proper accolades for its achievements.

VALUES OF THE EISENHOWER ADMINISTRATION

Presidents usually hope that their appointments to the Supreme Court will reflect the values of their administrations. Whether or not justices live up to the expectations of their presidential appointer, the political culture predominant at the time provides some predictive clues about how the appointees to the Court should behave.[5] A brief review of the Eisenhower years may help explain the ethos in which the Supreme Court operated in the 1950s.[6]

Eisenhower presided over eight years of prosperity, marred only by two minor recessions. By later standards, it was a decade of nearly full employment and no inflation. Indeed by almost every economic standard, it was one of the best decades of the century. Eisenhower's fiscal policies, his refusal to cut taxes or increase defense spending, his insistence on a balanced budget, played some role in creating this happy situation.

Under Eisenhower, the nation enjoyed domestic peace and tranquil-lity—at least as measured against the sixties. One of his goals was to lower the excesses of political rhetoric and partisanship. He managed to achieve that goal, in a negative way, by not dismantling the New Deal, as the Old Guard of the GOP wanted to do.

Ike wanted to see Senator Joseph McCarthy and his witch hunts eliminated from national public life, and he wanted it done without making the U.S. record and image on civil liberties issues worse than it already was. But his cautious approach to the McCarthy issue did harm to the president's reputation.

Eisenhower sought to provide a moral leadership that would both draw on and illuminate America's spiritual superiority to the USSR, indeed to the entire world. But on one of the great moral issues of the day, the struggle to eliminate racial segregation from American life, he provided almost no leadership at all. His failure to speak out, to indicate personal approval of *Brown*, did incalculable harm to the civil rights movement and to America's image.

On the other hand, Eisenhower completed the desegregation of the armed forces, and of the city of Washington, DC, as well as all federal property. He sponsored and signed the first civil rights legislation since Reconstruction. When he had to, he acted decisively, as he did in Little Rock in 1957. These were positive, if limited, gains. Ike boasted that they were made without riots and without driving the white South to acts of total desperation. Progress in desegregation, especially in the schools, was painfully slow during the Eisenhower years, but he was convinced that anything faster would have produced a much greater and more violent white southern resistance.[7]

Eisenhower was content to preside over a prosperous, satisfied nation that devoted itself to enjoying life, and especially the material benefits available in the greatest industrial power in the world. Perhaps the moderate jurisprudence of the justices he appointed to the Supreme Court reflected the values of that time.[8]

THE EISENHOWER COURT AS A SUBJECT OF STUDY

With the appointment of Earl Warren to the position of Chief Justice by President Eisenhower in October, 1953, the Supreme Court was in the news more often than at any time since the famous Court battle of 1937. The Warren Court was subjected to the most serious political attack on the integrity of the Court since the Franklin Roosevelt Court-packing proposals. During the first term under Chief Justice Warren, the Court found itself involved in a political controversy following the school segregation decision of 17 May 1954.[9] Individual justices were singled out for impeachment by legislators.[10] Southern members of Congress objected by issuing a *Declaration of Constitutional Principles* bearing the endorsement of nineteen Senators and seventy-seven Representatives.[11] Some of the justices even had fiery crosses burned on their lawns.

Southern opponents of desegregation were subsequently joined by other critics of the Court—those who contended that the Court had handicapped the fight against Communist subversion by its limitations on congressional investigating power and insistence on the procedural rights of "political offenders" and also by those critics who maintained that the Court had infringed on state authority over a wide range of activities, including economic regulation, procedure in criminal cases, and admission to the bar. At the same time that those criticisms were being made of "liberal" decisions by the Court, a less vocal group of critics possessing somewhat more "libertarian values" continued to find fault with its less libertarian decisions. Almost all of these critics centered their attacks on cases involving what can broadly be defined as "civil liberties."

The states-rights case against the Court on all issues except segregation was summed up in 1958 in a highly unusual document issued by the Conference of Chief Justices of the States.[12] This report specifically criticized several of the Court's decisions and also suggested that the Court had assumed "primarily legislative powers" and had come to exercise a dominance of authority incompatible with a system of checks and balances and a distribution of authority between national and state governments. The Conference of Chief Justices did not propose any restraints on the Court's authority but urged that the Court use its great powers with more self-restraint. The American Bar Association also expressed criticism of the Court[13] and lost the membership of Chief Justice Earl War-ren.[14] The Conservative press of the nation joined in the attack, charging judicial legislation on the part of a political Court composed of judges writing their biases into the Constitution.[15]

In Congress the assault on the Court reached its climax in the clos-ing days of the 1958 session, when a series of measures intended to re-verse or curb the Court were narrowly defeated.[16] Senate Majority Leader Lyndon B. Johnson persuaded several Senators who opposed the Court to be absent or "unavoidably detained on official business" during the crucial vote of the 85th Congress. Senators Jenner and Butler proposed measures[17] to deny the Court appellate authority in certain areas related to national security, which were defeated by the Senate forty-nine to forty-one.[18] An identical measure introduced in the House of Representa-tives[19] was also killed as were other proposals which would have reversed the Court's holdings in specific cases or changed the terms of office or qualifications and methods of selection of justices.[20] The Jenner–Butler bill was the high-water mark of congressional hostility to the Eisenhower Court. Similar bills were introduced in the 86th Congress, but proponents of these measures were unable to secure any positive action in either house.

The Court's opinions during the 1958 term rendered moot much of the criticism against it. There were still critics, but some of the Court's decisions concerning governmental control of "subversive activities" gave indication of a retreat from the former libertarian stand of the Court in that emotion-packed area, which had been a source of much public dis-satisfaction during the 1955 through 1957 terms.

The activities of the Court did result in positive congressional legis-lation following the *Jencks*[21] case. Other legislative "corrections" were in-troduced but not passed. Clarification of congressional intent, whether wise or not, is properly within the area of congressional discretion. But direct attacks on the Court, such as the Jenner bill seem destined to fail, just as the Court-packing plan of President Roosevelt failed in 1937.

Opposition to limitations on the Court's historic powers does not stem from the assumption that the Supreme Court is an infallible institu-tion incapable of error. Nor does anyone who understands the Court's role deny that it plays a part in the political processes of the nation and makes political decisions. Criticism based on honest thought should have some impact on the justices.[22] But much of the criticism of the Eisenhower Court was irrational and appeared to be based on no more profound prin-ciple than agreement or disagreement with the results of the Court's deci-sions.[23] There was frequently wide variation between what the Court was purported to have said and what was actually written in its opinion.[24] Of course, the Court was sometimes guilty of contributing to the confusion by saying more in dicta than it actually held, and for this, more literate critics properly pointed out the inconsistencies.[25]

By comparison with its immediate predecessor, the Eisenhower Court was bolder and frequently reached more libertarian results. This was not difficult, for the Vinson Court, after the deaths of Justices Rutledge and Murphy, exhibited such deference to the other branches of government in their substantive restrictions on free expression as to give the impression that the high tribunal had abdicated the field.[26] Perhaps this accounted for much of the clamor of the Court's critics, who became accustomed to a passive court and forgot that under the Constitution the judiciary has a positive, if limited, role to play in American society.

The activities of the Eisenhower Court in filling this role reveal three outstanding features: (1) Excluding Chief Justice Warren, the justices of the "liberal" Court appointed by Eisenhower were not ultra-libertarians of the Black–Douglas variety, but neither were they of the less-libertarian type exemplified by Justice Clark, who was the sole survivor of the Vinson Court majority. Instead, the Eisenhower justices fell into a middle ground between the two extremes with Justice Frankfurter occupying a central position in their midst. (2) Even though the Eisenhower justices could be classified as middle-of-the-road, they pushed the Court into a more libertarian position in the field of civil liberties. Their "hidden hand" techniques and indirect correction of oppressive actions of the government accomplished much more than was realized. In using this strategy the Court was conducting its business in a manner similar to that employed by President Eisenhower. Fred Greenstein described Eisenhower's hidden-hand ploy to conceal his activities "by adopting a crisis-minimizing demeanor in volatile situations." The president made careful use of language to create smoke screens for his successful actions. Frequently, the Court did too.[27] (3) Critics maintained that careful examination of the cases indicated that, other than in the field of segregation, the Court was effecting few constitutional changes at all and that its long-run influence on the course of American constitutional law might prove to be much less than intimated by the tumult.[28] The critics were very wrong.

This study will attempt to verify these findings and to examine their ramifications by (1) critically analyzing the important civil liberties cases decided by the Supreme Court under the Chief Justiceship of Earl Warren in the 1953–1961 terms, and (2) examining the politics and values of the justices as revealed in their voting behavior with particular attention to the justices appointed by President Eisenhower. This investigation will follow closely the statistical methods developed by Professor C. Herman Pritchett[29] and later augmented by Professor Glendon A. Schubert.[30] The source of statistics is Harold J. Spaeth's monumental *United States Supreme Court Judicial Data Base*[31] that has made possible much of the meaningful work involving numerical analysis of the Court. Divisions of the Court in nonunanimous opinions and the reasons for them will be analyzed. This work will be carried on with a full understanding of the limitation of statistical methods in dealing with materials of the kind involved here. Yet the work of Professors Pritchett, Schubert, and Spaeth indicates that such statistical methods have a positive contribution to make to an understanding of the motivations of the Court. This is especially so when statistical analysis is closely connected to a factual base—where fact gathering is given meaning by significant analysis. This study attempts to combine the two. The following chapter presents a brief introduction to the personnel of the Court, and Chapter 2 is devoted to the statistical record of the Eisenhower Court. Chapters 3 through 9 examine the decisions and the divisions of opinion in seven general areas where governmental regulation came in conflict with claims of individual freedom in cases involving political offenders, aliens and citizens facing possible loss of citizenship, First Amendment claimants, minority groups, defendants in federal and state criminal prosecutions, and voters. The concluding chapters tie together what has been presented before in an analysis of the voting behavior of the Eisenhower justices and their predecessors on the Court.

This study will be based on one major assumption—that the Supreme Court inevitably acts in a political context. This assumption has been so lucidly discussed in the past that there is no need to elaborate upon it here.[32]

One note of warning must be issued. A major barrier to understanding the work of the Court is the tendency to oversimplify the problems and to focus attention upon the immediate results of the decisions. In covering a topic so broad as civil liberties a brief review of cases can do little more than expose only a few of the difficult policy considerations that underlie decisions in the selected areas covered. It is hoped that this study will not convey a misunderstanding of the complexity of issues that form the daily work of the Court. For the justices there are no easy answers when competing claims in litigation are each supported by weighty considerations of public policy.

Finally, it must be remembered that the record of the Eisenhower Court covered here rests on litigation presented by only nine annual terms. Limitation of the study to a relatively brief period of the Court's history provides concentration of attention to the subject but leaves unanswered many questions which historians of a later day, reviewing the completed line of development of cases of the Warren Court and its successors, will be better prepared to answer.

NOTES

1. See, e.g., Alexander M. Bickel, *Politics and the Warren Court* (New York: Harper & Row, 1965); Leonard W. Levy, *The Supreme Court Under Earl Warren* (New York: Quadrangle Books, 1972); Mark Tushnet, ed., *The Warren Court in Historical and Political Perspective* (Charlottesville: University Press of Virginia,

1993); Bernard Schwartz, ed., *The Warren Court: A Retrospective* (New York: Oxford University Press, 1996); Lucas A. Powe, Jr., *The Warren Court and American Politics* (Cambridge, MA: Belknap Press, 2000); Melvin I. Urofsky, *The Warren Court: Justices, Rulings, and Legacy* (Santa Barbara, CA: ABC-CLIO, 2001).

2. Powe, pp. 209–12.

3. Kermit L. Hall, "The Warren Court in Historical Perspective," in Schwartz, p. 298.

4. Tushnet, pp.2–12; see also, Russell W. Galloway, Jr., "The Early Years of the Warren Court: Emergence of Judicial Liberalism (1953–1957)," 18 *Santa Clara L. Rev.* 609 (1978); "The Second Period of the Warren Court: The Liberal Trend Abates (1957–1961)," 19 *Santa Clara L. Rev.* 947 (1979); "The Warren Court: The Third Period of Liberal Dominance (1962–1969)," 20 *Santa Clara L. Rev.* 773 (1980); "The Supreme Court Since 1937," 24 *Santa Clara L. Rev.* 565 (1984).

5. Richard Funston, "The Supreme Court and Critical Elections," 69 *American Political Science Review* 810 (1975), finding that the Court is normally in line with popular majorities.

6. See Stephen E. Ambrose, *Eisenhower (Volume Two) The President* (New York: Simon and Schuster, 1984); David Halberstam, *The Fifties* (New York: Villard Books, 1993).

7. See Ambrose; Halberstam; Fred I. Greenstein, *The Hidden-Hand Presidency: Eisenhower as Leader* (New York: Basic Books, 1982).

8. Ambrose, pp. 190–91, 254, 282, 293–95.

9. *Brown v. Board of Education*, 347 U.S. 483 (1954).

10. *New York Times*, 19 February 1957, p. 63; and 8 July 1957, p. 15.

11. Ibid., 12 March 1956, p. 19.

12. Conference of Chief Justices, Committee on Federal-State Relationships as Affected by Judicial Decisions. Report 7 (1958); *New York Times*, 24 August 1958, p. 42.

13. Ibid., 25 February 1958, p. 20.

14. Ibid., 21 February 1958, p. 44.

15. "The Supreme Court and Liberty," (editorial), *Life*, 1 July 1957, p. 30; "Due Process vs. Survival," (editorial), *Dallas Morning News*, 19 June 1957, part 3, p. 2; "Efforts to Combat Communists Stymied by High Court Ruling," (editorial), *Dallas Times Herald*, 20 June 1957, part B, p. 2.

16. See generally, C. Herman Pritchett, *Congress Versus the Supreme Court, 1957–1960* (Minneapolis: University of Minnesota Press, 1961); Jack H. Pollack, *Earl Warren: The Judge Who Changed America* (Englewood Cliffs, NJ: Prentice-Hall, 1979), p. 196.

17. S. 2646, 85th Cong., 1st Sess. (1957).

18. Joseph L. Raugh, "The Truth about Congress and the Court," *The Progressive*, November 1958, p. 30.

19. H.R. 9207, 85th Cong., 1st Sess. (1957).

20. See generally, Sheldon D. Elliott, "Court-Curbing Proposals in Congress," 33 *Notre Dame Law* 597 (1958).

21. *Jencks v. United States*, 353 U.S. 657 (1957); see Chapter 3 this volume, *supra*.

22. "The Court Resumes," (editorial), *New York Times*, 5 October 1953, p. 26.

23. E.g., Rosalie M. Gordon, *Nine Men Against America: The Supreme Court and Its Attack on American Liberties* (New York: Devin-Adair, 1958).

24. See generally, Louis E. Pollack, "The Supreme Court Under Fire," 6 *J. Pub. L.* 428 (1957).

25. E.g., Philip B. Kurland, "The Supreme Court and Its Literate Critics," 47 *Yale Review* 596 (1958); "The Supreme Court and Its Judicial Critics," 6 *Utah L. Rev.* 457 (1959); Alexander M. Bickel and Harry H. Wellington, "Legislative Purpose and the Judicial Process: The Lincoln Mills Case," 71 *Harv. L. Rev.* 1 (1957); Robert B. McKay "The Supreme Court and Its Lawyer Critics," 28 *Fordham L. Rev.* 615 (1960); Anthony Lewis, "The Supreme Court and Its Critics," 45 *Minnesota L. Rev.* 305 (1961).

26. See generally, C. Herman Pritchett, *Civil Liberties and the Vinson Court* (Chicago: University of Chicago Press, 1954).

27. Greenstein, p. 232.

28. See generally, Daniel M. Berman, "Constitutional Issues and the Warren Court," 53 *Am. Pol. Sci. Rev.* 500 (1959).

29. C. Herman Pritchett, *The Roosevelt Court: A Study in Judicial Politics and Values, 1937–1947* (New York: MacMillan, 1948); "Divisions of Opinion among Justices of the U.S. Supreme Court, 1939–41." 35 *Am. Pol. Sci. Rev.* 890 (1941).

30. Glendon A. Schubert, *Quantitative Analysis of Judicial Behavior* (Glencoe, IL: The Free Press, 1959); "The Study of Judicial Decision-Making as an Aspect of Political Behavior," 52 *Am. Pol. Sci. Rev.* 1007 (1958).

31. Ann Arbor, MI, Inter-University Consortium for Political and Social Research, published and updated annually as study #9422.

32. E.g., Jack Peltason, *Federal Courts in the Political Process* (Garden City, NY: Doubleday, 1955); Victor G. Rosenblum, *Law as a Political Instrument* (Garden City, NY: Doubleday, 1955).

1

The Eisenhower Court

The New Deal Revolution of the 1930s was accompanied by a transilluminate change in the Supreme Court. In the early twentieth century the Court had been primarily concerned with defending the economic dogmas of the laissez-faire school of thought in protecting the property rights of the business community.[1] After the "switch-in-time-which-saved-nine" in 1937, which found the Court reversing its former anti-New Deal position and giving constitutional approval of the Roosevelt economic experiments, questions involving economic matters became of less and less importance in the business of the Court. The Court's old ideal of free enterprise and its profound distrust of governmental regulation of the economy gave way to a new role of the Court—defender of civil liberties.[2] The political characteristics of the era emphasized by the rise of "humane democracy" in the United States and totalitarianism in other parts of the world gave notice that domestic economic problems might well take a back seat in the constitutional order of a nation on the verge of entering a world war from which it would emerge the only great power capable of defending the values of the Western democracies.

The Supreme Court became the protector of the values enshrined by the political history of the New Deal. Organized labor, under the protecting wing of the Court, rose from an unfavorable position and flourished. The Court aided African-Americans in their movement toward racial equality in the eyes of the law through its decisions dealing with education, transportation, and voting rights. First Amendment protections were enlarged to cover a wide spectrum of activities by the states, from compulsory flag salutes in public schools to restraints on picketing.

In the postwar years the world of the New Deal changed. Labor unions, now powerful, no longer represented the underdogs of an earlier time. But more importantly, the spread of totalitarianism in the form of international communism cast a menacing shadow over most of the world.

The response of American democracy to totalitarianism showed signs of unpreparedness and misunderstanding, and this was especially so during the early days of the Cold War when government officials enforced laws that purported to combat totalitarianism by punishing freedom of expression and association.[3] What became obvious during the first postwar decade was that the threat of international communism was neither temporary nor an ordinary phenomenon.

The struggle of the American public and its representatives to come to grips with the problem of preserving traditional democratic values while combating a force which would subvert these values was reflected in the opinions of the Supreme Court under the Chief Justiceship of Vinson. The *American Communications Association v. Douds*,[4] *Dennis v. United States*,[5] and *Adler v. Board of Education*[6] cases gave evidence that there was no viable constitutional doctrine present. The majority opinions in those cases were tolerant of substantive government restrictions on free expression to the extent of giving the impression that the Court had abdicated the field. Constitutional tests of seditious activities of an earlier period were of little value in the mid-twentieth century. The "clear and present danger" test seemed unusable, although certain members of the Court attempted to apply it in their opinions. After the *Douds* and *Dennis* cases, there was doubt that it any longer had much meaning as a constitutional doctrine. The *Adler* decision, holding that public employment was a privilege and hence its deprivation not a punishment, was unrealistic. More controversial, however, was the majority's holding that in addition to one's conduct, "one's associates, past and present . . . may properly be considered in determining fitness and loyalty."[7] These statements gave indication that some members of the Court entertained grave doubts about judicial competence to evaluate the actual substance of antisubversive legislation.

Yet at the same time, "subversives" still received customary procedural protections. The Court preserved for suspected Communists such traditional American procedural safeguards as the privilege against self-incrimination,[8] rights to notice and a fair hearing,[9] prohibitions against excessive bail,[10] and strict adherence to the statute of limitations.[11] As for state law, *Wieman v. Updegraff*[12] struck down an Oklahoma loyalty oath for public employees on the ground that such a requirement could constitutionally apply only to those who knowingly join proscribed organizations.

While submitting to the substantive dictates of the popularly elected branches in dealing with "subversive activities," the Court continued to widen the scope of other constitutionally protected rights. State censorship of magazines and movies was given due warning by an expanded reading of First Amendment rights in that field. The scope of constitutional religious freedom was enlarged through interpretations of both the "free exercise" and "no establishment" clauses. State criminal procedures were found from time to time to be lacking due process. The Court's hostility to racial discrimination continued as seen in *Sweat v. Painter*,[13] *McLaurin v. Oklahoma State Regents*[14] and *Shelley v. Kraemer*.[15]

ACTIVITIES OF THE EISENHOWER COURT

This briefly was the history of the Supreme Court in the years leading up to the time of the appointment of Chief Justice Warren. In its first nine terms, the Eisenhower Court felt its way toward what might be called a "more mature" definition of its position in the field of private rights.[16] In the fields where the rights of alleged subversives were not involved, the Court was inclined to press the frontiers of constitutional liberty ahead fairly steadily even to the extent of laying substantive limitations on governmental power. This was especially true in race relations where the democratic ideal had long been undermined. The Court, realizing that the Communists made invaluable propaganda out of American discriminatory practices, played a major role in attempting to correct these inequalities.

When the Court was presented with the question of laws that circumscribed liberty for the very purpose of combating liberty's most menacing enemy, judicial response was less venturesome. The Eisenhower Court felt warranted to moderate the virulence of such laws in ways that did not challenge the substantive power, and the principal device for accomplishing this procedure was a strict reading of statutes so as to avoid the constitutional problems if at all possible. The result of this was that government might continue to "harass" subversives, but the judiciary had assumed the responsibility of holding the incidence and operation of the law to what the Court felt were reasonably narrow limits. This was an appropriately modest role, but no one who has grasped the significance of procedure in a system of ordered liberties would doubt its importance.[17]

AN ACTIVE ERA?

Upon the death of Chief Justice Vinson on 8 September 1953, President Eisenhower appointed Governor Earl Warren of California Chief Justice, and he was sworn in 5 October 1953. Many observers of the Court hoped that Warren's appointment would bring an end to the ineptness in the Chief Justiceship that had existed while the post had been filled by Vinson[18] and Harlan F. Stone.[19] The Court was still troubled by a division which dated back to the early days of Stone's Chief Justiceship. There was a great deal of ill-feeling between the so-called "judicial activists"—Justices Black and Douglas—and the "judicial restraintists"—Justices Frankfurter and Jackson. The divisions of the Court over issues were considerably more subtle and refined than those of the 1937 Court, but they were capable of generating heat and controversy. This is demonstrated by the fact that, based on the proportion of nonunanimous decisions, the Vinson Court had been the most divided in history.[20] Court statistics, documented by the data collected in Table 1.1, indicate that the division among the justices of the Eisenhower Court continued to be sharp. The number and percentage of nonunanimous decisions, the number of dissenting votes cast, and the number of five-to-four decisions became great again following a period of comparative harmony during the first three terms of the Eisenhower Court. Furthermore, if the Supreme Court under Vinson could be accused of being in a passive period,[21] then the Eisenhower Court must be considered to have been in an active era. More cases were being adjudicated, which indicated, among other things, that the Court was voting itself more work by writ of certiorari.

Table 1.1
Disagreement on the Supreme Court, 1950–1961 Terms

Term	Total Decisions by Full Opinion	Non-unanimous Decisions		Dissenting Votes		5 to 4 Votes
		Number	Percent	Number	Per Decision	
1950	98	62	66	168	1.71	15
1951	94	67	71	167	1.78	11
1952	108	87	81	204	1.90	9
1953	84	54	64	136	1.62	11*
1954	93	51	55	115	1.24	1**
1955	98	56	57	153	1.56	12
1956	121	86	71	205	1.69	13
1957	128	91	71	250	1.95	29
1958	118	69	59	199	1.69	24
1959	115	85	74	234	2.04	25
1960	128	87	68	235	1.84	26
1961	101	64	63	134	1.33	5

*Less than a full Court sitting during a considerable portion of the term.
**Includes 4 to 3 votes.

THE PERSONNEL OF THE EISENHOWER COURT

The Court, like any other group, consists of individuals, who, regardless of how detached or how scrupulously impartial, are part of the world in which they live. Judges are not automatons, and their values and prejudices influence their work on the bench. The personnel of the Court, then, make a difference in its decisions. It made a difference that the "Four Horsemen"—Justices Van Deventer, McReynolds, Sutherland, and Butler—were on the Court in the 1930s. It made a difference in civil liberties cases that the four "judicial activists" of the Roosevelt Court—Justices Black, Douglas, Murphy, and Rutledge—agreed on many libertarian values.

We must examine the thinking of the individual justices if we are to understand the civil liberty decisions of the Eisenhower Court or to appraise their significance in American life and politics. The fact of the relation between the judicial personality and the judicial decisions of a justice seems obvious. It is not so simple to develop means of appraising the influence of an individual justice upon the course or direction of the Court's decision-making.[22] He is subject to many contending forces and pressures when making up his mind, and possibly irrational thought patterns play an important part in his decisions.[23] It is, of course, impossible to reconstruct the thought processes of the justices, but in the judicial process, they impart some indications of their values and feelings. The votes of the justices and their reasoning in written opinions, whether for the majority, in concurrence, or in dissent, give us some clues.

Facts about the life of a justice may also indicate what matters will influence his decision-making process on the bench. His family background, education, organization memberships, and experiences are all potential sources of influence on his mind. For instance, a lawyer who has long been counsel for a railroad company may be very sympathetic, as a judge, to the cause of railroad company litigants. What a justice was, then, helps illuminate broad outlines of a pattern of thought and development that give direction to a judicial philosophy.

Chief Justice Warren, the son of a railroad worker, grow up in Bakersfield, California.[24] He took his law degree from the University of California and became Alameda County district attorney in 1925. Warren quickly made a name for himself as a racket buster and was elected state attorney general in 1938. He modernized that office but at the beginning of World War II, Warren was a strong advocate of the forced evacuation of persons of Japanese ancestry from the West Coast—an action he later regretted. In 1942 he was elected governor and served for an unprecedented three terms, once being nominated by both major parties under California's old system of cross-filing. The popularity of his administration made him a national figure in the Republican Party and its vice presidential nominee in

1948. As governor, Warren endeared himself to many of the "liberal" groups in the state by taking stands against racial prejudice and "loyalty" oaths for teachers and urging increased social security benefits. On the Court, Chief Justice Warren was described by *Fortune* as "calm, practical, hearty, persuasive, and stubborn."[25] He was also a modernizer. At the behest of Warren, the Court in 1956 began to record oral arguments—a long-overdue technological innovation. From that time on, historians could hear the voices of the justices and counsel in the give-and-take of the judicial process. During the Eisenhower Court era and throughout his service on the Court, Warren most often agreed with Justices Black, Douglas, and Brennan—especially in civil liberty cases.

According to Professor C. Herman Pritchett, a Chief Justice can exploit the potentialities of his position in two ways.[26] He can be the intellectual leader of the Court, dominating it by the strength of his personality and the coherence of his ideas. Such "task leaders" are justices who present their views with force and clarity, defend them successfully, and affect the Court's decisions and opinions. Chief Justice John Marshall was best described as this type. It is doubtful that Chief Justice Warren exerted his greatest influence in that manner, although he doubtlessly performed well as task leader upon occasion. More likely, he was, during his first three terms, a social leader, a compromiser or coordinator, the second important type. In such a role, the Chief Justice devises formulas on which disparate elements of the Court can agree and attempts to infuse his colleagues with a spirit of corporate response that is conducive to cooperative effort. In this regard, Warren's securing of a unanimous Court in the segregation cases was described as "a feat worthy of the greatest justices."[27] During his first three terms, while still learning the job of Chief Justice, Warren seems to have played some part in the marked degree of good will and cooperation evidenced by the great decline in the number and percentage of opinions with dissent. This was in sharp contrast to Chief Justice Vinson's last term which set a record in the percentage of dissents. The increase in dissents and five-to-four decisions beginning in the 1956 term may well be attributed to an accentuation in the polarization between Chief Justice Warren and Justices Black and Douglas on the one hand and the rest of the Court on the other,[28] with Justice Brennan a swing man between the two groups.

Public articulation of dissidence among the justices characterized several sessions of the Court during its post-1955 terms.[29] Fortunately this situation did not deteriorate into anything like that in the Court under Stone, when bitter personal feuds detracted from the prestige of the judiciary. Thus, Warren was credited with "massing the Court," holding it in line with some degree of agreement among the independent-minded justices. This was accomplished primarily through Warren's social leadership of the supreme tribunal.

The 1962 retirements of Frankfurter and Whittaker lessened some of the dissonance that had developed among the justices. By that time, Brennan had become Warren's closest colleague and the two shared both task and social leadership of the Court that was to transform the nation's constitutional law. During their terms together, the Chief came to Brennan's chambers every Thursday for a three-hour meeting to plan the Court's Friday conferences.

During the Eisenhower Court years, Warren developed a balanced leadership style that strengthened the Court as an institution. Warren's affability and dignity contributed to his being accepted as a leader by his colleagues. He presided firmly and politely during oral argument, in conference, and on opinion days. During the post-conference phase of decision-making, the Chief was the model of congeniality and was flexible in changing his dissenting and pass votes to majority votes, although he seldom defected from a majority. He was evenhanded in assigning opinions, assuring that each justice wrote approximately the same number of opinions, and he always took on a fair share of the more undesirable ones, the "dogs," himself. The Chief was respected for his rectitude, for his adherence to traditional American morality, and for his belief in the old-fashioned values of home, family, and country. Warren saw the law as an instrument to give effect to fairness, equality, and human dignity. He was decisive, yet he was willing to share leadership with others, letting Black preside over the first conference Warren attended and sharing task leadership with Frankfurter for a short time, and later with Brennan.[30]

The Eisenhower Court, during its first six terms, had several changes in personnel. Only during the 1955 and 1957 terms were no new justices appointed. Five Roosevelt and three Truman appointees served on the original Court over which Chief Justice Warren presided. Most were noted men of public affairs before their appointments to the Court. While on the Court, several of them, notably Black and Jackson had been considered for the chief justiceship, and Douglas and Jackson had nurtured presidential ambitions. Frankfurter and Douglas, both former Ivy League law professors, were active in trying to influence people in the executive branch and talked freely about cases pending before the Court. The reputation of the Court improved once Warren became Chief, and it was further enhanced by the caliber of justices appointed by Eisenhower.[31]

The senior associate justice was Hugo Black, who was President Roosevelt's first and most controversial appointee in 1937. Born in a cabin in Alabama, the son of a Civil War veteran, he had little formal education, including less than two years apprenticeship in a law office. Black practiced law in Birmingham, where he served briefly as judge of a police court. He was an able trial lawyer and was often in the service of the "little man" rather than corporations. Elected to the Senate in 1927, he built a reputation as a relentless investigator of lobbying and trusts. An ardent New Dealer, Black stood solidly for liberal values on the bench, although his critics liked to point to the fact that he had been a member of the Ku Klux Klan at an earlier time. Justice Black was the leader of "judicial activists" of the Court who were accused of being too concerned with making choices that gave the right result in each case. He was the outspoken champion of the "preferred position doctrine" (which will be explained in more detail later) and favored incorporation of all of the protections of the Bill of Rights into the Fourteenth Amendment.[32]

Justice Stanley Reed, the second Roosevelt appointee, retired on 25 February 1957, after nineteen years on the bench. A resident of Kentucky, he served in the Reconstruction Finance Corporation and as solicitor general when most of the major New Deal cases were argued. On the Court, Justice Reed was never labeled as either an "activist" or a "restraintist" but cast his vote with both groups at different times. He retained vestiges of the old South and purportedly refused to attend the Court's annual Christmas party when he learned that African-American staff was invited. In civil liberties cases, Reed usually supported government against claims of individual rights, especially if the case involved the loyalty-security programs. Perhaps Reed's greatest concern was the place of group liberty and individualism in a pluralistic society.[33]

Vienna-born, Justice Felix Frankfurter came to this country at the age of twelve and worked his way through City College of New York and the Harvard Law School where he was first in his class (1906). He worked briefly as a junior partner in a Manhattan law firm before assuming several positions in the federal government. In 1914 he returned to Harvard to teach and to encourage his students to seek public service. Frankfurter was known before his appointment to the bench by President Roosevelt in 1939 for his liberal reputation. His performance on the Court quickly departed from the expected liberal pattern, particularly in civil liberty cases. He appeared more concerned with developing a consistent philosophy of limited judicial power than in the social results of particular decisions.[34] At any rate Justices Frankfurter and Black became focal points and intellectual leaders of the two conflicting tendencies on the Court. Both justices were known as active "proselytizers" who tried to win over colleagues to their respective views until decisions finally were handed down.[35]

Justice William O. Douglas, appointed to the bench by President Roosevelt the same year as Frankfurter, spent his youth in Washington and came east to work his way through Columbia Law School. After a brief stint with a Wall Street law firm, he accepted a teaching position at Columbia and later became a professor at Yale. In 1937 he took a position with the Securities Exchange Commission and rose to its chairmanship before being elevated to the highest Court. He received consideration and support as a possible presidential candidate during the 1940s and as late as the 1952 Democratic convention. On the Court, Justice Douglas was a hard worker, turning out a large number of opinions each term, and beginning in 1955 he became the Court's champion dissenter. Over the years, Douglas, a staunch defender of the rights of the individual, frequently was in agreement with Justice Black on basic constitutional principles.[36]

The first vacancy on the Eisenhower Court was created by the death of Justice Robert H. Jackson prior to the opening of the Court's 1954 term. Jackson, a Roosevelt appointee, had served previously in the Internal Revenue Bureau and as solicitor general and attorney general. Jackson may well have been Roosevelt's heir apparent for the presidency had FDR not decided to seek a third term in 1940. When Chief Justice Stone died in 1945, both Jackson and Black were considered for the chief justiceship before President Truman appointed Vinson to the post. In 1945–1946 Jackson was chief counsel for the United States in the Nuremberg war trials. He possessed an acute mind and wrote with a pithy, brilliant style, often agreeing with Justice Frankfurter in expressing restraintist views. Jackson was accused, however, of being erratic in his civil liberty opinions.[37]

Justice Harold Burton, a onetime Republican mayor of Cleveland and senator from Ohio, was President Truman's first appointee to the Court in 1945. Truman so admired his former senatorial colleague that he attended Burton's swearing in as a justice—an unprecedented visit by a president to the Supreme Court. Burton was subject to criticism for his ineptness on the bench and held strong pro-government views in civil liberty cases.[38] In his latter years on the Court, Justice Burton suffered from Parkinson's disease that forced his retirement on 13 October 1958. His last three terms found him often in dissent from his more libertarian brethren.

President Truman appointed another former attorney general, Justice Tom Clark, in 1949. A Texas Democrat, he served as district attorney in Dallas County following his graduation from the University of Texas Law School. He left Texas for the Capitol in the late 1930s and worked his way up in the hierarchy of the Department of Justice. Subsequent congressional investigations questioned Clark's judgment in selecting some subordinates in the Department of Justice and caused criticism of his actions in connection with the Kansas City vote fraud investigations in 1946.[39] Clark also was criticized for his failure as attorney general to significantly advance civil rights issues. On the other hand, Attorney General Clark filed an amicus curiae brief in *Shelley v. Kraemer*, a landmark civil rights case in which the Court forbade judicial enforcement of racial restrictive covenants on the grounds that they violated equal protection. This was the first time an attorney general had filed an amicus brief in a case involving private parties. Clark, like Truman, clearly believed that communism was a real threat to American democracy, and he was particularly concerned with protecting government from communist subversion. As head of the Department of Justice, he organized the government's loyalty-security program and propagated the "Attorney General's List" of subversive organizations. Clark's judicial restraintist voting record on the Court indicated that he had little belief in the idea that the Court should prescribe boundaries between governmental power and civil liberties.

The last Truman appointee, Justice Sherman ("Shay") Minton, had been a senator from Indiana and an administrative assistant to President Roosevelt before his appointment to the Court of Appeals for the Seventh Circuit in 1941. After eight years of service on the lower court, he was appointed to the Supreme Court in 1949. Minton was the last New Dealer and last member of Congress to be appointed to the Court. Of the Truman justices, Minton was the most likely to believe in the beneficence of the government and the most willing to defer to decisions of the legislative and executive branches. Until his retirement on 15 October 1956, when he is purported to have said, "I'm an echo," Minton had established a reputation as one of the most illiberal justices in civil liberty cases.[40]

This, then, was the Court that Chief Justice Warren joined for the 1953 term. All of the justices were men of notable achievement in public affairs prior to their appointments to the Court. Several possessed prickly personalities as well as large egos. Whether the justices were considered nine scorpions in a bottle or nine opera singers who all wanted leading roles, the new Chief Justice faced a daunting task in leading this group. To use an operatic analogy, Warren, the accomplished director of a major provincial company, brought a record of outstanding accomplishment to the leading opera of the nation. There, in the midst of the full ensemble, he had to direct the Four Tenors, all of whom had sung leading roles and had their claques of followers. Lyric tenor, Hugo Black, in the company longer than any of the others, still had the high notes and rehearsed his roles very well; but he never commanded the following that he and his admirers thought he deserved. Dramatic tenor, William Douglas, could thrill audiences with his heartfelt phrasing; but he did not get along well with the members of the company and increasingly sang to himself. Spinto tenor, Felix Frankfurter, had a piercing voice that could be heard over any accompaniment. He probably sang too much and attempted too many roles, confident in his belief that his knowledge of *bel canto* surpassed that of any other singer. Frankfurter also was the most aggressive in trying to win new followers to his claque. Robert Jackson was a heroic or *helden* tenor of great talent, whose golden tones were among the most memorable heard in the house. Jackson, however, was never able to live up to the high expectations generated by his starring roles and rave reviews in his early years in the company. He was near the end of his career when Warren took over as director. The rest of the company primarily sang supporting roles. Under its two previous directors, the ensemble had real problems of intonation, and it rarely sang in harmony. The feuds, wrangling, and public backbiting among the strong-willed prima donna tenors produced a dissonance that had injured the reputation of the national opera. This was all to change, at least in the short term, under the new director and general manager, Earl Warren, who proved conclusively that he could restore harmony in the house and mount major new productions. After only a year at the helm, Warren faced changes in the company roster.

THE EISENHOWER ASSOCIATE JUSTICES

Upon the death of Jackson in 1954, President Eisenhower appointed John Marshall Harlan to the Court, and the personnel of the Court remained the same during the 1954 and 1955 terms. Justice Harlan, originally from Chicago, graduated from Princeton, went to Oxford as a Rhodes Scholar, graduated from New York Law School, and became a distinguished corporation lawyer. A staunch Republican, Harlan was named to the Second Circuit Court of Appeals in 1954, where he served for only a year before being elevated to the highest tribunal. During his brief tenure on the lower court, Harlan wrote some significant opinions which demonstrated that he possessed a sure instinct for the important question in a case.[41] On the Supreme Court, Justice Harlan concurred most often with Justice Frankfurter, and his clear and carefully worded and analytically sound opinions established his reputation as a "lawyer's judge" and the "conscience" of the Court. At the core of Harlan's jurisprudence was a strong desire to keep things on an even keel, to maintain a delicate balance in federal-state relations through forthright objectivity.

Upon the retirements of Justices Minton and Reed, two new appointments were made during the 1956 term. Minton's successor, Justice William J. Brennan, was a veteran of the New Jersey court system, having served on the state superior court and state supreme court. He was the first state judge to ascend to the Supreme Court since Benjamin Cardozo's appointment in 1932. Born in Newark, Brennan attended the University of Pennsylvania and Harvard Law School. A Democrat and a Roman Catholic, Justice Brennan was most closely allied with Justices Black and Douglas and the Chief Justice in civil liberty decisions. While agreeing with them in many instances, Justice Brennan often preferred to state his own reasoning in such cases. Eisenhower appointed Brennan to demonstrate to the public that partisan politics was not the major consideration in his judicial appointments. In reality, two groups probably influenced Eisenhower in his choice of Brennan: the Conference of Chief Justices of the State Courts, who pointed out that there were no sitting justices who had experience on a state court, and the Conference of Catholic Bishops led by Cardinal Francis Spellman, archbishop of New York, who noted that there was no Catholic on the Court although traditionally there had been (Frank Murphy being the last in 1949). Senator Joseph McCarthy opposed Brennan's appointment to the bench because of some public criticisms he had made of investigating committees for having indulged in what he had called "witch-hunting." Shortly after joining the Court, Brennan established a close working relationship with Warren, whom he referred to as "Super Chief."[42]

The mid-term retirement of Justice Reed was followed by the appointment of Charles Evans Whittaker. A graduate of the Kansas City School of Law, he practiced law as counsel for large corporations in Kansas City, Missouri. Whittaker's appointment apparently involved geographical considerations—the Middle West was underrepresented at the time. President Eisenhower appointed him to the U.S. District Court in Missouri and later to the Eighth Circuit Court of Appeals. On the lower courts, Whittaker showed an inclination to approve whatever the police considered necessary for combating crime and was generally tough on suspected Communists and aliens. A lifelong Republican, Whittaker boasted of having no political philosophy and being unconscious of any political leanings.[43] His voting record on the Supreme Court was somewhat erratic although he voted most often with the Frankfurter-Harlan bloc. With Whittaker's appointment, for the first time in the history of the Court, all sitting justices held law degrees.

Upon the retirement of Burton, President Eisenhower named the last of his appointees to the Court, Justice Potter Stewart (whose recess appointment was to be the last ever for a Supreme Court justice). The son of a judge of the Ohio Supreme Court, Stewart grew up in Cincinnati and was educated at Hotchkiss, Yale (where he was a Phi Beta Kappa), Cambridge, and the Yale Law School (from which he graduated cum laude). Stewart served in the Navy in World War II before going into the practice of law in Cincinnati. Appointed by President Eisenhower to the Court of Appeals of the Sixth Circuit in 1954, his opinions on that court served notice that he would not be a fire-eating libertarian.[44] Stewart turned out to be more libertarian than Burton had been, however, and became known as the Court's "swing justice" during the 1958–1961 terms. He was most often in concurrence with Justices Frankfurter, Harlan, and Whittaker. Of the justices, Stewart and Harlan probably were the most representative voices of the moderate Republican constituency that elected Eisenhower.

These men then were the justices through whom the Eisenhower Court spoke and who were responsible for balancing the claims of freedom and order in the civil liberty cases which the Court decided.[45] They had been appointed by the moderate, Eisenhower wing of the Republican Party and there was much more agreement between them and the liberals on the Court than would be true of Republican appointees today.[46]

All had been carefully selected. Eisenhower took an unusual personal interest in judicial appointments, and "unlike some of his successors in office, he did not rely on White House staff to screen potential nominees and to interview them about their judicial philosophy and legal views. Instead the Attorney General was the president's chief advisor on these matters."[47] Eisenhower had four basic criteria for selecting nominees. They had to be relatively young, have favorable recommendation from the American Bar Association's Committee on Judicial Appointments, have the approval of the local bar association in the candidate's home area, and pass a favorable background check by the FBI. Nominees for the Supreme Court were confined to those who had served on either a lower federal court or on a state supreme court, and their opinions were vetted by the attorney general. Most of all Eisenhower sought candidates of the highest possible standing in character, integrity, and ability—and who had "solid common sense."[48] The president also was concerned about balance on the Court between Democrats and Republicans.

Eisenhower regarded the Chief Justice's role as different from that of the associate justices. For example, the Chief Justice, as head of the judicial branch, is involved in matters of judicial organization and administration. In Eisenhower's selection of the Chief Justice, "previous experience in public affairs and administrative skill and abilities were qualities to be desired in addition to the usual requirements of judicial competence and integrity."[49] Although Eisenhower may have been reluctant to name Warren to head the Court, he honored a campaign promise to the former governor to appoint him to the Court at the first vacancy. When Warren was sworn in as Chief, the president made an unusual personal appearance.[50]

Before addressing the work of the Court, one myth concerning Eisenhower, Warren, and Brennan needs to be debunked. Many books about the Supreme Court or American government quote Eisenhower as saying his appointments of the liberal Warren and Brennan were "the biggest damned-fool mistakes" of his presidency. Eisenhower's Attorney General Herbert Brownell disputes such a statement. Eisenhower never made such a comment publicly, and the memoirs of the president and the Chief Justice do not support such a claim. It would not be in keeping with Eisenhower's temperment for him to make derrogatory comments about two of his most significant appointments. The only written source that Brownell could find for the alleged statement was in an oral history interview given by Ralph H. Cake, a former Republican national committeeman from Oregon and a longtime political enemy of Warren.

When Brennan resigned from the Supreme Court in 1990, the media reported that Eisenhower "is said to have said" that Brennan's appointment to the Court was one of the worst political mistakes he had ever made. Again, Brownell knew of no published basis for that report. Until someone publishes an "Eisenhower said to me . . . " report or better yet comes up with a recording of the president running down two of his appointees to the Court, the stories should be treated as apocryphal or at least not representative of Eisenhower's overall evaluation of the justices.[51]

NOTES

1. See generally, e.g., Roscoe Pound, "The Supreme Court and Responsible Government: 1864–1930," 40 *Neb. L. Rev.* 16 (1960).

2. See generally, e.g., J. Lee Rankin, "The Supreme Court, the Depression, and the New Deal: 1930–1941," Ibid., p. 35.

3. Robert G. McCloskey, "The Supreme Court Finds a Role: Civil Liberties in the 1955 Term," 42 *Va. L. Rev.* 735, 741–743 (1956).

4. 339 U.S. 382 (1950).

5. 341 U.S. 494 (1951).

6. 342 U.S. 485 (1952).

7. 342 U.S. 485 at 493.

8. *Blau v. United States*, 340 U.S. 159 (1950).

9. *Anti-Fascist Refugee Committee v. McGrath*, 341 U.S. 123 (1951).

10. *Stack v. Boyle*, 342 U.S. 1 (1951).

11. *Bridges v. United States*, 346 U.S. 209 (1953).

12. 344 U.S. 183 (1952).

13. 339 U.S. 629 (1950).

14. 339 U.S. 637 (1950).

15. 334 U.S. 1 (1948); see Clement E. Vose, *Caucasians Only: The Supreme Court, the NAACP, and the Restrictive Covenant Cases* (Berkeley: University of California Press, 1959).

16. McCloskey, "The Supreme Court Finds a Role."

17. Ibid., p. 745; Pritchett, *Congress Versus the Supreme Court 1957–1960*, pp. 128–133; Berman, "Constitutional Issues and the Warren Court."

18. John P. Frank, "Fred Vinson and the Chief-Justiceship," 21 *U. Chi. L. Rev.* 212 (1954).

19. Alpheus T. Mason, *Harlan Fiske Stone: Pillar of the Law* (New York: Viking Press, 1956), pp. 563–698; Robert J. Steamer, *Chief Justice: Leadership and the Supreme Court* (Columbia: University of South Carolina Press, 1986), pp. 240–292; Melvin I. Urofsky, *Division and Discord: The Supreme Court under Stone and Vinson, 1941–1953* (Columbia: University of South Carolina Press, 1997); Peter G. Renstrom, *The Stone Court: Justices, Rulings, and Legacy* (Santa Barbara, CA: ABC-CLIO, 2001).

20. C. Herman Pritchett, *Civil Liberties and the Vinson Court* (Chicago: University of Chicago Press, 1954), pp. 20–22.

21. John P. Frank, "Court and Constitution: The Passive Period," 4 *Vand. L. Rev.* 400 (1951).

22. Pritchett, *Civil Liberties and the Vinson Court*, pp. 15–16.

23. Chester I. Barnard, *The Functions of the Executive* (Cambridge: Harvard University Press, 1956), pp. 301–322. Masculine terms are used throughout this

book to describe the justices because there were no women among the brethren of the Eisenhower Court.

24. See generally, Irving Stone, *Earl Warren, A Great American Story* (New York: Prentice-Hall, 1948); Richard B. Harvey, "The Political Approach of Earl Warren, Governor of California," (unpublished Ph.D. dissertation, Dept. of Political Science, University of California, Los Angeles, 1959); G. Edward White, *Earl Warren, A Public Life* (New York: Oxford University Press, 1982); Bernard Schwartz, *Super Chief: Earl Warren and His Supreme Court: A Judicial Biography* (New York: New York University Press, 1983); Ed Cray, *Chief Justice: A Biography of Earl Warren* (New York: Simon & Schuster, 1997).

25. See the introductory comments accompanying Earl Warren, "The Law and the Future," *Fortune*, November, 1955, p. 107.

26. Pritchett, *Civil Liberties and the Vinson Court*, pp. 229–230; see also David J. Danelski, "The Influence of the Chief Justice in the Decisional Process," in Walter F. Murphy and Pritchett, eds., *Courts, Judges, and Politics* (New York: Random House, 1961), pp. 497–508; Danelski and Jeanne C. Danelski, "Leadership in the Warren Court," (Paper delivered at the 1986 Annual Meeting of the American Political Science Association, Washington, DC, 28–31 August, 1986).

27. C. Herman Pritchett, "The Supreme Court Today: Constitutional Interpretation and Judicial Self-Restraint," 2 *S. D. L. Rev.* 51, 59 (1958).

28. Bernard Schwartz, "The Supreme Court—October, 1957 Term," 57 *Mich. L. Rev.* 315, 345 (1958); "The Supreme Court—October, 1958 Term," 58 *Mich. L. Rev.* 165 (1959); "The Supreme Court—October 1959 Term," 59 *Mich. L. Rev.* 403 (1960).

29. E.g., John Osborne, "One Supreme Court," *Life*, 16 June 1958, pp. 92, 93; "Supreme Court: Dissenting Opinions," *Newsweek*, 8 May 1961, p. 27; Anthony Lewis, "Minor Cases Irk 2 on High Court," *New York Times*, 20 October 1959, p. 28; 15 December 1959, p. 25; Anthony Lewis, "Top Court Hears a Familiar Issue," 8 November 1960, p. 27; 21 March 1961, p. 1; *The Economist*, 13 May 1961, p. 674.

30. Danelski and Danelski, "Leadership in the Warren Court"; William J. Brennan, "Chief Justice Warren," 88 *Harv. L. Rev.* 5 (1974); Abe Fortas, "Chief Justice Warren: The Enigma of Leadership," 84 *Yale L. J.* 405 (1975); Schwartz, *Super Chief*, pp. 36, 47, 143–144; Schwartz, "Earl Warren," in *The Warren Court: A Retrospective*, pp. 256–275.

31. Herbert Brownell and John P. Burke, *Advising Ike: The Memoirs of Attorney General Herbert Brownell* (Lawrence: University Press of Kansas, 1993), p. 173.

32. See generally, e.g., John P. Frank, *Mr. Justice Black: The Man and His Opinions* (New York: Knopf, 1949); Fred Rodell, *Nine Men* (New York: Random House, 1955), pp. 263–66; Hugo Black and Elizabeth Black, *Mr. Justice and Mrs. Black: Memoirs* (New York: Random House, 1986); Tinsley E. Yarbrough, *Mr. Justice Black and His Critics* (Durham, NC: Duke University Press, 1988); Roger K. Newman, *Hugo Black: A Biography* (New York: Fordham University Press, 1994).

33. William S. J. O'Brien, "Mr. Justice Reed and Democratic Pluralism," 45 *Geo. L. J.* 364 (1957); *Justice Reed and the First Amendment: The Religion Clause* (Washington, DC: Georgetown University Press, 1958); Morgan D. Prickett, "Stanley Forman Reed: Perspectives on a Judicial Epitaph," 8. *Hastings Const. L. Q.* 343 (1981); John D. Fassett, *New Deal Justice: The Life of Stanley Reed of Kentucky* (New York: Vantage, 1994).

34. See generally, e.g., Wallace Mendelson, "Mr. Justice Frankfurter—Law and Choice," 10 *Vand. L. Rev.* 333 (1957); Clyde E. Jacobs, *Justice Frankfurter and Civil Liberties* (Berkeley: University of California Press, 1961); Philip B. Kurland, *Mr. Justice Frankfurter and the Constitution* (Chicago: University of Chicago Press, 1971); Melvin I. Urofsky, *Felix Frankfurter: Judicial Restraint and Individual Liberties* (Boston: Twayne, 1991).

35. Danelski and Danelski, "Leadership"; Wallace Mendelson, *Justices Black and Frankfurter: Conflict in the Court* (Chicago: University of Chicago Press, 1961); James F. Simon, *The Antagonists: Hugo Black, Felix Frankfurter and Civil Liberties in Modern America* (New York: Simon & Schuster, 1989); Jeffrey D. Hockett, *New Deal Justice: The Constitutional Jurisprudence of Hugo L. Black, Felix Frankfurter, and Robert H. Jackson* (Lanham, MD: Rowman & Littlefield, 1996).

36. See generally, e.g., Fred Rodell, "Justice Douglas: An Anniversary Fragment for a Friend," 26 *U. Chi. L. Rev.* 2 (1958); Vern Countryman, ed., *Douglas of the Supreme Court* (New York: Doubleday, 1959); James F. Simon, *Independent Journey: The Life of William O. Douglas* (New York: Harper and Row, 1980); Melvin I. Urofsky, ed., *The Douglas Letters* (Bethesda, MD: Adler & Adler, 1987). Douglas' 208 solo dissents during his career are the highest number of any of the justices.

37. Eugene C. Gerhart, *America's Advocate: Robert H. Jackson* (New York: Bobbs-Merrill, 1958), pp. 286–307; Walter F. Murphy, "Mr. Justice Jackson, Free Speech, and the Judicial Function," 12 *Vand. L. Rev.* 1019 (1959); Glendon Schubert, ed., *Dispassionate Justice: A Synthesis of the Judicial Opinions of Robert H. Jackson* (New York: Bobbs-Merrill, 1969).

38. Rodell, *Nine Men*, pp. 309–310; "Justice Harold Hitz Burton, United States Supreme Court," 40 *Kappa Beta Pi Q.* 35 (1956); Mary Frances Berry, *Stability, Security, and Continuity: Mr. Justice Burton and Decision-Making in the Supreme Court, 1945–1958* (Westport, CT: Greenwood Press, 1978); Frances H. Rudko, *Truman's Court: A Study in Judicial Restraint* (New York: Greenwood Press, 1988).

39. Pritchett, *Civil Liberties and the Vinson Court*, p. 20; C. B. Dutton, "Mr. Justice Tom Clark," 26 *Ind. L. J.* 169 (1951); Priscilla H. Machado and Mary P. Beeman, "Constitutional Reassessment: The Unheralded Role of Justice Tom C. Clark," (Paper delivered at the 1987 Meeting of the Southwestern Political Science Association, Dallas, 18–21 March 1987); Jan Palmer, *The Vinson Court Era* (New York: AMS Press, 1990).

40. Rodell, *Nine Men*, pp. 312–314; see also Harry L. Wallace, "Mr. Justice Minton—Hoosier Justice on the Supreme Court," (pts. 1–2), 34 *Ind. L. J.* 145, 378 (1959); George D. Braden, "Mr. Justice Minton and the Truman Bloc," 26 *Ind. L. J.* 153 (1951); Linda C. Gugin, *Sherman Minton: New Deal Senator, Cold War Justice* (Indianapolis: Indiana Historical Society, 1997), p. 282; Palmer, *The Vinson Court Era*, p. 13.

41. See generally, Arthur A. Ballantine, "John M. Harlan for the Supreme Court," 40 *Iowa L. Rev.* 391 (1955); Whitney N. Seymour, "Mr. Justice Harlan," 41 *A. B. A. J.* 434 (1955); Edward L. Friedman, Jr., "Mr. Justice Harlan," 30 *Notre Dame Law* 349 (1955); Tinsley E. Yarbrough, *John Marshall Harlan: Great Dissenter of the Warren Court* (New York: Oxford University Press, 1992); Norman Dorsen, "John Marshall Harlan," in Schwartz, *The Warren Court: A Retrospective*, pp. 236–255; "John Marshall Harlan and the Warren Court," in Tushnet, *The Warren Court*, pp. 109–122.

42. Francis P. McQuade and Alexander T. Kardos, "Mr. Justice Brennan and His Legal Philosophy," 33 *Notre Dame Law.* 321 (1958); Kim Isaac Eisler, *A Justice for All: William J. Brennan, Jr., and the Decisions that Transformed America* (New York: Simon & Schuster, 1993); Roger L. Goldman, *Justice William J. Brennan, Jr., Freedom First* (New York: Carroll & Graf Publishers, 1994); Hunter R. Clark, *Justice Brennan: The Great Conciliator* (Secaucus, NJ: Carol Publishing Group, 1995); David E. Marion, *The Jurisprudence of Justice William J. Brennan, Jr.: The Law and Politics of "Libertarian Dignity"* (Lanham, MD: Rowman & Littlefield, 1997); Frank I. Michelman, *Brennan and Democracy* (Princeton, NJ: Princeton University Press, 1999).

43. Daniel M. Berman, "Mr. Justice Whittaker: A Preliminary Appraisal," 24 *Mo. L. Rev.* 1 (1959); see also Marlin M. Volz, "Mr. Justice Whittaker," 33 *Notre Dame Law.* 159 (1958); Marlin M. Volz, "Charles Evans Whittaker—A Biographical Sketch" 40 *Tex. L. Rev.* 742 (1962); Barbara B. Christensen, "Mr. Justice Whittaker: The Man on the Right," 19 *Santa Clara L. Rev.* 1039 (1979); Richard L. Miller, *Whittaker: Struggles of a Supreme Court Justice* (Westport, CT: Greenwood Press, 2001).

44. J. Francis Paschal, "Mr. Justice Stewart on the Court of Appeals," 8 *Duke L. J.* 325 (1959); Daniel M. Berman, "Mr. Justice Stewart: A Preliminary Appraisal," 28 *U. Cin. L. Rev.* 401 (1959); Helaine M. Barnett and Kenneth Levine, "Mr. Justice Stewart," 40 *N. Y. U. L. Rev.* 526 (1965); Jerald H. Israel, "Potter Stewart," in Leon Friedman and Fred L. Israel, eds., *The Justices of the United States Supreme Court, 1789–1969, Volume IV* (Broomall, PA: Chelsea House, 1995); Potter Stewart, "Leaving the High Court," Sound Recording, Princeton University Library, Princeton, NJ.

45. For comment on prior judicial experience as a prerequisite to service on the Supreme Court, see Loren P. Beth, "Judge into Justice: Should Supreme Court Appointees Have Judicial Experience?" 58 *So. Atlan. Q.* 521 (1959).

46. Morton J. Horwitz, *The Warren Court and the Pursuit of Justice: A Critical Issue* (New York: Hill and Wang, 1998), p. 113.

47. Brownell, *Advising Ike*, pp. 176–77.

48. Harold W. Chase, *Federal Judges: The Appointing Process* (Minneapolis: University of Minnesota Press, 1972), pp. 91–94.

49. Brownell, pp. 163–175.

50. Ibid., p. 170.

51. Ibid., p. 175. In Merle Miller's biography, *Plain Speaking: An Oral Biography of Harry S. Truman* (New York: Berkley, 1973), President Truman is quoted as saying, "When you ask me what my biggest mistake was, that's it. Putting Tom Clark on the Supreme Court of the United States" (pp. 225–26).

2

Agreements and Differences

In the seven chapters that follow, the principal civil liberties decisions of the Eisenhower Court will be reviewed. An attempt also will be made to note the positions taken by individual justices in support of, or in opposition to, the doctrines announced by the Court. Identification of personal views will necessarily be subordinated to following the main lines of tendency. This chapter will be concerned with the positions taken by the members of the Court and their particularized participation rather than with the institutional product of the highest tribunal.

Professor Pritchett, a student of the Roosevelt and Vinson Courts, has probably been the most widely read statistician of the justices' voting behavior.[1] While admitting that there are difficulties in the path of any such effort, he rightly contends that his works are "at least a beginning" in the study of judicial voting behavior.[2] Most observers of the Court agree with Professor Pritchett that one of the most useful things to know about a justice is his location on the Court in relationship to his colleagues. His disagreements with the decisions of the Court and the company he keeps in his votes whether regular or by chance are also useful bits of knowledge, helpful in better understanding the work of the Court. Blocs of opinion have long existed on the Court, and statistical studies provide a systemic method of analyzing these associations. The large number of dissenting and concurring opinions handed down each term by the Eisenhower Court makes such studies desirable.

Data on judicial voting behavior can be effectively presented by a graphical arrangement, as in Table 2.1, giving the number of cases in which each pair of justices was in dissent together during the 1949–1952 terms of the Vinson Court.[3] In addition, the table indicates the total number of dissents for each justice. The names of the justices are arranged in such a manner as to indicate the bloc relationships by placing each justice as close as possible to those with whom he dissented most often and farthest from those with whom he had the fewest common dissents.

An Index of Cohesion, which reflects the average frequency of dissenting votes cast by bloc members in conjunction with other members of the same bloc is added at the bottom of the table. This index varies between zero, if there is no agreement, and 1.0, if all the justices dissented together. An Index of Cohesion of .50 or greater is considered to be high, .40–.49 is moderate, and less than .40 is low.[4]

Table 2.1

Participation of and Agreements Among Supreme Court Justice in Dissenting Opinions, 1949–1952 Terms

	Black	Douglas	Frankfurter	Jackson	Reed	Minton	Burton	Vinson	Clark
No. dissents	148	130	101	80	59	47	44	40	15
Black	(27)	79	49	27	11	16	16	13	6
Douglas	79	(18)	33	18	21	14	16	14	7
Frankfurter	49	33	(8)	46	13	10	13	2	1
Jackson	27	18	46	(13)	16	11	9	5	3
Reed	11	21	13	16	(6)	17	11	15	2
Minton	16	14	10	11	17	(3)	10	16	4
Burton	16	16	13	9	11	10	(2)	7	4
Vinson	13	14	2	5	15	16	7	(1)	8
Clark	6	7	1	3	2	4	4	8	--

Indices of Cohesion

Douglas–Black	.57 (high)
Frankfurter–Jackson	.51 (high)
Black–Frankfurther	.39 (low)

Such a table provides an insight into opinion on the Court. The total number of dissents for each justice indicates his disagreement with the general trends of the Court. Thus Justice Black with 148 dissents for this period was roughly ten times as dissatisfied with the work of the Court as was Justice Clark, who was in disagreement with the majority only fifteen times during the same period.

This table shows how the Truman appointees joined by Justice Reed dominated the Court. This Vinson Court majority forced the restraintists, Jackson and Frankfurter, into frequent agreement with the activists, Black and Douglas.

The charting of dissenting votes makes it clear that there were three separate blocs of dissenters. Placing the justices on the tables according to usual political designations, the activists are on the left, followed by the restraintists, with the Vinson majority on the right.

Another way to show basic agreements and disagreements among the justices is to indicate agreements in nonunanimous opinions between every pair of justices, whether on the majority or the minority side, on a percentage basis. Thus in Table 2.2 the blocs of the Vinson Court again emerge clearly.[5] Justices Black and Douglas had inter-agreement rates of 61 percent, while Justices Frankfurter and Jackson were at 69. The Vinson majority's agreement rate ran from 71 to 83 percent. This, then, was the lineup of the Court, excluding Vinson, over which Chief Justice Warren was called to preside.

Such tables reveal patterns of division, irrespective of the issues over which disagreement arose. A series of tables showing the alignments of the Warren Court traces shifts of judicial positions and the realignments resulting from the appointment of new justices to the Court.

Table 2.2
Agreement Among Supreme Court Justices in Nonunanimous Opinions,
1949–1952 Terms
(in percentages)

	Douglas	Black	Frankfurter	Jackson	Reed	Minton	Burton	Vinson	Clark
Douglas		61	40	33	42	36	42	39	40
Black	61		49	39	34	41	43	42	47
Frankfurter	40	49		69	51	52	58	51	59
Jackson	33	39	69		62	61	61	62	67
Reed	42	34	51	62		75	71	76	75
Minton	36	41	52	61	75		75	81	80
Burton	42	43	58	61	71	75		75	80
Vinson	39	42	51	62	76	81	75		83
Clark	40	47	59	67	75	80	80	83	

Indices of Inter-agreement

Vinson Majority	.77 (high)
Douglas—Black	.61 (moderate)
Frankfurter–Jackson	.69 (moderate)

Table 2.3 shows that the basic alignments of the Vinson Court held over into Chief Justice Warren's first term.[6] Justices Douglas and Black are still the leading dissenters and by far outstrip the others in their agreement in dissent. The Chief Justice rivals Justice Clark in the scarcity of his dissenting votes, and appears to have pulled Clark to the left of his former position on the Vinson Court. The small number of dissents in the 1953 term makes it difficult to adduce further conclusions.

Table 2.3
Participation of and Agreements Among Supreme Court Justices in Dissenting Opinions, 1953 Term

	Black	Douglas	Warren	Clark	Frankfurter	Jackson	Minton	Burton	Reed
No. of dissents	27	30	8	6	11	14	17	12	11
Black		21	6	2	4	3	5	1	0
Douglas	21		5	3	4	5	8	3	1
Warren	6	5		4	0	1	2	1	1
Clark	2	3	4		1	2	2	2	1
Frankfurter	4	4	0	1		6	3	2	0
Jackson	3	5	1	2	6		6	4	2
Minton	5	8	2	2	3	6		5	4
Burton	1	3	1	2	2	4	5		7
Reed	0	1	1	1	0	2	4	7	

Indices of Cohesion

Douglas–Black	.74 (high)
Reed–Burton	.61 (high)
Warren–Clark	.57 (high)
Frankfurter–Jackson	.48 (mod.)
Warren–Black	.34 (low)

The membership of the Court remained unchanged in the 1954 and 1955 terms following Jackson's replacement by Harlan, and these two terms can be represented in one table. Table 2.4 reveals a reasonably firm bloc of three justices on the left side of the Court with Chief Justice Warren finding himself most often in agreement with Justices Douglas and Black in dissent. On the other extreme, Justices Reed, Minton, and Burton were dissenting slightly more than the left wing (105 and 93 dissents respectively). The center of the Court was composed of Justices Frankfurter and Harlan who were most often in agreement with each other in dissent. Justice Burton had identical agreement records with these two justices and Justice Minton, although he agreed far more often with Reed. Justice Frankfurter's and especially Justice Harlan's records indicate that their leanings were much more toward the right of the Court than toward the left. Justice Reed, in his last two terms on the Court, dissented on the right almost as frequently as Douglas on the left. Justice Clark continued his established practice of seldom disagreeing with the Court.

The retirements of Justices Minton and Reed and their replacement by Brennan and Whittaker in 1957 caused a reorientation on the Court. Table 2.5 covers the voting alignments on the Court as remade in 1957. It shows clearly how the Court was basically divided into two camps. Justice Brennan joined the left branch of the Court while Justice Whittaker appeared to follow the pattern of his predecessor, Reed. An indication of

Table 2.4
Participation of and Agreements Among Supreme Court Justices in Dissenting Opinions, 1954–1955 Terms

	Douglas	Black	Warren	Frankfurter	Harlan	Burton	Minton	Reed	Clark
No. of dissents	46	29	18	33	24	34	27	44	13
Douglas		26	17	7	3	2	1	6	5
Black	26		15	5	0	0	1	2	5
Warren	17	15		2	0	0	1	1	5
Frankfurter	7	5	2		15	13	5	5	1
Harlan	3	0	0	15		13	8	7	1
Burton	2	0	0	13	13		13	23	2
Minton	1	1	1	5	8	13		22	5
Reed	6	2	1	5	7	23	22		7
Clark	5	5	5	1	1	2	5	7	

Indices of Cohesion

Douglas–Black–Warren	.62 (high)
Burton–Minton–Reed	.55 (high)
Frankfurter–Harlan	.53 (high)

a more libertarian tendency by the Court is evidenced by the increased number of dissents of Justice Clark who held the record for paucity of dissents on the Vinson Court and maintained it during the early years of the Warren Court. Under the pressure of more libertarian decisions by the Court, Justices Clark and Burton frequently found themselves the only dissenters, persisting in the pro-government view dominant during the Vinson era. The close voting tie of Justices Frankfurter and Harlan was reaffirmed during this period while their connection with Burton was somewhat higher than in the previous two terms. Justice Whittaker was closely allied with Justices Harlan and Burton, and never once during this two-term period was he in dissent with his fellow 1957 appointee, Justice Brennan.

One final change was made in the personnel of the Court when Justice Stewart replaced Justice Burton upon his retirement in 1958. The new appointee again fit nicely in his predecessor's relative position on the Court as seen in Table 2.6, but he joined the middle justices in dissent rather than Justice Clark. The less libertarian record of the Court is hinted at by Justice Clark's position of complacency, being in dissent only twenty five times during these terms. The other alignments remain primarily the same as those of the previous two terms. Justice Whittaker appears even more closely allied with Justices Frankfurter and Harlan. At the same time, the Chief Justice shows greater agreement with Justices Douglas and Black, while Justice Brennan shows a greater propensity to dissent with Chief Justice Warren and Justices Douglas and Black. Brennan also breaks from his moderate ties with Frankfurter established in the previous two terms.

Table 2.5
Participation of and Agreements Among Supreme Court Justices in Dissenting Opinions, 1956–1957 Terms

	Douglas	Black	Warren	Brennan	Frankfurter	Harlan	Burton	Whittaker	Clark
No. of dissents	71	55	39	30	58	64	61	31	38
Douglas		48	35	24	7	3	3	2	1
Black	48		36	22	5	2	3	2	1
Warren	35	36		19	0	1	1	2	0
Brennan	24	22	19		9	6	3	0	1
Frankfurter	7	5	0	9		40	27	12	8
Harlan	3	2	1	6	40		36	22	12
Burton	3	3	1	3	27	36		19	23
Whittaker	2	2	2	0	12	22	19		7
Clark	1	1	0	1	8	12	23	7	

Indices of Cohesion

Douglas–Black	.76 (high)
Douglas–Black–Warren	.72 (high)
Frankfurter–Harlan	.66 (high)
Douglas–Black–Warren–Brennan	.63 (high)
Burton–Harlan	.58 (high)
Frankfurter–Harlan–Burton–Whittaker	.49 (mod.)

Table 2.7 shows the voting alignments following the "Court-curbing" threats of Congress and other groups in 1959 and 1960 and the softening of the Court's approach to governmental antisubversive activities. Justices Frankfurter and Whittaker dissented much less frequently. Harlan and Clark were together in dissent as frequently as were Brennan and Warren. Clark dissented more often and was replaced by Brennan as the least frequent dissenter. By this time Brennan had established himself as a coalition builder and was successfully attracting at least four other votes to his side in many cases. The indices of cohesion declined for all of the blocs including associate justices appointed by Eisenhower. Especially noteworthy was the sharp decline in the Frankfurter–Harlan–Whittaker cohesion.

This rather complex pattern of alignments demonstrated by Tables 2.5, 2.6, and 2.7 calls for the additional clarification that can be supplied by translating these voting data into percentage figures. Table 2.8 gives the percentage of agreements in disputed cases during the three-year period 1956–1958 for every pair of justices. It indicates clearly a four-judge left, a four-judge right, regardless of whether the fourth justice is Burton or Stewart, and Justice Clark, with right leanings, playing the field. Justice Clark found the relatively incongruous group of the Chief Justice and

Table 2.6
Participation of and Agreements Among Supreme Court Justices in Dissenting Opinions, 1958–1959 Terms

	Douglas	Black	Warren	Brennan	Frankfurter	Harlan	Whittaker	Stewart	Clark
No. of Dissents	74	59	46	34	52	53	58	32	25
Douglas		49	41	30	5	2	6	5	2
Black	49		41	25	4	4	5	1	5
Warren	41	41		28	1	0	1	1	4
Brennan	30	25	28		3	3	0	2	0
Frankfurter	5	4	1	3		37	34	17	14
Harlan	2	4	0	3	37		33	21	13
Whittaker	6	5	1	0	34	33		23	13
Stewart	5	1	1	2	17	21	23		4
Clark	2	5	4	0	14	13	13	4	

Indices of Cohesion

Douglas–Black–Warren	.73 (high)
Douglas–Black–Warren–Brennan	.67 (high)
Frankfurter–Harlan–Whittaker	.64 (high)
Frankfurter–Harlan–Whittaker–Stewart	.56 (high)
Brennan–Frankfurter–Harlan–Whittaker–Stewart	.38 (low)

Table 2.7
Participation of and Agreements Among Supreme Court Justices in Dissenting Opinions, 1960–1961 Terms

	Douglas	Black	Warren	Brennan	Frankfurter	Harlan	Whittaker	Stewart	Clark
No. of Dissents	70	50	36	24	33	52	37	32	35
Douglas		38	31	22	3	4	7	7	2
Black	38		29	17	2	2	3	4	2
Warren	31	29		19	0	1	2	2	2
Brennan	22	17	19		1	1	1	4	2
Frankfurter	3	2	0	1		25	14	11	12
Harlan	4	2	1	1	25		17	16	19
Whittaker	7	3	2	1	14	17		11	12
Stewart	7	4	2	4	11	16	11		6
Clark	2	2	2	2	12	19	12	6	

Indices of Cohesion

Douglas–Black–Warren	.63 (high)
Douglas–Black–Warren–Brennan	.58 (high)
Frankfurter–Harlan–Whittaker	.46 (mod.)
Frankfurter–Harlan–Whittaker–Stewart	.41 (mod.)
Brennan–Frankfurter–Harlan–Whittaker–Stewart	.28 (low)

Justices Brennan, Frankfurter, and Harlan almost equally desirable to agree with. It is evident that Justice Brennan is the most likely of the four-judge left to join with the members of the right. His lowest agreement rate with any justice was a comparatively high 49 percent with Whittaker. The average inter-agreement rate of the left side of the Court was a high 79 percent, while the right, again counting either Burton or Stewart, was slightly lower at about 75 percent. More striking than either of these figures, however, is the index of inter-agreement of the Eisenhower associate justices and Justice Frankfurter. Their inter-agreement index, while moderate in comparison with the smaller left and right blocs, is higher than the inter-agreement rate of Black and Douglas in the 1949–1952 terms. Thus, a strong center bloc of five justices appears to have had significant influence on the course of the Court's work during the 1956–1958 terms.

Table 2.8
Agreement Among Supreme Court Justices in Nonunanimous Opinions, 1956-1958 Terms (in percentages)

	Douglas	Black	Warren	Brennan	Clark	Whittaker	Frankfurter	Burton	Harlan	Stewart
Douglas		83	78	69	37	29	28	28	24	22
Black	83		85	73	45	36	35	35	32	31
Warren	78	85		83	55	42	38	44	39	43
Brennan	69	73	83		59	49	54	51	51	54
Clark	37	45	55	59		67	56	71	60	67
Whittaker	29	36	42	49	67		71	76	73	79
Frankfurter	28	35	38	54	56	71		61	82	69
Burton	28	35	44	51	71	76	61		70	-
Harlan	24	32	39	51	60	73	82	70		77
Stewart	22	31	43	54	67	79	69	-	77	

Index of Inter-agreement

Douglas–Black–Warren–Brennan	79 (high)
Whittaker–Frankfurter–Stewart–Harlan	75 (high)
The Middle Bloc: Brennan–Whittaker– Frankfurter–Stewart–Harlan	66 (mod.)
Brennan–Whittaker–Stewart–Harlan	64 (mod.)
Warren–Brennan–Whittaker– Stewart–Harlan	59 (low)

The alignments of Table 2.9 remain basically the same for the major blocs during the 1959–1961 terms. There is high inter-agreement among the justices of the left and right blocs, but a moderate middle bloc of the Eisenhower associate justices plus Frankfurter remains in place. Stewart moves more to a centrist position while Whittaker, Harlan, and Frankfurter occupy the far right of the Court.

Table 2.9
Agreement Among Supreme Court Justices in Nonunanimous Opinions, 1959-1961 Terms (in percentages)

	Douglas	Black	Warren	Brennan	Clark	Stewart	Whittaker	Harlan	Frankfurter
Douglas		73	72	69	36	43	25	24	23
Black	73		85	75	49	47	33	33	33
Warren	72	85		85	59	54	38	39	39
Brennan	69	75	85		63	65	43	48	48
Clark	36	49	59	63		64	64	64	68
Stewart	43	47	54	65	64		66	66	68
Whittaker	25	33	38	43	64	66		69	69
Harlan	24	33	39	48	64	66	69		83
Frankfurter	23	33	39	48	68	68	69	83	

Index of Inter-agreement

Douglas–Black–Warren–Brennan	77 (high)
Whittaker–Frankfurter–Stewart–Harlan	70 (high)
The Middle Bloc: Brennan–Whittaker– Frankfurter–Stewart–Harlan	63 (mod.)
Brennan–Whittaker–Stewart–Harlan	60 (mod.)
Warren–Brennan–Whittaker– Stewart–Harlan	57 (low)

Table 2.10 recapitulates agreement among all the justices in nonunanimous opinions during the 1956–1961 terms. The Eisenhower associate justices agreed 61 percent of the time.

Table 2.11 shows inter-agreement between every pair of justices in all cases in which they were joint participants during the 1956–1961 terms. Agreements in opinions of the Court, concurring opinions, and dissenting opinions are included. This table further affirms the importance of the middle bloc, which has a high index of inter-agreement of 76 percent. The left bloc has a very high average of 85 percent while the justices of the right were only slightly lower with 81 percent.

Table 2.10
Agreement Among Supreme Court Justices in Nonunanimous Opinions,
1956–1961 Terms (in percentages)

	Douglas	Black	Warren	Brennan	Clark	Stewart	Burton	Whittaker	Frankfurter	Harlan
Douglas		78	75	69	37	39	28	27	25	24
Black	78		85	74	47	44	35	35	34	32
Warren	75	85		84	57	52	44	40	38	39
Brennan	69	74	84		61	62	51	46	51	49
Clark	37	47	57	61		64	71	65	61	62
Stewart	39	44	52	62	64		-	70	68	69
Burton	28	35	44	51	71	-		76	61	70
Whittaker	27	35	40	46	65	70	76		70	71
Frankfurter	25	34	38	51	61	68	61	70		82
Harlan	24	32	39	49	62	69	70	71	82	

Index of Inter-agreement

Douglas–Black–Warren–Brennan	78 (high)
Whittaker–Frankfurter–Stewart–Harlan	72 (high)
Brennan–Whittaker–Stewart–Harlan	61 (mod.)
The Middle Bloc: Brennan–Whittaker– Frankfurter–Stewart–Harlan	60 (mod.)
Warren–Brennan–Whittaker– Stewart–Harlan	58 (low)

Table 2.11
Agreement Among Supreme Court Justices in All Opinions, 1956–1961 Terms
(in percentages)

	Douglas	Black	Warren	Brennan	Clark	Whittaker	Frankfurter	Stewart	Harlan	Burton
Douglas		85	83	79	57	50	48	59	48	49
Black	85		90	82	64	56	54	63	54	55
Warren	83	90		89	70	60	57	68	59	60
Brennan	79	82	89		74	64	66	75	66	66
Clark	57	64	70	74		76	73	77	74	79
Whittaker	50	56	60	64	76		79	80	80	83
Frankfurter	48	54	57	66	73	79		78	88	72
Stewart	59	63	68	75	77	80	78		79	-
Harlan	48	54	59	66	74	80	88	79		79
Burton	49	55	60	66	79	83	72	-	79	

Index of Inter-agreement

Douglas–Black–Warren–Brennan	85 (high)
Whittaker–Frankfurter–Stewart–Harlan	81 (high)
The Middle Bloc: Brennan–Whittaker– Frankfurter–Stewart–Harlan	76 (high)
Brennan–Whittaker–Stewart–Harlan	74 (high)
Warren–Brennan–Whittaker– Stewart–Harlan	72 (high)

Finally, two additional tables will help to clarify the relation of individual justices to the Court since the 1953 term. Table 2.12 recapitulates the number of dissents each term, as well as the average per term, and Table 2.13 presents the record of dissents registered by each justice as a proportion of the total number of cases he participated in during each term. Varied reaction patterns are evident. Black and Douglas, beginning their Warren Court service with comparatively high percentages of dissenting votes, had a generally declining curve through the 1955 term, when they both began to climb again. During the 1961 term, however, their dissents again declined. Douglas, in the 1960 term, found himself in disagreement with the Court almost as frequently, percentage wise, as he had been in 1953. In the 1961 term, the pair of Harlan and Frankfurter compiled a higher percentage of dissents than did the Black–Douglas duo. The close tie of the Chief Justice with Black and Douglas also is affirmed by this table.

Frankfurter, later joined by Harlan, rose from low percentages during the 1954 term to highs in the 1956 and 1957 terms before starting a roller-coaster pattern by dropping considerably in the 1958 and 1960 terms while rising in the 1959 and 1961 terms. This would indicate an ebb and flow when the middle justices were more often in the majority during those terms. Until his retirement, Justice Burton roughly paralleled their pattern. Justice Clark hit all-time highs in 1957 and 1960 but dropped to relatively lower percentages in 1958, 1959, and 1961.

Table 2.12
Dissenting Records of Justices, 1953–1961 Terms (number of dissenting votes)

	1953	1954	1955	1956	1957	1958	1959	1960	1961	Average Per Term
Douglas	30	23	23	31	40	39	35	46	24	32
Black	27	14	15	25	30	30	29	30	20	24
Warren	8	6	12	12	27	24	22	22	14	16
Brennan	–	–	–	13	17	17	17	20	4	15
Harlan	–	4*	20	31	33	20	33	23	29	24
Frankfurter	11	11	22	29	29	20	32	22	11	21
Whittaker	–	–	–	6**	25	23	35	31	6	21
Burton	12	14	20	33	28	–	–	–	–	21
Stewart	–	–	–	–	–	14	18	20	12	16
Reed	11	25	19	8**	–	–	–	–	–	16
Minton	17	13	14	–	–	–	–	–	–	15
Jackson	14	–	–	–	–	–	–	–	–	14
Clark	6	5	8	17	21	12	13	21	14	13

*Justice Harlan participated in less than half of the decisions in the 1954 term.
**Justice Reed and his replacement Justice Whittaker did not participate during a
    considerable portion of the 1956 term.

Table 2.13
Dissenting Records of Justices, 1953–1961 Terms (in percentages)

	1953	1954	1955	1956	1957	1958	1959	1960	1961	Average Per Term
Douglas	38	25	24	26	31	33	31	36	24	30
Black	33	15	15	22	24	26	26	23	20	24
Warren	10	7	13	10	22	21	20	17	14	15
Brennan	–	–	–	12	14	14	15	16	4	13
Harlan	–	22*	25	26	26	17	29	18	29	24
Burton	14	15	20	27	22	–	–	–	–	21
Frankfurter	13	12	22	24	23	18	28	18	23	20
Minton	20	14	14	–	–	–	–	–	–	20
Whittaker	–	–	–	16*	20	20	30	24	17	19
Jackson	19	–	–	–	–	–	–	–	–	19
Stewart	–	–	–	–	–	13	16	16	12	16
Reed	14	27	19	17*	–	–	–	–	–	14
Clark	8	5	8	15	17	10	12	17	14	12

*Participated in only half or less of the decisions in this term.

Again the similarity in the number of dissents during the 1958 term of the Eisenhower associate justices plus Frankfurter indicates that there is substantial agreement within this group in the general performance of the Court. Whittaker's 20 percent is the highest of this bloc, while Stewart's 13 percent is the lowest. The percentages of Frankfurter, Harlan, and Brennan fall between those two, and their proportions of dissent are roughly half that of Douglas.

In summary, voting statistics of the Warren Court indicate the development of a moderate center bloc of justices, composed of the Eisenhower associate justices and Justice Frankfurter, which came to play an important role in the split decisions of the highest tribunal. This bloc was created during the 1954 term when Justice Harlan was appointed to the Court and developed close ties with Frankfurter. With the appointment of three more Eisenhower justices, this bloc became a dominant majority in many cases. Its influence on the decisions of the Warren Court perhaps explains the middle-of-the-road position characteristic of the Court during this period. Neither going as far in extending protection to civil liberties as Black, Douglas, and Warren would urge, nor retaining the less-libertarian attitude of Clark, which had been predominant under Vinson, the middle-of-the-road justices revitalized the role of the Supreme Court in protecting individual freedom while keeping this role within the proper bounds of the judiciary.[7] While this may not have been all that libertarian critics of the Court desired, it nevertheless was a major step forward from the Vinson Court's record.

NOTES

1. See also e.g., Glendon A. Schubert, *Quantitative Analysis of Judicial Behavior*; "The 1960 Term of the Supreme Court: A Psychological Analysis," 56 *Am. Pol. Sci. Rev.* 90 (1962); Fred Kort, "Predicting Supreme Court Decisions Mathematically: A Quantitative Analysis of the Right to Counsel Cases," 51 *Am. Pol. Sci. Rev.* 1 (1957); S. Sidney Ulmer, "Supreme Court Behavior and Civil Rights," 13 *W. Pol. Q.* 288 (1960).

2. Pritchett, *Civil Liberties and the Vinson Court*, p. 177.

3. Tables 2.1 and 2.2 are based upon Pritchett's tables, while the indices are based upon Schubert's methods: Pritchett, Ibid., p. 236; Schubert, *Quantitative Analysis*, pp. 89–91.

4. For instruction for computation of the Index of Cohesion as well as other indices useful in bloc identification, see Ibid. With Table 2.2 an Index of Inter-agreement is used, showing ratios rather than frequencies of paired agreement. For any given bloc, this index is computed by simply averaging the percentages of the included pairs. An Index of Inter-agreement of 70 percent or higher is considered to be high; 60–65 percent is moderate; less than 60 percent is low.

5. Pritchett, *Civil Liberties and the Vinson Court*, p. 184.

6. The count of cases used in these tables includes all those decided by full opinion appearing in the first section of the U.S. Reports, including per curiam opinions printed in this section among the formal opinions. Differences of policy in counting per curiam opinions may result in lack of uniformity in the statistics assembled by different commentators on the Court. Compare the figures of the annual reports of *U.S. Law Week* and *Harvard Law Review, Supreme Court Reporter* and the *Annual Report of the Administrative Office of the United States Courts*.

7. For other quantitative studies or suggested studies of Supreme Court voting behavior, see, e.g., Robert A. Horn, "A Quantitative Study of Judicial Review," 1 *Political Research: Organization and Design* 27 (1957); John Schmidhauser and David Gold, "Scaling Supreme Court Decisions in Relation to Social Background," Ibid., p. 6 (1958); S. Sidney Ulmer, "Label Thinking and the Supreme Court: A Methodological Note," Ibid., p. 25 (1958); "Judicial Review as Political Behavior: A Temporary Check on Congress," 4 *Adminis. Sci. Q.* 426 (1960); "The Analysis of Behavior Patterns on the United States Supreme Court," 22 *J. Politics* 502 (1960); "Supreme Court Behavior and Civil Rights," 13 *W. Pol. Q.* 288 (1960); "Polar Classification of Supreme Court Justices," 12 *S.C.L.Q.* 407 (1960); Harold J. Spaeth, "An Approach to the Study of Attitudinal Differences as an Aspect of Judicial Behavior," 5 *Mw. J. Pol. Sci.* 165 (1961); John Schmidhauser, "The Justices of the Supreme Court: A Collective Portrait," 3 *Mw. J. Pol. Sci.* 1 (1959); Eloise C. Snyder, "Political Power and the Ability to Win Supreme Court Decisions," 39 *Social Forces* 36 (1960); "A Quantitative Analysis of Supreme Court Opinions from 1921 to 1953: A Study of the Responses of an Institution Engaged in Resolving Social Conflict," unpublished Ph.D. dissertation, Pennsylvania State University, 1956; "The Supreme Court as a Small Group," 36 *Social Forces* 232 (1958); "Uncertainty and the Supreme Court's Decisions," 65 *Am. J. Sociol.* 241 (1959); Joseph Tanenhaus, "Supreme Court Attitudes Toward Federal Administrative Agencies,"

22 *J. Politics* 502 (1960); but see Franklin M. Fisher, "The Mathematical Analysis of Supreme Court Decisions: The Use and Abuse of Quantitative Methods," 52 *Am. Pol. Sci. Rev.* 321 (1958); John P. Roche, "Political Science and Science Fiction," 52 *Am. Pol. Sci. Rev.* 1026 (1958).

3

Anticommunist Activities

The response of American public opinion to political unorthodoxy has often been confused. In the cause of the preservation of democracy, public opinion has demanded restrictions and punishments for political deviates which in their enforcement have represented some of the darkest hours for American civil liberties.[1] The Alien[2] and Sedition[3] Acts of 1798 were the first "antisubversive" legislation of the national government. Although never tested in the Supreme Court, the Sedition Act was upheld in lower federal courts. Public opinion, expressed at the polls, however, showed disfavor with these Federalist acts more effectively than a judicial opinion.[4] Subsequent commentators regarded the act as unconstitutional, and the Supreme Court belatedly declared it so in 1964.

During the Civil War, when it might have been expected that repressive legislation would be enacted by Congress to control seditious publications and disloyal speeches, the matter was almost entirely handled by the executive and by military tribunals established by President Lincoln's authority.

It was not until World War I that Congress, responding to public hysteria, again resorted to antilibertarian controls over speech. The Espionage Act of 1917[5] and the Sedition Act of 1918[6] were used to prosecute socialists, pacifists, pro-Germans, Communists, and anarchists because of things they had said. The Supreme Court upheld convictions under these acts, and Justice Holmes justified them with his famous "clear and present danger" pronouncement in *Schenck v. United States*.[7] His statement emphasized that the circumstances in which words are used and the possible consequences which flow from their utterance are factors to be considered as well as the character of the words themselves. Two years later, Holmes, joined by Louis D. Brandeis, sought to demonstrate that this test also could be used to protect speech in *Abrams v. United States*,[8] but the seven-man majority found that there was a "dangerous tendency" in the defendants' words.

The Red Scare of the early 1920s furnished the public with another opportunity to harass radicals.[9] Some of the nation's leaders undertook to lead a crusade against the Communists. In the states, the laws passed to meet the supposed dangers of anarchists were used to restrict the activities of Reds and socialists. A conviction under one such law was upheld in *Gitlow v. New York*,[10] but the Court went on to say that it would assume the view that the freedoms guaranteed in the First Amendment are safeguarded against encroachment by the states by the due process clause of the Fourteenth Amendment.

In 1927, in *Whitney v. California*,[11] the majority upheld a conviction under a state criminal syndicalism law, primarily because conspiracy was not within the bounds of free speech.[12] The opinion of the Court gave indication that the Fourteenth Amendment extended a constitutional guarantee of freedom of speech against state interference. In concurring, Brandeis, this time speaking also for Holmes, reasserted the merits of the clear and present danger test and elaborated its protective features considerably beyond Holmes' previous explanations. These two justices contended that the state statute could be applied only after satisfying the clear and present danger test, which had not been properly raised as an issue in this case. The scope of this decision was narrowed, however, in *Fiske v. Kansas*,[13] in which a conviction under a similar Kansas statute was set aside because it was not known that the organization in which the defendant secured members advocated crime or violence.

In the 1930s, with some lessening of public fear of radicals, the Court reversed the convictions of admitted Communists in three important decisions—*Stromberg v. California*,[14] *DeJonge v. Oregon*,[15] and *Herndon v. Lawry*.[16] In each case the Court voided the conviction on the basis of well-established rules of criminal law rather than First Amendment grounds. These cases gave considerable support for associative freedom as applied to members of the Communist party and lessened the impact of the *Whitney* decision.

The House Un-American Activities Committee (HUAC) was created in 1938 to investigate the activities of "subversives" believed to be members of organizations controlled by the governments of the European dictatorships. During its existence, this committee was strongly motivated by a desire to influence public opinion concerning the nature and extent of subversive activity in the United States, while sometimes questioning beliefs or "exposing for the sake of exposing."[17] The Senate likewise set up committees concerned with making inquiries into the threat of subversive activity.

The most famous of the antisubversive measures passed by the federal government was the Alien Registration Act of 1940, better known as the Smith Act.[18] It was the first federal peacetime restriction on political speaking and writing by American citizens since the Sedition Act of 1798.[19] Section 2 of the statute makes it unlawful knowingly to advocate the overthrow of the government by force, to print or distribute written matter so advocating, or to organize or knowingly become a member of any group which so advocates.[20] Section 3 makes punishable conspiracy to accomplish any of these ends.

After World War II, the United States pursued a policy of containment of Soviet Union imperialism. In the ensuing Cold War, the anti-Communist rhetoric of government leaders, such as President Harry Truman, stirred up concerns about communism in America. Although there were few American Communists and they posed little real threat to national security, political demagogues, led by Senator Joseph R. McCarthy (R–WI), exploited this issue relentlessly. The ensuing Red Scare inspired both national and state governmental actions intended to thwart espionage and subversion but really aimed at hunting domestic Communists. Congress passed the Internal Security Act of 1950 and the Communist Control Act of 1954. Other government actions included criminal prosecutions and deportations of radicals, development of loyalty-security programs, official designation of certain organizations as subversive, loyalty oath requirements, and investigations by HUAC and other congressional committees. Both criminal and civil sanctions were used against suspected subversives. Many of these governmental actions infringed upon individual rights and were challenged in the courts.

One such challenge was made of the anti-Communist sections of the Labor Management Relations Act of 1947, the Taft–Hartley Act.[21] Section 9(h) of this act denies the protection and services of the act to any labor organization unless each of its officers files an affidavit with the National Labor Relations Board "that he is not a member of the Communist party or affiliated with such party, and that he does not believe in, and is not a member of or supports any organization that believes in or teaches, the overthrow of the United States Government."[22]

In *American Communications Association v. Douds*,[23] the Supreme Court upheld the validity of the oath. Chief Justice Vinson, writing in behalf of the Court, with the concurrence of only two other justices, treated the oath primarily as a measure for the control of interstate commerce rather than a regulation of opinion. Justices Jackson and Frankfurter, although agreeing that Congress could reasonably conclude that Communist party members could not be trusted as union leaders, felt that it was a different matter to permit Congress to inquire into belief. Justice Black, the sole dissenter of the six participating justices, voiced the view that the entire provision was unconstitutional, arguing that governmentally imposed civil

disabilities placed upon groups because of dislike for their political beliefs are just as dangerous to liberty as the imposition of criminal penalties.

The following term, the Court faced the first important test of the
Smith Act's constitutionality in *Dennis v. United States*.[24] Eight participating justices required five separate opinions to dispose of the issues, the
majority upholding the conviction of eleven leaders of the Communist
Party of the United States for advocating the violent overthrow of the
government. Chief Justice Vinson spoke for the six-man majority in an
opinion concurred in by three of the justices. He paid allegiance to Holmes'
statement and application of the clear and present danger test, but in reality adopted in its place Judge Hand's test of "clear and probable danger,"
practically reading the time element out of the Holmes' doctrine. Justice
Frankfurter felt that the legislative judgment embodied in the Smith Act
outweighed claims of violation of free speech protections. Justice Jackson
bluntly declared that the clear and present danger test had no applicability to a criminal conspiracy such as the Communist Party although he
thought the Smith Act constitutional in its punishment of conspiracy. Justices Black and Douglas dissenting, thought that the clear and present
danger test had been destroyed. Justice Douglas emphasized that the defendants were charged with no overt acts, only with speeches and publications. Justice Black concluded his opinion with the hope that "in calmer
time, when present pressures, passions and fears subside, this or some
later Court will restore the First Amendment liberties to the high preferred place where they belong in a free society." [25]

These Vinson Court decisions, perhaps made in response to emotional demands of outspoken segments of the American public,[26] were
subject to severe criticisms by lawyers, academicians, and the more "liberal" segments of society. [27] In fact the Vinson Court decisions pertaining
to antisubversive legislation were viewed as a "mass attack on civil liberties,"[28] and led Professor Eugene Rostow of the Yale Law School to state
in 1952 that "civil liberties in the United States are in a state of grave crisis." [29]

Although the Court's majority gave no indication of presenting a
strong challenge to the substantive restraints placed by Congress on
"subversives" during the 1946–1953 Vinson era, the Court in several decisions upheld procedural rights of accused Communists. In *Blau v. United
States*,[30] the Court held unanimously that a witness appearing before a
federal grand jury, claiming the privilege of immunity from self-incrimination, might refuse to answer questions concerning the Communist Party
and her employment by it. In *Stack v. Boyle*,[31] the Court unanimously ruled
that Communists could not be subjected to excessive bail. In testing the
federal loyalty program, the Court divided four to four, affirming the
decision of the Circuit Court which had approved the dismissal of a gov-

ernment employee and had held that the courts have no function to perform in such cases.[32] At the same time, the Court ruled that the loyalty-security program denied procedural due process to organizations listed as subversive by the Attorney General.[33] One great exception to the Court's sharp scrutiny of procedural guarantees in this area was presented in *Carlson v. Landon*[34] where the Court, by a five-to-four vote, approved the power of the Attorney General to hold alien Communists in jail without bail on the sole ground that they were security risks. Such imprisonment in deportation cases might last months or years. Thus the Court condoned indefinite confinement of aliens solely on the order of an administrative official.

This, then, was the record of the Supreme Court in cases dealing with "political offenders" at the time of the appointment of Chief Justice Warren. The convictions on which the Court had passed had not been for overt acts imperiling national security such as espionage, treason, or sabotage. The defendants' offenses were political, growing out of the opinions they expressed and the organizations they joined.[35]

SMITH ACT INTERPRETATIONS

After the *Dennis* decision, the Supreme Court refused to grant certiorari in other Smith Act cases until October 1955, when it agreed to review the conviction of fourteen "second-string" Communists by a federal court. The result was the shattering decision in *Yates v. United States*,[36] handed down on 17 June 1957, the day dubbed "Red Monday" by critics of the Court. By a vote of six to one the Court, while not challenging the constitutionality of the Smith Act as established by the *Dennis* decision, reversed the convictions of five of the fourteen defendants and laid down conditions for Smith Act trials which would make it considerably more difficult to secure future convictions.[37]

Justice Harlan, writing for the majority, pointed out three major issues. First was the definition of the term "organize." The Smith Act makes it unlawful to "organize" a group that advocates the overthrow of the government by force and violence. Justice Harlan held that the term "organize" in the act referred to the actual formation of the Communist Party in the United States in its present form, which had occurred in 1945, and that since the date of the indictment was 1951, the three-year statute of limitations had expired. Since the Court was unable to tell whether the jury would have rendered a verdict of guilty if only the advocacy charge had been before them, the elimination of the organizing charge required the entire verdict to be set aside.

Justice Harlan's second point concerned the trial judge's instructions to the jury. The trial judge had failed to charge the jury in the same terms as Judge Harold Medina had used in the *Dennis* trial. The lower court, Justice Harlan said, had erroneously supposed that the *Dennis* case had "obliterated the traditional dividing line between advocacy of abstract doctrine and advocacy of action."[38] To show that the Communists advocated the necessity and desirability of violent overthrow was not sufficient. According to Justice Harlan: "That sort of advocacy even though uttered with the hope that it may ultimately lead to violent revolution is too remote from concrete action to be regarded as the kind of indoctrination preparatory to action which was condemned in *Dennis*. . . . The essential distinction is that those to whom the advocacy is addressed must be urged to do something, now or in the future, rather than merely to believe in something."[39] Because the trial court had failed so to instruct the jury, another reason for reversal of the conviction was supplied.

Third, Justice Harlan passed on the evidence on which the conviction had been secured, determining whether evidence in the record was "palpably insufficient" to justify a new trial. All of the evidence relating to the "organizing" aspect of the conspiracy had been thrown out and the evidence relating to the advocacy point was valueless to the extent that it was intended only to prove advocacy of the abstract doctrine of violent overthrow. The Court found the record "strikingly deficient" in such evidence. The government had relied heavily on the theory that conspiracy on the part of the defendants was proved by their connections with the Party. But the Court insisted that evidence of activity in the Communist Party would not meet the requirements of this case. Some of the activities of the Party might be completely lawful. The defendants could be convicted only on the basis of their individual acts other than their relations with the Party. On this basis, the Court ordered the outright acquittal of five of the petitioners and ordered new trials for nine others. Six months later the Department of Justice "reluctantly" requested the trial court to dismiss the indictments against the remaining nine defendants on the ground that "the evidentiary requirements laid down by the Supreme Court" could not be satisfied. Also on the basis of the *Yates* ruling, indictments were dismissed against other Communists. The *Dennis* case dissents of Justices Black and Douglas were somewhat vindicated by the *Yates* decision, although these justices would have gone further than the majority by holding the Smith Act completely unconstitutional and directing the acquittal of all defendants.

The sole dissenter in *Yates*, Justice Clark, attacked the Court's limited construction of the "organize" provision and went on to argue more generally that the Court's distinction between *Yates* and *Dennis* was "too subtle and difficult to grasp." He insisted that the *Dennis* doctrine, which he supported, required for conviction merely "a finding that 'the Party advocates the theory that there is a duty and necessity to overthrow the government by force and violence . . . as a policy to be translated into action' as soon as circumstances permit."[40]

The Court's new position in the *Yates* case was to some extent a consequence of changes in personnel, four of the six-justice majority in *Dennis* having died or retired. The *Yates* decision also reflected a lessening of tensions in the social and political order. By 1957, there were many indications that the American people were in a somewhat calmer mood with respect to the Communist threat. To be sure, there were many voices of protest against the Court's decision, but there appeared also to be a sizeable segment of society which approved more conservative constitutional techniques against Communists rather than some of the methods used in the "scare" period of the Cold War.[41] The Court, although making an about-face from the thinking of the Vinson Court, had not really ventured too far afield. Here, the Court merely construed the Smith Act, and Congress might have changed that law if it liked. In order to convict under the Smith Act, all the government apparently needed to do under the *Yates* dictum was to present evidence that the Communists advocated or conspired to advocate specific violent acts, then or in the future. The *Yates* opinion suggests that Congress might exceed its constitutional power if it attempts to punish mere abstract doctrine, which is not a new or startling idea, but a needed reminder to the American public.

During the 1960 term, in two decisions, the Court held that mere membership in the Communist Party did not violate the Smith Act. Scales and Noto were convicted of having "knowing membership" in an organization that advocated the overthrow of the government. Justice Harlan, writing for a five-justice majority in *Scales v. U.S.*, upheld Scales' conviction but interpreted the membership clause as requiring proof of "active" as distinguished from merely "nominal" or "passive" membership in the Communist Party.[42] The Court held that the membership clause did not violate the due process clause of the Fifth Amendment or the free speech guarantee of the First Amendment. The Communist Party was considered an organization that engaged in criminal activity, and the majority saw no constitutional reason why a person, who actively and knowingly worked in its ranks with intent to contribute to the success of its illegal objectives, could not be prosecuted. But punishment could be applied only against members who actively advanced the Party's aims. It was therefore no longer a crime to advocate, as an abstract doctrine, the forcible overthrow of government. Harlan's opinion was the last one to uphold a conviction of someone sent to prison under the Smith Act. Justices Brennan, Black, and Douglas and the Chief Justice dissented.

A unanimous Court reversed Noto's conviction. Five of the justices decided that the evidence at the trial was insufficient to show the Communist Party engaged in advocacy of the doctrine of forcible overthrow of the government and in advocacy of action to that end, as distinguished from advocacy of mere abstract doctrine. Justice Harlan, writing for the Court, found that there must be substantial evidence of a call to violence "now or in the future" and also substantial evidence to justify a finding that the call to violence could fairly be imputed to the Party as a whole and not merely to a segment of it. Justices Black and Douglas found the conviction invalid as a violation of the First Amendment. Justice Brennan, joined by Warren, claimed that the Subversive Activities Control Act (SACA)—which stated that the holding of office or membership in a communist organization constituted a violation of the SACA or "any other criminal statute"—superseded the Smith Act's membership provisions.

The Smith Act remains on the statute books and is available for use by the government, provided it meets the requirements of the Court. The fact is, of course, that those requirements are less than what many libertarians, including two justices of the Eisenhower Court, believed necessary to meet the requirements of the First Amendment, since the Smith Act prosecutions primarily punished speech in teaching and advocating, an activity supposedly protected by the First Amendment. During the Cold War, 141 persons were indicted for violating the Smith Act, but because of the more liberal standards applied by the Court in *Yates* and *Scales*, only twenty-nine of those indicted served prison terms. The Court had successfully defanged the Smith Act.

A majority of the Eisenhower Court justices found the danger of communism was not isolated speeches or statements of doctrine, but rather the organizational setting within which the teaching and advocacy were carried out. It was the existence in the United States of a tightly organized group controlled by an unfriendly foreign power that made the Communist Party a grave concern of the FBI. But instead of punishing activity to achieve the forceful overthrow of government through an organization set up and controlled by a foreign power, the Smith Act centered its attack on speech regardless of its setting.

Congress chose to combat the communist conspiracy by punishing speech as a crime. The Court upheld the constitutionality of this section of the Smith Act, in spite of the First Amendment, when speech was an important factor in a situation that was perceived as threatening to the security of the nation. But because the First Amendment was involved, the Court could not abdicate its responsibility to judge whether there had been proof by judicial standards that the speech which was the basis of the offense took place in a setting which alone could justify punishment for use of the freedom guaranteed by the First Amendment.[43]

During the 1955 term, the Supreme Court had placed some limitations on the states' ability to combat subversives through the use of state sedition laws. In *Pennsylvania v. Nelson*,[44] the Court struck down the Pennsylvania Sedition Act[45] on the ground that congressional action bearing on this matter had superseded the state law.[46] Chief Justice Warren delivered the opinion of the Court for the six-justice majority. He contended that Congress had intended, when it passed the Smith Act, the Internal Security Act of 1950,[47] and the Communist Control Act of 1954,[48] to "occupy the field" leaving no room for the states to supplement national efforts. Although Congress had not specifically stated its intent to occupy the field, the Chief Justice found the "pervasiveness" of the federal regulation, the "dominant federal interest" in the problem, and the possibly "serious danger of conflict" between state and federal laws in this field sufficient to justify this decision. The Court cited *Hines v. Davidowitz*,[49] in which it had been held that the federal Alien Registration Act of 1940 superseded a Pennsylvania alien registration law.[50]

Justices Reed, Burton, and Minton dissented, denying that the federal government's interest in protection against sedition was dominant over that of the states. Since Congress had not forbidden the states to legislate in this area, the courts should not. Neither the Chief Justice nor Justice Reed was entirely convincing in supporting his position in this case. This uncertainty was reflected in the law journal comments written about *Nelson*.[51] Some clarification of the scope of this decision was provided by the Court three years later, however, in *Uphaus v. Wyman*. [52]

The *Nelson* decision brought an immediate end to several state prosecutions and was bitterly attacked in Congress and the states. The author of the Smith Act, Congressman Howard Smith (D–VA), denied that he had ever intended the act to preempt state actions. He introduced legislation in Congress in 1958 and again in 1959 forbidding the Court to interpret any law of Congress as precluding state legislation unless it specifically so provided. Although the House of Representatives passed this measure in consecutive years, it died in the Senate.

ACCESS TO FBI FILES

The case of *Jencks v. United States*,[53] decided two weeks prior to *Yates*, also aroused great controversy, since it involved an apparent invasion of the secrecy of FBI files. Jencks, a labor union official, filed a non-Communist affidavit with the National Labor Relations Board in 1950. The government charged that the affidavit was false, and it presented two witnesses, paid FBI informants, in court to establish Jencks' connection with the Party both before and after that date. The witnesses made oral and written reports to the FBI during this period concerning Jencks' alleged participation in Communist Party activities. Jencks' counsel desired to see these reports to compare them with the testimony given by the witnesses at the trial several years later, hoping that discrepancies or contradictions could be found which would impeach their testimony. Counsel requested that the reports be produced by the government for the inspection of the trial judge, who would examine them for materiality and relevancy and turn over to the defense such materials as met these tests. This request was refused.

The Court, by a vote of seven to one, held that this refusal invalidated the conviction. Pointing out that Jencks was not required to show inconsistency first, Justice Brennan, for the Court, held that it was sufficient that these witnesses had made reports of events and activities concerning which they testified in court. Since the testimony of the informants was crucial, its impeachment was of the utmost importance to the defendant. "Every experienced trial judge and trial lawyer," said Justice Brennan, "knows the value for impeaching purposes of statements of the witness recording the events before time dulls treacherous memory."[54] Justice Brennan also made the commonsense observation that unless the witness himself admits conflict between his reports and his court testimony, the defendant cannot prove it without inspecting the reports. He added a reminder to the government that its interest in a criminal case is not to win it, but to see that justice is done.

Justice Brennan's opinion held, perhaps unwisely, that defense counsel was entitled to more than he had requested. The reports that the government was ordered to produce would have to go first to the accused, and only after that to the judge to determine admissibility. Justices Burton and Harlan disagreed with this part of the decision, contending that the trial judge would have the responsibility and the discretion to protect the interests of all involved in the case—"the legitimate public interest in safeguarding executive files"[55] as well as the interest of the accused "to receive all information necessary to his defense."[56]

Justice Clark again dissented, asserting that the Court had fashioned a "new rule of evidence which is foreign to our federal jurisprudence."[57] He warned: "Unless the Congress changes the rule announced by the Court today, those intelligence agencies of our Government engaged in law enforcement may as well close up shop for the Court has opened their files to the criminal and thus afforded him a Roman holiday for rummaging through confidential information as well as vital national secrets."[58] This cry was taken up by Congress in its attacks on the decision.

Although the majority opinion had pointed out that the demand must be for specific documents supplied by informants actually offered as witnesses, and that indiscriminate file-rummaging would not be permitted, uncertainties remained.[59] The finding of the majority that materials from FBI files should be selected by the prosecution and handed directly to the defense, not the judge, had not been argued by either side before the Court. Justice Brennan did not specifically say that the disclosure was to be made only after witnesses had testified for the prosecution.

To clarify these points of procedure, Congress enacted a statute on 2 September 1957,[60] which provided that when reports of witnesses were demanded, the judge should make a preliminary examination of them in private, and exclude those portions which did not relate to the subject matter of the testimony of the witness. The act was made applicable only to prior written statements signed or approved by the witness, or oral statements in substantially verbatim form. Notes made by an FBI agent on a witness's oral statement would not be subject to enforced inspection under these provisions.[61]

Nevertheless, under the *Jencks* decision as implemented by this legislation, the government, when it used informers in Communist prosecutions, had to be willing to have their relevant reports to the FBI made available to the defense. If the government thought it was important to have Communists in jail, this was part of the price it had to pay. The Court affirmed the principle that all Americans, even Communists, are entitled to due process of law before they go to jail.

During the 1958 term, the Court made three decisions in non-seditious cases clarifying the *Jencks* rule.[62] In *Palermo v. United States*,[63] a unanimous Court sustained the conviction of an income tax evader who requested to see government documents but was denied the use of texts of governmental interrogation of a witness whose testimony he sought to impeach. In *Rosenberg v. United States*,[64] however, a bare majority of the Court upheld the conviction of the plaintiff, who had been indicted for carrying fraudulent checks in interstate commerce. The trial judge withheld documents from FBI files requested by Rosenberg, who contended that the decision should be reversed under the *Jencks* doctrine. Justices Brennan, Black, Douglas, and the Chief Justice, in dissent, would have applied the *Jencks* rule. Finally, the Court held that the Jencks Act does not apply to federal grand jury minutes in *Pittsburg Plate Glass Co. v. United States*.[65]

JUDICIAL PUNISHMENTS FOR CONTEMPT

The judicial power to punish subversives for contempt was also a concern of the Eisenhower Court. A judge without a jury has historically exercised this summary power. In *Green v. United States*,[66] an unusually severe sentence of three years for contempt was affirmed by a five–four vote of the Court.[67] After their conviction in the *Dennis* case, two of the Communist defendants, who had remained free on bail until their appeals were adjudicated, failed to appear in court when the surrender order was signed. The two remained fugitives for more than four years before voluntarily surrendering. The government brought criminal contempt proceedings in the district court, which found them guilty. Justice Black's dissent, with the concurrence of the Chief Justice and Justice Douglas, contended unsuccessfully that summary punishment for criminal contempt was despotic, and that indictment by grand jury and trial by jury were a constitutional necessity in such prosecutions just as for other crimes.

In *Yates v. United States*,[68] on the other hand, the Court made an unusual use of its supervisory power over the administration of justice in the federal courts by itself reducing a sentence for contempt of court after the district judge who imposed the original sentence had failed to respond to the Supreme Court's "gentle intimations" that the sentence should be reduced. In this case, a Communist had been found guilty of eleven separate contempts. The Supreme Court found only one contempt and ordered a reduction in the defendant's sentence accordingly.

FAIR TRIALS

In another demonstration of its power as supervisor of justice in the federal courts, the Court ordered a new trial for five convicted Communists in *Mesarosh v. United States*,[69] After the Supreme Court had granted certiorari to these violators of the Smith Act, the Solicitor General filed a motion calling the Court's attention to the testimony given by one of the government's seven witnesses, a paid informer, and expressing serious doubt regarding his truthfulness. The aim of the government was to remand the case to the district court for a determination as to the informer's truthfulness. But a five-justice majority, speaking through Chief Justice Warren, held that the Supreme Court should itself order a new trial since "the dignity of the United States Government will not permit the conviction of any person on tainted testimony."[70] With only seven government witnesses, it would be impossible for any court to determine conclusively that the testimony of this particular one had been insignificant. The jury and not the judge had made the original finding of fact that would preclude him from deciding that the conviction could have been sustained by the other evidence. Without referring to any constitutional question, the Court ordered a new trial "to see that the waters of justice are not polluted."[71] The three dissenters argued that reversal of the convictions was "an unprecedented and dangerous departure from sound principles of judicial administration,"[72] for here the Court overturned the results of a complex, lengthy, and expensive trial before any investigation had been made of the suspicions of the Solicitor General.[73]

In *Gold v. United States*,[74] the Court required a new trial of a union president convicted of filing a false non-Communist affidavit. During the trial an FBI agent telephoned or visited three members of Gold's petit jury or their families to inquire whether they had received any propaganda literature. The Court ruled in a per curiam decision that these contacts were so prejudicial as to require reversal even though the intrusion was unintentional.[75]

LEGISLATIVE INVESTIGATIONS

Legislative investigating committees have long used their implied power of investigation to provide Congress with information for proposed legislation. This power has without doubt been of great importance to Congress in carrying out its specifically assigned legislative responsibilities. At times the exercise of investigatory powers have been characterized by such abuses as to discredit the entire legislative branch. Procedures of committees often have been criticized because of their failure to provide adequate safeguards or effective remedy against damaging but unwarranted charges. This has been particularly true in investigations subjecting political offenders to obloquy by exposure and publicity.[76]

The record of the Supreme Court in reviewing cases involving congressional investigatory committees has been one of judicial timidity and confusion. During the early years of the Cold War, the Vinson Court, by acquiescence, did nothing to curb serious committee abuses of power and invasions of individual rights, which became standard operating procedures with some committees.[77]

Under these circumstances, the Eisenhower Court's decision in *Watkins v. United States*[78] on 17 June 1957, rebuffing congressional investigatory power, had a great impact on the public opinion of the country even though its doctrine was not an extreme one. Watkins, appearing before the House Committee on Un-American Activities, testified fully about his past, denying that he had ever been a card-carrying Communist. He admitted, however, that from 1942 to 1947 he had cooperated with the Party and had participated in its activities to such a degree that some persons might honestly have thought that he was a Party member.

But when committee counsel read him a list of names and asked him to tell whether he knew these persons to have been members of the Party, he refused to answer. Watkins did not plead the Fifth Amendment, but refused to answer since he did "not believe that such questions are relevant to the work of this committee." He said that he would answer questions about people who he knew were still members of the Party, but not about the others who might suffer from "public exposure of their past activities."[79] Watkins was then convicted of contempt of Congress under a statute making it a crime to refuse to answer "any questions pertinent to the question under inquiry." Lower federal courts affirmed the conviction.

The Supreme Court, by a vote of six to one, reversed Watkins' conviction. Chief Justice Warren's majority opinion decided the case on the

narrow ground that a witness can be compelled to answer only those questions that are pertinent to a matter under proper investigation and that
the purpose of the inquiry must be stated with sufficient clarity so that a
witness can intelligently judge whether he is being asked a relevant or an
irrelevant question.

In a far-ranging opinion the Chief Justice made many ringing declarations that went much further then needed to dispose of this case. He
stated that there was "no general authority to expose the private affairs of
individuals without justification in terms of the functions of the Congress,"[80] and that there was no congressional power "to expose for the
sake of exposure."[81] Pointing out that committees could not usurp executive and judicial powers by serving as a law enforcement or trial agency,
the Chief Justice contended that "investigations conducted solely for the
personal aggrandizement of the investigators or to 'punish' those investigated are indefensible"[82] A congressional inquiry, then, "must be related
to, and in furtherance of, a legitimate task of the Congress."[83]

Chief Justice Warren's opinion found the 1938 resolution authorizing the committee to investigate "un-American activities" so vague that
"it would be difficult to imagine a less explicit authorization."[84] For, he
said, "who can define the meaning of 'un-American'?" The Chief Justice
stated that in authorizing the committee's work, Congress must instruct
the committee members "on what they are to do with the power delegated
to them."[85] Such authorization must "spell out that group's jurisdiction
and purpose with sufficient particularity" so that a witness and a reviewing court may have some basis of judging the pertinency of questions to
the committee's legislative purpose. Yet it is interesting to note that Warren did not say that Congress had failed to do this in the *Watkins* case.

Turning to possible threats to First Amendment rights of witnesses
by committee action, Chief Justice Warren stated: "Clearly, an investigation is subject to the command that the Congress shall make no law abridging freedom of speech or press or assembly. While it is true that . . . an
investigation is not a law, nevertheless an investigation is part of law
making. . . . The First Amendment may be invoked against infringement
of the protected freedom by law or by law making."[86]

Then in a broad dictum describing the possible dangers of congressional investigatory abuses, the Chief Justice added:

> Abuses of the investigative process may imperceptibly lead to
> abridgement of protected freedoms. The mere summoning of a
> witness and compelling him to testify, against his will, about his
> beliefs, expressions or associations is a measure of governmental
> interference. And when those forced revelations concern matters that
> are unorthodox, unpopular, or even hateful to the general public,
> the reaction in the life of the witness may be disastrous. . . . Nor does
> the witness alone suffer the consequences. Those who are identified

by witnesses and thereby placed in the same glare of publicity are equally subject to public stigma, scorn and obloquy. Beyond that, there is the more subtle and immeasurable effect upon those who tend to adhere to the most orthodox and uncontroversial views and associations in order to avoid a similar fate at some future time.[87]

Chief Justice Warren's broad essay on congressional investigatory authority did not completely close the door on such inquiries, however, for he said: "It is manifest that despite the adverse effects which follow upon compelled disclosure of private matters, not all such inquiries are barred. . . . The critical element is the existence of, and the weight to be ascribed to, the interest of the Congress in demanding disclosures from an unwilling witness."[88]

There was a great deal of confusion as to the rights of witnesses resulting from the failure of many to distinguish the actual holding of *Watkins* from the broad language of Warren's opinion. The former was a needed check upon legislative investigation, while the latter could have led to the emasculation of the informing function of Congress. The actual result of this decision was quite modest while much of the Warren dictum was irrelevant.

State legislative investigations also came under Court perusal at this time. In *Sweezy v. New Hampshire*,[89] decided the same day as *Watkins*, the Supreme Court invalidated a contempt conviction by a six-to-two vote. The New Hampshire legislature had designated the attorney general of the state as a one-man legislative committee and directed him to investigate "subversive persons" as defined within the state subversive activities act. Sweezy, subpoenaed to broad inquiries about his activities and beliefs by the attorney general, answered many questions that he regarded as unconstitutional. While denying membership in the Communist Party, he refused to answer questions which he regarded not pertinent to the subject under inquiry as well as any questions about his opinions or beliefs, which he considered within the protection of the First Amendment. His contempt charge was based on his refusal to answer questions about his activities in the Progressive Party in 1948 and the ideas he had expressed as a guest lecturer at the University of New Hampshire in 1954. The Chief Justice, speaking for the Court, reaffirmed the doctrine of the *Watkins* opinion that legislative investigation, like laws themselves, may encroach on the right of free expression and declared that the Attorney General's investigation had so done "in the areas of academic freedom and political expression."[90] He added that academic freedom and the right to form new political parties are of special importance and should be protected from investigatory abuses. Warren also based his decision on the narrower ground of the "separation of the power of a state legislature to conduct investigations from the responsibility to direct the use of that power."[91]

Justice Frankfurter, in a concurring opinion in which Justice Harlan joined, maintained that whether the Attorney General had acted within the scope of the authority given to him by the legislature was for the state courts to decide. He contended that the state had invaded both the academic and political freedom of Sweezy: "For a citizen to be made to forego even a part of so basic a liberty as his political autonomy, the subordinating interest of the State must be compelling."[92] Justice Frankfurter found no such justification in the circumstances of this case, since the threats to the security of New Hampshire involved here were too remote to justify the inquiries. The concept of a compelling state interest was to become one of the most significant Court tests in a number of areas in later years. Frankfurter's concurrence also included one of the finest statements ever written by a justice about the meaning of academic freedom.

Justice Burton, who had not participated in *Watkins*, joined the dissent of Justice Clark, who took the position that the state's interest in investigating subversive activities outweighed Sweezy's First Amendment rights and that the Supreme Court was bound by the state supreme court's determination of the relevancy of the questions to the legislative purpose.

The *Watkins* and *Sweezy* opinions seemed to indicate a new vigor of the Court in reviewing criminal prosecutions for failure to cooperate with legislative committees, although in their strict holdings they made little inroad on legislative power to investigate subversion. In *Sacher v. United States*,[93] the Court followed the *Watkins* theory, and in *Flaxer v. United States*,[94] the Court gave notice that Congressional investigators must be explicit in their orders to witnesses.

Again in *Raley v. Ohio*,[95] where witnesses were misled as to their duty to testify, convictions for contempt were reversed. Under the authority of the *Watkins* case, it appeared that Congress would be required to prove contempt before federal judges who could exercise their own judgment in determining whether Congress is entitled to the information it is seeking. Some clarification in this matter was provided when the Court indicated in two decisions in the 1958 term that much of the wide-ranging Warren opinions was dicta.

In *Barenblatt v. United States*,[96] the Court made what conservatives thought was a needed corrective to the extreme implication of the *Watkins* dicta on committee inquiries. Barenblatt, a college professor, appeared before a subcommittee of the House Un-American Activities Committee investigating communism in education and operating under the same authorizing resolution that had been attacked in *Watkins*. He refused to answer questions about his affiliation with the Communist Party on the ground that the committee had no authority to inquire into his political and religious beliefs or any "other personal and private affairs" or associational activities. He expressly disclaimed any reliance on the Fifth Amendment protection against self-incrimination and made no objections to the inquiry on First Amendment grounds. For this, Barenblatt was found guilty of contempt of Congress, and the Court affirmed the conviction by a five-to-four vote.[97]

Justice Harlan, for the majority, confined *Watkins* to its narrow factual holdings, while finding that Barenblatt had been clearly informed of both the subject matter under inquiry and the pertinency of the questions asked. Although the authorizing resolution alone was still insufficient for this purpose, remarks made by the committee chairman during the proceeding provided the witness with the requisite information. Barenblatt, unlike Watkins, well knew the Committee's purpose. The witness had been informed by the Committee about the intended aim of its questioning. At least some of the questions he refused to answer were plainly relevant to the purpose. The original grant of power should now, according to the majority, be read in the light of the "persuasive gloss of legislative history" that had been added in the years since the Committee's creation. Thus, this investigation was within the intended scope, as it had come to be understood through political usage. The Committee was investigating the potential overthrow of the government and "an investigation of advocacy of or preparation for overthrow certainly embraces the right to identify a witness as a member of the Communist party"—which the opinion noted has been found not to be "an ordinary political party at all."[98] Justice Harlan went on to state that the special nature of the Communist Party was the basis for upholding federal legislation directed at subversive activities "which in a different context would certainly have raised constitutional issues of the gravest character."

Having decided that the House of Representatives had empowered the Committee to ask the questions it did, the Court considered Barenblatt's objection that the whole undertaking was beyond the pale of constitutionality. Justice Harlan emphasized that the Court's function in passing on that grave issue was "purely one of constitutional adjudication in the particular case and upon the particular record," not one of "judgment upon the general wisdom or efficacy of the activities of this committee in a vexing and complicated field."[99] He contended that the "resolution of the issue always involves a balancing by the courts of the competing private and public interests at stake in the particular circumstances shown."[100] Here Barenblatt's private interest in secrecy to avoid public censure following disclosure was weighed against congressional interest in obtaining information necessary for effective legislation against subversive activities. In this case, the majority held that the individual's rights to privacy in connection with one's associational memberships had to yield to the nation's interest in self-preservation.

Justice Black, joined in dissent by the Chief Justice and Justice Douglas, thought that the resolution itself must contain specific authority from Congress to conduct the particular investigation involved. He argued that the witness, in order to make a meaningful decision whether to answer the Committee's questions, must be informed not only of the subject matter of the inquiry and the pertinency of the questions asked, but also of the importance to the government of the information sought, so that he can make an on-the-spot appraisal of the constitutionality of the proceedings. Since witnesses could not be expected to examine lengthy legislative history before testifying, they could not make this determination unless guided by an explicit mandate from Congress to the Committee.

As Justice Brennan's separate dissent noted, the motive of a committee is often admittedly exposure for its own sake rather than the desire to lay the framework for legislation. Congress has generally refrained from repressing such an attitude on the part of the committees, thus perhaps indicating approval. Exposure alone hardly seems an adequate legislative end to justify subordination of First Amendment guarantees, but the majority pointed out "so long as Congress acts in pursuance of its constitutional power, the judiciary lacks authority to intervene on the basis of the motives which spurred the exercise of that power."[101]

The Court faces grave difficulties when dealing with challenges to legislative power. A basic problem is that the exigencies of the congressional calendar make it impossible for the mandates of committees to be laid down in other than broad terms. The justices have an onerous task in determining whether the congressional commands are too broad or whether the committee is pursuing a legitimate concern of Congress. If an investigation is related to a valid legislative purpose, it cannot be invalidated because the Court feels that its real purpose is the exposure of those being investigated.[102] Regardless of how offensive the motives of individual legislators, legislative investigations have great values. [103]

In the same term the Court also ruled again on state legislative investigations. In *Uphaus v. Wyman*,[104] a five-justice majority upheld the contempt conviction of a witness for failure to produce a list of guests at a summer camp suspected of being a "Communist front" when ordered to do so by the attorney general of New Hampshire, again acting as a one-man legislative investigating committee. Uphaus contended that the Smith Act had superseded the New Hampshire Subversive Activities Act of 1951 and that the *Nelson* decision had barred all state action in the field of subversion. In this case Justices Frankfurter and Harlan, who had disagreed with the theory of the Court while concurring in *Sweezy*, joined Justices Clark, Whittaker, and Stewart to affirm the conviction. The issue of authorization was mentioned only in passing by the majority, which tacitly adopted Frankfurter's concurring opinion in *Sweezy* and accepted the finding of the New Hampshire Supreme Court as controlling. Thus the Court held that a state could investigate subversive activities against itself. To this extent state and federal sedition laws could coexist.

Justice Brennan, for the four dissenters, wrote a strongly worded opinion demonstrating that exposure was the sole purpose of *Uphaus*. The dissent vigorously argued violation of due process and only incidentally referred to Uphaus' contention of federal preemption of the field. Brennan contended that the state should make some plausible disclosure of its law-making interest so that the relevance of its inquiries could be tested. Although the opinion of the majority did not satisfy Brennan, it did make it clear in *Uphaus* that the "academic and political freedoms discussed in *Sweezy* . . . are not present here in the same degree, since . . . (the camp) is neither a university nor a political party."[105] The questions Sweezy had refused to answer did not touch areas closely related to Communist activities. On the other hand, nineteen speakers at the summer camp in *Uphaus* were or had been members of one or more Communist or Communist-front organizations on the U.S. Attorney General's list.

Another aspect of the *Uphaus* decision was the fact that the New Hampshire statute required all public lodging houses to maintain a guest book open to police inspection. The Court reasoned that since the statute required the guest list to be "public," the private interest in maintaining associational privacy was minimal.

Justice Clark in his *Sweezy* dissent had argued preemption,[106] and in *Uphaus* the Court made explicit one of its tacit assumptions in *Sweezy*, holding that the New Hampshire Subversive Activities Act had not been superseded by the federal Smith Act, since the former was intended to control subversive activity directed at the state, whereas the Smith Act was designed to protect the federal government. The majority stated further that the important state power to deal with internal disturbances and the correlative interest in preserving itself by the investigation of subversion are such important state interests that they could not be superseded without a clear congressional expression of intent to do so. The state power to preserve itself includes the power to investigate subversive activities and the power to prosecute follows a fortiori from the investigatory powers. *Uphaus*, then, supplied an essential clarification of the general language of the *Nelson* case. The majority opinion was consistent with the requirements of the federal system that allows the state to retain the power to preserve itself through enactment of anti-sedition statutes.[107]

The change from *Sweezy* to *Uphaus* was not great considering that the Chief Justice spoke for only four members of the Court (Black, Douglas, Brennan, and himself) in the former. Justices Frankfurter and Harlan had concurred in the judgment but not the opinion of the Court; Justice Whittaker did not participate, and Justices Clark and Burton had dissented.

The net result of these decisions was that all the justices closely reviewed cases involving legislative investigations. This was noteworthy since for some years, the Court appeared disinclined to examine such cases at all.[108] What the Court seemed to be asking in 1957 was for Congress to provide some limits for the comparatively few committees to which vague instructions and indefinite jurisdiction had been given, and some measure of supervision for the few committees whose activities indicated the need for such. Such self-imposed restriction by Congress would have been preferable to judicial supervision, but the Court gave indication that there were limits to this rule of legislative supremacy. The 1959 decisions appeared to have reaffirmed rather than to have destroyed the view that exposure and punishment were not permissible objectives of legislative inquiries. Neither the majority nor the minority of the justices said that the legislative purposes of these cases were irrelevant. Nothing in these cases diminished the restraints on legislative investigators that had previously been established, such as the obligation to recognize a witness's right to avoid self-incrimination, the duty to remain within the scope of authority conferred by the parent legislative body, or the need to enlighten the witness as to the pertinency of questions asked. What the Court demonstrated was that it would question legislative committee authority where there was obvious denial of process due a witness under such circumstances. But the Court wisely chose to tread warily on the path of censorship of the internal functioning of a coordinate branch.[109]

During the 1960 term, the Court reviewed two HUAC cases involving contempt convictions of critics of the Committee rather than Communists.[110] Braden was an officer of a civil rights organization that believed that HUAC was being used by segregationists to attack their opponents as Communists. Wilkinson was a member of the Emergency Civil Liberties Committee, which lobbied for HUAC's abolition. Both were subpoenaed by the Committee and refused to answer whether they were Party members. Justice Stewart, for the Court, ruled that the First Amendment claims of Braden and Wilkinson were "indistinguishable" from those of Barenblatt. The Court, with the same voting alignment as in *Barenblatt*, again relied upon the government's interest in self-preservation outweighing the individual's right not to answer whether he was a Communist. In dissent, Justice Black saw the Court's decisions as a "dangerous trend" in need of correction and used the occasion to blast the majority's balancing doctrine. Said Black: "Where First Amendment freedoms are left to depend upon a balance to be struck by this Court in each particular case, liberty cannot survive. For under such a rule, there are no constitutional rights that cannot be 'balanced' away."

FIFTH AMENDMENT PRIVILEGES

The Eisenhower Court also made important rulings on the use of the Fifth Amendment privilege against self-incrimination by witnesses before congressional committees.[111] Although the use of this privilege is an effective method of justifying silence before a committee, it almost invariably does great damage to the reputation of the claimant and may also be the basis for punitive actions of various kinds against him. Witnesses have lost their jobs both in public and private employment as a result of an unfavorable public attitude toward claimants of the privilege. In two cases decided on the same day in 1955, *Emspak v. United States*[112] and *Quinn v. United States*,[113] the Supreme Court defended the use of this controversial right.[114]

Both Quinn and Emspak had refused to answer questions before the House Committee on Un-American Activities, but their pleas under the Fifth Amendment had been "deliberately phrased in muffled terms." The government charged that they were trying to "obtain the benefit of the privilege without incurring the popular opprobrium which often attaches to its exercise."[115] The Supreme Court majority held that they had given adequate notice of their intention to invoke the privilege. Chief Justice Warren noted in the *Quinn* case that "no ritualistic formula is necessary."[116] If the Committee had been in any doubt as to the ground on which refusal to testify was based, it should have asked the witness whether he was in fact relying on the Fifth Amendment. In *Emspak*, the Chief Justice added: "If it is true that in these times a stigma may somehow result from a witness' reliance on the Self-Incrimination Clause, a committee should be all the more ready to recognize a veiled claim of the privilege. Otherwise, the great right which the Clause was intended to secure might be effectively frustrated by private pressures."[117]

The frequent blockage of government inquiries into "subversive activities" by claims of the privilege against self-incrimination[118] led the Eisenhower administration to propose, and Congress to adopt, the Immunity Act of 1954,[119] under which witnesses could be compelled to testify before courts, grand juries, or congressional committees in national security cases by granting them immunity from prosecution for any criminal activities they may confess. This law was upheld by the Court in *Ullmann v. United States*.[120] Ullmann, a senior economic analyst in the Treasury Department, had pleaded the Fifth Amendment before a congressional committee and a grand jury when questioned about a wartime espionage ring in Washington, and had been granted an immunity under the 1954 act so that a grand jury could secure his testimony. Justice Frankfurter, for the Court, warned that the protection of this privilege should not be downgraded or its effectiveness diminished. However, he found the act constitutional, holding that the protection of the amendment related only to the infliction of penalties affixed to criminal acts.

Justice Douglas, with whom Justice Black concurred, dissented, arguing that this interpretation was too narrow. The immunity act protected individuals from criminal punishment but exposed them to the obloquy of public "infamy" and other informal penalties. Douglas, in what was called "the twentieth century's most eloquent apologia for the right to remain silent," contended that "the Framers put it beyond the power of Congress to compel anyone to confess his crimes. The evil to be guarded against was partly self-accusation under legal compulsion. But this was only a part of the evil. The conscience and dignity of man were also involved."[121]

Apologists for the *Ullmann* decision did not view it as an indication that the Court was disrespectful of the self-incrimination guarantee.[122] Justice Frankfurter's opinion insisted that the problem should be approached in the "spirit of strict, not lax, observance of the constitutional protection of the individual."[123] Such a statement indicated that the Court, while not going as far as Justice Douglas and Justice Black suggested, was aware of the problems in this touchy area. It should also be noted that although *Ullmann* dealt with testimony before a grand jury under the Immunity Act of 1954, the constitutional considerations in compelling disclosures before a congressional committee would be the same.

CLASSIFICATION OF ORGANIZATIONS

In *Communist Party v. Subversive Activities Control Board*,[124] the Court again carried its fastidious concern for procedural regularity in this field to great lengths and sidestepped the determination of thorny constitutional questions. The case involved an order of the Board that the Party register as a "Communist action organization" under the Subversive Activities Control Act of 1950.[125] Among the grounds asserted by the Party for challenging the order was the argument that three of the witnesses on whom the Board had relied in making its determination had been perjurers. The Court of Appeals had concluded that the evidence supporting the order was ample without reference to the testimony of these three. But the Supreme Court, speaking by Justice Frankfurter, declared that it could not "pass upon a record containing such challenged testimony."[126] The case was returned to the Board "to make certain that the Board bases its findings on untainted evidence."

The argument of the dissenters that the Board's new judgment would precisely duplicate the old and that the remand would accomplish nothing beyond making the process of review longer, was rejected in characteristic restraintist language by Justice Frankfurter:

> The untainted administration of justice is certainly one of the most cherished aspects of our institutions. Its observance is one of our proudest boasts. This Court is charged with supervisory functions in relation to proceedings in the federal courts. . . . Therefore, fastidious regard for the honor of the administration of justice requires the Court

> to make certain that the doing of justice be made so manifest that
> only irrational or perverse claims of its disregard can be asserted.[127]

These words might be taken as the credo of the restraintists' attitude toward governmental action aimed at subversion. The judiciary may hesitate to substitute its judgment for that of Congress in deciding whether laws like these should be passed. But it can make sure that no one, Communist or other, is able to say that the laws were unfairly enforced in American courts. The Court perhaps leaned over backward to clinch that result in some cases, but this result was probably the greatest contribution of the restraintists in this area.[128]

Five years later, the Court, by a five-to-four vote, affirmed the Board's finding that the Communist Party was a Communist-action organization and therefore required to register with the Attorney General.[129] Avoiding constitutional questions of free speech, bill of attainder, and self-incrimination, Justice Frankfurter, for the Court, concluded that the statute was "regulatory," rather than prohibitory. But the Court postponed any decision on the constitutionality of the statutory sanctions until they were actually enforced. Warren, Brennan, Black, and Douglas again dissented. The Subversive Activities Control Board eventually was allowed to die in 1973 when Congress refused to appropriate funds for it.

CONTROL OVER PASSPORTS

From 1947 until 1958, the State Department adopted a policy of refusing passports to Communists or persons engaged in activities which would advance the movement, or whose travel would "prejudice the orderly conduct of foreign relations" or "otherwise be prejudicial to the interests of the United States."[130] Ever since the Russian revolution, the Secretary of State had occasionally restricted foreign travel of U.S. citizens on "political" grounds.[131] A number of applicants who were denied passports brought suits against the State Department to compel their issuance, but none of these controversies reached the Supreme Court until 1958.[132]

The refusal to grant passports to two men on the ground that they were alleged to be Communists was reviewed in *Kent v. Dulles*.[133] The Secretary of State purported to be acting under the authority of a law codified in 1926, which stated that he "may grant and issue passports . . . under such rules as the President shall designate."[134] For a bare majority, Justice Douglas denied him this discretionary authority, and in the course of reaching that conclusion made two important points. First was that "the right to travel is a part of the 'liberty' of which the citizen cannot be deprived without due process of law under the Fifth Amendment."[135] This being the first such declaration by the Supreme Court, it represented an important pronouncement. However, this right was declared only as an aid to statutory construction. A holding that the Secretary had been granted the power to withhold passports to citizens on the basis of beliefs and associations would raise "important constitutional questions."[136] The Court avoided the constitutional questions in this case involving the well-known artist Rockwell Kent and held that the power was not granted by the law.

Following the *Kent* decision, the State Department announced that passport applicants would no longer be required to answer questions about Communist Party membership, and passports were immediately granted to alleged subversives who had been denied passports for years. Shortly thereafter, legislation was introduced in Congress that would bar the issuance of passports to persons who had been members of the Communist Party or who had engaged in "pro-Communist activity" within the previous ten years. Congress failed to enact such laws during the 1958 "Court-curbing" session. Were such bills passed, the Court would doubtlessly have been faced with the constitutional questions that were dodged in *Kent*.

The Court probably would have been hesitant to contend that the right of a citizen to leave the country was an absolute right which Congress could not deny under any circumstances.[137] More likely the justices would have admitted the right of Congress to subject the granting of passports to "reasonable regulation under law," meaning that any legislative delegation to the Secretary of State would have to state fairly specific standards for the denial of passports. The main problem confronting the Court here was the requisite specificity that might be attributed to delegation by silence.[138]

Due process requirements in passport denial cases would probably necessitate open hearings to substantiate evidence of illegal activity on the part of the applicant. To the Court majority, evidence merely of the applicant's past opinions or associations would not be acceptable for this purpose. The Court gave indication that a passport denial could not consistently with due process rest on a confidential file which was not disclosed to the applicant in *Dayton v. Dulles*;[139] but the Court preferred not to reach the constitutional question, holding, on the authority of *Kent*, that the denial exceeded the Secretary's statutory authority.[140]

THE FEDERAL LOYALTY PROGRAM

One of the special concerns of the Cold War period was the loyalty of governmental employees.[141] The federal loyalty program was set up in 1947 by President Truman, and President Eisenhower continued it in a somewhat revised form in 1953. All employees and applicants for employment were required to undergo a loyalty check, in which the FBI assisted in investigations. The Department of Justice prepared a list of subversive organizations to help guide the decisions of agency loyalty boards. These boards held hearings when damaging information was received concerning an employee or applicant, but some of the customary protections of the American hearing procedure tradition—such as the right to be informed of the source of the charges and the right to confront the persons making the accusations—were not guaranteed.

The loyalty-security program was widely attacked as denying procedural due process. The Supreme Court held that the Attorney General had not accorded necessary procedural protections to the organizations he labeled as subversive, but an evenly divided Court affirmed the ruling of the lower court that it is not the business of the courts to question the decisions of administrative superiors about the fitness of their employees to perform their assigned tasks. The relevant federal statutes require only notice of removal and an opportunity to reply to charges.

This is without doubt the proper policy under usual conditions. It would be outlandish to require a quasi-judicial hearing and provide for judicial review in order to discharge a federal employee for inefficiency. But the loyalty-security program removals were not this type. A loyalty charge put an employee on trial not only for his job but for his reputation and his professional standing. Such removals might make it extremely difficult for him to secure any other employment for which he was fitted, since he was condemned as a person unworthy of trust and confidence. Administrative hearings having such severe consequences would appear to merit the protective requirements of judicial process.

The Eisenhower Court carefully avoided constitutional questions in subsequent loyalty cases it handled.[142] When favoring the injured employee in these cases, the Court restricted its rulings to rather narrow grounds. The first loyalty case adjudged by the Eisenhower Court was *Peters v. Hobby*,[143] involving a professor of medicine at Yale University who was employed part-time as a consultant by the U.S. Public Health Service in work of a nonsensitive or nonconfidential character. After being twice cleared by agency loyalty boards, Peters was discharged on loyalty grounds and barred from the federal service for three years by the president's Loyalty Review Board post-audit of his case four years after the original charges had been successfully met.

Chief Justice Warren, speaking for the Court, held that the post-audit conducted by the Board was in violation of President Truman's executive order setting up the loyalty system. The order was construed by the Court to limit the Board's jurisdiction to appeals from adverse rulings, but the regulations issued by the Board under the order asserted authority over appeals from favorable rulings as well. Likewise the regulations permitted the Board to review cases on its own motion, and since Dr. Peters had not been recommended for dismissal by the agency board, and neither he nor his agency referred his case to the Loyalty Review Board, the Court ruled that in the absence of a prior dismissal and proper referral, the Loyalty Review Board had exceeded its delegated authority by providing for a hearing on its own motion.[144] By these technicalities the Court was able to evade the constitutional questions presented by the case.

In *Cole v. Young*,[145] the Court held invalid a dismissal under President Eisenhower's Executive Order 10450 of a food and drug inspector employed by the Department of Health, Education and Welfare. Justice Harlan, speaking for a six-man majority, argued that the 1950 act under which the order was promulgated prescribed summary dismissal only for employees in positions which were "sensitive" in terms of their possible effects on national security.[146] A dismissal of a preference-eligible veteran made without considering the special sensitivity of the position thus violated the Veterans Preference Act.[147] The president had extended the act to all departments and agencies of the government without regard for any criteria of sensitivity. In the Court's opinion this wholesale extension was at variance with congressional intent as revealed by the wording of the act and in its legislative history. Thus the Court endowed Congress with presumptive good intentions and invested it with the same concern for procedural regularity as the judiciary.

Service v. Dulles[148] involved a foreign service officer who was subjected to six inquiries by the State Department Loyalty-Security Board and was cleared each time over a six-year period. The last three clearances were post-audited by the president's Loyalty Review Board, which twice remanded the case to the State Department for further consideration, and the third time decided to conduct a hearing itself, resulting in the removal of John Stewart Service, an "Old China Hand," from office.

The Supreme Court found a procedural reason for reversing the ouster and restoring Service to his position. The majority found that the State Department had not followed its own regulations in handling this case. The government contended that the Secretary of State had been given "absolute discretion" to "terminate the employment of any officer or employee" whenever he deemed it necessary or advisable in the interests of the United States under the so-called "McCarran rider,"[149] that had been attached annually to the State Department appropriation act since 1947. The Court thought that the department and also the president had recognized an obligation to operate under procedural requirements even in McCarran rider cases. With Justice Clark not participating, the Court was unanimous in its decision.

The following term, the Court again avoided the due process problem in holding that the army lacked statutory authority to give other than honorable discharges to servicemen because of allegedly subversive pre-induction activities in *Harmon v. Brucker*.[150] Justice Clark again demonstrated his opposition to curtailment of Congress's antisubversive measures in his sole dissent.

Again in *Vitarelli v. Seaton*,[151] the Court unanimously agreed on nonconstitutional grounds that a discharge under the federal security program was invalid. In this case, charges against an employee of the Department of the Interior failed to specify the "subversive" persons and organizations with whom the employee had allegedly associated, thereby violating the program's requirement of specificity of charges. At his loyalty hearing, Vitarelli was asked questions concerning his religious, educational, social, and political beliefs in violation of the program's requirements of relevancy. Nor was the accused confronted with derogatory witnesses whose names were in the record and thus were not confidential informants, in violation of another regulation that gave employees the right to cross-examine opposing, nonconfidential witnesses.

Constitutional overtones were less muted in *Greene v. McElroy*.[152] Greene, the vice president of a private manufacturing corporation engaged in producing goods for the armed forces, was denied access to classified governmental information in the "interests of national security," although he had been granted the required clearances for a number of years previously. As a result, Greene was discharged from his position and was unable to obtain other employment in the field. Greene requested reconsideration and a year later received a hearing before the Eastern Industrial Personnel Security Board. At the hearing, he was not permitted to examine reports made by investigatory agencies and was not allowed to confront and cross-examine any of the government's informants. The Board affirmed the action of the Secretary of the Navy in denying Greene his clearance, and the lower federal courts affirmed this decision.

The Supreme Court reversed, holding that neither the president nor Congress had given the Defense Department authority to establish a program by which persons might lose their jobs on the basis of determinations made in proceedings in which they were denied confrontation and cross-examination. The Chief Justice, writing for the majority, reasoned that when administrative program and procedures present a strong possibility of infringement of constitutionally protected rights, explicit congressional or presidential authorization for them is necessary. Such authorization could not be assumed by acquiescence or nonaction. Thus the Court could not reach the constitutional issues unless the requisite specificity was present. Frankfurter, Harlan, and Whittaker denied that even if the nonconfrontation procedures had been authorized, they might still be invalid.

There was some dispute as to whether the right to work for a living in a chosen field constituted a constitutional right. Those in government service had no vested right to their jobs and could be dismissed without judicial process. The government's power to cause a civilian's dismissal from a classified job without trial had not been seriously disputed by the lower courts.[153] Appeal from an administrative board to the courts required damage resulting from action by the government which constituted an invasion of a recognized legal right or injury resulting from an act of a government official in excess of his powers. Assuming that employment was a constitutional right not to be invaded without due process, a question was presented whether due process was achieved in the summary type of hearing utilized where the government claimed the privilege to withhold its investigative sources and files from the accused. Although a person might have no constitutional right to view confidential documents, he should be protected in his right to pursue his chosen private employment and to maintain his reputation and standing in the community without arbitrary governmental interference. A person's freedom to work would seem to be part of his protected "liberty" and his reputation and community standing, a part of "property" within the meaning of the Fifth Amendment.[154] The dicta of the *Greene* opinion indicated that where private employment was involved, the individual could not be deprived of his job by governmental action except after a hearing which comported with our traditional ideas of fair procedure—including the safeguards of confrontation and cross-examination.[155]

A more difficult problem was determining the procedure that was sufficient to satisfy the requirements of due process within the context of the government security program. The government was faced with the dilemma of either revealing the identity of important informants or allowing suspected subversives to remain in sensitive positions. On the other hand, the employee had less chance of obtaining a favorable administrative finding if he was denied the opportunity to confront his accusers. In determining which was more important, the Court had to be guided by such variables as the extent of actual harm incurred by the affected employee, the sensitivity of his position in relation to the national security, or the relative importance of the information provided by "confidential" sources to the factual determination.[156]

The *Greene* decision cast doubt on the constitutionality not only of the Industrial Security Program but also of the closely related Employee Loyalty Program, under which government employees could be discharged for security reasons after hearings that did not afford the protections of confrontation and cross-examination. Although the right of persons to secure and retain public employment appeared less clear than their right to pursue a private profession, the right to be free from arbitrary subjection to the public stigma inevitably attached to government disloyalty proceedings was equally present in both situations. While government may surely hire and fire as it desires in the absence of restrictions imposed by statute or regulation, it was questionable whether this privilege could be extended to permit the arbitrary dismissal of a public employee when the government's reasons seriously impaired an employee's reputation.[157]

Excluding *Harmon* and *Greene*, these decisions involving federal loyalty and security programs had little practical effect beyond the individual cases involved.[158] The *Peters* decision came after the Loyalty Review Board had been abolished. The review guaranteed veterans by the Civil Service Commission in the *Cole* case was of little value as long as the loyalty-security standards for removal remained as broad as they were. The State Department regulations involved in the *Service* decision could have been changed at any time and the *Vitarelli* case was limited to its factual setting. Thus, the Court had actually said little of lasting value in this important area although the *Peters* and *Greene* pronouncements by Chief Justice Warren indicated a tendency to insist on a high degree of formalism in the relations between the president and his assistants in the executive branch. If such formalism were extended beyond questionable executive procedures, the Court would have been guilty of a serious encroachment upon executive authority. On the other hand, the force of these opinions might well have affected the administration of the loyalty-security program in a manner that might have made it more equitable and more effective.[159]

In 1961 the Court for the first time wrote on the constitutional question of a summary discharge of a federal employee—a short-order cook at a naval gun factory who needed a security badge to enter the premises.[160] Justice Stewart's majority opinion upheld the constitutional basis of the summary discharge of Rachel Brawner because there was no stigma attached, and she could find other employment elsewhere. Brennan, Black, Douglas, and Warren dissented finding the government's action arbitrary and intrusive upon Brawner's property interest in her job.

REMOVAL OF PUBLIC EMPLOYEES

During the Cold War, several states adopted statutes for the removal of public employees on loyalty grounds. The New York law[161] was upheld by the Court in *Adler v. Board of Education of City of New York*.[162] The law required the Board of Regents to make a listing of organizations which it found to adhere to the doctrine that government should be overthrown by force or violence. Membership of a schoolteacher in any such listed organization was "prima facie evidence for disqualification for appointment to or retention in" any school employment, although the accused was to be given a full hearing and the right of judicial review before a final decision could be rendered. The Court upheld the law by a six-to-two vote, with Justices Black and Douglas in dissent, warning of the dangers of guilt by association and censorship of teachers.

Another rather common state action was the removal of employees who refused to give information about alleged subversive connections by taking the Fifth Amendment before a legislative committee or some other governmental body. In *Slochower v. Board of Higher Education*,[163] however, a five-justice majority held that a state violated the due process clause when it discharged an employee merely because he had invoked the Fifth Amendment before a committee of the U.S. Senate. Under the challenged provision of the city charter, "the assertion of the privilege against self-incrimination" was equivalent to a resignation and employees lost their jobs without "notice, hearing or opportunity to explain."[164]

The Court's decision was restricted to a narrow range, leaving open the possibility that Slochower, a tenured associate professor at Brooklyn College, could have been dismissed if the refusal to answer had occurred in the course of an inquiry into an employee's fitness by the city officials themselves or if, having invoked the privilege before any body, he was unable to provide a satisfactory explanation when given an opportunity to do so. The majority opinion appeared to hold that the fact of invoking the privilege before a federal committee could not be made the sole ground for dismissal, since the terms of government employment must be "reasonable, lawful, and non-discriminatory"[165] to satisfy the requirements of due process. Justice Clark went on to express the view that Slochower had no "constitutional right" to his job, and that it would be perfectly proper for "the city authorities themselves to inquire into Slochower's fitness."[166]

Such was the case in *Lerner v. Casey*[167] and *Beilan v. Board of Public Education*.[168] Lerner was a New York subway conductor who refused to tell New York City authorities whether he was a member of the Communist Party, and was dismissed as a person of "doubtful trust and reliability" because of his "lack of candor." Beilan, a Philadelphia schoolteacher, refused to tell his superintendent whether he had held a certain position in the Communist Party in 1944, and later took the Fifth Amendment before a House committee. He was then dismissed for "incompetency."

A five-justice majority upheld the official action in both cases, contending that the employees were not removed because of a Fifth Amendment plea, or because of their beliefs or associations, or because they were "security risks," but only because their refusal to answer questions put by their employers constituted evidence of their unreliability and incompetence. The four dissenters could not accept such "transparent denials" of the real reasons for the removals. Justice Brennan, joined by the Chief Justice, contended that each petitioner had been branded a "disloyal American" on the basis of evidence and through a procedure which could not possibly support such a finding, and so had been denied due process of law.[169] Justices Black and Douglas thought that people were being punished for their beliefs in these cases. They reasserted the principle that government should "concern itself only with the actions of men, not with their opinions or beliefs."[170]

These cases seemed to give the states broad powers of removal for suspected subversives in public employment. What they made clear was that the privilege of the Fifth Amendment did not protect from discharge a state employee who stood mute before an inquiry by his superior, even though the state could not discharge him merely for invoking this right before a federal authority such as a congressional committee.[171] On the other hand, one could make a strong case for the requirements of notice and a full and fair hearing before administrative action was taken that adversely affected the private individual. Such would appear to be fundamental to due process. Also, the threat of dismissal after a valid invocation of the privilege might so undermine the effective use of it that dismissal for mere refusal to answer might become impermissible.[172]

Although the state might carefully label the reason for its action in releasing employees, the public generally attached a lack-of-loyalty stigma. The Court construed the privilege against self-incrimination to protect a person from the necessity of giving evidence that could lead to a criminal charge, but not from public opprobrium.

The judicial attitude appeared to be that the Court would adhere scrupulously to what it deemed to be the explicit command of the self-incrimination clause, but would not extend this right beyond those strict limits. The majority would not enlarge the protection into a general "right to silence," or apply it in any form as a restriction on the states.[173] Indeed these cases should not be distinguished from others where dismissal was made for refusal to answer other relevant questions relating to such matters as immorality, drug addiction, and alcoholism. To hold otherwise would appear to lead to the questionable result that an employee interrogated as to matters involving disloyalty was less vulnerable to dismissal than one asked about matters which involved comparable stigma.[174]

REMOVAL FROM PRIVATE EMPLOYMENT

The policy of avoiding substantive constitutional issues was again exemplified in Black v. Cutter Laboratories,[175] though here the logic of Justice Clark's majority opinion was somewhat confusing. The Cutter Laboratories had discharged an employee on the stated ground, among others, that she was an active Communist Party member, but an arbitration board had found this charge "stale" and had concluded that she was in fact being discharged for union activity. The collective bargaining agreement between company and union recognized Communist Party membership as "just cause" for dismissal, but the board pointed out that the company had known of the alleged affiliation for two years and argued that the right to invoke this cause had been waived by the delay in doing so. Upon affirmation by a lower court, the Supreme Court of California reversed, holding that the employee had been discharged for her Communist Party activities and that it was against the public policy of the state to apply the doctrine of waiver in a case involving discharge for that reason.

For the Supreme Court, Justice Clark dismissed the writ, declaring that the state supreme court had merely construed a local contract under local law and that the cause therefore raised no federal question. But in dissent, Justice Douglas insisted that the state decision seemed to involve enforcement of a contract barring Party members from employment and if so the question was raised as to whether this state action violated the Fourteenth Amendment. Justice Clark's opinion was such that the dissenters could be justified in assuming that the Court was approving state court enforcement of a contract that barred Communists and thus deciding a significant constitutional question by its silence. Since the Court stated that no constitutional question was presented, it left the issue of enforcing non-Communist provisions of collective bargaining agreements in suspense.[176] Thus the Court again dodged the substantive problem presented by subversion and the law.

Two years later, Justice Frankfurter, for the Court, ruled in *International Association of Machinists v. Gonzales*[177] that the Wagner and Taft–Hartley Acts did not preempt a state law that provided a remedy for wrongful expulsion from a union. Douglas and Warren dissented.

STATE LOYALTY OATHS

One of the most common state legislative reactions to the subversive problem has been to require a loyalty oath of public employees. Oaths that relate to actual membership of government employees in the Communist Party have received the Supreme Court's approval. In *Garner v. Board of Public Works*,[178] the Vinson Court had upheld a Los Angeles ordinance requiring the filing of an affidavit by city employees that they were not and never had been members of the Party. On the other hand, the Court has been stricter on oaths with less definite standards of disloyalty. In *Wieman v. Updegraff*,[179] the Court had unanimously invalidated an Oklahoma oath for state employees that adopted a guilt by association test. Persons who were or had been members of proscribed organizations were excluded from the state service, regardless of their degree of knowledge concerning the organizations to which they had belonged.

In 1958 other questions were faced by the Court in tax exemption cases. In *Speiser v. Randall*[180] and *First Unitarian Church of Los Angeles v. County of Los Angeles*,[181] two war veterans and two churches had claimed property tax exemptions under the California constitution.[182] The state law provided that applicants for such exemption must take an oath that they do not advocate violent overthrow of the government. The applicants refused to subscribe to the oath, and the assessors denied the exemptions.[183] The Supreme Court limited itself to the question of whether the state provisions deny "freedom of speech without the procedural safeguards required by the Due Process Clause of the Fourteenth Amendment."[184] Justice Brennan, for the Court, held that "a discriminatory denial of a tax exemption for engaging in speech is a limitation on free speech."[185] The provisions of the California tax exemptions laws impose on the taxpayer the burden of proving that he belongs in the exempt category. Such an allocation of the burden of proof on an issue concerning free speech was a denial of due process according to the Court. If the state wished to deny tax exemptions to persons or organizations on grounds of disloyalty, it would have to "bear the burden of persuasion to show that the appellants engaged in criminal speech."[186]

The opinion of the Court perhaps indicated that the justices might have had some doubts about the ability of governments to inculcate loyalty through security measures. The Court appeared to believe that loyalty was a matter of individual conscience and individual competence to appraise questions of moral obligation.[187]

ADMISSION TO THE BAR

Several states refused admission to the bar to candidates suspected of some kind of subversive association. In 1955 the Court denied certiorari in the case of *In re Anastaplo*,[188] involving a lawyer who had been refused admission to the bar in Illinois because of his insistence that the examiners had no right to inquire into his political beliefs. He put his refusal solely on First and Fourteenth Amendment grounds, not on the Fifth Amendment. The Illinois Supreme Court said it could attach whatever conditions to the practicing of law that it might reasonably select and that if an applicant could not meet these conditions he was "free to retain his beliefs and go elsewhere."[189]

Two years later, however, the Court reviewed two state denials of admission to the bar. In *Schware v. New Mexico Board of Bar Examiners*,[190] the applicant had been denied admission because he did not meet the requirement of "good moral character." The reasons for this were that he had used certain aliases during the Depression, that he had been arrested during labor disputes, and that he had been a member of the Communist Party from 1932 to 1940. The Supreme Court, in unanimously reversing the state action, accepted the explanations of the applicant who maintained that the aliases had been assumed to secure a job in businesses which discriminated against Jews and that in each instance of arrest he had been released with no charges filed. As for his membership in the Communist Party, Justice Black, for the Court, pointed out that at the time in question it was "a lawful political party with candidates on the ballot in most States." While some members might have engaged in illegal activities, Justice Black added "it cannot automatically be inferred that all members shared their evil purposes or participated in their illegal conduct."[191] No longer could it be assumed under the loyalty-security program that all who had been Communists were necessarily evil.

In a companion case, *Konigsberg v. State Bar of California*,[192] the applicant had been refused certification to state practice on the ground that he had not met the burden of proving that he was of good moral character and that he did not advocate the overthrow of government by unconstitutional means. Konigsberg had declined on constitutional grounds to answer questions concerning his political beliefs. The Court did not uphold or deny this claim of privilege, but instead addressed itself to the question of whether the record supported any reasonable doubt as to Konigsberg's good character or loyalty and concluded that it did not.[193] His character references were favorable with the main spokesman against him being an ex-Communist who testified that Konigsberg had attended meetings of a Communist organization in 1941. In 1950 Konigsberg had written newspaper articles criticizing the Korean War, big business, some decisions of the Supreme Court, and racial discrimination, but Justice Black, speaking for the five-justice majority, could not see how this was an indication of "bad moral character."[194] According to the majority, the state bar examiners could not draw unfavorable inferences from his refusals to answer if those refusals were based on his conviction that the questions invaded a constitutionally privileged area.[195] The majority opinion ignored the situation confronting the bar examiners. California law required that no one be certified for admission to the bar who advocated the overthrow of government by force and violence.[196] Konigsberg denied that he advocated such, and to test the reliability of this disavowal, the examiners questioned him about organizations to which he belonged and especially about current or past membership in the Communist Party. Konigsberg refused to answer on the basis that the examiners were limited to asking him whether he advocated the forcible overthrow of the government, and having asked that question, they could ask no related questions. The Court asserted that the plaintiff was not denied admission simply because he refused to answer the questions. As the majority of the Court stated the issue, it was whether the record contained evidence demonstrating as a factual matter that Konigsberg had a bad moral character. The bar examiners thought that the plaintiff's refusal to answer questions bearing upon the truth of his denial of advocacy was clear affirmative evidence of lack of moral character required for admission to the bar.

The question for the Court should have been as Justice Harlan's dissent stated: "Whether it violated the Fourteenth Amendment for a state bar committee to decline to certify for admission to the bar an applicant who obstructs a proper investigation into his qualifications by deliberately, and without constitutional justification, refusing to answer questions relevant to his fitness under valid standards, and who is therefore deemed by the State, under its law, to have failed to carry his burden of proof to establish that he is qualified."[197] The three dissenters, Harlan, Frankfurter, and Clark, contended that the examiners barred Konigsberg because of his noncooperation and should be affirmed in their action.

The case was remanded to the California Supreme Court, which vacated its previous order denying review and referred the matter to the bar committee for further consideration. At the ensuing hearings, Konigsberg again refused to answer any question relating to his membership in the Communist Party. The committee again declined to certify him, this time on the ground that his refusals to answer had obstructed a full investigation into his qualifications. The state supreme court refused review and also denied Konigsberg's motion for direct admission to practice.[198] The Supreme Court of the United States granted certiorari and this time ruled that the Fourteenth Amendment did not prevent a state from denying bar membership to an applicant who refused to answer questions about Communist Party membership after having been warned of the consequences of continuing refusal to answer.[199] Justice Harlan, for the five-man majority (the three dissenters of the earlier decision joined by Whittaker and Stewart, who had not participated in the first case), maintained that Konigsberg had been denied admission for obstructing the committee in performance of its necessary functions of examination and cross-examination. Justice Black, joined by Douglas and Warren, wrote a strong dissenting opinion, arguing that Konigsberg's freedom of association and speech had been abridged by the denial of admission. Black castigated the majority for using a balancing approach to free speech issues. Justice Brennan, joined by the Chief Justice, dissented on more limited grounds, contending that the procedural requirements of *Speiser* placing the burden of proof on the state to justify inhibition of speech, should be the controlling authority.

A companion case of *Konigsberg* was *In re Anastaplo* revisited.[200] Following the U.S. Supreme Court's denial of certiorari in 1955, the Illinois bar queried George Anastaplo about his membership in the Communist Party after he had written a short mandatory essay on principles underlying the Constitution. Anastaplo made the "mistake" of paraphrasing the Declaration of Independence and stating that when government did not protect citizens' liberties, the people had the right to alter or abolish it and establish a new government. Bar examiners read the statement and held a hearing during which Anastaplo was asked if he was a member of the Party. Anastaplo again declined the invitation of the examiners to inquire into his political beliefs. Justice Harlan, for the majority, used the balancing test and found the state's interest far outweighed Anastaplo's interest in not answering. The Court maintained that Anastaplo could quit obstructing the examiners and thus held "the key to admission in his own hands." Justice Black, in a dissent joined by Brennan, Douglas, and Warren, stated: "The effect of the 'balancing' here is that any State may now reject an applicant for admission to the bar if he believes in the Declaration of Independence as strongly as Anastaplo and if he is willing to sacrifice his career and his means of livelihood in defense of the freedoms of the First Amendment."

The net result of the confusing array of bar cases decided by the Eisenhower Court appeared to be that: (1) State occupational requirements must comply with the due process clause; (2) Refusal to answer questions about political connections can be a grounds for denying admission to the bar if such refusal obstructs investigation into the applicant's qualifications; (3) To a limited, if uncertain, degree, state factual determinations will be reviewed as to the validity of the standards used and perhaps as to the actual correctness of their results.[201] The last point—that the Supreme Court may reassess state factual determinations—was a disturbing extension of power in the first *Konigsberg* decision, and this was attacked in the Jenner–Butler bills to curb the Court. The proposed legislation would have withdrawn from the Supreme Court appellate jurisdiction in cases involving state regulations for admission to the bar and would have left to the states the enforcement of their own interpretations of the constitutional standards applicable in such cases. The second *Konigsberg* decision, distinguishing and limiting the prior ruling, in effect accomplished the purposes of the proposed legislation.

CONCLUSIONS

It is difficult to summarize the holdings of the Eisenhower Court in the types of controversial cases involving "subversives" covered in this chapter. One thing stands out—even though its opinions made ringing declarations that sometimes wandered from the legal point at hand, where the Court took a positive stand in invalidating official action, it was usually for rather narrow reasons. To quote Professor Pritchett, the Court revealed its concern for the threat of the misuse of zealous governmental antisubversive activities "by going as far as possible in protecting against the denial of rights and privileges without challenging the basic constitutional positions that such denials are not punishment or without creating new constitutional doctrines to justify wider judicial review. . . . The libertarian effects which the Court has . . . achieved have been secured for the most part through the interpretation of statutes, not through the interposition of constitutional barriers."[202] Even when the Court reached constitutional questions, it tended to treat them in as limited a fashion as possible.

It was a daunting task for the Eisenhower Court to attempt to work out the relationship of the judiciary to the Cold War. In assuring procedural regularity for accused subversives, even on narrow grounds, the Court took a positive, giant step forward from the position of the Vinson Court. In pursuance of this more positive role, the Court interposed certain restraints on a popularly supported legislative and administrative program aimed at restraining persons considered to be subversive. These decisions were offensive to those Americans who believed that the Communist threat was so great that constitutional protections had to yield to the necessity of national self-preservation. Such views were held widely enough to present in a very real way a challenge to the Court's rulings in several of these cases—as demonstrated by the congressional attack on the Court.[203]

On the basis of his votes and his written opinions, Justice Clark appeared to find the limited judicial role of the Eisenhower Court too broad in scope.[204] Perhaps he best exemplified the values of the Vinson era, which gave a strong presumption to the idea that the community's demands were nearly always more imperative than the individual's rights (a view supported by a fair number in the United States at that time). His judicial stance had the merit of clarity and gave one a strong indication of how he was likely to stand in political offender cases. Complete acceptance of this view would have devitalized the concept of constitutional freedom in the United States.

On the other hand, the civil liberties position adopted by Justices Black and Douglas would have gone much further than the majority in considering constitutional questions in many of these cases. In *Peters v. Hobby*, these Justices would have considered the constitutionality of the federal loyalty program and in *Yates v. United States*, they would have declared the Smith Act unconstitutional. Their philosophy was well summarized by Justice Douglas: "Our real power is our spiritual strength, and that spiritual strength stems from our civil liberties. If we are true to our traditions, if we are tolerant of a whole market place of ideas, we will always be strong. Our weakness grows when we become intolerant of opposing ideas, depart from our standards of civil liberties, and borrow the policeman's philosophy from the enemy we detest."[205]

The Justices appointed by Eisenhower were sharply divided in most of these cases. Chief Justice Warren, this group's outstanding protagonist

of civil liberties, cast only three votes against the claims of alleged procedural violations in the forty-four nonunanimous decisions discussed in
this chapter in which he participated,[206] notably in *Ullmann* where the
opinion of the Court accompanied its denial of certain claimed rights with
a reaffirmation of certain others. In cases in which both participated, Justice Brennan markedly differed from the Chief Justice only in the *Yates*
contempt case. Whittaker's zeal was considerably less intense than that
of Warren and Brennan, and on several occasions he was willing to support a restriction that was objectionable to them. Specifically, he approved
the government's passport policy, the dismissals of Beilan and Lerner, the
contempt convictions of Sacher, Barenblatt, Uphaus, Wilkinson, and
Braden, and the summary contempt sentence of Greene. Justice Harlan
rarely differed from Whittaker, as he did in *Sacher*, but in addition, he
opposed the Chief Justice in two Fifth Amendment cases and in *Slochower*,
Black, *Konigsberg*, and *Mesarosh*. In the last three cases, he concurred with
Justice Frankfurter with whom he was in agreement in all but a very few
of the cases where they were joint participants. Frankfurter's view that
the legislature should be allowed the benefit of every doubt did not prevent him from joining with Justices Black and Douglas in finding violations of due process in several cases including *Yates* and *Jencks*. Frankfurter and Harlan were the only members of the Court who were in the
majority in the *Watkins*, *Barenblatt*, *Sweezy*, and *Uphaus* series of cases. These
two justices also swung the balance of power toward the states by their
votes in *Beilan* and *Lerner*. The importance of Justice Frankfurter's vote is
demonstrated by the fact that he was in the majority in all of the cases
covered in this chapter with the exceptions of *Konigsberg I* and *Mesarosh*.[207]
Justice Stewart participated in only eighteen of the cases, usually holding
for the government's claims. He voted with Harlan, Frankfurter, Whittaker,
and Clark in the majority in *Barenblatt* and *Uphaus*, but he subscribed to
the opinion of the Chief Justice in *Greene v. McElroy*, rather than the concurring opinion of Frankfurter, Harlan, and Whittaker.

One needs only to compare cases to see the different trend of the
Eisenhower Court from that of the Vinson era. Although some of the decisions in this field were severely criticized as hampering the nation's security program, a careful reading of the strict holdings in these cases indicates that governmental power to combat subversion was not far from
where it was before the rulings of the Eisenhower Court. In fact "the Court
leaned over backward to keep from impeding the legislative and administrative program against subversion."[208] The Court, however, cleared the
way for judicial supervision of subjects that had once seemed immune.
The right to travel was pronounced a part of liberty under due process in
the passport cases. The protection of federal employees from arbitrary
dismissal under the Federal Loyalty-Security Program was enhanced, al-

though not guaranteed by the decisions of the Court. The highest tribunal likewise continued to insist upon fair trial procedures and other procedural guarantees for suspected subversives. In *Ullmann* the Court gave fair warning to Congress that although the immunity technique was constitutional, Fifth Amendment protection must not be downgraded or its effectiveness diminished. The Court in *Watkins* and *Barenblatt*, while granting continued broad investigatory powers, also required congressional committees to stay within the confining restraints of due process. If the Court misread the intent of Congress in the *Yates* or *Nelson* cases, the legislature needed only to amend the statutes in question to state its purposes in unmistakable fashion. What the Court's actions did was to force Congress to rethink these issues and to decide whether it really intended the more punitive standards in each instance. The *Jencks* case, as already noted, resulted in such positive congressional action.

The fact that the Court was more hesitant to find procedural violations in state cases is seen in Table 3.1. In this table, forty-seven important nonunanimous cases involving alleged subversives are divided into two categories according to their origin in federal or state proceedings. While procedural irregularity was found in 63 percent of the federal cases, only 40 percent of the state cases were decided favorably to the claims of the defendant. Considerations of federalism appear to have been of especial importance to Stewart, who did not uphold a single alleged subversive in five state cases, and to Burton, who voted against the states almost twice as much as against the federal government.

In federal cases through the 1958 term, Justice Frankfurter and the justices to his left formed a libertarian majority that frequently upheld charges of procedural irregularity. These justices were often joined by Harlan and Burton and later, Stewart. In state cases, Frankfurter, Harlan, and Whittaker formed a core group that upheld actions against political offenders in about half of the cases.[209] When these justices found violations in state procedures they were joined by Douglas, Black, Brennan, and Chief Justice Warren. After the serious Court-curbing threats from Congress in 1958, Frankfurter led what he might have considered a strategic retreat from libertarian outcomes in domestic security cases—and he usually won over Harlan, Whittaker, and Stewart in the process. With Clark maintaining the less libertarian Vinson Court attitude, a "right wing" majority prevailed from 1959–1962. Junius Scales was called a sacrificial lamb in the Court's effort to avoid a direct challenge to congressional authority after its close call with Court-curbing proposals. The rightwing retreat proved to be only temporary. After the retirements of Frankfurter and Whittaker in 1962, the Court proceeded to invalidate a number of legal leftovers from the Cold War era.

Table 3.1
Voting Records of Supreme Court Justices in 46 Selected Nonunanimous Cases Involving Alleged Subversives, 1953–1961 Terms (in percentages)

	For Claims of Defendants		
	Federal Cases	States Cases	Total
No. of cases	31	15	46
Douglas	100	100	100
Black	100	100	100
Warren	97	83 (12)	93 (44)
Brennan	91 (23)	91 (11)	91 (34)
COURT	63	40	56
Frankfurter	47	40	45
Burton	53 (17)	30 (10)	44 (27)
Harlan	38	29 (14)	35
Stewart	31 (13)	0 (5)	22 (18)
Whittaker	30 (20)	22 (9)	28 (29)
Clark	16	13	15

Justices Reed, Minton and Jackson are not included in this table, which represents the
   following cases:
Federal cases (31): For defendants' claims (19): *Quinn v. U.S.* (1955); *Emspak v. U.S.* (1955);
   Bart v. U.S. (1955); *Peters v. Hobby* (1955); *Communist Party v. Subversive Activities Control
   Board* (1956); *Cole v. Young* (1956); *Mesarosh v. U.S.* (1956); *Yates v. U.S.* (1957); *Jencks v.
   U.S.* (1957); *Watkins v. U.S.* (1957); *Harmon v. Brucker* (1958); *Sacher v. U.S.* (1958); *Dayton
   v. Dulles* (1958); *Kent v. Dulles* (1958); *Greene v. McElroy* (1959); *Vitarelli v. Seaton* (1959);
   Campbell v. U.S. (1961); *Clancy v. U.S.* (1961); *Deutch v. U.S.* (1961).
Against defendants' claims (12): *Ullmann v. U.S.* (1956); *Yates v. U.S.* (1957); *Green v. U.S.*
   (1958); *International Association of Machinists v. Gonzales* (1958); *Barenblatt v. U.S.* (1959);
   Gonzales v. U.S. (1960); *McPhaul v. U.S.* (1960); *Wilkinson v. U.S.* (1961); *Braden v. U.S.*
   (1961); *Communist Party v. Subversive Activities Control Board* (1961); *Scales v. U.S.* (1961);
   Cafeteria Workers v. McElroy (1961).
State cases (15): For defendants' claims (6): *Pennsylvania v. Nelson* (1956); *Slochower v. Board
   of Education* (1956); *Konigsberg v. State Bar* (1957); *Sweezy v. New Hampshire* (1957); *Speiser
   v. Randall* (1958); *First Unitarian Church v. Los Angeles* (1958).
Against defendants' claims (9): *Barsky v. Board of Regents* (1954); *Black v. Cutter Laboratories*
   (1956); *Beilan v. Board of Education* (1958); *Lerner v. Casey* (1958); *Uphaus v. Wyman* (1959);
   Nelson v. County of Los Angeles (1960); *Nostrand v. Little* (1960); *Konigsberg v. State Bar*
   (1961); *In re Anastaplo* (1961).

The lesson of these political offender cases adjudged by the
Eisenhower Court was obvious at the time: we must be wary of easy an-
swers when the totalitarian threat to democracy is under consideration.
The Court could not ignore the problem posed by the conflict between

our libertarian premises and totalitarian fact without shirking its historic duty. The problem of the Court was in determining what part it could best play in this process. The choice of roles was important. The Vinson Court chose a path of abstention—and individual civil rights suffered. The Eisenhower Court appeared to have selected an appropriate role in protecting procedural rights of the accused—a role for which the courts would seem especially well-suited. The power of the legislative and executive arms still existed, if those objectives continued to recommend themselves and if their sponsors were willing to observe the canons of procedural decency. Most of the Court's opinions served to remind the public that the greatest threat to American security was not from "miserable merchants of unwanted ideas"[210] but rather from weakness in American character in yielding to emotion and showing increased readiness to minimize and disregard the fundamental rights of the individual. What the decisions of the Eisenhower Court in this field did was to give the nation and its representatives a chance for a second look and to give them and the world at large a salutary reminder that the American tradition prescribed fair play, even in what was perceived as the perilous times of Cold War.[211]

NOTES

1. E.g., Zechariah Chafee, Jr., *Free Speech in the United States* (Cambridge: Harvard University Press, 1941).

2. 1 Stat. 570 (1798).

3. 1 Stat. 596 (1798).

4. See generally, James M. Smith, *Freedom's Fetters* (Ithaca, NY: Cornell University Press, 1956); Leonard W. Levy, *Legacy of Suppression* (Cambridge, MA: Belknap Press of Harvard University Press, 1960); John C. Miller, *Crisis in Freedom: The Alien and Sedition Acts* (Boston: Little, Brown & Co., 1951). The Sedition Act of 1798 was declared unconstitutional in *New York Times v. Sullivan*, 376 U.S. 254 (1964).

5. 40 Stat. 217 (1917).

6. 40 Stat. 553 (1918).

7. 249 U.S. 47 (1919).

8. 250 U.S. 616 (1919).

9. See generally, Robert K. Murray, *Red Scare: A Study in National Hysteria, 1919–1920* (Minneapolis: University of Minnesota Press, 1955).

10. 268 U.S. 652 (1925).

11. 274 U.S. 357 (1927).

12. See generally, Eldridge F. Dowell, *A History of Criminal Syndicalism in the United States* (Baltimore: Johns Hopkins Press, 1939).

13. 274 U.S. 380 (1927).

14. 283 U.S. 359 (1931).

15. 299 U.S. 353 (1937).

16. 301 U.S. 242 (1937).

17. Robert K. Carr, "Constitutional Liberty and Congressional Investigations," in *Foundations of Freedom in the American Constitution*, ed. Alfred H. Kelly (New York: Harper, 1958), pp. 140–192; Carr, *The House Committee on Un-American Activities, 1945-1950* (Ithaca, NY: Cornell University Press, 1952); *The Constitution and Congressional Investigating Committees: Individual Liberty and Congressional Power* (New York: Carrie Chapman Catt Memorial Fund, 1954); Alan Barth, *Government by Investigation* (New York: Viking Press, 1955); Telford Taylor, *Grand Inquest: The Story of Congressional Investigations* (New York: Simon & Schuster, 1955); Daniel H. Pollit, "Pleading the Fifth Amendment Before a Congressional Committee: A Study and Explanation," 32 *Notre Dame Law.* 43 (1956).

18. 54 Stat. 670 (1940).

19. Other important security legislation includes the Internal Security Act of 1950, 65 Stat. 987 (1950) and the Communist Control Act of 1954, 68 Stat. 775 (1954); see generally, Carl A. Auerbach, "Communist Control Act of 1954: A Proposed Legal-Political Theory of Free Speech," 23 *U. Chi. L. Rev.* 173 (1956); *cf.* 53 *Mich. L. Rev.* 1153 (1955).

20. See "Communism and the First Amendment: The Membership Clause of the Smith Act," 52 *Nw. U. L. Rev.* 527 (1957).

21. Labor Management Relations Act, 61 Stat. 156 (1947).

22. See generally, Walter L. Daykin, "The Operation of the Taft–Hartley Act's Non-Communist Provisions," 36 *Iowa L. Rev.* 607 (1957).

23. 339 U.S. 382 (1950).

24. 341 U.S. 494 (1951); for analysis of the various opinions with special emphasis on the concurring opinion of Justice Frankfurter, see Jacobs, *Justice Frankfurter*, pp. 114–121; see also Robert A. Horn, *Groups and the Constitution* (Stanford, CA: Stanford University Press, 1956), pp. 136–141; Wallace Mendelson, "Clandestine Speech and the First Amendment," 51 *Mich. L. Rev.* 553 (1953); "Clear and Present Danger—From *Schenck* to *Dennis*," 52 *Colum. L. Rev.* 313 (1952); Nathaniel L. Nathanson, "The Communists Trial and the Clear and Present Danger Test," 63 *Harv. L. Rev.* 1167 (1950); Edward S. Corwin, "Bowing Out 'Clear and Present Danger'," 27 *Notre Dame Law.* 329 (1952).

25. 341 U.S. 494 at 581.

26. See Samuel A. Stouffer, *Communism, Conformity, and Civil Liberties: A Cross-Section of the Nation Speaks Its Mind* (New York: Doubleday, 1955); but see Horn, *Groups and the Constitution*, pp. 122–151; see also John A. Gorfinkel and Julian W. Mack, "*Dennis v. United States* and the Clear and Present Danger Rule," 39 *Calif. L. Rev.* 475 (1951).

27. E.g., Harold W. Chase, *Security and Liberty: The Problem of Native Communists, 1947-1955* (New York: Doubleday, 1955); Thomas I. Cook, *Democratic Rights versus Communist Activity* (New York: Doubleday, 1954).

28. Rodell, *Nine Men*, p. 314.

29. Eugene V. Rostow, "The Democratic Character of Judicial Review," 66 *Harv. L. Rev.* 193, 223 (1952); *cf.* John Lord O'Brian, "New Encroachments on Individual Freedom," 66 *Harv. L. Rev.* 1 (1952).

30. 340 U.S. 159 (1950).

31. 342 U.S. 1 (1951).

32. *Bailey v. Richardson*, 341 U.S. 918 (1951).

33. *Anti-Fascist Refugee Committee v. McGrath*, 341 U.S. 123 (1951).

34. 342 U.S. 524 (1952).

35. C. Herman Pritchett, *The Political Offender and the Warren Court* (Boston: Boston University Press, 1958), p. 13.

36. 354 U.S. 298 (1957); see Pritchett, *Congress Versus the Supreme Court, 1957–1960*, pp. 59–71.

37. For a powerful argument against section 2a (3), which punishes membership, see Chafee, *Free Speech*, pp. 470–485; but see Horn, *Groups and the Constitution*, pp. 142–147; see also Arthur J. Sabin, *In Calmer Times: The Supreme Court and Red Monday* (Philadelphia: University of Pennsylvania Press, 1999).

38. 354 U.S. 298 at 320.

39. 354 U.S. 298 at 321–325.

40. 354 U.S. 298 at 349.

41. See 71 *Harv. L. Rev.* 123 (1957); 5 *U.C.L.A. L. Rev.* 316 (1958); *cf.* 42 *Minn. L. Rev.* 301 (1957).

42. *Scales v. United States*, 367 U.S. 203 (1961), upholding a conviction under the membership the Smith Act; *cf. Noto v. United States*, 367 U.S. 203 (1961).

43. See, e.g., Jack W. Peltason, "Constitutional Liberty and the Communist Problem," in Alfred H. Kelly, ed., *Foundations of Freedom in the American Constitution* (New York: Harper, 1956), pp. 88–139.

44. 350 U.S. 497 (1956).

45. 18 P.S. sec. 4207.

46. Actually the Court upheld the decision of the Pennsylvania Supreme Court and in doing so did not set a Communist free, but left him where he was— in a federal penitentiary. Mendelson, "Clandestine Speech," p. 103; see also Pritchett, *Congress Versus the Supreme Court*, pp. 72–85; Walter Gelhorn, ed., *The States and Subversion* (Ithaca, NY: Cornell University Press, 1952); Lawrence Chamberlain, *Loyalty and Legislative Action: A Survey of Activity by the New York State Legislature, 1919–1949* (Ithaca, NY: Cornell University Press, 1951).

47. 64 Stat. 987 (1950).

48. 68 Stat. 775 (1954).

49. 312 U.S. 52 (1941).

50. 35 P.S. secs. 1801–1806.

51. Some thought that the field was entirely preempted by the federal government: Alan R. Hunt, "State Control of Sedition: The Smith Act as the Supreme Law of the Land," 41 *Minn. L. Rev.* 287, (1957); "The Supreme Court, 1955 Term," 70 *Harv. L. Rev.* 95, 119 (1956); others thought the question of preemption had been unanswered in *Nelson*: 45 *Ill. B. J.* 178, 182 (1956); 32 *N.Y.U. L. Rev.* 1302–1303 (1957); others thought *Nelson* left the door open for state prosecution of sedition against the state: 2 *Vill. L. Rev.* 127 (1956); 31 *Wash. L. Rev.* 300, 301 (1956).

52. 360 U.S. 72 (1959).

53. 353 U.S. 657 (1957).

54. 353 U.S. 657 at 667.

55. 353 U.S. 657 at 676.

56. 353 U.S. 657 at 677.

57. 353 U.S. 657 at 680.

58. 353 U.S. 657 at 681–682.

59. See 5 *U.C.L.A. L. Rev.* 147 (1958).

60. 71 Stat. 595 (1957).

61. For criticism of this statute, see Note, "The Jencks Legislation: Problem in Prospect," 67 *Yale L. J.* 674 (1958).

62. See 73 *Harv. L. Rev.* 179 (1959); 48 *Geo. L. J.* 173 (1959); but see 108 *U. Pa. L. Rev.* 141 (1959). See also *Gonzales v. United States*, 364 U.S. 59 (1960); *Clancy v. United States*, 365 U.S. 312 (1961); *Campbell v. United States*, 365 U.S. 85 (1961).

63. 360 U.S. 343 (1959).

64. 360 U.S. 367 (1959).

65. 360 U.S. 395 (1959).

66. 356 U.S. 165 (1958).

67. See 72 *Harv. L. Rev.* 153 (1958).

68. 356 U.S. 363 (1958); 7 *DePaul L. Rev.* 260 (1958). Here the middle bloc justices, Frankfurter, Harlan, Brennan, and Whittaker, were in the majority with Burton and Clark.

69. 352 U.S. 1 (1956). Mesarosh was the real name of Steve Nelson of the *Pennsylvania v. Nelson* case.

70. 352 U.S. 1 at 9.

71. 352 U.S. 1 at 14.

72. 352 U.S. 1 at 20.

73. See 71 *Harv. L. Rev.* 106 (1957); but see 45 *Geo. L. J.* 508 (1957).

74. 352 U.S. 985 (1957).

75. See 71 *Harv. L. Rev.* 108 (1957).

76. E.g., Harold W. Chase, "Improving Congressional Investigations: A No Progress Report," 30 *Temp. L. Q.* 126 (1957); Robert A. Horn, "Book Review," 18 *U. Chi. L. Rev.* 883 (1951).

77. *Eisner v. Macomber*, 252 U.S. 189 (1949); *United States v. Bryan*, 339 U.S. 323 (1950); *United States v. Fleischman*, 339 U.S. 349 (1950); *Dennis v. United States*, 339 U.S. 162 (1950); *Morford v. United States,* 339 U.S. 258 (1950). *Cf. United States v. Rumely*, 345 U.S. 41 (1953); *United States v. Josephson*, 165 F.2d 82 (1947).

78. 354 U.S. 178 (1957); see Pritchett, *Congress Versus the Supreme Court, 1957-1960*, pp. 41–58.

79. 354 U.S. 178 at 185.

80. 354 U.S. 178 at 187.

81. 354 U.S. 178 at 200.

82. 354 U.S. 178 at 187.

83. Ibid.

84. 354 U.S. 187 at 202.

85. 354 U.S. 187 at 201.

86. 354 U.S. 187 at 197.

87. 354 U.S. 187 at 197-198.

88. 354 U.S. 187 at 198.

89. 354 U.S. 234 (1957).

90. 354 U.S. 234 at 250.

91. 354 U.S. 234 at 255.

92. 354 U.S. 234 at 265.

93. 354 U.S. 576 (1958).

94. 358 U.S. 147 (1958).

95. 360 U.S. 423 (1959); but see *Slagle v. Ohio*, 366 U.S. 259 (1961).

96. 360 U.S. 109 (1959).

97. Harlan, Frankfurter, Whittaker, Stewart, and Clark formed the majority. Harlan and Frankfurter were accused of switching their votes from *Watkins* to *Barenblatt*, in Glendon A. Schubert, *Constitutional Politics* (New York: Holt, Rhinehart & Winston, 1960), p. 636, but this seems unjustified in light of the *Sweezy* opinions.

98. 360 U.S. 109 at 130.

99. 360 U.S. 109 at 125.

100. 360 U.S. 109 at 126.

101. 360 U.S. 109 at 132.

102. 38 *Texas L. Rev.* 330 (1960); 28 *Geo. Wash. L. Rev.* 457 (1960); *contra* 47 *Calif. L. Rev.* 930 (1959).

103. But see Harold W. Chase, "The Warren Court and Congress," 44 *Minn. L. Rev.* 595, 599-604 (1960).

104. 360 U.S. 72 (1959); 364 U.S. 388 (1960).

105. 360 U.S. 72 at 77.

106. 354 U.S. 234 at 269.

107. 38 *Texas L. Rev.* 330 (1960); 20 *La. L. Rev.* 595 (1960); but see 44 *Minn. L. Rev.* 555 (1960); 21 *Ohio St. L. J.* 17 (1960); see also Roger C. Cranton, "Supreme Court and State Power to Deal With Subversion and Loyalty," 43 *Minn. L. Rev.* 1025 (1959).

108. During the 1960 term, the Court ruled on two additional contempt of Congress cases, ruling against the defendant in one and for the defendant in the other. In *McPhaul v. United States*, 364 U.S. 372 (1960), the same voting alignment of the *Barenblatt* decision affirmed a contempt conviction. In *Deutch v. United States*, 367 U.S. 456 (1961), however, Justice Stewart joined the *Barenblatt* dissenters to form a majority ruling in favor of the witness.

109. Walter Gellhorn, *American Rights* (New York: MacMillan Co., 1960), pp. 114-131; but see Alexander Meiklejohn, "The Balancing of Self-Preservation Against Political Freedom," 49 *Calif. L. Rev.* 4 (1961); "The *Barenblatt* Opinion," 27 *U. Chi. L. Rev.* 329 (1960); *cf.* Harry Kalven, Jr., "Mr. Alexander Meiklejohn and the *Barenblatt* Opinion," 27 *U. Chi. L. Rev.* 315 (1960); see also Note, "The Constitutional Right to Anonymity: Free Speech, Disclosure and the Devil," 70 *Yale L. J.* 1084 (1961).

110. *Wilkinson v. United States*, 365 U.S. 399 (1961) and *Braden v. United States*, 365 U.S. 431 (1961).

111. See generally, O. John Rogge, *The First and the Fifth, With Some Excursions into Others* (New York: T. Nelson, 1960); Sidney Hook, *Common Sense and the Fifth Amendment* (New York: Criterion Books, 1957).

112. 349 U.S. 190 (1955).

113. 349 U.S. 155 (1955).

114. See 69 *Harv. L. Rev.* 131 (1955); *cf.,* 21 *Mo. L. Rev.* 66 (1956).

115. 349 U.S. 190 at 194.

116. 349 U.S. 155 at 164.

117. 349 U.S. 190 at 195.

118. See generally, O. John Rogge, "Compelling the Testimony of Political Deviants," (pts. 1–2), 55 *Mich. L. Rev.* 163, 375 (1956–1957); *cf.* Erwin W. Griswold, *The 5th Amendment Today* (Cambridge, MA: Harvard University Press 1955). More

than three hundred witnesses refused to testify before congressional committees during a single year: Samuel H. Hofstadter, *The Fifth Amendment and the Immunity Act of 1954* (New York: Fund for the Republic, n.d.), p. 20.

119. 68 Stat. 745 (1945).

120. 350 U.S. 422 (1956).

121. 350 U.S. 422 at 445–446; Powe, *The Warren Court*, p. 83.

122. But see Maxwell Brandwen, "Reflections on *Ullmann v. United States*," 58 *Colum. L. Rev.* 500 (1957).

123. 350 U.S. 422 at 429.

124. 351 U.S. 115 (1956); 43 *Geo. L. J.* 507 (1955).

125. Title I of the Internal Security Act of 1950, 65 Stat. 987 (1950); see generally, 51 *Colum. L. Rev.* 606 (1951).

126. 351 U.S. 115 at 125.

127. 351 U.S. 115 at 124.

128. McCloskey, "The Supreme Court Finds a Role," p. 751.

129. *Communist Party v. Subversive Activities Control Board*, 367 U.S. 1 (1961).

130. 22 CFR sec. 51. 135.

131. See Robert A. Horn, "The Warren Court and the Discretionary Power of the Executive," 44 *Minn. L. Rev.* 639, 665–668 (1960).

132. For a collection of views on the passport problem, see Staff of Senate Committee on the Judiciary, 85th Cong., 2d Sess., *The Right to Travel* (1958).

133. 357 U.S. 116 (1958).

134. 44 Stat. 887.

135. 357 U.S. 116 at 125.

136. 357 U.S. 116 at 130.

137. 43 *Minn. L. Rev.* 126 (1958); *cf.* 37 *Texas L. Rev.* 235 (1958); but see 27 *Fordham L. Rev.* 426 (1958).

138. Horn, "The Warren Court," p. 668; a similar problem is posed in *Greene v. McElroy*, 360 U.S. 474 (1959).

139. 357 U.S. 144 (1958).

140. For a study of a field closely related to the right to travel, see Allan D. Vestal, "Freedom of Movement," 41 *Ia. L. Rev.* 7 (1955); *see also* Pritchett, *Congress Versus the Supreme Court*, p. 95.

141. See generally, e.g., Ralph S. Brown, Jr., *Loyalty and Security: Employment Tests in the United States* (New Haven, CT: Yale University Press, 1958); Eleanor Bontecou, *The Federal Loyalty-Security Program* (Ithaca, NY: Cornell University Press, 1953).

142. Horn, "The Warren Court," pp. 645–656; Pritchett, *Congress Versus the Supreme Court*, pp. 96–106; Glendon A. Schubert, *The Presidency in the Courts* (Minneapolis: University of Minnesota Press, 1957), pp. 21–33; David Fellman, *The Defendant's Rights* (New York: Rhinehart, 1958), pp. 213–235.

143. 349 U.S. 331 (1955).

144. Horn, "The Warren Court," p. 646.

145. 351 U.S. 536 (1956); 44 *Geo. L. J.* 132 (1955).

146. 64 Stat. 476 (1950).

147. 58 Stat. 390 (1944).

148. 354 U.S. 363 (1957).

149. 60 Stat. 458 (1947).

150. 355 U.S. 579 (1958).

151. 359 U.S. 535 (1959); Frankfurter wrote a concurring opinion in which he was joined by Stewart, Whittaker, and Clark, at 535. This was the last loyalty-security case in which Frankfurter voted against upholding the government's claims until his retirement in 1962.

152. 360 U.S. 474 (1959).

153. *Von Knorr v. Griswold*, 156 F.2d 287 (1st Cir. 1946); *Sperry Gyroscope Co. v. Engineering Associates*, 304 N.Y. 582, 107 N. E. 2d 78 (1958).

154."The Supreme Court, 1958 Term," 73 *Harv. L. Rev.* 128, 198 (1959).

155. Joseph L. Rauh, "Nonconfrontation in Security Cases: The Greene Decision," 45 *Va. L. Rev.* 1175 (1959).

156. 73 *Harv. L. Rev.* 128, 199 (1959).

157. Ibid. 200; but *cf.* 46 *Calif. L. Rev.* 828 (1958).

158. Note, "Constitutional Shadows and Security Clearances—The Right to Confrontation," 48 *Geo. L. J.* 576 (1960).

159. Horn, "The Warren Court," pp. 646–653.

160. Powe, *The Warren Court*, pp. 153–154.

161. N.Y. Laws 1949 c. 360.

162. 342 U.S. 485 (1952).

163. 350 U.S. 551 (1956); see Pritchett, *Congress Versus the Supreme Court, 1957–1960*, pp. 107–115.

164. *City of New York, Charter*, sect. 903.

165. 350 U.S. 551 at 555.

166. 350 U.S. 551 at 558–559.

167. 357 U.S. 468 (1958).

168. 357 U.S. 399 (1958); see also *Nelson v. County of Los Angeles*, 362 U.S. 1 (1960).

169. 357 U.S. 399 at 417.

170. 357 U.S. 399 at 415.

171. See e.g., Robert G. McCloskey, "Tools, Stumbling Blocks, and Stepping Stones: Civil Liberties in the 1957 Term of the Supreme Court," 44 *Va. L. Rev.* 1029 (1958).

172. 72 *Harv. L. Rev.* 188 (1958); 44 *Cornell L. Q.* 244 (1959); but see 57 *Mich. L. Rev.* 412 (1959); 12 *Vand. L. Rev.* 273 (1958); *cf.* 2 *Geo. Wash. L. Rev.* 581 (1959).

173. McCloskey, "Tools, Stumbling Blocks," p. 1029.

174. 72 *Harv. L. Rev.* 191–192 (1958).

175. 351 U.S. 292 (1956).

176. 55 *Mich. L. Rev.* 871 (1957); *cf.* 103 *U. Pa. L. Rev.* 983 (1956).

177. 356 U.S. 617 (1958).

178. 341 U.S. 716 (1951).

179. 344 U.S. 183 (1952).

180. 357 U.S. 513 (1958).

181. 357 U.S. 545 (1958).

182. Art. XX sec. 19 (Nov. 4, 1952).

183. See Note, "Punishment: Its Meaning in Relation to Separation of Power and Substantive Constitutional Restrictions and Its Use in the Lovett, Trop, Perez, and Speiser Cases," 34 *Ind. L. J.* 231 (1959).

184. 357 U.S. 513 at 517.

185. 357 U.S. 513 at 518.

186. 357 U.S. 513 at 526.

187. 42 *Marq. L. Rev.* 560 (1959); 10 *Syracuse L. Rev.* 135 (1958); but see 12 *Vand. L. Rev.* 275 (1958); *Nostrand v. Little*, 362 U.S. 474 (1960).

188. 348 U.S. 946 (1955); but he was finally denied admission by the U.S. Supreme Court. *In re Anastaplo*, 366 U.S. 82 (1961).

189. 3 Ill. 2d 471, 121 N.E. 2d 826 (1954).

190. 353 U.S. 232 (1957).

191. 353 U.S. 232 at 246; Powe, *The Warren Court*, p. 93.

192. 353 U.S. 252 (1957).

193. Robert G. McCloskey, "Useful Toil or the Paths of Glory? Civil Liberties in the 1956 Term of the Supreme Court," 43 *Va. L. Rev.* 803, 815 (1957).

194. 353 U.S. 252 at 269.

195. For comment favorable to the majority position, see John T. McTernan, "*Schware, Konigsberg*, and Independence of the Bar: The Return to Reason," 17 *Law. Guild Rev.* 149 (1957).

196. *Deering's Calif. Code*, B. & P.C.A., Sect. 6064.1.

197. 353 U.S. 252 at 279–280.

198. 52 Cal. 2d 769 (1959).

199. 366 U.S. 36 (1961).

200. *In re Anastaplo*, 366 U.S. 82 (1961).

201. Compare this analysis with that of Professor McCloskey in McCloskey, "Useful Toil," p. 816.

202. Pritchett, *The Political Offender and the Warren Court*, pp. 60, 62; see Jacobs, *Justice Frankfurter*, pp. 149–151; Berman, "Constitutional Issues and the Warren Court," p. 500; McCloskey, "Useful Toil"; Joseph O. Losos, "The Supreme Court and Its Critics: Is the Court Moving Left?" 21 *Rev. of Politics* 495 (1959); J. Patrick White, "The Warren Court Under Attack," 19 *Md. L. Rev.* 181 (1959); Robert J. Steamer, "Statesmanship or Craftsmanship: Current Conflict Over the Supreme Court," 11 *W. Political Q.* 265 (1958); Paul A. Freund, "Storm Over the American Supreme Court," 21 *Modern L. Rev.* 345 (1958); Bernard Schwartz, "Is Criticism of the High Court Valid?" *New York Times Magazine*, 25 August 1957, p. 14.

203. Pritchett, *The Political Offender and the Warren Court*, p. 61.

204. McCloskey, "Tools, Stumbling Blocks, and Stepping Stones," p. 1053; Jacobs, *Justice Frankfurter*, pp. 148–149.

205. William O. Douglas, "The Black Silence of Fear," *New York Times Magazine*, 13 January 1952, p. 38.

206. But see *Barsky v. Board of Regents*, 347 U.S. 442 (1954), where the Chief Justice was in a majority voting against the defendant's claims.

207. Frankfurter was also in a libertarian minority with Black and Douglas in *Barsky v. Board of Regents*.

208. Pritchett, *The Political Offender*, p. 24.

209. Notably in *Beilan* and *Lerner* where Frankfurter, Harlan, and Whittaker were joined by Clark and Burton and in *Uphaus* where Clark and Stewart completed the majority.

210. McCloskey, "The Supreme Court Finds a Role," p. 760.

211. *Dennis v. United States*, 341 U.S. 494, 589 (1951) (Douglas, dissenting); see the excellent analysis of the Court's decisions in national security cases in Alan I. Bigel, "The First Amendment and National Security: The Court Responds to Governmental Harassment of Alleged Communist Sympathizers," 19 *Ohio N.U.L. Rev.* 885 (1993); see also Albert Fried, ed., *McCarthyism: The Great American Red Scare, A Documentary History* (New York, Oxford University Press, 1997).

4

The Rights of Citizens and Aliens

The Eisenhower Court handed down an important series of opinions dealing with loss of citizenship of U.S. citizens and deportation of aliens. Alleged subversive activities on the part of the defendants were important aspects in several of these cases, and the Court tended to follow the tactic of avoiding the subversive issues but finding fault with government practice on procedural or statutory points.

DENATURALIZATION

American citizenship can be lost in two ways: denaturalization and expatriation.[1] Denaturalization is the process of canceling a certificate of naturalization by official action for cause, and is, of course, employed only against persons who have secured their citizenship by naturalization. Statutes dealing with denaturalization were originally enacted to prevent fraud in naturalization proceedings and to ensure the political loyalty of naturalized citizens. During World War I and World War II a substantial number of naturalized citizens who expressed sympathy for the cause of the United States' enemies were denaturalized or had proceedings brought against them.[2] The Immigration and Nationality Act of 1952,[3] passed over President Truman's veto, controlled the denaturalization process during the Eisenhower presidency.[4] This statute set forth ten acts by which nationals of the United States, whether native born or naturalized, might lose their nationality. It provided that any naturalized person who had taken the oath to support and defend the Constitution must have had no concealed beliefs or affiliations that would disqualify him by law. If mental reservations or memberships could be proved in judicial proceedings, a naturalized citizen might have his certificate canceled. The act also provided that if a naturalized citizen, within five years after his naturalization, became a member of an organization which would have precluded his naturalization, "it shall be considered prima facie evidence that such person was not attached to the principles of the Constitution of the United States and was not well disposed to the good order and happiness of the United States at the time of naturalization." This prima facie evidence, if not met, was sufficient to cancel a certificate as having been obtained by "willful misrepresentation."

In *United States v. Zucca*,[5] the Court by a five-to-three vote took a rather strict view of the statutory requirement that denaturalization proceedings be begun by affidavit showing good cause therefor.[6] The government contended that this was rarely a practice which it could follow or not as it saw fit, but the Chief Justice replied: "We think that the public interest is not served by taking such liberties with a specific statutory requirement designed for the protection of naturalized citizens."[7] Two years later, the Court reaffirmed this ruling in *Mattes v. United States*.[8]

In 1958 the Supreme Court was faced with two cases dealing with denaturalization proceedings under the McCarran Act. The most important of these, *Nowak v. United States*,[9] involved alleged fraud and illegal procurement in a naturalization proceeding. Stanislaw Nowak had entered the United States at the age of ten in 1913, and had been naturalized in 1938. He had been asked whether he believed in anarchy or whether he belonged to an association which taught or advocated anarchy or the overthrow of government. Though a member of the Communist Party at the time, he answered "no" to both parts of the question. In 1952 the government brought a denaturalization suit against him. The Court held, six-to-three, that on these facts fraud had not been proved.[10]

Justice Harlan, speaking for the Court, took the position that Nowak could reasonably have interpreted the question as dealing with anarchy alone and as such it had been answered truthfully. The issue of illegal procurement turned on the government's assertion that during the five years preceding his naturalization, Nowak had not been "attached" to the principles of the Constitution. On this point the Court held that the government had failed to prove that Nowak knew of the Communist Party's advocacy of force, and that the fact that he had been an active member did not establish this significant point in the government's case. At no point in the record was there any indication that Nowak had himself advocated action for the violent overthrow of government or even understood that the Communist Party took this position. The Court seemed to serve notice that the government must be held to a strict standard of proof when an attack upon citizenship is made many years after the certificate was granted and the citizen has since been well behaved. Justices

Burton, Clark, and Whittaker argued that the issues were factual in nature; and since the facts amply supported the conclusions of the lower courts, the findings of the two lower courts should not be set aside.

The Court reached a similar conclusion in a companion case, *Maisenberg v. United States*.[11] Rebecca Maisenberg had been naturalized the same year as Nowak, and the other facts of the case were very similar. Justice Harlan stated for the Court: "We are of the opinion that the Government has failed to prove by 'clear, unequivocal and convincing' evidence . . . that Maisenberg was not 'attached to the principles of the Constitution'."[12]

In these cases the Court ruled that proof neither of attendance at closed Party meetings,[13] nor of concealment of Communist Party membership,[14] nor of service as a Party functionary,[15] were evidence of guilt. In addition, the Court maintained that the making of sporadic statements which are equivocal in that "they can be taken as merely the expression of opinions or predictions about future events, rather than as advocacy of violent action for the overthrow of government"[16] were not adequate to show awareness by petitioners that the party advocated illegal overthrow. Not thought or opinion but personal advocacy or personal knowledge of proposed action by the Communist Party would be needed to justify cancellation of citizenship on grounds of fraud in concealment of Party membership at the time of, or prior to, naturalization.[17]

The Eisenhower Court passed on an important procedural ruling in denaturalization proceedings in the 1958 case, *Brown v. United States*.[18] The provision in the Fifth Amendment that no one "shall be compelled in any criminal case to be a witness against himself" had been a subject of great controversy during the Cold War. Dividing five-to-four, the Court ruled that where a person involved in a denaturalization proceeding voluntarily answered some questions, he might not refuse to answer related questions on the ground of self-incrimination. In this case, Brown had voluntarily taken the stand and testified in his own behalf regarding his beliefs, activities, and memberships. The government then asked him questions about membership in the Communist Party on cross-examination, and it was ruled that Brown had abandoned the privilege not to testify on grounds of self-incrimination due to his previous remarks. The Court held that if the witness was a party, he determined the area of disclosure and therefore of inquiry. The witness had the choice of weighing the advantages of the privilege against the advantages of presenting his version of the facts. If he elected to give testimony, he had no immunity from cross-examination on the matters he himself had put in dispute.

Justices Black and Douglas and the Chief Justice regarded this as another erosion of the privilege and expressed opposition to extending the waiver rule of criminal cases, which at best had long been debatable, to civil proceedings such as those concerned with denaturalization. Justice Brennan dissented on the theory that the trial judge had incorrectly informed the witness that he had waived his privilege by the simple act of taking the stand, arguing that this was derived from criminal cases and had no application in civil cases.

The Eisenhower Court libertarians contended that requirements of process in a civil proceeding such as this should have been reexamined where a defendant is placed in the untenable position of having to elect between waiving his privilege or prematurely invoking it.[19] In such circumstances it would seem that the protection of the Fifth Amendment should outweigh the desirability of cross-examination which might lead to injurious testimony. Justice Black pointed out in dissent that the civil defendant's testimony was in a sense not completely voluntary, since in a civil trial, inferences may be drawn from silence and comment be made. Viewed in this light, the civil defendant would appear to be in the same untenable position as an involuntary witness summoned by a grand jury or congressional committee. The libertarian justices contended that it would be a good policy to allow Fifth Amendment protections to extend to all citizens who face penalties as stiff as denaturalization. Although there had been no indictment for a crime in such cases, Black, Douglas, and Warren worried that the penalty that might result from self-incriminating testimony was more severe than that in many criminal proceedings.

EXPATRIATION

Expatriation refers to the loss of citizenship as the result, intended or unintended, of voluntary action taken by a citizen, either natural born or naturalized.[20] In the United States, Congress has since 1907 prescribed various circumstances under which one may lose his citizenship. The Citizenship Act of 1907[21] augmented by the Nationality Act of 1940[22] provides twelve conditions under which individual action results in expatriation. At least six of these conditions could cause loss of citizenship contrary to the intention of the individual. Three of these involve relationships with a foreign country: serving in the armed forces of a foreign nation without authorization and with consequent acquisition of foreign nationality; holding a public office under the government of a foreign state, for which only nationals of that state are eligible; and voting in a foreign election.

The constitutionality of this last provision was upheld by a five-to-four vote of the Supreme Court in *Perez v. Brownell*.[23] Justice Frankfurter, speaking for the majority,[24] held that Congress was entitled under its implied powers to enact legislation for the regulation of foreign affairs. This authority might "reasonably be deemed to include a power to deal generally with the active participation, by way of voting, of American citizens in foreign political elections."[25] Congress could reasonably believe that such activities "might well become acute, to the point of jeopardizing the successful conduct of international relations."[26] Frankfurter added that loss of nationality was one of the consequences which Congress could attach to such voting as a means of avoiding this potential embarrassment in the conduct of foreign relations. Frankfurter reemphasized that Congress' power to terminate citizenship does not depend upon the citizen's assent or consent.[27]

Chief Justice Warren, joined by Justices Black and Douglas, dissented, contending that the Fourteenth Amendment literally makes citizenship the constitutional birthright of every person born in the country. Thus, according to these three justices, citizenship may be relinquished voluntarily, but Congress cannot take it away. They argued that the real issue was whether voting in a foreign election invariably involves a diminution of allegiance sufficient to show voluntary abandonment of citizenship. They felt that it might in some circumstances, where one must become a foreign citizen before voting. But the Chief Justice felt that Congress had gone too far in saying that any act of participation in any foreign election supports the inference of a voluntary abandonment of American citizenship.

Justice Whittaker agreed with the majority that Congress may expatriate a citizen for an act which it may reasonably find to endanger the involvement of our government in international disputes or to embarrass the conduct of foreign relations. He dissented, however, contending that the statute in question was too broadly written, since it extended to any voting in foreign elections.

On the same day *Perez v. Brownell* was decided, the Court passed upon another ground for expatriation—conviction and discharge from the armed services for desertion in time of war. In *Trop v. Dulles*,[28] Justice Brennan joined the four dissenters of the *Perez* case to provide a five-justice majority which declared a section of the Nationality Act of 1940 unconstitutional. Speaking for the Court, Chief Justice Warren pointed out that military authorities had complete discretion in issuing dishonorable discharges or readmitting offenders to military service, thus restoring their citizenship. For practical purposes this made the military authorities the arbiters of citizenship. The Chief Justice added that conviction for desertion is not rare, since all it entails is absence from duty plus the intention not to return, which may be prompted by many motives, such as fear, laziness, hysteria, or emotional unbalance. The offense was the same whether in a combat zone or in training camps in the United States. During World War II, there were 21,000 convictions for desertion in the Army alone, and 7,000 were actually separated from the service and expatriated. The Chief Justice argued that even though desertion in wartime may merit a stiff penalty, it does not necessarily signify allegiance to a foreign state. The statute was not limited to desertion to the enemy, and there was no such element in Trop's case. Chief Justice Warren contended: "Citizenship is not a license that expires upon misbehavior. . . . And the deprivation of citizenship is not a weapon that the Government may use to express its displeasure at a citizen's conduct, however reprehensible that conduct may be. As long as a person does not voluntarily renounce or abandon his citizenship . . . his fundamental right of citizenship is secure."[29]

To the Chief Justice this was plainly a penal statute with denaturalization inflicted as punishment. To take away the citizenship of a convicted deserter was punishment since no claim was made that denaturalization would have any effect upon foreign affairs.[30] The Chief Justice then held this to be a cruel and unusual punishment forbidden by the Eighth Amendment. Admitting the offense of desertion may be punished by death, Chief Justice Warren still thought this did not authorize the government to devise any punishment short of death within the limit of its imagination. "The basic concept underlying the Eighth Amendment," he said, "is nothing less than the dignity of man."[31] The Chief Justice contended that the Court should determine the meaning of the Eighth Amendment from "the evolving standards of decency that mark the progress of a maturing society." The power to punish must be exercised within the limits of civilized standards, and denaturalization means "the total destruction of the individual's status in organized society," a punishment more primitive than torture. The expatriate loses "the right to have rights."[32]

Justice Brennan concurred only because he thought that expatriation as a punishment for desertion did not have the "requisite rational relation" to the war power that voting in a foreign election had to the power to regulate the conduct of foreign relations.[33] Considering his view and that of Justice Whittaker in the *Perez* case, this pronouncement weakened the authority of the *Trop* majority.

Speaking for the four dissenters, Justice Frankfurter insisted that the underlying issue is a matter of policy for Congress to decide, that it is within allowable legislative judgment to deal so severely with the problem of wartime desertion, and that like denaturalization, expatriation is not "punishment" in any valid constitutional sense. But even assuming that it is punishment, it is not contrary to the Eighth Amendment, he argued, since no punishment can possibly be worse than death.

In the same term, the Court held that when there is a question of the voluntary nature of conduct resulting in expatriation, the burden is upon the government to prove that such conduct was voluntary by "clear, convincing and unequivocal" evidence.[34] Nishikawa, who was born in California and hence an American citizen, was also considered a citizen of Japan under Japanese law because of the nationality of his parents. At the time of the Pearl Harbor attack, he was a student in Japan and was inducted into the Japanese army. The U.S. State Department took the position that he had forfeited his American citizenship by serving in the Japanese army. Nishikawa brought suit for a declaratory judgment. At his trial, he testified that he had been inducted under a compulsory service law, that he had not protested to the American Embassy or Consulate because a friend had told him that the American authorities would not help him, and that he was afraid to protest because of fear of the brutality of the Japanese secret police. The district judge, after hearing this testimony, announced that he did not believe it and concluded that Nishikawa's entry into the Japanese army had been a free and voluntary act.

Noting the drastic nature of the consequences of denationalization, the Chief Justice, for the Court, held that the government had failed in this instance to carry the burden of proof, because Congress had not intended to create a conclusive presumption of voluntariness in cases involving dual nationals under these facts.[35] It was not enough for the trial judge to say merely that he did not believe the petitioner's story. Justices Black and Douglas concurred separately to argue that insofar as the statute created involuntary expatriation, it was unconstitutional. They argued that Congress had no power to destroy citizenship, whether for acts bearing a rational nexus to some substantive power or for acts showing a transfer of allegiance. In their view the question was whether an individual himself intended to relinquish his citizenship, and Congress could do no more than establish rebuttal presumptions that certain acts evidenced that intent.

Justices Frankfurter and Burton, also concurring, contended that the government ought to have a further opportunity to bring forward the necessary proof, if able to do so. Justices Harlan and Clark dissented, arguing that the issue was mainly one of credibility, as to which the trial court's findings should not normally be disturbed, and that the general rule was that consciously performed acts are presumed to be voluntary.

Throughout these cases ran a line of disagreement as to the basic policy the Court should follow in reviewing expatriation acts of Congress.[36] Justice Frankfurter continuously advocated a policy of judicial restraint: "To deny the power of Congress to enact the legislation challenged here would be to disregard the constitutional allocation of governmental functions that it is this Court's solemn duty to guard."[37] The Chief Justice, on the other hand, asserted the Court's responsibility to enforce the Constitution's prohibitions as it understood them: "Courts must not consider the wisdom of statutes but neither can they sanction as being merely unwise that which the Constitution forbids. When the Government acts to take away the fundamental rights of citizenship, the safeguards of the Constitution should be examined with special diligence."[38]

The proposition that the government had inherent power as an attribute of sovereignty to deal with foreign affairs seemed to be firmly accepted by the Court. In *Perez*, both the majority and minority appeared to accept the doctrine. As international relations became more complex, the doctrine became increasingly important.[39]

At the same time, it is evident that the nature of expatriation itself was in question. The *Perez* majority, speaking through Justice Frankfurter, maintained that expatriation was merely a regulatory technique that need bear only a rational relationship to the exercise of a substantive power—the regulation of foreign affairs. On the other hand, the *Perez* minority contended that expatriation is itself a substantive subject for legislation requiring a specific grant of power, failing which it can only be applied when an individual's acts approach voluntary expatriation. The latter view would seem preferable since the Court could thus prevent involuntary denationalization and statelessness without being charged with disregarding the constitutional allocation of governmental functions. In 1967 in *Afroyim v. Rusk*, the Court overruled *Perez* and adopted Warren's broad argument that citizenship could only be voluntarily relinquished.[40]

DEPORTATION

Congress has absolute power to provide for the deportation of aliens if they are found to have entered the country illegally or to have become members of specific excluded classes.[41] The first American deportation statute was part of the notorious Alien and Sedition Acts of 1798. In the name of national security, and probably as a political measure, the president was given the power, by these acts, to expel aliens who were citizens of an enemy nation in time of war or who were thought to be dangerous to the peace and safety of the nation.

No new deportation laws were added until almost a century later, after the United States had adopted a policy of Chinese exclusion.[42] An act of 1892[43] required all Chinese laborers in this country who were entitled to remain to secure a certificate of residence. A person without such a certificate was considered to be unlawfully within the country and subject to arrest and deportation.

Congress next sought to use deportation to remove aliens who had entered legally but had subsequently violated a condition attached to continued residence. The Immigration Act of 1917[44] provided for the deportation of aliens convicted of a crime involving moral turpitude committed within five years of entry, where a sentence of one year or more was levied, and also of aliens convicted and sentenced more than once for crimes involving moral turpitude, regardless of how many years had elapsed before deportation proceedings were instigated.

The Immigration and Nationality Act of 1952 provided for deportation of aliens who violated alien registration requirements, who were dealers in or peddlers of narcotic drugs or were narcotic addicts, or who became a public charge within five years after entry. The Subversive Activities Control Act of 1950[45] provided for the deportation of aliens who were members of or affiliated with the Communist Party. The Alien Registration Act of 1940[46] provided for the deportation of aliens whose membership in the Communist Party had terminated prior to 1940.[47]

Deportation proceedings are civil and administrative in nature and thus need not be attended by all the safeguards of a criminal trial.[48] Involved too, is American policy in foreign relations, a subject which the courts recognize as being in the domain of the popularly elected branches of the government and hence the pressure for judicial acceptance of legislative or administrative decisions is particularly strong in this field.

Judicial review can insist that administrative determinations of liability to deportation be made according to due process of law, but the substantive provisions have not been open to question.[49] The Eisenhower Court did not seek to effect any change in this respect.

The first important case dealing with deportation proceedings faced by the Eisenhower Court was the 1954 case, *Galvan v. Press*,[50] that well illustrates that an alien's freedom to remain in this country was largely at the mercy of Congress. A seven-justice majority held that an alien who joined the Communist Party without knowledge of its advocacy of violence was deportable as a Party "member."[51] Robert Galvan, an alien from Mexico, entered the United States in 1918 and was a "member" of the Party from 1944 until 1946. He contended that there was insufficient evidence that he knew of the Party's purpose. Justice Frankfurter, for the majority, replied that the statute did not require such proof and that, although deportation may "deprive a man of all that makes life worth living," it is not an unconstitutional "punishment."[52]

Justices Black and Douglas dissented, contending that a resident alien is entitled to the protections of due process. To them, it was unconstitutional to "punish" by deportation for a past membership in an organization that was at the time legal and on the ballot. For those aliens who had been in this country many years, such deportation could only be described as sheer tragedy, equivalent to banishment or exile. The Court declined to follow Justices Douglas and Black into such an extension of substantive due process. Although the Court did not challenge Congress' substantive powers, it insisted rather strictly on procedural due process. Where a statute might reasonably be interpreted in two different ways, the Court tended to choose the less harsh interpretation. In *United States v. Minker*,[53] the Court ruled unanimously that the Immigration Service could not use its statutory powers to subpoena aliens as "witnesses" when the purpose was actually to secure information about them on which a deportation case could be based. There was a clear difference between a witness and a defendant, the Court thought.

The next term, the Court held that there had to be a substantial basis for the finding that an alien was conscious of what the Communist Party stood for at the time of his joining.[54] An alien, Rowoldt, had been ordered deported under Section 22 of the Internal Security Act of 1950 because of past membership in the Communist Party. On appeal, Rowoldt alleged that he had not been a "member" of the Communist Party within the meaning of the statute. He had come to the United States from Germany in 1914. Testifying before an immigration inspector in 1947, Rowoldt related that he had joined the Party to fight for bread and that he did not join because he was dissatisfied with democracy. He stated that he had never advocated violence or force to change the government.

By a five-to-four vote,[55] the Court decided that Rowoldt's membership did not fall within the statute.[56] It was asserted that there must be a substantial basis for the finding that an alien had committed himself to the Communist Party in the consciousness that he was joining an organization which operated as an active political organization, and that solidity of proof was required for a judgment entailing deportation, especially in the case of an older person who had lived in the United States for forty years. The Court ruled that the unchallenged account given by Rowoldt of his relations with the Communist Party did not establish the kind of meaningful association required by the 1950 act. His reason for joining might well have had no connection with politics at all, according to Justice Frankfurter, who wrote the opinion of the Court.

Justice Harlan, for his fellow dissenters, Burton, Clark, and Whittaker, felt that while the effort of the majority "to find a way out from the rigors of a severe statute has alluring appeal," this was done by taking "impermissible liberties" with both the statute and the record.[57]

The legal consequences of *Rowoldt* were to compel the Immigration Department to supply more positive proof of an alien's affiliation with the Communist Party than had previously been the case. Proof that an alien joined knowing it to be a political party would be sufficient, under *Galvan*, even though membership was thirty years earlier, long terminated, and legal at the time. But under *Rowoldt*, the sufficiency of the proof of membership was a matter of close scrutiny, and since deportation is a harsh act, if there was doubt in this matter it would be construed more favorably to the alien than to the government.[58]

The Court also showed great concern for the enforcement of procedural guarantees in deportation hearings. The first important case before the Eisenhower Court in this category was *United States ex rel. Accardi v. Shaughnessy*.[59] In that case the district judge in a habeas corpus action had denied offer of proof that an application for suspension of deportation was prejudged by the Attorney General's issuance of a list of "unsavory characters" including Accardi's name. According to a bare majority, speaking through Justice Clark, such evidence should have been heard. If proved, it would show that the Appeal Board had failed to exercise its own discretion as required by statute.

In the next term, the Court reviewed the same case, this time on the merits of Accardi's procedural claim.[60] In the district court to which the case had been remanded, the court found that the Board of Immigration Appeals had reached its decision to deny Accardi's application for suspension of deportation free from influence by the Attorney General. The Court of Appeals reversed the district court decision. Judge Frank, for the majority, thought it "incredible . . . that the Attorney General's statements . . . did not unconsciously influence the Board members."[61] Judge (now Justice) Harlan had dissented, maintaining that, before the district court, Accardi was entitled only to a hearing on "whether the Board's denial of discretionary relief represented its own untrammeled decision or one dictated by the Attorney General."[62]

The Supreme Court adopted the views of Judge Harlan, in reversing the Court of Appeals. Justice Clark, again speaking for the Court, found that the testimony of the Board members showed that they consciously believed, when they testified, that the Attorney General's statements had no effect upon their decisions:[63] "In the face of such evidence, we do not believe that speculation on the effect of the subconscious psychological pressures provides sufficient justification for rejecting the District Court's finding as clearly erroneous."[64]

Justices Black and Frankfurter dissented, contending that the Attorney General's action, which proclaimed a strong desire and purpose to deport, among others, Accardi, placed the Board, the members of which hold office completely at the Attorney General's will, in a position which no administrative agency should be. To Justice Black: "The Attorney General's publicized program made it impossible to expect his subordinates to give Accardi's application . . . fair consideration. . . . The use of administrative bodies as agencies of justice under law is seriously weakened by proceedings such as these."[65]

When prejudgment is charged, it is extremely difficult for the party having the burden of proof to win. It seems inconceivable, as the Court observed, that the members of the Board would not be influenced by so strong a series of statements as those made by their superior in this case. An independent decision, the Court insisted, is particularly necessary in suspension proceedings, which provide the alien his only opportunity to show that despite the early offense, his subsequent conduct demonstrated his fitness for residence and that extreme hardship would result from deportation.[66]

The Eisenhower Court ruled upon several cases dealing with the application of certain sections of the Administration Procedure Act

(A.P.A.)[67] in deportation hearings. The Immigration and Nationality Act of 1952 did not deal expressly with the question of the applicability of the A.P.A. to the deportation proceedings provided for therein. In *Marcello v. Bonds*,[68] the Court considered whether deportation hearings must be conducted in accordance with section 5(c) of the A.P.A., which proscribed the use of adjudicatory officers who were also prosecutors or were under the supervision of investigative or prosecutory sections of an agency. Enforcement officers had ordered Marcello deported at a hearing before a special inquiry officer who, although not a prosecutor, was subject to supervision. A majority of the Court held that Congress intended the Immigration Act of 1952 to provide exemption for deportation proceedings from section 5 of the A.P.A., although the act made no specific reference to it. For the majority, Justice Clark pointed to "clear and categorical language" that the procedure set out in the 1952 act "shall be the sole and exclusive procedure for determining the deportability of an alien."[69] Further, he continued, the detailed procedure provided by the act, much of which duplicated provisions of the Administrative Act Procedure, would have been unnecessary had the entire A.P.A. procedure, including section 5(c), been intended to apply. The Court also summarily dismissed Marcello's contention that supervision of the special inquiry officer by the prosecutory staff of the Immigration Service denied the defendant due process, citing the long-standing practice of Congress of concentrating the functions of investigation, prosecution, and adjudication in the same administrative agency.

In the Court's view, it was the task of Congress, not the judiciary, to remedy the evil—even though such concentration of function was unsatisfactory. The majority was willing to concede this power to the legislature even though it meant that litigants would feel that they had lost all opportunity to argue their cases to an unbiased official and that they had been deprived of the safeguards which Americans are taught to revere.

Justices Black and Frankfurter again dissented together, arguing that the alleged exemption from section 5(c) was not sufficiently explicit. Justice Douglas also dissented, declaring that Marcello's deportation on the basis of a crime he had committed before passage of the Immigration Act was a violation of the ex post facto clause of the Constitution.

The Court majority felt it was correct in concluding that Congress did not intend section 5(c) to apply to deportation proceedings. There was little reason to interpret "expressly" in section 12 of the A.P.A. as requiring that Congress always referred specifically to sections of that act in order to indicate exemptions. Even though such specific reference may be omitted, congressional intent may be clear; and considerations of political expediency may often explain the lack of specificity where the applicability of the A.P.A. was subject to controversy.[70]

Interpretation of the Administration Procedure Act was also involved in *Shaughnessy v. Pedreiro*.[71] Here the Court ruled that an alien may test a possibly invalid deportation order in court prior to detention under section 10 of the A.P.A. The Court rejected the contention that the provision of the Immigration and Nationality Act of 1952 that deportation orders of the Attorney General shall be "final" expressed a congressional purpose to deprive those subject to deportation orders of all rights of judicial review except by habeas corpus. For the majority, Justice Black stated that "such a restrictive construction of the finality provision of the present Immigration Act would run counter" to sections 10 and 12 of the A.P.A. "Their purpose was to remove obstacles to judicial review of agency action under subsequently enacted statutes like the 1952 Immigration Act."[72]

The government also urged that the plaintiff's suit be dismissed because the Commissioner of Immigration, who issued the deportation order, had not been made a party. It was argued that if suit is brought only against a particular district director instead of the Commissioner of Immigration, the decision would not be res judicata in other districts, and the alien would be subject to deportation upon entering another district. The Court did not find this argument persuasive and held that the Commissioner need not be a party. Purporting to base its decision on "practical considerations," the majority pointed out that it was unlikely that any district director would disregard a judicial decision invalidating an order and that, even if the alien were again arrested, the first decision would have to be considered by the reviewing court.[73] Justices Minton, Reed, and Burton dissented.

The following year, in *Brownell v. We Shung*, the Court ruled that the legality of an exclusion order under the Immigration Act of 1952 may be challenged either by a habeas corpus proceeding or by an action for a declaratory judgment under Section 10 of the A.P.A.[74] The Court held that the difference between the constitutional status of an alien in a deportation case and in an exclusion case, which in the former puts the burden of proof on the government, and in the latter on the alien, does not justify making a straitjacket out of forms of judicial action.

From a practical point of view, the *We Shung* case was of great importance to an alien. For a habeas corpus proceeding, the alien must be detained, or at least be in technical custody. On the other hand, a declaratory judgment action requires no such basis and the undesirable elements of arrest and detention are not present. Habeas corpus may be a far more expeditious remedy than that of declaratory judgment, but that fact may be weighed by the alien against the necessity of arrest and detention, after which he may choose a form of action to challenge his expulsion.[75]

The Immigration and Nationality Act of 1952 authorized the Attorney General to retain an alien in custody for an additional period of six months after the final order of deportation is issued in order to "effect the alien's departure." During this six months' period the alien was subject to the "supervision" of the Attorney General, and might be required "to give information under oath as to his nationality, circumstances, habits, associations, and activities, and such other information, whether or not related to the foregoing, as the Attorney General may deem fit and proper." In *United States v. Witkovich*,[76] the Court reviewed a case involving an attempt of the Attorney General to compel an alien under "supervision" to answer questions as to whether he subscribed to the *Daily Worker*, was a member of the Communist Party, and numerous others aimed at establishing possible Communist connections. For his refusal to answer these questions, Witkovich was indicted. The Supreme Court upheld the district court in finding these questions invalid. Justice Frankfurter for the Court, noted that to uphold the statute as it literally read would "generate constitutional doubts," since it would infringe upon the civil rights of the alien at the will of the Attorney General, and might exact a long-lasting penalty if deportation were impossible.[77] The statute should be interpreted to authorize only questions "reasonably calculated to keep the Attorney General advised regarding the continued availability for departure of aliens whose deportation is overdue."[78] The Court indicated that any broader interpretation of the statute would raise constitutional questions. Justices Clark and Burton dissented,[79] contending that the majority's opinion suggested that the government might not constitutionally prevent an alien from engaging in activities such as those for which he had been ordered deported. They also felt that the opinion stripped the Attorney General of the power of supervision over aliens that they regard as valuable. While the dissent exaggerated the result of the decisions, since aliens still had to report regularly and submit to interrogation having some relevance to their availability for deportation, the decision did provide aliens, in their general day-to-day activities, the same rights as all other persons and exempted them from special penalties for exercising those rights solely because they were aliens.

In two other 1957 decisions, the Eisenhower Court reaffirmed a well-established rule that since deportation is not a criminal proceeding, the ex post facto doctrine does not apply,[80] and Congress might legislate retrospectively to provide for deportation of aliens for committing offenses which were not deportable when committed.[81]

In *Jay v. Boyd*,[82] the Court again took a strict view of the rights of aliens, ruling that it was not improper for administrative officials to make an adverse finding on the basis of confidential information. The regulations of the Attorney General provided that when an alien qualified for suspension of deportation under Section 244 of the Immigration and Nationality Act applied for relief, the determination might be made on confidential information without disclosure to the applicant, if in the opinion of those making the determination disclosure, of the information would be prejudicial to the public interest, safety, or security. Jay, a sixty-five-year-old Canadian World War I veteran who had come to this country in 1914, admitted at a fair hearing that he had been a voluntary member of the Communist Party from 1935 to 1940. Being able to demonstrate good behavior for at least ten years since the ground for deportation arose, and also exceptional hardship, Jay met the statutory prerequisites for applying for suspension of deportation. But a special inquiry officer found against him on the basis of confidential information, and the Board of Immigration Appeals dismissed an appeal after reviewing the whole record, including the undisclosed information. There was no statutory grant of the right to a hearing on an application to the Attorney General for discretionary suspension of deportation. A badly divided Supreme Court affirmed the action of the Board.

Speaking for a bare majority,[83] Justice Reed held that the Attorney General did not have to exercise his discretion personally in suspension cases, for, since the discretion was conferred upon him as an administrator, under his rule-making power he might delegate this responsibility to special inquiry officers. Furthermore, he held that Section 244 of the Immigration Act did not require the Attorney General to give a hearing with all the evidence spread upon an open record. While the statute might implicitly require a hearing on an open record as to the specified statutory prerequisites to a favorable action, it did not follow, according to Justice Reed, that there was such a right with regard to the ultimate decision, this being left to the sound discretion of the Attorney General.[84] He maintained that this was a matter of grace, not requiring a hearing, as in the case of probation, parole, pardon, or suspension of a criminal sentence. He brushed aside the appeal to the principles of free government with the observation that "we must adopt the plain meaning of the statute, however severe the consequences."[85] There was no right to a suspension of deportation, and the Attorney General's discretion was described as being "unfettered."

This was met by strong objection from the four dissenters, each of whom wrote an opinion. The Chief Justice argued that the majority opinion "sacrifices to form too much of the American spirit of fair play."[86] He felt that the Attorney General's discretion was not unfettered, but only administrative, and could be exercised only on the basis of an administrative hearing in the American tradition. A hearing where the decision rested on confidential information was no hearing at all and violated due process according to Chief Justice Warren.

Justice Black thought that the Attorney General's regulation went beyond his statutory power, since the statute said that the alien must be given a chance to "prove" that he is eligible for relief, and this meant a full and fair hearing. He also argued that this procedure was unconstitutional and a departure from the ideal of liberty under law. Unfettered discretion was arbitrary power, and life and freedom should never have to depend upon it.

Justice Frankfurter took the position that the Attorney General could not delegate his discretionary power to subordinates, but that if he did, he was then bound by the basic regulations of administrative law, for administrative agencies could not be authorized to defy the presupposition of a fair hearing. Justice Douglas maintained that this sort of procedure violated the due process requirement of a fair hearing, and was so un-American that the Court should lean over backwards to avoid imputing to Congress a purpose to sanction it.

In a case of this type it would seem that an explicit congressional command should be required before a deportable alien was denied an important procedural protection. Had Congress intended to permit the use of such evidence, it should have expressly authorized its use, in view of consistent judicial criticism of findings based on evidence not subject to rebuttal. After this decision was handed down, the Immigration Service amended its regulations so as to preclude the use of confidential information except in extraordinary cases where the Commissioner himself had determined that its use was in the interest of national security and safety.[87]

In 1960 the Court ruled against a deported alien's claim to social security benefits.[88] Ephram Nestor, a Bulgarian immigrant to the United States in 1913, had lived in the United States for forty-three years but had never become a citizen. He had belonged to the Communist Party during the 1930s. Under the McCarran Act's retroactive application to membership provision, Nestor was deported in 1956. Two years earlier, the Social Security Act was amended to deny social security benefits to aliens who had been deported because of their subversive activities in the past. Nestor had begun to receive social security payments in 1955. His wife, who remained in the United States, received notification of the termination of Nestor's payments. Justice Harlan, for a five-justice majority, upheld the action. Harlan found nothing wrong with the retroactivity of the cutoff and rejected the argument that a social security payment was a property right that could be protected under the Takings Clause of the Fifth Amendment. He found the result harsh but not unconstitutional. Black, Brennan, Douglas, and Warren dissented and found the retroactive application of the social security amendments to be an ex post facto law, punishing behavior that was legal when committed. Justice Black, in dissent, worried about "the extent to which people are willing to go these days to overlook violations of the Constitution perpetrated against anyone who has ever even innocently belonged to the Communist Party."

CONCLUSION

The Eisenhower Court, in several of its cases dealing with the rights of citizens and aliens, made an effort to bring American practice up to its democratic ideals. Again the Court's method was to invalidate official action for narrow reasons rather than challenging basic constitutional theories. Such an effort, involving the application of the principles of the Bill of Rights to administrative powers over individual liberty was in the best tradition of the highest tribunal. Where the result was favorable to the government, it was usually rationalized in restraintist terms—that the courts should not interfere with a valid exercise of legislative or executive power in dealing with what Justice Reed called "denizens."[89] And while procedural and statutory interpretations were used by the Court to justify official action, they frequently served to protect the alien or citizen.

By the late 1950s, denaturalization proceedings required the government to meet strict standards of proof, which was desirable where such a stern consequence was involved. The *Brown* decision approving waiver of Fifth Amendment rights in civil suits was an unfortunate step backward from the libertarian gains in *Zucca, Matles, Nowak,* and *Maisenberg.* The major problem of denaturalization was that there were two classes of citizens. Those fortunate enough to be native-born were secure in their citizenship as long as they did not perform certain acts amounting to forfeiture. The naturalized citizens, on the other hand, were insecure in their status since conduct subsequent to naturalization could open the door to loss of citizenship. Naturalized citizens could exercise First Amendment freedoms only with risks not incurred by native-born citizens. Correction of this condition did not require an end to the power of denaturalization, but only that its use be limited to cases where willful and material fraud was involved in procuring naturalization papers.[90]

The cases involving expatriation indicated that there were several opposing views on that subject.[91] One view, expounded by Justices Harlan and Clark who voted against all four petitioners, was that the citizenship of native-born Americans was a "license" which Congress could revoke when it believed such action would further the legitimate purposes of government. Justices Frankfurter and Burton joined with this bloc when constitutional rather than statutory construction was involved. Justices Brennan and Whittaker would uphold the government's claim if they saw any rational relation between expatriation and the goal of Congress. These two Justices disagreed as to what a "rational nexus" was, however. Whittaker could find none in *Trop* or *Perez* while Brennan, on the other hand, saw a rational relationship between expatriation and the foreign relations power, but not between expatriation and the war power. Still another view was that supported by the Chief Justice and Justices Black and Douglas that if expatriation was necessary, it would be a better policy to allow involuntary expatriation only where acts of most serious detriment to the nation were involved. The *Trop* decision, in this area, was noteworthy as one of the few instances in which the Eisenhower Court found a national statute unconstitutional, and this by only a bare majority.

The cases involving aliens made it clear that Congress had extremely broad powers over deportation. Yet by statutory interpretation and by comparing deportation procedures in certain instances to those of criminal prosecutions, the Eisenhower Court softened somewhat the absolutism of the congressional power over aliens. This was in contrast to the Vinson Court practice of generally upholding both the statutory interpretations and the procedures of the Immigration Service.[92] Although *Jay, Accardi, Marcello,* and *Nestor* demonstrated that there was still strong sentiment in favor of such a policy, the Court also showed resistance to over-officious bureaucratic zeal. Again, these decisions did not cause irreparable damage. If the Court misread the intent of Congress in *Witkovich*, as Justices Clark and Burton thought, then Congress only had to amend the statute to give the Attorney General "unbounded authority" to require information from aliens. The change in attitude of the Court in *Rowoldt* and *Galvan*, requiring more positive proof of Communist connections for aliens, was in keeping with the Court's position in denaturalization cases. Other interpretations of the A.P.A. also allowed aliens to face the possibility of deportation in a manner in keeping with civilized standards. The deportation cases demonstrated that the immigration laws and their administration needed some degree of flexibility in dealing so importantly with human beings.

Table 4.1 graphically presents the voting record of the Eisenhower Court in this area[93] and indicates that the Eisenhower associate justices and Justice Frankfurter did not have the same degree of cohesion here that was present in other areas. Brennan, Frankfurter, Harlan, and Whittaker voted as a bloc in only five of the twenty cases in which they were joint participants.[94] As would be expected, the greatest resistance to legislative and administrative policy toward aliens and those facing a possible loss of citizenship came from Justices Black and Douglas, who, as the preceding chapter demonstrated, displayed the greatest concern for the protection of civil liberties of alleged subversives. In ruling on deportation cases, however, these justices lost their usual voting comrade, Warren, who joined Brennan and Frankfurter to form a center bloc which upheld aliens' claims in approximately half of the cases. The remaining justices appeared to give preference to the claims of the government in most instances. In this respect, Harlan and Whittaker differ little from Clark and Burton. In denaturalization proceedings, Douglas, Black, and Warren were reunited, while Brennan, Frankfurter, and Harlan formed a center bloc. The expatriation cases, as indicated earlier, present a more complicated pattern. Whittaker's votes with Douglas, Black, and Warren in this area are in sharp contrast to his record in denaturalization cases. Clark remained consistently less libertarian in all three categories, and Stewart never voted in favor of individual claimants in any of the seven cases included in this table.

Table 4.1
Alignments of Justices in Nonunanimous Cases Involving Rights of Aliens and Litigants in Denaturalization and Expatriation Proceedings, 1953–1961 Terms (in percentages)

Decisions Favorable to the Individual

	Deportation	Denaturalization	Expatriation
No. of cases	18	6	4
Douglas	95	100	100
Black	95	100	100
Warren	58	100	100
Brennan	58 (12)	83 (5)	75
Frankfurter	42	50	50
COURT	40	50	75
Harlan	15 (14)	40 (5)	0
Whittaker	10 (11)	0 (5)	75
Burton	6 (16)	25 (4)	3
Stewart	0 (4)	0 (2)	0 (1)
Clark	11	0	0

Justices Reed and Minton participated in eight cases included in this table without once voting against the government's claims. Justice Jackson participated in three deportation cases included and voted for the claim of the individual in one. The cases included in Table 4.1 are as follows:

Deportation (18): For alien claims (4): *Barber v. Gonzales* (1954); *Shaughnessy v. Pedreiro* (1955); *Rowoldt v. Perfetto* (1957); *U.S. v. Witkovich* (1957).

Against alien claims (14): *Longshoreman's Union v. Boyd* (1954); *Galven v. Press* (1954); *Marcello v. Bonds* (1955); *Shaughnessy v. Accardi* (1955); *Jay v. Boyd* (1956); *Hintopoulos v. Shaughnessy* (1957); *Rabang v. Boyd* (1957); *Lehman v. Carson* (1957); *Mulcahey v. Catalanotte* (1957); *Rodgers v. Quan* (1958); *Leng May Ma v. Barber* (1958); *U.S. v. Cores* (1958); *Niukkanen v. McAlexander* (1960); *Kim v. Rosenberg* (1960).

Denaturalization (6): For citizens' claims (3): *U.S. v. Zucca* (1956); *Nowak v. U.S.* (1958); *Maisenberg v. U.S.* (1958).

Against citizens' claims (3): *Brown v. U.S.* (1958); *Tak Shan Fong v. U.S.* (1959); *Fleming v. Nestor* (1960).

Expatriation (4): For citizens' claims (3): *Kent v. Dulles* (1958); *Trop v. Dulles* (1958); *Nishikawa v. Dulles* (1958).

Against citizens' claims (1): *Perez v. Brownell* (1958).

In conclusion, the Eisenhower Court showed more sensitivity toward the rights of citizens and aliens than its predecessor.[95] Although there were still many worthwhile corrections that could have been made, the Court had at least demonstrated that the American sense of "fair play" could be extended to those so unfortunate as to be involved in denaturalization, expatriation, or deportation proceedings.

NOTES

1. See generally, Walter H. Maloney, Jr., "Involuntary Loss of American Citizenship," 3 *St. Louis U. L. J.* 168 (1956).

2. *Schneiderman v. U.S.*, 320 U.S. 118 (1943); *Baumgartner v. U.S.*, 322 U.S. 695 (1944); *Knauer v. U.S.*, 328 U.S. 654 (1946).

3. McCarran Act, 66 Stat. 163 (1952).

4. Comment, *Denaturalization under the Immigration and Nationality Act of 1952*, 51 *Mich. L. Rev.* 881 (1953).

5. 351 U.S. 91 (1956).

6. See, 55 *Colum. L. Rev.* 75 (1955); 3 *Wane L. Rev.* 68 (1956).

7. 351 U.S. 91 at 98; Clark, Reed, and Minton disagreed with this view in dissent.

8. 356 U.S. 256 (1958).

9. 356 U.S. 660 (1958).

10. See, 13 *Rutgers L. Rev.* 361 (1958).

11. 356 U.S. 670 (1958).

12. 356 U.S. 670 at 672.

13. 356 U.S. 660 at 666.

14. 356 U.S. 670 at 673.

15. Ibid.

16. 354 U.S. 660 at 666–67.

17. "Civil Liberties and the Supreme Court: October Term 1957," 18 *Law. Guild Rev.* 93, 102 (1958).

18. 356 U.S. 148 (1958). The majority was composed of Frankfurter, Whittaker, Harlan, Clark, and Burton.

19. See 37 *Texas L. Rev.* 343 (1959); 61 *W. Va. L. Rev.* 79 (1958).

20. See generally, Leonard B. Boudin, "Involuntary Loss of American Nationality," 73 *Harv. L. Rev.* 1510 (1960).

21. 34 Stat. 1228.

22. 54 Stat. 1137 [amended by 58 Stat. 746 (1944)].

23. 356 U.S. 44 (1958).

24. Justices Frankfurter, Harlan, Brennan, Clark, and Burton.

25. 356 U.S. 44 at 59.

26. Ibid.

27. But see 47 *Geo. L. J.* 177 (1958); 25 *Brooklyn L. Rev.* 113 (1958).

28. 356 U.S. 86 (1958).

29. 356 U.S. 86 at 92–93.

30. See 12 *Sw. L. J.* 511 (1958); 44 *Cornell L. Q.* 593 (1959).

31. 356 U.S. 86 at 100.

32. 356 U.S. 86 at 101.

33. 356 U.S. 86 at 114.

34. *Nishikawa v. Dulles*, 356 U.S. 129 (1958).

35. See 14 *Wyo. L. J.* 258 (1960).

36. See Robert E. Goostree, "Denationalization Cases of 1958," 8 *Am. U. L. Rev.* 87 (1959).

37. 354 U.S. 44 at 62.

38. 356 U.S. 86 at 103.

39. Comment, 56 *Mich. L. Rev.* 1142, 1167 (1958).

40. 387 U.S. 253 (1967); see 47 *Geo. L. J.* 177 (1958); 44 *Cornell L. Q.* 593 (1959); 25 *Brooklyn L. Rev.* 113 (1958); cf. 34 *Ind. L. J.* 231 (1959); but cf. 72 *Harv. L. Rev.* 167 (1958).

41. See generally, Common Council for American Unity, *The Alien and the Immigration Law*, a study under the direction of Edith Lowenstein (New York: Oceana Publications, 1956).

42. For historical studies of the impact of immigration on American history, see Henry Steele Commanger, ed., *Immigration and American History* (Minneapolis: University of Minnesota Press, 1961); see also Milton R. Konvitz, *Civil Rights in Immigration* (Ithaca, NY: Cornell University Press, 1953); *The Alien and the Asiatic in American Law* (Ithaca, NY: Cornell University Press, 1946).

43. Chinese Exclusion Acts [repealed by 57 Stat. 600 (1943)].

44. 39 Stat. 874.

45. 64 Stat. 987 (1950); for a thorough treatment of laws in this field in the 1960s, see Frank L. Auerbach, *Immigration Laws of the United States* (Indianapolis, IN: Bobbs-Merrill, 1961).

46. 54 Stat. 670 (1940).

47. Note, "Rights of Communist Aliens Subject to Deportation," 30 *Notre Dame Law.* 438 (1955).

48. Note, "Rights of Aliens in Deportation Proceedings," 31 *Ind. L. J.* 218 (1956).

49. See generally, Will Maslow, "Recasting our Deportation Laws: Proposals for Reform," 56 *Colum. L. Rev.* 309 (1956); see also Charles Gordon and Harry N. Rosenfield, *Immigration Law and Procedure* (Albany, NY: Banks, 1959).

50. 347 U.S. 522 (1954).

51. See 1 *Wayne. L. Rev.* 132 (1955); cf. 8 *Vand. L. Rev.* 121 (1954).

52. 347 U.S. 522 at 530.

53. 350 U.S. 179 (1956).

54. *Rowoldt v. Perfetto*, 355 U.S. 115 (1957).

55. The majority was composed of Warren, Black, Douglas, Brennan, and Frankfurter.

56. See 56 *Mich. L. Rev.* 803 (1958); 10 *Ala. L. Rev.* 470 (1958).

57. 355 U.S. 115 at 121.

58. See 22 *Geo. Wash. L. Rev.* 756 (1954); 7 *U. Fla. L. Rev.* 328 (1954); see also William B. Ball, "Judicial Review in Deportation and Exclusion Cases," *Interpreter Releases*, 10 June 1957.

59. 347 U.S. 260 (1954).

60. *Shaughnessy v. United States ex rel. Accardi*, 349 U.S. 280 (1955).

61. *United States ex rel. Accardi v. Shaughnessy*, 219 F.2d 77, 80 (2d Cir. 1955).

62. 219 F.2d 77 at 90.

63. 69 *Harv. L. Rev.* 168 (1955).

64. 349 U.S. 280 at 283.

65. 349 U.S. 280 at 292–93.

66. 69 *Harv. L. Rev.* 168 (1955).

67. 60 Stat. 237 (1946).

68. 349 U.S. 302 (1955).

69. 349 U.S. 302 at 309, 317.

70. 69 *Harv. L. Rev.* 165 (1955); but see, 35 *Neb. L. Rev.* 138 (1955).

71. 349 U.S. 48 (1955).

72. 349 U.S. 48 at 51.

73. See 3 *U.C.L.A. L. Rev.* 86 (1955); 28 *So. Cal. L. Rev.* 407 (1955); but see, 40 *Minn. L. Rev.* 497 (1956).

74. 352 U.S. 180 (1956).

75. Bernard Schwartz, "Administrative Law," 33 *N.Y.U. L. Rev.* 154, 163 (1958).

76. 353 U.S. 194 (1957).

77. 353 U.S. 194 at 199.

78. 353 U.S. 194 at 202.

79. In opposition to the majority composed of Frankfurter, Harlan, Brennan, Warren, Douglas, and Black.

80. Note, "Ex Post Facto Clause and Deportations" 11 *Wyo. L. J.* 32 (1956).

81. *Lehmann v. U.S. ex rel. Carson*, 353 U.S. 685 (1957); *Mulcahey v. Catalanotte*, 353 U.S. 692 (1957).

82. 351 U.S. 345 (1956).

83. Reed, Minton, Burton, Clark, and Harlan.

84. But see, 59 *W. Va. L. Rev.* 199 (1957).

85. 351 U.S. 345 at 357.

86. 351 U.S. 345 at 361.

87. 8 C.F.R. 242.17(c) (1956).

88. *Fleming v. Nestor*, 363 U.S. 603 (1960).

89. In *Carlson v. Landon*, 342 U.S. 524 at 536.

90. C. Herman Pritchett, *The American Constitution* (New York: McGraw-Hill, 1959), p. 637.

91. Comment, 56 *Mich. L. Rev.* 1142 (1958).

92. Pritchett, *Civil Liberties and the Vinson Court*, p. 107; but see *Kimm v. Rosenbert*, 363 U.S. 405 (1960); *Niukkanen v. McAlexander*, 362 U.S. 390 (1960).

93. Including several cases not discussed in the text.

94. *Rabang v. Boyd*, 353 U.S. 427 (1957); *Lehmann v. Carson*, 353 U.S. 685 (1957); *Mulcahey v. Catalanotte*, 353 U.S. 692 (1957); *U.S. v. Cores*, 356 U.S. 405 (1958); *Tak Shan Fong v. U.S.*, 359 U.S. 102 (1959). In *Tak Shan Fong*, Justice Stewart joined the center bloc.

95. "Only 29 percent of the Vinson Court's decisions were favorable to the aliens, while 45 per cent of the Warren Court's decisions were pro-alien" (through the 1957 term). Schubert, *Quantitative Analysis*, p. 305.

5

First Amendment Freedoms

Excluding cases dealing with control of "subversive activities," the Eisenhower Court faced few cases dealing with First Amendment freedoms—the right to free speech, press, religion, and assemblage—and derived from these rights, the freedom of association. In comparison with the Roosevelt and Vinson Courts, the Eisenhower Court's adjudication in this area was greatly reduced quantitatively.[1] Yet the Court was confronted with and decided many of the principal questions relating to obscenity. In doing this, the Court developed constitutional doctrine with major implications transcending the immediate problem. The Court also moved boldly in placing substantive limitations on governmental actions by formally recognizing rights of association, Although the Court made no significant church–state rulings during Eisenhower's administration, in 1961 the Eisenhower Court got religion and handed down landmark decisions involving Sunday closing laws and prayer in schools.

The largest number of First Amendment cases dealt with by the Eisenhower Court concerned censorship of books, magazines, and motion pictures. At that time, obscenity was punishable under state laws and when sent through the mail, by federal statute.[2] The judicial problem has traditionally been to find and apply standards for determining what is obscene.[3]

The Vinson Court ruled on two important cases that gave indication that state statutes dealing with First Amendment rights would have to be carefully drawn to avoid being struck down for being too vague. In 1948 in *Winters v. New York*,[4] the Court held invalid a New York statute which made it a crime to publish or distribute books, magazines, or papers "principally made up of criminal news, police reports, or accounts of criminal deeds, or pictures or stories of deeds of bloodshed."[5] Since the crime was defined in terms so vague "that men of intelligence must necessarily guess at its meaning,"[6] it denied due process of law. Also, since the statute was so broad that it forbade acts fairly within the protection of a free press, it was also void on that ground.

In *Burstyn v. Wilson*, the Vinson Court ruled that motion pictures are part of the press protected by the First and Fourteenth Amendments.[7] In rescinding a New York ban of the Rossolini movie, "The Miracle," the Court ruled that "sacrilegious" was too vague a standard to meet the requirements of due process. The Court did not, however, rule out the possibility of valid prior censorship of motion pictures, provided sufficiently definite standards could be drawn so that reasonable people could know what the law forbade.[8]

The *Winters* decision and particularly the *Burstyn* opinion suggested skepticism about any sweeping use of the obscenity standard. In 1957 the Supreme Court, for the first time in a full opinion, passed on the conviction of persons charged with publishing or selling obscene publications. In the first case, *Butler v. Michigan*,[9] the facts were such that the Court was able to dispose of it without facing the more difficult issues involved. Butler was convicted of violating a Michigan obscenity statute by selling a copy of a paperback edition of John Griffin's *The Devil Rides Outside* to a policeman. The statute penalized the selling of printed materials or pictures "tending to incite minors to violent or depraved or immoral acts (or) manifestly tending to the corruption of the morals of youth."[10] The trial judge found that the book would have a "potentially deleterious influence upon youth." The Supreme Court found it unnecessary to consider the standards the trial judge employed in reaching this conclusion, since the book had been sold to an adult. Said Justice Frankfurter for the unanimous Court:

> The State insists that, by thus quarantining the General reading public against books not too rugged for grown men and women in order to shield juvenile innocence, it is exercising its power to promote the general welfare. Surely, this is to burn the house to roast the pig. . . . We have before us legislation not reasonably restricted to the evil with which it is said to deal. The incidence of this enactment is to reduce the adult population of Michigan to reading only what is for children. It thereby arbitrarily curtails one of those liberties of the individual, now enshrined in the Due Process Clause of the Fourteenth Amendment, that history has attested as the indispensable conditions for the maintenance and progress of a free society.[11]

In the same term, in *Roth v. United States* and its companion case, *Alberts v. California*, a divided Court upheld both federal and state criminal obscenity laws.[12] Roth, a New York bookseller, was convicted in a federal court of violating the federal statute which forbade the mailing of "every obscene, lewd, lascivious, or filthy book, pamphlet, picture, paper, letter, writing, print or other publication of an indecent character,"[13] by sending through the mail a publication called *American Aphrodite*.[14] Alberts was convicted for advertising such books as *Sword of Desire*, *She Made It Pay*, and *The Business Side of the Oldest Business* in violation of a California law which forbade the writing, publishing, or selling of "any obscene or indecent writing, paper or book."[15]

Justice Brennan, speaking for the majority, pointed to numerous expressions in many opinions indicating that the Court had always assumed that obscenity is not protected by the constitutional guaranty of freedom of speech and press. The First Amendment extends to "all ideas having even the slightest redeeming social importance—unorthodox ideas, controversial ideas, even ideas hateful to the prevailing climate of opinion. . . . But implicit in the history of the First Amendment is the rejection of obscenity as utterly without social importance."[16] Since obscenity is not "protected speech," there is no necessity to show any connection with unlawful action in order to justify criminal punishment. The clear and present danger standard does not apply, and therefore it is unnecessary for the government to prove that the particular literature on which a prosecution rests will perceptibly create a clear and present danger of antisocial conduct.

Justice Brennan defined obscene material as that "which deals with sex in a manner appealing to prurient interest." In a footnote he added, "i.e., material having a tendency to excite lustful thoughts."[17] Justice Brennan admitted that prosecutors and judges might misuse or misconstrue their freedom to punish discussions of sex, "a great and mysterious motive force in human life. . . . It is therefore vital that the standards for judging obscenity safeguard the protection of freedom of speech and press for material which does not treat sex in a manner appealing to prurient interest."[18] Justice Brennan made it clear that sex and obscenity are not synonymous and the portrayal of sex in art and literature is not in itself bad. He stated that the test of obscenity is not the possible effect the publication might have upon the most susceptible person in the community. The Court thus rejected the famous *Hicklin* test of the courts of England.[19] The proper standard was now "whether to the average person, applying contemporary community standards, the dominant theme of the material taken as a whole appeals to prurient interest."[20] The Court majority thought it unnecessary to make any independent determination of the obscene character of the material. What the Court had announced was a constitutional formula more protective of artists' freedom than any that previously had been proposed.

The Court rejected the argument that the statutes were void for vagueness. Although it agreed that the terms used were not precise, it was pointed out that lack of precision is not itself offensive to due process since the Constitution does not require impossible standards. It was held that the federal statute fell within the authority delegated to the national government by the postal clause of the Constitution, and that insofar as the California statute was applied to a man who ran a mail-order business, the state was neither burdening nor interfering with the federal postal functions, since it was punishing for "keeping for sale" or "advertising."

When *Roth* was before the Court, Professor Alexander Meikeljohn lead a movement seeking to restrict the scope of free speech protection only to "political" speech on the grounds that the First Amendment was limited to fostering democratic politics. Brennan's opinion in *Roth* rejected this distinction and acknowledged the relationship between culture and politics.[21]

The Chief Justice, a strong opponent of what he considered "smut," concurred, although he thought that the language of the opinion was too broad. He feared that the Court's test might be applied to the arts and sciences and freedom of communication generally. He insisted that the central issue was the conduct of the individual defendant, since a person and not a book was on trial. Both defendants were "plainly engaged in the commercial exploitation of the morbid and shameful craving for materials with prurient effect."[22]

Justice Harlan dissented in part, fearing that the Court's standard might result "in a loosening of the tight reins which State and federal courts should hold upon the enforcement of obscenity statutes."[23] He concurred in the state case, feeling that the Court should accept as not irrational the state legislature's conclusion that distribution of certain types of literature might induce criminal or immoral sexual conduct. But Justice Harlan dissented in the federal case on the grounds that "Congress has no substantive power over sexual morality," and that federal censorship should be discouraged because of its nationwide impact. "The fact that the people of one State cannot read some of the works of D. H. Lawrence seems to me, if not wise or desirable, at least acceptable. But that no person in the United States should be allowed to do so seems to me to be intolerable, and violative of both the letter and spirit of the First Amendment."[24]

Thus Justice Harlan would have construed the federal obscenity law to regulate only "hard-core" pornography, which he did not think was present in this case. Roth had been charged with selling a book that tended to "stir sexual impulses and lead to sexually impure thoughts." Harlan thought that much of the great literature of the world sent through the mail could lead to conviction under such a view of the statute. "The Federal Government has no business, whether under the postal or commerce power, to bar the sale of books because they might lead to any kind of 'thoughts'."[25] Harlan would not deny Congress the power to protect the country from "hard-core" pornography, but the present statute, as here construed, "defines obscenity so widely that it encompasses matters which might very well be protected speech." He concluded: "I am very much afraid that the broad manner in which the Court has decided these cases will tend to obscure the peculiar responsibilities resting on State and Federal courts in this field and encourage them to rely on easy labeling and jury verdicts as a substitute for facing up to the tough individual problems of constitutional judgment involved in every obscenity case."[26]

Justices Black and Douglas dissented in both cases since they believed that the standards invoked punished thoughts rather than overt acts or antisocial conduct. "The test of obscenity the Court endorses today gives the censor free range over a vast domain. To allow the State to step in and punish mere speech or publication that the judge or the jury thinks has an *undesirable* impact on thoughts but that is not shown to be a part of unlawful action is drastically to curtail the First Amendment."[27] Black and Douglas maintained that the Court should have confidence in the ability of the American people to make up their own minds as to what they want to read or believe.

The Court also disposed of an important procedural question in connection with the enjoining of distribution of obscene literature in *Kingsley Books, Inc. v. Brown*.[28] A bookseller was charged with displaying for sale some fourteen paperback booklets having the general title "Nights of Horror." A New York statute authorized the chief executive or legal officer of any city or town in the state to bring an injunction action against the sale of any indecent books or other materials.[29] A person so enjoined was entitled to a trial of the issues within one day, and the court was to give its decision two days after the trial ended. If the injunction was granted, the material was to be surrendered to the sheriff or seized by him and destroyed. The appellant argued that the statute was an unconstitutional prior censorship of literature. The Court upheld the act by a narrow five-to-four margin.[30] Pointing out that due process does not limit the state to the criminal process in seeking to protect its people against the dissemination of pornography, Justice Frankfurter, for the majority, maintained that the phrase "prior restraint" is neither a "self-wielding sword" nor a "talismanic test."[31] The kind of prior restraint applied in this case seemed to him no more restrictive an interference with freedom of publication than criminal punishment after the event would be. Instead of running the risk of a criminal prosecution without prior warning, book dealers were assured by this civil procedure that they would not be punished criminally unless they ignored a court order specifically directed to them that lead to a prompt and carefully circumscribed determination of the issue of obscenity. Justice Frankfurter distinguished the *Near* case, which had condemned on constitutional grounds the imposition of prior restraints upon the publication of a newspaper as being the very essence of censorship.[32] The Court in the *Near* case was enjoining future issues of a publication because its past issues had been found to be offensive and derogatory to a public official. In the case at hand, a court was enjoining circulation of material already published, which had been found in a judicial proceeding to be obscene.

The four dissenting justices filed three different opinions. Chief Justice Warren pointed out that police first summarily seized the books that in their opinion were obscene, and then obtained a court order. Such book seizure, in his opinion, "savors too much of book burning." The New York statute, totally ignoring the "manner of use" of the book, or the "setting in which it is placed," put the book itself on trial, not its seller. The Chief Justice concluded: "It is the conduct of the individual that should be judged, not the quality of art or literature. To do otherwise is to impose a prior restraint and hence to violate the Constitution. Certainly in the absence of a prior judicial determination of illegal use, books, pictures and other objects of expression should not be destroyed."[33]

Justice Douglas, joined by Justice Black in dissent, contended that the provision for temporary injunction against the sale of a book, issued simply on complaint and without a hearing or a finding of obscenity, was "prior restraint and censorship at its worst."[34] Furthermore, he attacked this use of equity power because it made one conviction the basis for a statewide decree against the particular publication, without considering the total context of the case (for example, to whom the sales were made— to juveniles or adults). Justice Douglas insisted on the need for a separate trial for separate offenses. He also contended that trial should be by jury. Justice Brennan likewise thought that the absence in this statute of the right to jury trial was a fatal defect, especially since in such cases as these the jury is peculiarly well fitted to appraise the challenged publication "according to the average person's application of contemporary community standards."[35]

In the next term the Court made it clear that these decisions had not given government a blank check in the area of censorship of obscene publications. In three unanimous per curiam decisions, the Court set aside convictions in cases involving nudist magazines[36] and a magazine devoted to the subject of homosexuality,[37] in each instance on the authority of the Roth case. This would indicate that the barriers to censorship spelled out in the Roth case were apparently quite substantial. Significant in the Sunshine Book case was the fact that the Court found no difficulty in substituting its own finding on the issue of obscenity for that of the Postmaster General, the District Court, and the Court of Appeals. It remained unsettled whether the Court would exercise the same independence in reviewing a finding of obscenity if made by a jury upon proper instruction or by a state tribunal which was normally entitled to great deference on matters of fact.

From these decisions, it can be seen that a firm majority, with only Justices Black and Douglas dissenting, was willing to sustain the power of the states to prosecute criminally the deliberate and willful purveyor of matter, the dominant theme of which "taken as a whole appeals to prurient interest." This majority was reduced by one, Justice Harlan, when the federal government asserted the power so to prosecute. Where such restraints were imposed without particular reference to the context of the utterance, the majority lost the support of Chief Justice Warren; and where no jury trial was guaranteed, Justice Brennan would likewise dissent. While the Court disappointed those seeking total eradication of the censorship that was promoted by obscenity legislation, the Court sought to narrowly define the area of permissible restraint.

The language in these holdings fell short of solving the problem at hand, which was to set understandable limits on governmental interference with individual freedom in this area without depriving it of power to protect legitimate community and individual interests in combating evils associated with commercialized pornography. The primary argument appears to have been reduced by the Court to its definition of "obscenity." Justice Brennan's definition of "obscene" in the *Roth* case was far from satisfactory. "Prurient" and obscene are synonymous along with some of the older statutory standbys, lewd, lascivious, filthy, or disgusting. These words have always been used to define each other. A great deal of case-by-case litigation would be necessary to give "obscenity" an understandable meaning. The solution to this problem did not lie in the formulation of some foolproof definition, however. Since attempts to define what appears to be the indefinable are futile, the Court's formal commitment to procedural safeguards in the *Roth* case was to be far more significant in the future.[38]

The *Kingsley Books* decision was likewise unsatisfactory. The dangers of misuse of the powers allocated by this case were obvious. The more vocal groups in a community might rant and rave until certain books might be enjoined over an entire state as "bad" under all circumstances. The seizure and destruction of such books would surely smack more of book burning than a "closely confined" exception to the general constitutional rule against censorship.

Many persons feel that society has a positive interest in preventing those forms of expression that are particularly offensive from being thrust upon its members.[39] It has a further interest in prohibiting speech which incites a listener to illegal conduct. Certain forms of speech that are obscene or libelous have been held not to be speech within the meaning of the First Amendment. It is thus possible that such speech could be subject to prior restraint. But in the *Kingsley Books* case, the Court showed an unwillingness to make rigid doctrinal distinctions between prior restraint and subsequent punishment, instead preferring a pragmatic consideration in each case of the extent to which a particular sanction inhibited speech.

One wonders whether the transition from the law at issue in *Roth* to that at issue in *Kingsley* was as easy as the Court stated. The distinction between previous restraints and subsequent punishment is one that has always been fundamental in our constitutional law.

Kingsley tended to blur this fundamental distinction. More than that, defendants were deprived of their right to jury trial, which they were clearly entitled to under the *Roth* statute. All things considered, however, the "obscenity decisions" of the Court, in application, left the affected field of expression in a better condition than the Court found it.[40]

MOTION PICTURES

Following the *Miracle* case, the Eisenhower Court invalidated censorship as applied to four different films, but in none of these cases was an opinion written for the Court. In *Superior Films v. Ohio Department of Education,*[41] the Court cited the *Burstyn* case while reversing Ohio's ban on the film *M*, which had been found to "undermine confidence in the enforcement of law and government" and which could lead "unstable persons to increased immorality and crime." At the same time the Court reversed New York's ban on the French film *La Ronda* on grounds of obscenity.[42] *Holmby Productions v. Vaughn* was concerned with the Kansas State Board of Review's ban of the American motion picture, *The Moon Is Blue*.[43] The Court cited both the *Burstyn* and *Superior Films* cases in striking the action of the Board. In *Times Film Corp. v. Chicago,*[44] the Court struck down a Chicago ban of the French movie, *Game of Love*, basing its decision on the *Alberts* case.

During the 1958 term, the Court reversed a decision of the New York Court of Appeals that upheld the denial of a license for the motion picture made of D. H. Lawrence's novel, *Lady Chatterley's Lover*, another French movie, because it portrayed "acts of sexual immorality . . . as desirable, acceptable, or proper patterns of behavior."[45] The Court held that the statute[46] was, on its face, an unconstitutional abridgment of freedom of speech since, as interpreted by the state court, it prevented, under any circumstances, the advocacy of certain ideas, without regard to the method of portraying these ideas or without regard to whether the ideas incited to unlawful conduct.

The Court was unanimous in holding the denial of a license unconstitutional, but it was greatly divided as to the grounds that should justify this opinion. Justice Stewart wrote the opinion of the Court and expressly declined to reach the issue of prior restraint. He held in effect that New York had no legitimate interest in banning the movie merely because it alluringly presented adultery as socially acceptable conduct. His theory was that an abridgment of speech on the ground that the ideas portrayed by a motion picture are not shared by a majority of the community can never be justified under the First Amendment. To Justice Stewart, the First Amendment's basic guarantee is freedom to advocate ideas.

Justice Harlan, with whom Justice Frankfurter and Justice Whittaker concurred, contended that the majority erred in declaring the statute unconstitutional on its face, since the New York Court of Appeals had read the statute as proscribing only speech that was obscene or an incitement of illegal action and not words that merely advocated an immoral line of conduct. They based their conclusion on the ground that application of the statutory prohibition to this particular film was unconstitutional.

Justices Black and Douglas concurred with the Court but stated that prior restraints on any form of speech could not be upheld. Justice Clark would have held the statute void since it set up a standard too vague for the censor to apply: "This is nothing less than a roving commission in which individual impressions become the yardstick of action, and result in regulation in accordance with the beliefs of the individual censor rather than regulation by law."[47] Thus Clark, like Stewart, found the statute unconstitutional on its face.

In another 1959 case, the Court ruled that a city ordinance was unconstitutional because its effect would allow a store owner to sell only the books he had inspected.[48] Under such a scheme, restrictions affected the distribution of constitutionally protected as well as obscene literature.

The question of prior restraint returned in 1961 in *Times Film Corp. v. Chicago*, where the Court in a five-to-four decision upheld the examination of movies before their showing. The Court held that licensing could be used to suppress ideas—not only obscene but social and political views as well. For the majority, the issue was not the standards for censorship but the act of censorship itself. Justice Clark, joined by Frankfurter, Harlan, Whittaker, and Stewart, supported the screening of movies, a procedure that would be intolerable for newspapers or even broadcasting.[49]

The net effect of the cases dealing with motion pictures adjudicated by the Eisenhower Court was to require it to make independent determinations whether a movie should be censored, which was no doubt, a salutary assurance against overzealous guardians of the public morality, but which brought the Court uncomfortably close to the role of super-critic.[50]

Justice Black, in a separate concurrence in the *Lady Chatterley's Lover* decision, made some pungent comments about the Supreme Court as a board of movie critics:

> This Court is about the most inappropriate Supreme Board of Censors that could be found. So far as I know, judges possess no special expertise providing exceptional competency to set standards and to supervise the private morals of the Nation. In addition, the Justices

of this Court seem especially unsuited to make the kind of value
judgments—as to what movies are good or bad for local
communities—which the concurring opinions appear to require. . . .
The end result of such decisions seems to me to be a purely personal
determination by individual Justices as to whether a particular picture
viewed is too bad to allow it to be seen by the public. . . . In my
judgment, this Court should not permit itself to get into the very
center of such policy controversies, which have so little in common
with lawsuits.[51]

The problem of the Court as a board of censors is obvious. Determinations as to whether a movie should be censored would be made without guidance of reasonably fixed and certain standards. Thus, neither the
states nor moving picture makers could know in advance whether a given
work might be censored.

Some members of the Court appeared to think that reliance on the
Roth definition might establish a sufficiently definite standard for "obscene" film. The *Times Film* decision did not refer to the previous cases
invalidating a prior restraint because of indefiniteness of the standard
employed. Instead, the validity of the licensing system appeared to be
assumed; only the particular application was held bad. In the *Lady
Chatterley* case, the ground relied upon by the Court appeared equally
applicable in both prior restraint and subsequent punishment cases. From
this, it might be concluded that the states were authorized to withhold
licenses for the exhibition of film on grounds of obscenity as defined in
Roth. The use of any other less permissive standard would likely have
resulted in striking down the statute as in *Lady Chatterley* or in reversal as
in *Times Film*.

The problem still remained—regardless of how words were defined,
the courts had to invoke somebody's sense of moral values to determine
the legal consequences of the definition. Whose sense of decency, or good
taste, or delicacy is controlling? The opinions of these cases indicated that
the justices differed on this question and that there was also disagreement about free-speech doctrine between those justices who favored a
particularized case-by-case balancing that was inevitably personal. The
effects of this disagreement would have a major influence not only on
future obscenity regulation, but also on general free-speech doctrine as
well.[52]

PRIOR RESTRAINT ON FREEDOM OF SPEECH

In 1958 the Court reviewed the conviction of a salaried trade union organizer for violating an ordinance of Baxley, Georgia.[53] The ordinance provided that no person could solicit membership in any organization or

union which required payment of dues without first securing a permit from the mayor and council. In addition to paying a stiff license fee—$2,000, plus $500 for each member obtained—the mayor and council were directed to consider the character of the applicant, the nature of the organization, and "its effects upon the general welfare" of the city. The fact that a municipality would have such an ordinance is amazing considering that the Supreme Court had struck down, as unconstitutional, a Texas statute requiring a feeless registration of union organizers.[54] The Court of Appeals of Georgia affirmed lower state courts in holding that the constitutional question could not be considered since the petitioner, Rose Staub of the International Ladies' Garment Workers Union, should have attacked specific sections of the ordinance rather than the whole, and because she had not made an effort first to secure a license.

Reversing the state courts, the Supreme Court held that the decision below did not rest upon an adequate nonfederal basis. Justice Whittaker, speaking for the Court,[55] noted that when a defense is based on federal law, the Supreme Court is not precluded by the state court's view of pleading. The assertion of federal rights, when made plainly and reasonably, should not be defeated by local practice. The Court had previously held that failure to apply for a license under an ordinance which on its face violates the federal constitution does not prevent its review of the case. Justice Whittaker added that to force the plaintiff to challenge all sections of the ordinance, one by one, when they were interdependent and constituted one complete act of the licensing power, was to compel her to "an arid ritual of meaningless form."[56]

The Court held the ordinance unconstitutional on its face as a prior restraint on freedom of speech. The mayor and council were authorized to refuse a license "without semblance of definitive standards or other controlling guides."[57] An ordinance which makes the enjoyment of constitutional freedom contingent on the uncontrolled will of an official is an unconstitutional censorship or prior restraint upon the enjoyment of such freedoms.[58] What the Court still failed to answer was to what extent the state might regulate union organizers engaged in occupational or fund-securing activities in addition to their speech. Any attempt to impose a prior restraint on, "pure" speech, or to interfere with federally regulated labor–management relations, would be subject to judicial invalidation.[59]

Justice Frankfurter, with whom Justice Clark concurred, dissented on the theory that the case rested upon adequate nonfederal grounds. Justice Frankfurter, in characteristically restraintist language, argued that the Court ought to recognize that the states have a wide discretion in formulating procedures, even though their procedures may seem crude, awkward, or even unnecessarily formal, so long as they are not used to stifle a federal claim.

RADIO STATIONS, POLITICAL CANDIDATES, AND LIBELOUS BROADCASTS

Closely related to state laws dealing with prior restraint and subsequent punishment of speech are state libel statutes.[60] During the 1958 term, in *Farmers Educ. and Co-op. Union v. WDAY, Inc.*, the Court settled a vexing problem in this area involving radio broadcasts by political candidates.[61]

Section 315 of the Federal Communications Act [62] required all FCC licensees to grant "equal opportunities" to all "legally qualified candidates for a public office" if the licensee had allowed any "legally qualified" candidate for that office to use its facilities. The licensee had "no power of censorship over the material broadcast under the provisions of this section."

A candidate for U.S. senator from North Dakota, A. C. Townley, demanded radio time under Section 315. The managers of station WDAY knew that Townley's speech defamed the Farmers Educational and Co-operative Union, but they allowed him to broadcast the speech without deletions. The Supreme Court of North Dakota held that under Section 315, the station was immune from liability for defamation. The Supreme Court affirmed this in a five-to-four decision. All nine justices agreed that the censorship prescription barred a licensee from censoring or removing defamatory speeches covered by its provisions. For the majority,[63] Justice Black held that the station's inability to prevent the defamatory statements created an immunity from defamation actions under state law, since without such immunity, either an underlying purpose of the Communications Act would be frustrated or an unreasonable burden would be imposed on licensees. Justice Frankfurter, for the dissenters, Harlan, Whittaker, and Stewart, maintained that there were insufficient grounds for finding that Section 315 made the state defamation law inapplicable.

A contrary decision might have defeated the apparent purpose of Section 315—to provide all candidates with equal opportunities to engage in free debate prior to an election. If licensee stations were empowered to delete allegedly defamatory material, speeches might be delayed or kept off the air by licensees acting in good faith because the complexities and jurisdictional differences concerning the law of defamation made it difficult to determine quickly and accurately whether any critical statement was actionable. Stations attempting to promote the interests of one candidate by unduly delaying and censoring the speeches of his opponent might be able to do so without apprehension, since if reasonable grounds existed for believing that the speech was defamatory, it would be difficult to prove bad faith. In addition, the prospect of having a speech delayed while its defamatory nature was examined would be likely to induce candidates to avoid sharp attacks, particularly when only a short time remained before the election.[64]

FEDERAL REGULATION OF LOBBYING

Attempts to control lobbying activities of interest groups in the United States have a long history. The Georgia constitution of 1877 stated simply that "lobbying is declared to be a crime."[65] Many of the states today have acts to regulate lobbyists.[66] Most of these measures require that legislative counsel or agents officially register as such, and that they file statements of expenses paid in promoting legislation. The Federal Regulation of Lobbying Act of 1946 (Title III of the Legislative Reorganization Act of 1946) followed this pattern.[67] One provision required reports to Congress from every person "receiving any contributions or expending any money" for the purpose of influencing the passage or defeat of any legislation by Congress. Any person "who shall engage himself for pay or for any consideration for the purpose of attempting to influence the passage or defeat of any legislation" is required to register with Congress and to make specified disclosures. Another provision sought to clarify the coverage of the statute by stating that it applied to any person who "directly or indirectly" solicited or received money to be used "principally" to aid in the passage or defeat of legislation by Congress, or "to influence, directly or indirectly, the passage or defeat" of such legislation.[68]

In *United States v. Harriss*,[69] the Eisenhower Court showed great concern over the breadth and vagueness of this language and its impact on the rights to free speech and to petition the government. Chief Justice Warren, speaking for a five-man majority,[70] managed by interpretation to narrow the coverage of the act to constitutional dimensions. The Chief Justice construed the law to refer only to "lobbying in its commonly accepted sense" (i.e., "direct communication with members of Congress on pending or proposed Federal legislation"). It was not intended to apply more broadly "to organizations seeking to propagandize the general public."[71] If it had such breadth of scope, it might be unconstitutional. To the narrower power, there was no constitutional objection.

> Present-day legislative complexities are such that individual members of Congress cannot be expected to explore the myriad pressures to which they are regularly subjected. Yet full realization of the American ideal of government by elected representatives depends to no small extent on their ability to properly evaluate such pressures. Otherwise the voice of the people may all too easily be drowned out by the voice of special interest groups seeking favored treatment while masquerading as proponents of the public weal. This is the evil which the Lobbying Act was designed to help prevent.[72]

Justices Douglas, Black, and Jackson, dissenting, could not approve what they regarded as a rewriting of the act in order to make it constitutional. Said Justice Jackson: "The clearest feature of the Court's decision is that it leaves the country under an Act which is not much like any Act passed by Congress. Of course, when such a question is before us, it is easy to differ as to whether it is more appropriate to strike out or to strike down. But I recall few cases in which the Court has gone so far in rewriting an Act."[73]

Although "lobbying" may have unpleasant connotations to the average citizen, it must not be forgotten that petitioning the government is a constitutional right and an integral part of the American system of government. Of course, Congress is entitled to information on the origin and financing of pressures brought upon it; but should it resort to an act that is so vague on its face as to force the Court practically to rewrite it? Congress could have legislated more precisely, and a refusal to uphold the present statute, indicating some of its faults, might have produced a new statute stating in fact what the Court so tortuously construed the act to mean. Here the Court construed the statute in such a way that it perhaps went beyond the acceptable scope of statutory interpretation to uphold the act. [74]

Five years after the *Harriss* decision, a unanimous Court upheld Treasury Department regulations that forbade income tax deductions of sums expended for "the promotion or defeat of legislation." [75] The Court held that the regulations applied to expenditures made in connection with efforts to promote or defeat legislation by persuasion of the general public (as in initiative measures and referenda), as well as efforts to influence legislative bodies directly through "lobbying."

The Eisenhower Court also reviewed a decision defining the legal status of a political party, ruling in *United States v. Shirey*[76] that a political party could be considered a "person" in statutes. The law involved in this case provided that: "Whoever pays or offers or promises any money or thing of value, to any person, firms or corporation in consideration of the use or promise to use any influence to procure any appointive office or place under the United States for any person, shall be fined not more than $1,000 or imprisoned not more than one year, or both."[77]

George Donald Shirey proposed to Congressman S. Walter Stauffer of Pennsylvania that he would contribute $1,000 a year to the Republican Party in consideration of Stauffer's use of influence to procure for him the postmastership of York, Pennsylvania. Shirey was indicted and convicted of violating the statute. Justice Frankfurter, for the five-justice majority,[78] affirmed the convictions contending that the Republican Party was an organization of such nature as to satisfy the requirements of the statute. The majority held that the person promising political influence need not be the recipient of the money and that a political party is a "person" for purposes of the statute. The unusual combination of Justices Harlan, Black, Whittaker, and Stewart dissented on the ground that whether or not a political party is a "person" is essentially ambiguous, thus requiring a strict construction of the statute. According to the minority, the payee (the person receiving the contribution) must be the party exerting the influence.

THE RIGHT TO PICKET AND THE FIRST AMENDMENT

Since 1940 and the case of *Thornhill v. Alabama*,[79] the Supreme Court has maintained that peaceful picketing in labor disputes is protected by the free speech clause of the First Amendment. Justice Murphy, speaking for the majority in that case, declared that picketing was a form of communication and a method of circulating information. This opinion did not consider whether the state would be justified in regulating picketing where the communication process results in damage to other social values protected by law or the Constitution. Since that time, the Court, in a series of cases, spelled out instances where state regulation of such communication rights was permissible.[80]

In 1957 the Eisenhower Court was faced with a case involving these problems. When local Teamsters resorted to peaceful "stranger" picketing (that carried on by people not having a direct economic interest in the labor dispute) to induce a group of employees to join the union, the Wisconsin courts granted an injunction under a state law which prohibited picketing in the absence of a "labor dispute." The state supreme court held the picketing was for an unlawful purpose under a state law,[81] which made it an unfair labor practice for workers to coerce or induce any employer to interfere with the right of any of his employees to join or not to join a union. Here pickets had been used to coerce an employer to coerce his employees into joining the union.

By a five-to-three vote, the Supreme Court affirmed.[82] Justice Frankfurter stated that it was established that even peaceful picketing involved something more than merely the communication of ideas and could not be immune from all state regulation. He contended that there was "a broad field in which a State, in enforcing some public policy, whether of its criminal or its civil law, and whether announced by its legislature or its courts, (could) constitutionally enjoin peaceful picketing aimed at preventing effectuation of that policy."[83] While a blanket state prohibition of all picketing would be invalid, the Court felt that the Wisconsin policy that the injunction was designed to enforce was a valid one.

Justice Douglas, joined by Justice Black and the Chief Justice in dissent, maintained that such picketing as this could "be regulated or prohibited only to the extent that it forms an essential part of a course of conduct which the State can regulate or prohibit."[84] Since there was no violence, disorder, or coercion in this case, the dissenters thought that the communications activity was within the protection of the free speech guaranty of the Constitution. Thus, for all practical purposes, a state could actually bar all picketing, according to Douglas.

This was the first case in which the Supreme Court upheld a state injunction specifically against stranger picketing for organizational purposes. This holding together with earlier decisions established the principle that such organizational picketing could be state enjoined, not only if the "means" (i.e., violence) were illegal, but also if any objective of the picketing was held by a state court to be against state policy. This did not mean, of course, that picketing was to be given no constitutional protection by the First Amendment against state action. Conduct to achieve an illegal end has never been clothed with constitutional immunity by that amendment. The most valid objection to the "unlawful purpose" test involved here was that it seemed to be applied mechanically by the Supreme Court. Though the characterization of the picketers' purpose was said to be subject to judicial inquiry by the Court, the state court's finding on this matter was generally treated as conclusive. Here the Wisconsin court drew the "inference" that the picketing was for the purpose of forcing employers to coerce union membership among their employees. Such an inference could always be drawn since any organization picketing exerts some economic pressure on employers that can be relieved by their employee's acceptance of union membership. Thus, as to constitutional objections, it seemed that a state might suppress any particular type of picketing for any reason other than a blanket prohibition of picketing per se. The result was that labor's right "to organize" by peaceful stranger picketing was one which had essentially been rendered innocuous.[85]

In the next term, in *Youngdahl v. Rainfair, Inc.*,[86] the Court reaffirmed the states' power to enjoin picketing that takes the form of violent conduct. At the same time, it reasserted that states may not constitutionally forbid peaceful picketing.[87] In this case, the violent conduct took the form of violent speech. The Court ruled that abusive language such as the word "scab" was not protected speech.[88] According to Justice Burton, "If a sufficient number yell any word sufficiently loudly showing an intent to ridicule, insult or annoy, no matter how innocuous the dictionary definition of that word, the effect may cease to be persuasion and become intimidation and incitement to violence."[89] A state court, then, may enjoin threats and intimidation, but it is not free to go so far as to forbid all picketing. Chief Justice Warren and Justices Black and Douglas dissented, maintaining that Congress had given the National Labor Relations Board exclusive jurisdiction over the controversy.

In 1960 in *Talley v. California*, the Court recognized the First Amendment right to distribute anonymous handbills.[90] The decision facilitated a boycott on behalf of an organization protesting denial of "equal employment opportunities to Negroes, Mexicans, and Orientals" in a struggle to end discrimination by certain merchants and businessmen.

These free speech and labor cases indicated that the Eisenhower Court continued to keep the *Thornhill* principle confined to narrow limits, invalidating flat restraints against all picketing, but leaving legislatures and judges free in many respects to define public purposes which override picketing rights. Thus picketing was, at best, a dubious form of speech. It is interesting to note that Justice Brennan, the former labor lawyer, deserted his usual companions in opinion—the Chief Justice and Justices Black and Douglas—in these labor cases.[91]

FREEDOM OF ASSOCIATION

Most modern human activities are carried on in groups and associations. Although there is no express provision in the Constitution protecting freedom of association, the right of individuals to organize into groups for political, economic, religious, and social purposes is widely recognized. Professor Robert A. Horn, in his study, *Groups and the Constitution*,[92] contends: "Freedom of association is one of the most important civil liberties guaranteed by the Constitution of the United States, that we already have a substantial corpus of constitutional law on the freedom of association, and that the rapid creation of this body of law in the twentieth century by the United States Supreme Court is one of the most significant acts of American constitutional development."[93]

Professor Horn postulates five principles of the law of association which he believes to have emerged from Supreme Court interpretation of the Constitution, one of the most important of which is that there are limitations which a state may legitimately impose on groups to prevent them from performing acts injurious to other persons or even to their own members. This type of regulation could pose a real threat to associative freedom and provide reviewing courts the opportunity to consider the competing claims of interests in our pluralistic society.[94] The Eisenhower Court ruled unanimously on this problem in *National Association for the Advancement of Colored People v. Alabama*.[95]

Alabama, like other states, had a statute requiring out-of-state corporations to register and meet specified requirements before carrying on business in the state.[96] The NAACP, organized under the laws of New York as a nonprofit organization, maintained a regional office in Alabama, but it never attempted to comply with the Alabama foreign corporations act, from which it considered itself exempt. After the 1954 Supreme Court ruling against segregation in public schools, the NAACP became particularly active in the state, seeking enforcement of the Court's decree. In 1956 the Attorney General of Alabama brought an equity suit in the state court to enjoin the NAACP from further activity in the state. The court granted an immediate restraining order. The state then ordered the organization to produce its records, including names and addresses of all members in Alabama. The association filed the qualifying forms required by the statute and produced all of the records requested by the State except the membership lists, the disclosure of which the NAACP contended could not be constitutionally compelled. For its failure to comply with the production order, the association was held in civil contempt and fined $100,000.

When the U.S. Supreme Court took up the case, Justice Harlan played a significant role behind the scenes. In a memo to the conference, Harlan argued for a fully reasoned opinion rather than a per curiam one as had been the case since the original segregation cases were decided. Harlan urged that the opinion be "written (1) with utmost dispassion, (2) within an orthodox constitutional framework and (3) as narrowly as possible." [97] The Chief Justice agreed with these ideas and assigned the writing of the majority opinion to Harlan.

The Supreme Court ruled that the NAACP could assert the constitutional rights of its members, who were not parties to the suit, since their rights could not be vindicated effectively except through an appropriate representative. To require each member to claim his right himself would have defeated the purpose of the NAACP's action.[98] The Court stated that, for practical purposes, the NAACP and its members were identical.

Justice Harlan's opinion held that the production order violated due process. Compelled disclosure of the membership lists would abridge the rights of the members to engage in lawful association in support of their common beliefs. Justice Harlan said: "It is beyond debate that freedom to engage in association for the advancement of beliefs and ideas is an inseparable aspect of the 'liberty' assured by the Due Process Clause. . . . Of course, it is immaterial whether the beliefs sought to be advanced by the association pertain to political, economic, religious or cultural matters."[99]

The association had pointed out "that on past occasions revelation of the identity of its rank-and-file members has exposed these members to economic reprisal, loss of employment, threat of physical coercion, and other manifestations of public hostility."[100] Under such circumstances, the Court believed "that compelled disclosure of . . . membership is likely to affect adversely the ability of petitioner and its members to pursue their collective effort to foster beliefs which they admittedly have the right to advocate, in that it may induce members to withdraw from the Association and dissuade others from joining it because of fear of exposure of their beliefs shown through their associations and of the consequences of this exposure."[101]

It was irrelevant that "private community pressures" rather than state action would penalize disclosure of membership. "The crucial factor is the interplay of governmental and private action, for it is only after the initial exertion of State power represented by the production order that private action takes hold."[102] Thus there was a "vital relationship between freedom to associate and privacy in one's associations." When a group expresses unpopular beliefs, it may be absolutely essential to preserve the inviolability of privacy in group association.[103] The Court went on to rule that Alabama did not demonstrate an interest in obtaining the disclosures which was sufficient to justify the deterrent effect which these disclosures would have on the free exercise of the constitutionally protected right of association. The exclusive announced purpose of the court action was to determine whether the association was doing business in Alabama in violation of the state act. This was not, according to Justice Harlan, "a controlling justification for the deterrent offset on the free enjoyment of the right to associate which disclosure of membership lists is likely to have."[104]

The Court distinguished the case from *Bryant v. Zimmerman*,[105] which had upheld New York in requiring the Ku Klux Klan to supply a list of its members in 1928. That decision was based on the character of the Klan's activities, "involving acts of unlawful intimidation and violence." Here the organization was seeking to protect "the right of the members to pursue their lawful private interest privately and to associate freely with others in so doing." These rights, the Court held, came within the protection of the Fourteenth Amendment. The Court set aside the judgment of civil contempt and the $100,000 fine, but directed that the validity of the temporary restraining order remained to be adjudicated on the merits in the state courts.

On remand the Supreme Court of Alabama affirmed its previous judgment[106] and the Association again petitioned for a writ of certiorari. The Supreme Court in a per curiam decision[107] held that where its prior decision was based on the fact that the Association had complied with state court orders except as to its records of membership lists, and the state did not deny the Association's compliance with the court order except as to its records of membership, the state is bound by its position previously taken and it could not now claim that the Association failed in other respects to comply with the court order. In reversing the decision, the Supreme Court held that the Alabama Supreme Court was foreclosed from reexamining the grounds of disposition and added: "We assume that the State Supreme Court, thus advised, will not fail to proceed promptly with the disposition of the matters left open under our mandate for further proceedings."[108] Unfortunately the Alabama Supreme Court did fail to proceed promptly, and it was not until June 1964 that the state supreme court finally recognized the NAACP's constitutional rights.

In *Harrison v. NAACP*,[109] the high Court reversed the decision of a federal district court restraining the state of Virginia from proceeding under Virginia statutes admittedly aimed directly at the NAACP and its efforts to achieve compliance with the *Brown* decision. Even though the action was brought under the civil rights statutes, the Supreme Court thought that the district court should have abstained from deciding the merits of the issue in order to afford Virginia an opportunity to construe the statutes.[110] Justice Harlan, for the majority, held "that these enactments should be exposed to state construction or limiting interpretation before the federal courts are asked to decide upon their constitutionality, so that the federal judgment will be based on something that is a complete product of the State, the enactment as phrased by its state legislature and as construed by its highest court."[111]

Justice Douglas, joined by Justice Brennan and the Chief Justice, wrote a strong dissent, stating: "Where state laws make such an assault as these do on our decisions and a State has spoken definitely against the constitutional rights of the citizens, reasons for showing deference to local institutions vanish. The conflict is plain and apparent; and the federal courts stand as the one authoritative body for the enforcing of the constitutional rights of the citizens."[112]

In two other NAACP cases in the 1958 term, the Court moved with caution remanding them to lower courts for further proceedings.[113] Southern state legislative investigating committees concerned with integration activities also raised questions concerning freedom of association. In *Scull v. Commonwealth of Virginia*,[114] the Supreme Court unanimously reversed Scull's conviction of contempt for refusing to obey the decision of the county court ordering him to answer a number of questions put to him by the Virginia legislative committee concerning his membership and activities in the NAACP, the PTA, the American Civil Liberties Union, American Friends Service Committee, B'nai B'rith, the Communist Party, and others. The Court ruled that Scull was never given a fair opportunity to determine whether he was within his rights in refusing to answer because he was never able to find out from the committee which of its purposes the questions were pertinent to. The Court did not reach Scull's contentions that the committee was part of a legislative program of "massive resistance" to the desegregation decisions with the aim of harassing and publicly embarrassing members of the NAACP and that the questions asked violated his rights of freedom of speech, assembly, and petition and constituted unjustified restraint upon his associations with others and could serve no legitimate legislative purpose. Justice Black, for the Court, added a footnote that four members of the Court adhered to their views expressed in *Sweezy* and could not conceive of any circumstances wherein a state interest would justify infringement of rights in those fields.[115]

In the *Sweezy* case, Chief Justice Warren wrote one of the classic statements of the right of association: "Our form of government is built on the premise that every citizen shall have the right to engage in political expression and association. This right was enshrined in the First Amendment of the Bill of Rights. Exercise of these basic freedoms in America has traditionally been through the media of political associations. Any interference with the freedom of a party is simultaneously an interference with the freedom of its adherents."[116]

Arkansas also tried to force the NAACP to make public its membership lists. In *Bates v. Little Rock*, decided in 1960, the Court unanimously rejected compulsory disclosure of the organization's memberships as an unconstitutional interference with the freedom of association.[117] Justice Stewart, for the Court, found that Little Rock had no compelling interest in forcing the NAACP to disclose its members' identities simply because the organization was required to pay a licensing fee.

Arkansas statutes banned NAACP members from state employment and required teachers to declare the organizations to which they belonged. Teachers who were members of the NAACP were in a catch-22 situation. If they admitted membership, they lost their jobs; if they failed to file the requisite disclosure, they also would be fired. When the NAACP contested these laws, a federal judge struck down the membership statute but upheld the disclosure provisions because they did not specifically mention the NAACP. In *Beilan* and *Barenblatt*, the Supreme Court had indicated that membership in some organizations could legitimately be investigated by the state.

Thus, in *Shelton v. Tucker*, the Court had to decide whether it should be consistent in its treatment of the Communist Party and the NAACP.[118] In a five-to-four decision, the Court struck down the Arkansas disclosure requirement. Justice Stewart, for the Court, found that although the state had a legitimate interest in the integrity of its employees, those asked to disclose their memberships also had considerable interests at stake. Said Stewart: "Public exposure, bringing with it the possibilities of public pressures upon school boards to discharge teachers who belong to unpopular or minority organizations, would simply operate to widen and aggravate the impairment of constitutional liberty." Stewart's opinion was noteworthy because it enunciated two important First Amendment doctrines: "overbreadth," recognizing that any speech regulation must be fine-tuned so as not to threaten expression that should be protected; and "less restrictive alternatives," the concept that the Court should strike down any measure abridging speech if the government purpose could be effectively served by some other measure posing less danger to free speech.[119]

Harlan, Frankfurter, Clark, and Whittaker dissented believing the statute valid until Arkansas misused it. Harlan found "it impossible to determine *a priori* the place where the line should be drawn between what would be permissible inquiry and overbroad inquiry in a situation like this." This decision was the first of the NAACP desegregation cases in which the Eisenhower Court justices were divided.

Judicial recognition of association as a right protected by the Constitution against unreasonable restraint by government closely mirrors the importance of formal organization in American life.[120] Government action requiring organizations to make their membership lists public is a restraint on that right. Even without specific evidence, one would be entitled to assume that an association formed to advance views that invade emotionally held beliefs of a large part of the population would be hampered, if not altogether frustrated, by such measures.

The NAACP made a strong factual case that hostility in some areas had reached the point where exposure would make it not merely difficult, but impossible to operate. There were cases, of course, where an organization might be required to make known its membership if it were reasonably necessary to attain some proper societal objective, such as exposure to suppress crime or subversion or disclose financial sources of lobbyists. If the sole justification for such action was the intent to restrain the activities of persons or groups exposed, then the state action would merit closer surveyance. It was not enough simply to state that the activity in question was bad.[121]

The Court was correct in ruling the efforts of the states to force disclosures unconstitutional since such action could be used against any organization which espoused permissible views that were opposed by an influential part of the general public. Such activity would appear to be a direct violation of the protections of the First Amendment.[122]

The formal recognition given the right of association by the Eisenhower Court was, in the long run, one of its most important contributions to American constitutional law. The Court's decisions protecting associational rights made it possible for the NAACP to survive repeated attacks by state and local officials in the South and to continue its vital role in the Civil Rights Movement.[123]

FREE EXERCISE OF RELIGION AND ESTABLISHMENT CLAUSE CASES

Prior to Warren's appointment to the Chief Justiceship, the Court had incorporated the First Amendment religions clauses to apply to the states through the Fourteenth Amendment Due Process Clause. In 1940 in *Cantwell v. Connecticut*, the Court incorporated the free exercise clause,[124] and the establishment clause followed seven years later in *Everson v. Board of Education*.[125] Black, Douglas, and Frankfurter participated in both cases. Free exercise cases typically involved conflicts between governmental regulations with secular purposes and individuals' religious beliefs. Before 1960 the Court relied on the belief-action doctrine, also called the secular regulation rule, in evaluating free exercise claims. Under this doctrine, legislation was held to be invalid if it did not serve legitimate nonreligious governmental ends or if it was directed at particular religious sects. If those requirements were met, the fact that the legislation conflicted with some persons' perceived religious beliefs did not invalidate it or qualify them for exemptions. According to this interpretation, the Constitution did not require government to accord special recognition to religious beliefs or behavior.

In a great majority of establishment clause cases the question is how to distinguish between acceptable and unacceptable cooperation between the state and religion. In *Everson,* the Court upheld the cooperation on grounds that its primary purpose was secular and intended to benefit school children. In addition the Court affirmed a separationist reading of the establishment clause. Justice Black wrote: "The First Amendment has erected a wall between church and state. That wall must be kept high and impregnable. We could not approve the slightest breach."

In 1961, the Eisenhower Court decided four cases involving Sunday closing laws, or "blue laws," that brought together aspects of both the free exercise and establishment clauses. The most important of these, *Braunfeld v. Brown,*[126] marked a major shift in the Court's interpretation of the free exercise clause. A kosher grocery store owner in Pennsylvania challenged a law that placed his business at a competitive disadvantage: it was closed Friday evenings and all day Saturday to observe the Sabbath and then forced by the state to be closed on Sunday as well. Chief Justice Warren, for a six-justice majority, upheld Pennsylvania's Sunday closing law, noting that the state could not achieve its important secular goal of a uniform day of rest through any alternative means that was less burdensome on religious practice. The Court reasoned that the law did not inconvenience all members of the Orthodox Jewish faith, but only those who chose to work on Sunday. While dodging the question of why Sunday would be chosen as the official day of rest, Warren argued that any law was likely to result in an economic disadvantage to some religious group.

In a companion case, the Court upheld a Massachusetts law that allowed kosher markets to sell kosher meats until 10 A.M. on Sunday even though the plaintiffs argued that it was economically impractical for them to stay open from Saturday at sundown until 10 A.M. the following day.[127] The Court upheld the law because it had lost its original religious character. A corporation claiming economic injury was likewise unsuccessful in challenging the Sunday closing laws.[128]

In reviewing the history of Sunday "blue laws" in *McGowan v. Maryland,* Chief Justice Warren found that the original motivation had gradually changed from a religious character to a secular purpose in setting aside a day for rest and recreation.[129] Warren affirmed that if the purpose of such laws was to support a particular religion, they would be unconstitutional. But he found that was not the case in the state's proclaiming a "family day of rest." The fact that the day selected was Sunday, "a day of particular significance for the dominant Christian sects, does not bar the State from achieving its secular goals." Justice Douglas dissented in all four cases on Establishment Clause grounds maintaining that Sunday closing laws "force minorities to obey the majority's religious feelings of what is due and proper for a Christian community." Brennan and Stewart joined him in dissent in the cases involving Orthodox Jews on free exercise grounds. Stewart thought the Orthodox Jewish merchants were being given a "cruel choice."

Also in 1961 a unanimous Court in *Torcaso v. Watkins* invalidated Maryland's constitutional provision requiring all public officers to affirm a belief in God.[130] According to Justice Black, writing for the Court, the provision invaded the freedom of belief and religion guaranteed by the First Amendment. The opinion explicitly protected the irreligious, and in a footnote, listed Buddhism, Taoism, Ethical Culture, and Secular Humanism as among religions in America that did not teach "what would generally be considered in the existence of God."[131]

The Court handed down the most controversial establishment clause case in 1962. In *Engel v. Vitale*, the Court invalidated the New York "Regents' Prayer" that state law required to be recited at the beginning of each day in the public schools.[132] The relatively short nondenominational prayer read: "Almighty God, we acknowledge our dependence upon Thee, and we beg Thy blessing upon us, our parents, our teachers and our Country." The six-to-one decision (Frankfurter was no longer sitting, and although Byron White had replaced Whittaker, he did not participate), written by Justice Black, argued that the establishment clause "must at least mean that in this country it is no part of the business of government to compose official prayers for any group of the American people to recite as a part of a religious program carried on by the government." Stewart's dissent rehearsed a different history of religion in America than did Black's opinion, and he cited many examples of governmental accommodation and recognition of religion. Stewart's opinion strayed from the issue before the Court—as did critics of the Court for decades after *Vitale* was decided. The issue was the constitutionality of state officers composing an official prayer for children in public schools.

Engel set off a heated nationwide debate on school prayer that has continued to the present. Many schools ignored the Court's ruling, and obligatory prayers in public schools have remained a part of the ritual beginning the school day in some parts of the country. Critics of the Court added the school prayer decision to their litany of complaints of a Court too activist in pushing civil rights and too soft on subversives. Congressman George Andrews of Alabama is purported to have complained that the justices had "put Negroes in the school and now they've driven God out."[133] But all the Court had done was invalidate New York's effort to aid religion on the ground that it violated governmental neutrality between religion and irreligion.

CONCLUSIONS

In the split decisions involving First Amendment questions discussed in this chapter the middle bloc justices exhibited strong agreement. In *Alberts* and *Roth*, they were joined by the Chief Justice and Justice Clark, although Justice Harlan left their ranks in the federal case, as noted earlier. *The Kingsley Books* decision found Warren and Brennan leaving the majority to write separate dissenting opinions. Brennan rejoined the middle bloc plus Clark in the picketing cases, while the Chief Justice dissented with Black and Douglas. Justice Stewart was considerably above the Court's average in upholding claims of defendants. Justice Clark also maintained a much more libertarian outlook in these cases than he did in First Amendment cases involving subversives. Among the justices, he was most frequently in the majority in the cases in which he participated, including *Shirey* and the *WDAY* case. The absolutist opinions of Justices Douglas and Black were not convincing to any of the other justices in the obscenity cases, although they were joined by the Chief Justice in the labor case dissents.

Table 5.1 indicates that in the split decisions in this area the Court has usually ruled against First Amendment claims. This is offset, of course, by the several instances where the Court reached unanimous agreement that governmental activity had infringed upon constitutional rights of speech or press—although the justices were frequently in disagreement in their reasoning. The omission of important unanimous decisions from statistical tables of this type illustrates the difficulty of presenting an accurate picture of the record of the Court by quantitative methods only. Table 5.1 might be interpreted to mean that the Eisenhower Court had little sympathy for persons claiming abridgments of First Amendment rights. Analysis of all the cases in this area makes it clear, however, that such was hardly the case. What Table 5.1 does point out is the cohesion of certain blocs of justices in this area. Here, Brennan and Warren emerge almost as statistical equals in their libertarian sympathies, while Frankfurter and Whittaker are identical in percentages at the less libertarian end of the scale.

Table 5.1
Voting Records of Supreme Court Justices in 15 Selected Nonunanimous
Cases Involving First Amendment Questions, 1953–1961 Terms (in percent-
ages)

For Claims of Defendant

No. of cases	15
Douglas	100
Black	73
Brennan	64 (14)
Warren	60
Stewart	44 (9)
COURT	33
Harlan	29 (14)
Burton	17 (6)
Clark	14 (14)
Frankfurter	7 (14)
Whittaker	7 (13)

The following cases are represented:
Federal cases (2): Against defendants' claims (2): *U.S. v. Harriss* (1954); *Roth v. U.S.* (1957).
State cases (13): For defendants' claims (5): *Staub v. City of Baxley* (1958); *Farmer's Union v.
    WDAY* (1959); *Talley v. California* (1960); *Shelton v. Tucker* (1960); *Engle v. Vitale* (1961).
Against defendants' claims (8): *Kingsley Books v. Brown* (1957); *International Brotherhood of
    Teamsters v. Vogt* (1957); *Youngdahl v. Rainfair* (1957); *Times Film Corporation v. Chicago*
    (1961); *McGowan v. Maryland* (1961); *Two Guys from Harrison–Allentown v. McGinley*
    (1961); *Braunfield v. Brown* (1961); *Gallagher v. Crown Kosher Super Market* (1961).

NOTES

1. See generally, C. Herman Pritchett, *The Roosevelt Court Civil Liberties* and
The Vinson Court; Walter Berns, *Freedom, Virtue and The First Amendment* (Baton
Rouge: Louisiana State University Press, 1957).

2. See generally, Edward DeGrazia, "Obscenity and the Mail: A Study of
Administrative Restraint," 20 *Law & Contemp. Prob.* 608 (1955).

3. For general discussions of obscenity and the law, see Leo M. Alpert, "Judicial Censorship of Obscene Literature," 52 *Harv. L. Rev.* 40 (1937); "Symposium: Obscenity and the Arts," 20 *Law & Contemp. Prob.* 531 (1955); Norman St.
John-Stevas, *Obscenity and the Law* (London: Secker and Warburg, 1956); Harry
Kalven, Jr., "Book Review," 24 *U. Chi. L. Rev.* 769 (1957); 12 *Syracuse L. Rev.* 58
(1960).

4. 333 U.S. 507 (1948).

5. N.Y. Penal Code, Sec. 1141, subsec. 2.

6. 233 U.S. 507 at 518.

7. 343 U.S. 495 (1952).

8. Note, "Entertainment: Public Pressures and the Law," 71 *Harv. L. Rev.* 326 (1957); *cf.* 30 *Ind. L. J.* 462 (1955); Note, "Extralegal Censorship of Literature," 33 *N.Y.U. L. Rev.* 989 (1958).

9. 352 U.S. 380 (1957).

10. Mich. Penal Code, Sec. 343.

11. 352 U.S. 380 at 383–84.

12. 354 U.S. 476 (1957). See Dwight Leland Tester, "The Supreme Court and Obscene Literature: *Roth v. United States*" (unpublished Master's thesis, Journalism, University of California, Berkeley, 1959).

13. 62 Stat. 768 (1948); 27 *U. Chi. L. Rev.* 354 (1960).

14. Comment, "Obscenity and the Post Office: Removal from the Mail under Section 1461," 27 *U. Chi. L. Rev.* 354 (1960).

15. Calif. Penal Code Ann., sec. 311.

16. 354 U.S. 476 at 484. For an analysis of writing without social importance, see James J. Kilpatrick, *The Smut Peddler* (New York: Doubleday, 1960).

17. 354 U.S. 476 at 487.

18. 354 U.S. 476 at 487–88.

19. *Regina v. Hicklin*, Law Reports, 3 Q.B. 360, 371 (1868). Here Justice Cockburn said: "I think the test of obscenity is this, whether the tendency of the matter charged as obscenity is to deprave and corrupt those whose minds are open to such immoral influences, and into whose hands a publication of this sort may fall."

20. 354 U.S. 476 at 489.

21. Horwitz, *Warren Court*, pp. 99–101. See 7 *Duke L. J.* 116 (1958); but see 36 *Texas L. Rev.* 226 (1957); 36 *N.C.L. Rev.* 16 (1958); *cf.* 7 *DePaul L. Rev.* 111 (1957).

22. 354 U.S. 476 at 496.

23. Ibid.

24. 354 U.S. 476 at 506.

25. 354 U.S. 476 at 507.

26. 354 U.S. 476 at 498.

27. 354 U.S. 476 at 509.

28. 354 U.S. 436 (1957).

29. N.Y. Code of Cr. Proc., sec. 22-a.

30. The majority was composed of Frankfurter, Harlan, Whittaker, Clark, and Burton.

31. 354 U.S. 436 at 441.

32. *Near v. Minnesota*, 283 U.S. 697 (1931).

33. 354 U.S. 436 at 446.

34. Ibid.

35. 354 U.S. 436 at 448.

36. *Mounce v. U.S.*, 355 U S. 180 (1957); *Sunshine Book Co. v. Summerfield*, 355 U.S. 372 (1958).

37. *One, Inc. v. Olesen*, 355 U.S. 371 (1957).

38. 6 *J. Public L.* 548 (1957); but see 42 *Cornell L. Q.* 256 (1957); see also *Smith v. California*, 361 U.S. 147 (1959); compare *Talley v. California*, 362 U.S. 60 (1960);

Marcus v. Search Warrants, 367 U.S. 717 (1961).

39. See generally, "Censorship: A Symposium," 3 *Catholic Law*. 283 (1957).

40. For analysis of the decisions of the Eisenhower Court in this area, see Harry Kalven, Jr., "The Metaphysics of the Law of Obscenity," *1960 The Supreme Court Review,* ed. Philip B. Kurland (Chicago: University of Chicago Press, 1960); *cf.* William B. Lockhart and Robert C. McClure, "Censorship of Obscenity: The Developing Constitutional Standards," 45 *Minn. L. Rev.* 5 (1960); 35 *Notre Dame Law.* 537 (1960).

41. 346 U.S. 587 (1954).

42. *Commercial Pictures Corp. v. Regents of University of New York*, 346 U.S. 507 (1954).

43. 350 U.S. 870 (1955).

44. 355 U.S. 35 (1957); 106 *U. Pa. L. Rev.* 132 (1957); *cf.* 42 *Va. L. Rev.* 154 (1956).

45. *Kingsley International Picture Corp. v. New York,* 360 U.S. 684 (1959).

46. N.Y. Educ. Law, sec. 122-a (Supp. 1959).

47. 360 U.S. 684 at 701.

48. *Smith v. California*, 361 U.S. 147 (1959).

49. 365 U.S. 43 (1961).

50. 14 *Sw. L. J.* 102 (1960); but see 13 *Vand. L. Rev.* 54 (1960).

51. 360 U.S. 684 at 690–91.

52. Kalven, "The Metaphysics of the Law," p. 34.

53. *Staub v. City of Baxley*, 355 U.S. 313 (1958).

54. *Thomas v. Collins*, 323 U.S. 516 (1945).

55. Whittaker, Black, Douglas, Warren, Brennan, Harlan, and Burton composed the majority.

56. 355 U.S. 313 at 320.

57. 355 U.S. 313 at 322.

58. *Cantwell v. Connecticut*, 310 U.S. 296 (1940).

59. 9 *Syracuse L. Rev.* 317 (1958); *cf.* 12 *Ark. L. Rev.* 209 (1958).

60. See generally, Walter B. Emery, *Broadcasting and Government: Responsibilities and Regulations* (East Lansing: Michigan State University Press, 1961).

61. 360 U.S. 525 (1959).

62. 48 Stat. 1088 (1934).

63. Black, Douglas, Warren, Brennan, and Clark.

64. 73 *Harv. L. Rev.* 234 (1959); *cf.* 44 *Minn. L. Rev.* 787 (1960); 13 *Vand. L. Rev.* 423 (1959).

65. *Ga. Const.*, Art I, Sec. 2–205 (1877).

66. E.g., *California Gov. C.A.* 9900-9911 (1958).

67. 60 Stat. 839 (1946).

68. See generally, Belle Zeller, "The Federal Regulation of Lobbying Act," 42 *Am. Pol. Sci. Rev.* 329 (1948).

69. 347 U.S. 612 (1954).

70. Warren, Frankfurter, Burton, Minton, and Reed.

71. 347 U.S. 612 at 620–21.

72. 347 U.S. 612 at 625.

73. 347 U.S. 612 at 633.

74. 53 *Mich. L. Rev.* 616 (1955); but see 39 *Minn. L. Rev.* 214 (1955).

75. *Cammarano v. United States*, 358 U.S. 498 (1959).

76. 359 U.S. 255 (1959); 13 *Vand. L. Rev.* 558 (1960); *cf.* 20 *Ohio S. L. J.* 693 (1959).

77. 62 Stat. 694 (1948).

78. Frankfurter, Douglas, Warren, Brennan, and Clark.

79. 310 U.S. 88 (1940).

80. See generally, Pritchett, *The American Constitution*, pp. 424–28; Morris D. Forkosch "Analysis and Re-evaluation of Picketing in Labor Relations," 26 *Fordham L. Rev.* 391 (1957); Guy Farmer and Charles G. Williamson, Jr., "Picketing and the Injunctive Power of State Courts—From *Thornhill* to *Vogt*," 35 *U. Det. L. J.* 431 (1958); see also O. John Rogge, "State Power Over Sedition, Obscenity, and Picketing," 34 *N.Y.U. L. Rev.* 817 (1959); Albion G. Taylor, *Labor and the Supreme Court* (Ann Arbor, MI: Braun-Brumfield, 1961).

81. W.S.A. 103, 535.

82. *International Brotherhood of Teamsters v. Vogt*, 354 U.S. 284 (1957).

83. 354 U.S. 284 at 293.

84. 354 U.S. 284 at 297.

85. 11 *Vand. L. Rev.* 627, 631–32 (1958); *cf.* 26 *Fordham L. Rev.* 580 (1957); but see 11 *Sw. L. J.* 531 (1957); 1958 *Wis. L. Rev.* 154 (1958).

86. 355 U.S. 131 (1957).

87. See generally, William J. Isaacson "Organizational Picketing: What Is the Law?—Ought the Law to Be Changed?" 8 *Buffalo L. Rev.* (1959).

88. 9 *Syracuse L. Rev.* 299 (1958).

89. 355 U.S. 131 at 138.

90. 362 U.S. 60 (1960).

91. The same voting blocs split in *United States v. U.A.W.*, 352 U.S. 567 (1957), where the majority failed to find a constitutional question while the three dissenters argued that there had been an abridgment of freedom of political expression. See generally, Bernard L. Samoff, "Picketing and the First Amendment: 'Full Circle' and 'Formal Surrender'," 9 *Lab. L. J.* 889 (1958); but see Herman Stein, "Enjoinable Organizational Picketing: A Phantasy on the Constitutional Doctrine of *International Teamsters v. Vogt*," 31 *Temp. L.Q.* 12 (1957).

92. Horn, *Groups and the Constitution*.

93. Ibid., p. 1.

94. Glen Abernathy, *The Right of Assembly and Association* (Columbia: University of South Carolina Press, 1961), pp. 239–244.

95. 57 U.S. 449 (1958); see also *Bryan v. Anstin*, 354 U.S. 933 (1957).

96. Ala. Code, Tit. 10, Secs. 192–198 (1940).

97. Harlan, Memo to the Conference, 22 April 1958, Warren Papers, I:10, No. 91, Library of Congress, Manuscripts Division, Washington, D.C.

98. "Freedom of Association," 4 *Race Rel. L. Rep.* 207 (1959); see also *Louisiana v. NAACP*, 366 U.S. 293 (1961).

99. 357 U.S. 449 at 460.

100. 357 U.S. 449 at 462.

101. 357 U.S. 449 at 462–63.

102. 357 U.S. 449 at 463.

103. 5 *How. L. J.* 112 (1959); 13 *Rutgers L. Rev.* 370 (1958); *cf.* 13 *Ark. L. Rev.* 79 (1958–1959).

104. 357 U.S. 449 at 466.

105. 278 U.S. 63 (1928).

106. 109 So. 2d. 138.

107. 360 U.S. 240 (1959).

108. 360 U.S. 240 at 245.

109. 360 U.S. 167 (1959).

110. 20 *La. L. Rev.* 614 (1960); but see 14 *Rutgers L. Rev.* 185 (1959).

111. 360 U.S. 167 at 178.

112. 360 U.S. 167 at 182.

113. *NAACP v. Bennet*, 360 U.S. 471 (1959); *NAACP v. Williams*, 359 U.S. 550 (1959).

114. 359 U.S. 344 (1959).

115. 359 U.S. 344 at 353.

116. 354 U.S. 234 at 250.

117. 361 U.S. 516 (1960).

118. 364 U.S. 479 (1960).

119. Nadine Strossen, "Freedom of Speech in the Warren Court," in Schwartz, ed., *The Warren Court*, p. 69.

120. Lloyd McAulay and Carroll Brewster, "In re Application of the Association for the Preservation of Freedom of Choice," 6 *How. L. J.* 169 (1960); *cf.* William J. Hotes and Catherine H. Hotes, "Freedom of Association," 10 *Clev.- Mar. L. Rev.* 104 (1961); see also Anthony C. Vance, "Freedom of Association and Freedom of Choice in New York State," 46 *Cornell L. Q.* 290 (1961).

121. 54 *Nw. U. L. Rev.* 390 (1959); *cf.* 27 *Geo. Wash. L. Rev.* 653 (1959).

122. Joseph B. Robison, "Protection of Associations from Compulsory Disclosure of Membership," 58 *Col. L. Rev.* 614, 647–649 (1958); but see Fred S. Ball, "The Tyranny of Ideas," 20 *Ala. L. Rev.* 418 (1959).

123. The Eisenhower Court, by a five-to-four vote in conference, had actually approved McCarthyite tactics by a Florida Legislative Investigating Committee to force the NAACP to disclose its membership. Justice Whittaker's retirement in 1962 resulted in a tie vote, however, and during the next term, the case was subsequently decided in favor of the NAACP. *Gibson v. Florida Legislative Investigating Committee*, 372 U.S. 539 (1963).

124. 310 U.S. 296 (1940).

125. 330 U.S.1 (1947)

126. *Braunfeld v. Brown*, 366 U.S. 599 (1961).

127. *Gallagher v. Crown Kosher Super Market*, 366 U.S. 617 (1961).

128. *Two Guys From Harrison-Allentown v. McGinley*, 366 U.S. 582 (1961).

129. 366 U.S. 420 (1961).

130. 367 U.S. 488 (1961).

131. 367 U.S. 488 at 495.

132. 370 U.S. 421 (1962); see "The Supreme Court 1961 Term," 76 *Harv. L. Rev.* 78 (1962); Benjamin F. Wright, "The Rights of Majorities and Minorities in the 1961 Term of the Supreme Court," 57 *Am. Pol. Sci. Rev.* 98 (1963).

133. John D. Weaver, *Warren: The Man, the Court, the Era* (Boston: Little, Brown, 1967), p. 258.

6

The Rights of Minorities

The post-World War I era witnessed the beginnings of a remarkable alteration of the position of the African-American in American society. This change was almost as remarkable as that following the Emancipation Proclamation and the adoption of the Fourteenth and Fifteenth Amendments during the Reconstruction period.[1] Public opinion concerning the African-American's role in the social order following the Civil War was such that the "freedman" became a "second-class citizen," lacking equal opportunities in education and employment, and segregated in the South into a separate caste. The Supreme Court in turn reflected this view and in 1896 gave its blessing to the "separate but equal" doctrine, which became the legal basis of segregation practices and Jim Crow laws.[2]

By the beginning of World War II, however, it became apparent that the ideas of "humane democracy" of the New Deal were having an important effect in bettering the position of the African-American in American life. Growing numbers of African-Americans began to improve their economic status by entering professions, businesses, and higher paying occupations. During the war, the color line was abolished by many employers and labor unions, while the manpower shortage, the government's hiring of African-Americans for federal positions and requiring "no discrimination" clauses in war contracts all contributed to this development.[3]

Except for certain areas in the "deep" South, segregation was being brought to an end in public places such as hotels, theaters, restaurants, and recreational facilities. African-Americans all over the country were voting in larger numbers—sometimes requiring the aid of the Supreme Court to accomplish this. The lot of the African-American in transportation, education, and housing was likewise improved by the Court's decisions. The ideas of the New Deal became a force creating a deep-seated change in American mores, with many people convinced that the maintenance of a caste system was inconsistent with the twentieth-century idea of America as a constitutional democracy. Despite these changes, Swedish sociologist Gunnar Myrdal wrote in 1944 that "the status accorded the Negro in America represents nothing more and nothing less than a century-long lag of public morals."[4]

In its first term, the Eisenhower Court rendered perhaps the most fateful judicial decision of the twentieth century—in the segregation cases, decided on 17 May 1954.[5] For the first time, the Court met head-on the moral challenge of the separate but equal doctrine in public schools.[6] The Vinson Court had dodged the question in 1950 although it had opened the issue to discussion and action in graduate professional and university training.

The question of segregation in public education at the primary and secondary levels was brought before the Vinson Court in December 1952, when hearings were held on five appeals involving cases in which the lower courts had upheld segregation but had indicated that educational facilities should be made equal. On 8 June 1953, the Court announced that the cases would be reargued the following October and requested counsel to address themselves to a series of five questions, two of which related to the intent of Congress and the state legislatures which drafted and ratified the Fourteenth Amendment and whether they understood that the amendment would abolish segregation in public schools. By that time, the Eisenhower administration's Justice Department had demonstrated its support of civil rights by filing crucial briefs in *Brown* and other cases.

The following term, the Court unanimously declared the separate but equal doctrine unconstitutional.[7] The unanimous vote was considered a diplomatic victory for Chief Justice Warren who presided over the same Court, excluding Vinson, that had swept the doctrine under the rug so as to avoid having to consider its constitutional implications.[8]

The Chief Justice, writing the opinion of the Court, noted that the historical background and the circumstances surrounding the adoption of the Fourteenth Amendment were "inconclusive" as to the intention of the drafters since the Court could not "turn the clock back to 1868 when the Amendment was adopted, or even to 1896 when *Plessy v. Ferguson* was written." The Court had to consider public education "in the light of its full development and its present place in American life throughout the Nation."[9] The Chief Justice pointed out the importance of education in American society, saying:

> Today, education is perhaps the most important function of state and local government. Compulsory school attendance laws and the great expenditures for education both demonstrate our recognition of the

importance of education to our democratic society. It is required in the performance of our most basic public responsibilities, even service in the armed forces. It is the very foundation of good citizenship. Today it is a principal instrument in wakening the child to cultural values, in preparing him for later professional training, and in helping him to adjust normally to his environment. In these days, it is doubtful that any child may reasonably be expected to succeed in life if he is denied the opportunity of an education. Such an opportunity, where the state has undertaken to provide it, is a right which must be made available to all on equal terms.[10]

To the Court, it was obvious that in the light of twentieth-century conditions, school segregation imposed an inferior status upon African-American children: "Does segregation of children in public schools solely on the basis of race, even though the physical facilities and other 'tangible' factors may be equal, deprive the children of the minority group of equal educational opportunities? We believe that it does."[11] Segregation, said the Chief Justice, generated a "feeling of inferiority" in African-American children as to their status in the community. Such damage to their minds and hearts might well be so grave that it could never be undone. Since "separate educational facilities are inherently unequal," school segregation laws violated the equal protection clause of the Fourteenth Amendment.[12]

Bolling v. Sharpe[13] was handled in a separate decision from the four state cases, since it involved segregation in the District of Columbia where the equal protection clause was not applicable. Chief Justice Warren found that segregation was not "reasonably related to any proper governmental objective" and that it amounted to an improper restriction of "liberty under law," in violation of the due process clause of the Fifth Amendment. It would be absurd to suppose that the Constitution permitted the national government to maintain segregated schools when it forbade that practice to the states. Thus segregation in the District of Columbia also was unconstitutional.

The Court issued no enforcement order. Instead, it asked counsel to reargue once more the means of implementing the decision. In 1955 the Court delivered a further opinion, that came to be called *Brown II*, conceding that there were many complexities connected with the transition to a system of public education freed of racial discrimination.[14] This led the Court to recognize that the tribunals best equipped to determine the specific relief to be granted in each case where the *Brown* principle was invoked were the trial courts themselves which were closest to the local conditions in each case. If time were needed in the public interest before the *Brown* principle could be implemented in practice in a locality, the lower courts were authorized to grant such time. The lower courts were instructed to take such action in each case as necessary to ensure that

African-Americans were admitted to public schools on a racially nondiscriminatory basis "with all deliberate speed"—a phrase from a Holmes opinion in a 1911 equity case that Frankfurter successfully urged the Court to use in *Brown II*. The Court rejected the advice of the Justice Department's brief that desegregation plans had to be filed within ninety days. Instead, the Court's opinion left certain matters undecided, allowing room for discussion and dialogue by other officials in other forums.[15]

The Southern states immediately began denunciation of the Court's decisions and prepared various plans of resistance. Harking back to the historical doctrine of interposition, some of these states "interposed" state sovereignty against "encroachment" upon their reserved powers. The legal effect of such pronouncements was, of course, insignificant.[16]

Pupil placement laws quickly were adopted by ten Southern states.[17] Such statutes laid down broad principles such as nearness to schools, the wishes of parents, psychological qualification of the pupil for the type of teaching and association involved, or the possibility of economic retaliation within the community. The North Carolina[18] and Alabama[19] statutes were upheld while those of Virginia,[20] Louisiana,[21] and Arkansas[22] were invalidated. The Supreme Court, in affirming a district court decision upholding the Alabama law, ruled such regulations were valid on their face, so long as race was not used as a placement factor. The district court had indicated, however, that any use of the statute to achieve racial discrimination would bring a declaration of unconstitutionality.

By the end of 1958 the Eisenhower Court had handed down its last significant cases dealing with desegregation in public schools. In several instances the Court indicated that it would give local communities maximum opportunity to proceed on their own toward the constitutional goal of integration. For example, in *Slade v. Board of Education of Hartford County*,[23] the Court refused to interfere with a plan for gradual desegregation of public schools in Maryland which the NAACP attacked as too gradual. In 1958 the Court also refused to review the transformation of Girard College in Philadelphia, which it had held the year before to be a public institution bound by the Fourteenth Amendment, into a private college by the substitution of private for public trustees.[24]

In *Florida ex rel. Hawkins v. Board of Control*,[25] the Court required the admission of an African-American to a graduate professional school of the state university, holding that delay permitted in achieving integration in primary and secondary education was not tolerable in higher education. Hawkins then sought a writ of mandamus from the Florida Supreme Court to require his immediate admission. When this writ was denied, he sought relief in the federal courts. Although the district court denied him admission, the Court of Appeals issued an injunction restraining the state "from enforcing any policy, custom or usage of limiting admission to the graduate schools and graduate professional schools of the University of Florida to white persons only."[26] Other decisions affirmed lower court decrees ordering admission of African-American college applicants in North Carolina,[27] Louisiana,[28] and Tennessee.[29]

In the fall of 1958 racial strife in Little Rock required the Court to reinterpret and apply the principles of its 1954 decision. In June 1958, the federal district judge in Little Rock had ordered a two-and-a-half-year delay in the modest program of integration in the city's high schools, which had been the scene of riotous activity in 1957 when state troops had been used to defeat a federal court order, followed by the president's sending in federal troops. The Federal Court of Appeals reversed the order in August. The Supreme Court, meeting in special session, unanimously affirmed the judgment of the appellate court in *Cooper v. Aaron* on September 12.[30] The Court made it clear that if there is state participation through "any arrangement, management, funds or property," no scheme of racial discrimination against African-Americans attending schools can be squared with the equal protection clause of the Fourteenth Amendment. The Court found that the violence attending integration in Little Rock was "directly traceable to the actions of legislators and executive officials of the State of Arkansas . . . which reflect their own determination to resist the Court's decision."[31] In the face of such defiance, the Court's reply was strong: "The constitutional rights of respondents are not to be sacrificed or yielded to the violence and disorder which have followed upon the actions of the Governor and Legislature. . . . Thus law and order are not here to be preserved by depriving the Negro children of their constitutional rights."[32]

The Court likewise gave notice that any and all integration-dodging laws would meet close surveillance. "State legislators, or state executive or judicial officers" cannot nullify "the constitutional rights of children not to be discriminated against in school admission on grounds of race or color" openly and directly or "through evasive schemes for segregation, whether attempted 'ingeniously or ingenuously'."[33]

In announcing the Court's unanimous judgment, Chief Justice Warren noted that all nine members of the Court were joint authors of it, and to emphasize the point he looked at each of the justices as he read their names. This was the first and only Supreme Court opinion ever to be signed individually by all nine justices underlining their unanimity. The opinion of the Court noted that "Since the first *Brown* opinion three new Justices have come to the Court. They are at one with the Justices still on the Court who participated in the basic decision as to its correctness, and that decision is now unanimously reaffirmed."[34] The opinion thus presented the southern states with the alternatives of beginning desegregation "with all deliberate speed" or facing the termination of public education.[35]

In announcing the unconstitutional nature of public school segregation and in standing firmly behind it, the Court brought the law of the
American Constitution into line with the conscience of the world.[36] The
Court could hardly have done otherwise. As Professor Pritchett stated:
"Here were nine men, sworn to defend a Constitution which guarantees
equal protection of the laws, living in a country which declared its independence on the proposition that all men are created equal, and fighting
for moral leadership in a world predominantly populated by people whose
skin color is other than white."[37]

The opinions of the Court were attacked for being "sociological"
rather than "legal."[38] They rejected the presuppositions underlying *Plessy
v. Ferguson* and repudiated the views that had for many years in many
quarters been regarded as logical extensions of that decision. It should be
pointed out, however, that the *Brown* case was the first litigation in which
the validity of the "separate but equal" doctrine in the field of public education was squarely before the highest tribunal. In reaching its decision
the Supreme Court demonstrated that it is more than a court of law—it is
also a court of justice. Segregation could not be tested in a vacuum, and
thus the Court had to look beyond the narrow confines of its past decisions. Where operation of the political process is corrupted or clogged at
the state level, particularly as here, in the area of civil liberties, the Court
is bound to uphold the national majority over a defiant local majority
will.[39] As long as the doctrine of separate but equal had judicial sanction,
those who considered it morally wrong and socially unsound had no alternative, consistent with the rule of law, but to accept it. With the situation then reversed, advocates of the antiquated doctrine were presented
with the choice of accepting the reversal or expounding an abstract right
of revolution and resistance to law, taking full responsibility for the subversive nature of such declarations.[40]

Critics who pointed with derision to the sociological and psychological basis of the segregation decisions ignored the sociological theory
accepted in the separate but equal doctrine. The Court, citing "psychological knowledge" not available when *Plessy v. Ferguson* was decided,
did mention seven works, including those of psychologist Kenneth B. Clark
and Gunnar Myrdal's *An American Dilemma,* in a footnote backing up the
contention that segregation "has a detrimental affect upon the colored
children."[41] Perhaps the best reply to this criticism and the best defense of
the views of those who realized that law does not exist in a vacuum was
given by Justice Brennan at the time of his appointment to the Court: "The
mind of the layman unfamiliar with the judicial process supposes it to
exist in the air, as a self-justifying and wholly independent process. The
opposite is of course true, that judicial decision must be nourished by all
the insights that scholarship can furnish and legal scholarship must in
turn be nourished by all the disciplines that comprehend the totality of
human experience."[42]

According to Justice Brennan, judges, in order to understand the law of their society, should "turn their minds to the knowledge and experience of the other disciplines, and in particular to those disciplines that investigate and report on the functioning and nature of society."[43] This the Justices of the Supreme Court did by necessity, in cases dealing with the rights of African-Americans, since the legal precedents of an earlier society could no longer meet the constitutional tests of American society in the mid-twentieth century.

By criticizing the Eisenhower Court for utilizing psychological and sociological evidence not available in 1896, the segregationists revealed their reliance upon traditional dogma and their distaste for rational analysis of social problems.[44] Indeed, their contempt for empirical evidence bearing on the problem of segregation put them in a position of preferring "theory" to "fact," an untenable posture for those who denounced their opponents as "sentimentalists" and took pride in their own "realism." But the hypocritical concept that integration of the races in a public schoolroom amounted to "forced association" which would lead to intermarriage and the "mongrelization of the race" was at once so speculative, so "theoretical," and so tainted by racist mythology as to have no place within government-sanctioned activities.[45]

These opinions struck at the very core of the South's way of life, and prolonged litigation was expected.[46] Actual desegregation in the southern states was slow—and in some cases, for a number of years, nil. By the end of the Eisenhower Court era in 1962, only 0.24 percent of African-Americans were attending elementary and secondary schools with white children in the eleven Southern states. There were many violent forms of resistance to court-ordered desegregation, but the South gradually accepted the authority of the federal courts. The Supreme Court had made a powerful pronouncement that affected public opinion. In the long run, school segregation was doomed.[47]

OTHER SEGREGATION CASES

Once the "separate but equal" doctrine was discarded as unconstitutional in public education, it was inevitable that the courts would rule it inapplicable in other fields.[48] The Supreme Court had earlier ruled against segregation in public transportation as a burden on interstate commerce and had drastically reduced the effect of restrictive covenants in housing by declaring that state court enforcement of such covenants was a violation of the equal protection clause. The Eisenhower Court continued to broaden constitutional protections against segregation. Following the *Brown* decision, the Interstate Commerce Commission ordered several railroads to "terminate their rules and practices maintaining segregation." In 1956 the

Supreme Court affirmed without opinion lower court decrees ordering the end of segregation in purely local bus transportation, thus rendering invalid all forms of segregation in public transportation.[49] The local bus company in one of the cases was that of Montgomery, Alabama, whose policies had caused the bus boycott led by Rosa Parks.

The Court also held that when blacks travel on an interstate bus, and the bus stops at a terminal and restaurant that function as an integral part of the bus system, the restaurant might not be segregated by race.[50] The freedom riders of the Congress of Racial Equality and the Student Non-Violent Coordinating Committee courageously tested the validity of that ruling in southern states in 1961. A per curiam decision likewise granted the right of African-Americans to admission on the same basis as white persons to a municipal golf course.[51] The right to use public bathing facilities was similarly asserted.[52] Similar rulings by lower courts were made with respect to parks, public housing, and other public facilities.[53] The Court ruled that a restaurant in a building owned by the state of Delaware that refused to serve blacks was acting as an agent of the state and thus could not discriminate against African-Americans.[54]

The first sit-in case, *Garner v. Louisiana*, to reach the Supreme Court affirmed the right of African-Americans to challenge the policy of lunch counter owners to deny them service.[55] In a concurring opinion, Harlan was the only justice to perceive that the sit-in by African-Americans in a segregated southern restaurant could be a form of free expression protected by the Constitution. The Court also affirmed, without opinion, a federal district court's opinion declaring unconstitutional a Louisiana law prohibiting interracial sports activity.[56] In addition, the Eisenhower Court also kept close scrutiny on state discrimination in jury selection.[57]

On the other hand, the Court did not go as far in upholding African-American defendants' claims as some desired. The Court was presented with the opportunity to rule on the constitutionality of Virginia's antimiscegenation law in 1955 but finally refused to review the judgment of the state's highest court because the case was "devoid of a properly presented federal question."[58] Miscegenation was too controversial a subject for the Supreme Court to rule favorably for either side at that time. Twelve years later when Southern resistance to *Brown* had subsided, the Court unanimously invalidated the Virginia law as an invidious racial discrimination prohibited by the equal protection clause. For the Court, Chief Justice Warren wrote, "Under our Constitution, the freedom to marry, or not marry, a person of another race resides with the individual and cannot be infringed by the State."[59]

When in 1956 a North Carolina real estate owner willed some property to a city park commission to be used for recreational purposes, with the proviso that if the park was not used by the white race exclusively, the land would revert to the grantor or his heirs, the state supreme court ruled that the restriction was enforceable. The Supreme Court refused certiorari, probably on the basis that the law of property and estates outweighed the claims of alleged discrimination.[60] In 1958 the Court in like manner declined to review a Tallahassee ordinance giving bus drivers authority to seat passengers on nonracial grounds, which had been attacked by the NAACP as a subterfuge for continuing racial segregation on buses.[61] If discrimination in the practice of a regulation which on its face is valid can be proved, however, the Court did not hesitate to rule against it. In the 1958 term, the Court denied certiorari in three suits brought by African-American railroad workers,[62] oil workers,[63] and doctors,[64] charging discrimination by white unions and hospitals in working conditions and other matters. The Chief Justice and Justices Brennan and Douglas would have granted certiorari in the railroad workers' case indicating the presence of values which they weighed heavily in that instance which were not present in the other two. By a denial of certiorari, the Court permitted segregation against Native Americans in a cemetery in *Rice v. Sioux City Memorial Park Cemetery*.[65] Chief Justice Warren and Justices Black and Douglas filed dissents indicating that their libertarian sympathies probably extended even to opposition to discrimination against the deceased.

The Supreme Court also ruled that a state might consistently, with the Fourteenth, Fifteenth, and Seventeenth Amendments, apply a literacy test to all voters irrespective of race or color.[66] Such a North Carolina law did not on its face violate the Constitution, but the Court warned that improper administration or application of the law might.

During the Eisenhower administration, Congress passed the Civil Rights Act of 1957 to protect the voting rights of African-Americans. Under this act, the U.S. Attorney General could seek an injunction against anyone engaged in a practice to deprive a person of the right to vote. A unanimous Court upheld this provision in *United States v. Raines*.[67] In another voting rights case, *Hannah v. Larche,* the Court upheld the broad investigatory powers of the Commission on Civil Rights established by the Civil Rights Act of 1957.[68] The voting rights cases gave promise that African-Americans might be helped in registering to vote but did little immediately to change states' patterns of keeping blacks from the polls.

In 1960 a unanimous Court struck down the political boundaries drawn by the Alabama legislature for the city of Tuskegee.[69] African-American citizens challenged the legislature's decision to change the boundaries "from a square to an uncouth twenty-eight sided figure." Through this elaborate gerrymandering, the state had eliminated all but a handful of the city's four hundred black voters without eliminating a single white voter. Justice Frankfurter, for the Court, stated that the Fifteenth Amendment, which forbids a state to deprive any citizen of the right to vote because of race, "nullifies sophisticated as well as simple-minded modes of discrimination."[70]

CONCLUSION

Problems of racial discrimination remain a pressing social issue. One distinguished observer noted that it is perhaps a misnomer to speak of a race "problem" since this implies that there is some solution to it.[71] The difficulty lies in the fact that prejudice is a private, personal feeling with little basis in objectivity. This personal prejudice, highly responsive to emotional appeals, is responsible for acts of private segregation. Such actions, feelings, and thoughts are properly in the sphere of individual conscience—beyond governmental control. Perhaps increased education and rational thought will play an important part in ending private, de facto segregation and prejudice of this nature. If government was helpless to control private segregation, however, it could act positively in preventing its practice under the color of law as de jure segregation.

Governmental actions, however, should not be based on the lowest common standard. If in the international ideological struggle of the Cold War, the United States presented itself as the embodiment of a moral code, which among other things ensured "justice and equality for all," but failed to enforce such a code, it was not surprising that other peoples were suspicious of the American position. Adhering to that code was not easy—few important changes are. But the challenge for America to become a more democratic nation and to end *apartheid* in the United States had been presented. The Court had sown the seeds of freedom that would be harvested in the 1960s in the Civil Rights Act of 1964, the Voting Rights Act of 1965, significant decisions of the Warren Court, and other victories of the Civil Rights Movement.

The complexities of civil rights cases and the emotions they aroused during the Eisenhower era prompted the Court to avoid any major desegregation pronouncement for a decade after *Brown I & II*, except for its exceptional opinion in the Little Rock case. The Court was unanimous in granting or refusing to grant certiorari in cases involving alleged segregation of African-Americans between 1954 and 1959. During the 1958 term, however, the unanimity was broken when four of the justices found occasion to dissent from denials of certiorari. The high tribunal's caution in requiring state statutes and actions to be construed and interpreted by state courts before federal courts were asked to decide upon their constitutionality, brought occasional dissents from the Chief Justice and Justices Douglas and Brennan, who preferred to review the constitutional questions involved, believing that the federal courts and especially the Supreme Court had to act if the rights of minorities were to be protected.[72] It is interesting to note that Justice Black did not join his usual colleagues on those occasions. Perhaps his knowledge of Southern mores and traditions influenced his decision to move with greater caution in that area.[73] Yet when state legislative investigations involving the NAACP came before the Court for review, Justice Black joined Warren and Douglas in voting to grant certiorari, while Justice Brennan, who did not share the same opinion as the other three on that subject, joined the majority in denying certiorari.[74] Looked at in this respect, Chief Justice Warren and Justice Douglas emerged as the most libertarian members of the Court in this area, urging even greater judicial action.

The members of the Court were, of course, in basic agreement that segregation sanctioned by law had no place under the Constitution, as evidenced by the unanimous stand of the justices in important equal protection–racial discrimination cases which was in sharp contrast to a generally divided Court in other fields. The Court evidenced a striking boldness in its handling of discrimination issues by placing substantive restraints on governmental powers, and this trend continued as long as state action or law was involved in segregation. One of the major contributions of the Eisenhower Court to American constitutional law was its role in facilitating the end of legalized segregation. In doing so the Court enunciated what Professor Horn described as the "novel and socially useful principle that government actions admittedly less than constitutional may under appropriate circumstances be given temporary judicial sanction."[75] This represents constitutional relativism at its best.

Solving the race problem to many people meant jobs for the African-American "without discrimination, free use of the ballot without intimidation, the right to worship and join churches without embarrassment, freedom to learn without segregation, freedom to use the recreational facilities available to other citizens, freedom to live in hotels and motels when on business trips or vacations, freedom to travel unsegregated on boats, buses, trains, and planes, freedom to use rest rooms in public places, and freedom to pay taxes without having to stand in segregated lines."[76]

In brief, it meant integration of the African-American into American life. Many observers believed that this was possible and desirable. The Eisenhower Court tossed this moral question squarely into the forum of public opinion. The result was rational thought and action in an area where only a decade before there had been silence and complacency.[77]

NOTES

1. See generally, John P. Frank and Robert F. Munro, "The Original Understanding of 'Equal Protection of the Laws'," 50 *Colum. L. Rev.* 131 (1950); see also Ralph T. Jans, "Negro Civil Rights and the Supreme Court 1865–1949" (unpublished doctoral dissertation, Political Science, University of Chicago, 1950); John P. Roche, "Education, Segregation, and the Supreme Court—A Political Analysis," 99 *U. Pa. L. Rev.* 949 (1951); Donald G. Nieman, *Promises to Keep: African-Americans and the Constitutional Order, 1776 to the Present* (New York: Oxford University Press, 1991).

2. *Plessy v. Ferguson*, 163 U.S. 537 (1896).

3. Jack Greenberg, *Race Relations and American Law* (New York: Columbia University Press, 1959); see also "Racial Desegregation and Integration," 304 *Annals of the Am. Academy of Pol. & Soc. Science* 1 (1956).

4. Gunnar Myrdal, *An American Dilemma* (New York: Harper & Bros., 1944), p. 24.

5. *Brown v. Board of Education*, 347 U.S. 483 (1954); *Bolling v. Sharpe*, 347 U.S. 497 (1954).

6. Alexander M. Bickel, "Original Understanding and the Segregation Decision," 69 *Harv. L. Rev.* 1 (1955).

7. See generally, "Symposium: Legal Framework of Desegregation," 34 *Notre Dame Law.* 718 (1959).

8. Ira M. Heyman, "The Chief Justice, Racial Segregation, and the Friendly Critics," 49 *Cal. L. Rev.* 104 (1961). This article criticizes two scholarly attacks on the segregation decision by law professors who abhor segregation: Herbert Wechsler, "Toward Neutral Principles of Constitutional Law," 73 *Harv. L. Rev.* 1 (1959); *cf.* Louis Pollak, "Racial Discrimination and Judicial Integrity: A Reply to Professor Wechsler," 108 *U. Pa. L. Rev.* 1 (1959).

9. 347 U.S. 483 at 492.

10. 347 U.S. 483 at 493.

11. Ibid. See John L. Fletcher, *The Segregation Case and the Supreme Court* (Boston: Boston University Studies in Political Science, No. 1, 1958).

12. *But see* Eugene Cook and William I. Potter, "School Segregation Cases: Opposing the Opinion of the Supreme Court," 42 *A.B.A.J.* 313 (1956); Southern Regional Council, *Schools in the South: Answers for Action* (Atlanta: Southern Regional Council, 1954); see also Charles J. Bloch, *States' Rights, the Law of the Land* (Atlanta, GA: Harrison Co., 1958).

13. 347 U.S. 497 (1954).

14. 349 U.S. 294 (1955).

15. Cass R. Sunstein, *One Case at a Time: Judicial Minimalism on the Supreme Court* (Cambridge, MA: Harvard University Press, 1999), p. 38; Berry, *Stability, Security, and Continuity*, p. 160–61. Extensive citation of the voluminous literature dealing with the segregation cases seems unnecessary here. See, e.g., Arthur E. Sutherland, "American Judiciary and Racial Desegregation," 20 *Modern L. Rev.* 201 (1957); Alfred H. Kelly, "Fourteenth Amendment Reconsidered: The Segregation Question," 54 *Mich. L. Rev.* 1049 (1956); Robert J. Harris, "The Constitution, Education, and Segregation," 29 *Temp. L. Q.* 409 (1956); Richard Kluger, *Simple Justice* (New York: Knopf, 1976); Jack W. Peltason, *Fifty-eight Lonely Men: Southern Federal Judges and School Desegregation* (New York: Harcourt, Brace & World, 1961); James T. Patterson, *Brown v. Board of Education: A Civil Rights Milestone and Its Troubled Legacy* (New York: Oxford University Press, 2001).

16. See generally, Lloyd M. Wells, "Interposition and the Supreme Court," 41 *Southwest Review* 305 (1956); Charles Fairman, "Attack on the Segregation Cases," 70 *Harv. L. Rev.* 83 (1956).

17. Alabama, Arkansas, Florida, Louisiana, Mississippi, North Carolina, South Carolina, Tennessee, Texas, and Virginia. Georgia pursued other means to end school segregation.

18. *Carson v. Warlick*, 238 F.2d 724 (4th Cir., 1955); *cert. denied* 353 U.S. 910

(1957).

19. *Shuttlesworth v. Birmingham Board of Education*, 162 F. Supp. 372 (N.D. Ala, 1958); *aff'd*, 358 U.S. 101 (1958).

20. *Adkins v. School Board*, 148 F. Supp. 430 (E.D. Va, 1957); *aff'd* 246 F.2d 325 (4th Cir., 1957); *cert. denied*, 355 U.S. 855 (1957).

21. *Orleans Parish School Board v. Bush*, 242 F.2d 156 (5th Cir., 1957); *aff'd per curiam*, 351 U.S. 946 (1957); 365 U.S. 569 (1961).

22. *Dove v. Parham*, 176 F. Supp. 430 (E.D. Ark. 1959); 282 F.2d 256 (8th Cir., 1960).

23. 252 F.2d 291 (4th Cir., 1955), *cert. denied*, 357 U.S. 906 (1958).

24. *Pennsylvania v. Board of Directors of City Trusts of City of Philadelphia*, 357 U.S. 570 (1958); see generally, Elias Clark, "Charitable Trusts, the Fourteenth Amendment and the Will of Stephen Girard," 66 *Yale L. J.* 979 (1959); *cf.* 71 *Harv. L. Rev.* 150 (1957); 11 *Sw. L. Rev.* 518 (1957); see also Arthur S. Miller, *Racial Discrimination and Private Education* (Chapel Hill: University of North Carolina Press, 1957).

25. 350 U.S. 413 (1956); 93 So. 2d 354 (1957); 355 U.S. 839 (1957); 253 F.2d 752 (5th Cir., 1958); 162 F. Supp. 851 (N.D. Fla. 1958).

26. 162 F. Supp. 851 at 853 (N.D. Fla. 1958); Thomas M. Jenkins, "Judicial Discretion in Desegregation: The Hawkins Case," 4 *How. L. J.* 193 (1958); 3 *Race Relations L. Rep.* 657 (1958).

27. *Board of Trustees v. Frasier*, 134 F. Supp. 589 (M.D.N.C. 1955), *aff'd per curiam* 350 U.S. 979 (1956).

28. *Board of Supervisors of L.S.U. v. Tureaud*, 225 F.2d 434 (5th Cir., 1955), *cert. denied*, 351 U.S. 924 (1956).

29. *Booker v. Board of Education*, *motion denied*, 351 U.S. 948 (1956); 240 F.2d 689 (6th Cir., 1957); see also *Lucy v. Adams*, 350 U.S. 1 (1955).

30. *Cooper v. Aaron*, 358 U.S. 1 (1958).

31. 358 U.S. 1 at 15; see Richard P. Longaker, *The Presidency and Individual Liberties* (Ithaca, NY: Cornell University Press, 1961), pp. 152–73.

32. 358 U.S. 1 at 16.

33. 358 U.S. 1 at 17.

34. 358 U.S. 1 at 19.

35. For a detailed account of the aftermath of the Court's decisions, in the segregation cases, see Albert P. Blaustein and Clarence Ferguson, *Desegregation and the Law* (New Brunswick, NJ: Rutgers University Press, 1957); Longaker, pp. 214–220.

36. For comment by foreign observers on the segregation decisions, see, e.g., H. E. Groves, "Problems of Integration Following the School Desegregation Cases in the United States," 2 *J. Indian L. Institute* 507 (1960); B. M. Carl, "Problema de la Segregacion Racial en los Estados Unidos," 26 *Revista de Derecho* (Chile) 469 (1958).

37. Pritchett, *The Political Offender and the Warren Court*, p. 10.

38. For discussion of this issue, see Herbert Garfinkel, "Social Science Evidence and the School Segregation Cases," 21 *J. of Politics* 37 (1959); *cf.* Charles L. Black, Jr., "Lawfulness of the Segregation Decisions," 69 *Yale L. J.* 421 (1960); see also Benjamin M. Ziegler, *Desegregation and the Supreme Court* (Boston: D.C. Heath, 1958); Ray D. Henson, "Study in Style: Mr. Justice Frankfurter," 6 *Vill. L. Rev.*

377, 384 (1961).

39. On May 17, 1961, the seventh anniversary of the *Brown* decision, United Press International reported the following figures on African-Americans in de-segregated classes in states which prior to 1954 required segregated schools: District of Columbia 82,000; Missouri 35,000; Kentucky 16,239; West Virginia 14,000; Oklahoma 9,822; Delaware 6,734; Texas 3,500; Maryland 2,800; Tennessee 342; Virginia 208; Arkansas 113; North Carolina 82; Florida 27; Louisiana 4; and none in South Carolina, Alabama, Mississippi, or Georgia (although Atlanta schools were subsequently integrated in the autumn of 1961). See Robert G. McCloskey, "Deeds Without Doctrines: Civil Rights in the 1960 Term of the Supreme Court," 56 *Am. Pol. Sci. Rev.* 71 (1962).

40. Wells, "Interposition and the Supreme Court," p. 312.

41. 347 U.S. 483 at 494.

42. *New York Times*, 27 November 1957, p. 17; the *Brown* decision represents the application of the best techniques of the American Realists and the American school of sociological jurisprudence: see generally, Julius Stone, *The Province and Function of Law* (Cambridge, MA: Harvard University Press, 1950), pp. 406–417.

43. *New York Times*, 27 November 1957, p. 17.

44. Bella S. Abzug, "Legislative Proposals in the South Against Integration," 16 *Law. Guild Rev.* 45 (1956).

45. Wells, "Interposition and the Supreme Court," p. 312.

46. Walter F. Murphy, "Desegregation in Public Education—A Generation of Future Litigation," 15 *Md. L. Rev.* 221 (1955).

47. George W. Spicer, *The Supreme Court and Fundamental Freedoms* (New York: Appleton-Century-Crofts, 1959), p. 114; segregation in Southern public schools came to an end under financial and legal pressures put on school districts by the passage of the Civil Rights Act of 1964 and the Elementary and Secondary Education Act of 1965.

48. See generall, "Symposium: Equality Before the Law," 54 *Nw. U. L. Rev.* 354 (1959).

49. *South Carolina Electric & Gas Co. v. Flemming*, 351 U.S. 901 (1956); *accord*, *Gayle v. Browder*, 352 U.S. 903 (1956); *Morrison v. Davis*, 356 U.S. 968 (1958); *cert. denied*; *Evers v. Dwyer*, 358 U.S. 202 (1958).

50. *Boynton v. Virginia*, 364 U.S. 454 (1960).

51. *Holmes v. Atlanta*, 350 U.S. 879 (1955); *accord*, *Muir v. Louisville Park Theatrical Assoc.*, 347 U.S. 971 (1954); *St. Petersburg v. Alsup*, 353 U.S. 924 (1957).

52. *Dawson v. Baltimore City*, 350 U.S. 877 (1955).

53. Segregation in a restaurant in a Texas county courthouse was ended by court action in *Casey v. Plummer*, 353 U.S. 924 (1957).

54. *Burton v. Willmington Parking Authority*, 365 U.S. 715 (1961).

55. 368 U.S. 157 (1961).

56. *Louisiana State Athletic Commission v. Dorsey*, 359 U.S. 533 (1959).

57. See Chapter 8.

58. *Naim v. Naim*, 350 U.S. 891 (1955), *motion den.* 350 U.S. 985 (1955).

59. *Loving v. Virginia*, 388 U.S. 1 (1967).

60. *Leeper v. Charlotte Park Commission*, 350 U.S. 983 (1956), *cert. denied*.

61. *Speed v. City of Tallahassee*, 356 U.S. 913 (1958), *cert. denied*.

62. *Oliphant v. Brotherhood of Locomotive Fireman and Enginemen*, 359 U.S.

935 (1959), *cert. denied.*

63. *Syres and Warrick v. Oil Workers International Union*, 358 U.S. 929 (1959), *cert. denied.*

64. *Eaton v. Board of Managers*, 359 U.S. 984 (1959), *cert. denied.* Warren, Brennan, and Douglas would have granted certiorari.

65. 349 U.S. 70 (1955).

66. *Lassiter v. Board of Elections*, 360 U.S. 45 (1959).

67. *United States v. Raines*, 362 U.S. 17 (1960).

68. *Hannah v. Larche*, 363 U.S. 420 (1960).

69. *Gomillion v. Lightfoot*, 364 U.S. 339 (1960).

70. 364 U.S. 339 at 346.

71. Edward S. Corwin, *Total War and the Constitution* (New York: Knopf, 1947), p. 181; *but see* Jacob K. Javits, *Discrimination—U.S.A.* (New York: Harcourt, Brace & Co., 1960); Peltason, *Fifty-eight Lonely Men*; see also John H. Griffin, *Black Like Me* (New York: Houghton Mifflin, 1961); McCloskey, *The American Supreme Court* (Chicago: University of Chicago Press, 1960), pp. 208–19.

72. *Harrison v. NAACP*, 360 U.S. 167 (1959); *NAACP v. Bennet*, 360 U.S. 471 (1959); *Eaton v. Board of Managers*, 359 U.S. 984 (1959), *cert. denied*; see also the separate opinion of Justice Douglas in *NAACP v. Williams*, 359 U.S. 550 (1959).

73. See Daniel M. Berman, "Hugo Black: The Early Years," 8 *Catholic U. L. Rev.* 103 (1959); "Hugo Black and the Negro," 10 *Am. U. L. Rev.* 35 (1961); Clifford J. Durr, "Hugo Black, Southerner," 10 *Am. U. L. Rev.* 27 (1961).

74. *Gibson v. Florida Legislative Investigation Committee*, 360 U.S. 919 (1959).

75. Horn, "The Warren Court and the Discretionary Power of the Executive," p. 672.

76. Benjamin Mays, "Race in America: The Negro Perspective," in *The Search for America*, ed. Huston Smith (Englewood Cliffs, NJ: Prentice-Hall, 1959), p. 65.

77. See also *NAACP v. Bates*, 361 U.S. 516 (1960); *Thompson v. Louisville*, 362 U.S. 199 (1960); *United States v. Alabama*, 362 U.S. 602 (1960).

Republican presidential nominee Dwight Eisenhower and wife Mamie campaigning in California with governor Earl Warren. *Photo courtesy the Collection of the Supreme Court of the United States.*

Justice Hugo Black, who served on the Supreme Court from 1937–1971, was the intellectual leader of the judicial activists. *Photo courtesy the Library of Congress.*

Justice Felix Frankfurter served on the Court from 1939–1962 and led the judicial restraintist bloc. *Photo courtesy the Library of Congress.*

Justice William O. Douglas, the restless spirit of the Court, served on the high tribunal from 1939 to 1975. *Photo courtesy the Library of Congress.*

Justice Tom Clark, appointed by President Truman, was a supporter of the government's internal security programs. He served on the Court from 1949 to 1967. *Photo courtesy the Collection of the Supreme Court of the United States.*

"Super Chief" and his top lieutenant: Chief Justice Earl Warren and Associate Justice William Brennan became good friends and close colleagues on the Court. *Photo courtesy the Library of Congress.*

John M. Harlan II was the first Associate Justice appointed by President Eisenhower. He served on the Court from 1954 to 1971 and was a close ally of Frankfurter. *Photo courtesy the Library of Congress.*

President Dwight Eisenhower and nominee for Associate Justice William J. Brennan, Jr., who served on the Court from 1956 to 1990. *Photo courtesy the Collection of the Supreme Court of the United States.*

Charles E. Whittaker, who had the shortest tenure of the Eisenhower associate justices on the Court, serving from 1957 to 1962. *Photo courtesy the Library of Congress.*

Potter Stewart was the last Eisenhower appointee to the Court and the young-est. He served on the court from 1958 to 1981. *Photo courtesy the Library of Congress.*

The Eisenhower Court, October 1958 Term. *Photo courtesy the Library of Congress.*

7

Fair Trial Procedures

One of the most important functions of the Supreme Court is the maintenance of constitutional standards for criminal prosecutions conducted in both federal and state courts. Fair trial procedures were considered of such importance as to be included in five of the first ten amendments to the Constitution. These Bill of Rights provisions include the broad guarantee of due process of law as well as a number of specific procedural protections that were thought to be fundamental and beyond invasion by the national government. In addition to enforcing these constitutional provisions, the Supreme Court, as the apex of the federal judicial system, has general responsibility for the administration of justice in the federal courts. In the words of Justice Frankfurter: "Judicial supervision of the administration of criminal justice in the federal courts implies the duty of establishing and maintaining civilized standards of procedure and evidence."[1]

With respect to the state courts, the Supreme Court's authority had historically been less extensive, since it had long held that the specific provisions of the Bill of Rights dealing with judicial procedure did not apply to the states. Because of the difference in constitutional theory as to federal and state prosecutions, the two areas will be examined separately. This chapter will discuss federal cases while Chapter 8 will examine state cases. Since the facts of a given case may involve several matters related to fair trial procedures, these cases have been arranged arbitrarily into categories for convenience.

FEDERAL SEARCHES AND SEIZURES

The Fourth Amendment protection against unreasonable searches and seizures presented the Supreme Court with some of its most difficult questions. That amendment contains an unqualified prohibition against violation of "the rights of the people to be secure in their persons, houses, papers, and effects, against unreasonable searches and seizures." Justice Frankfurter characterized the provision as central to enjoyment of the other guarantees of the Bill of Rights.[2] Searches and seizures at the discretion of government officials have characterized totalitarian police states. Although the Court has had difficulty in determining whether, in individual cases, federal officers have engaged in illegal search or seizure, there is no doubt that it is quick to intervene when it feels that the Fourth Amendment has been violated. Justice Black referred to this difficulty when he stated that "in no other field has the law's uncertainty been more clearly manifested."[3] But the Court has been consistent in applying the accepted sanction inherent in the Fourth Amendment. It has since 1914 made evidence secured as the result of illegal search and seizure generally inadmissible in the federal courts.[4] This exclusion of illegally procured evidence is not, strictly speaking, an integral part of the search and seizure concept. Rather it is a rule of evidence adopted for the federal courts by the Supreme Court in the *Weeks* case. Until 1961, this prohibition on the use of illegally secured evidence in federal courts applied only if federal agents were the guilty parties in procuring the evidence. If the evidence was illegally secured by state police officers and turned over to federal agents, or if it was stolen by private parties and then passed on to the government, it might be employed in a federal trial. These exceptions to the exclusionary rule were known as "the silver platter doctrine."

In 1956 the Eisenhower Court handed down one of its most important rulings in this area in *Rea v. United States*.[5] Here the majority (Douglas, Warren, Black, Frankfurter, and Clark) held that a federal agent could be enjoined from testifying in a state court prosecution with respect to evidence obtained by him in the course of an unlawful search that had been suppressed in a prior federal prosecution under the federal rule barring illegal evidence.[6] The majority decided the case on the basis of the Court's supervisory responsibility for the administration of justice in the federal courts and ruled that federal policies forbade the agent's conduct. For the Court, Justice Douglas pointed out that the federal policy would be defeated if a federal agent could use the fruits of his unlawful act in a state proceeding. But could federal courts continue to admit evidence obtained solely from illegal state searches, a practice permitted under the silver platter exception to the exclusionary rule? The Eisenhower Court would answer that question four years later. For the four *Rea* dissenters,

Justice Harlan maintained that the Court's ruling would encourage races "between a state prosecution and a federal injunction proceeding."[7]

A 1960 decision laid the groundwork for applying *Weeks* to the states and abandoning the silver platter doctrine. In *Elkins v. United States*, the Supreme Court, by a five-to-four majority, decided that the silver platter doctrine had become intolerable, and that it did not matter to the victim of police abuse "whether his constitutional right has been invaded by a federal agent or by a state officer."[8] The justices concluded that the silver platter doctrine undermined federalism. Justice Stewart's majority opinion asserted that the protections provided by the Fourth and Fourteenth Amendments against unreasonable searches were equivalent. By that time, almost half of the states had adopted the exclusionary rule, so admitting illegally seized evidence in federal courts defeated state court efforts to uphold Fourth Amendment standards. In 1961 the Eisenhower Court would take the next step and require state courts, like federal courts, to exclude unconstitutionally seized evidence.

In *Kremen v. United States*,[9] the Court held that the seizing, inventory, and removing to FBI headquarters two hundred miles away, of the entire contents of a secluded cabin was unreasonable and unconstitutional. The Court noted that this seizure of the entire contents of the house, and its removal to such a great distance for the purpose of examination, went beyond the sanction of any precedents. Justices Burton and Clark dissented on the ground that the validity of a seizure should not be tested by the quantity of items seized.

Further restrictions on searches and seizures by federal officers had been added in the 1957 term of the Court. In *Miller v. United States*,[10] a seizure was invalidated because officers who had broken in the door of the suspect's apartment without giving the required notice of their authority and purpose had made an arrest. The rule that before an officer is permitted to break down the door of a house to affect an arrest, he must first state his authority and purpose in demanding admission, holds whether the arrest is made with or without a warrant. *Jones v. United States*[11] reaffirmed the settled doctrine that probable cause for belief that certain articles subject to seizure are in a dwelling does not of itself justify a search without a warrant. *Giordenello v. United States*[12] held that a warrant of arrest is insufficient if it does no more than merely recite the elements of the crime charged. The main point of these cases with regard to both arrest and search warrants was that a neutral and detached magistrate, not a policeman, should judge the persuasiveness of the facts relied on by the complaining officer, and therefore the magistrate must have the facts before him and not the complainant's mere conclusion. Justices Burton and Clark dissented in all three cases, and Justice Whittaker joined them in *Giordenello*. In its most significant venture into the troubled area of searches of automobiles, the Eisenhower Court ruled that if probable cause was lacking, automobile searches were illegal.[13]

The process of investigation necessarily involves other types of interference with the privacy of suspected offenders. The doctrine of "probable cause" can be used to justify the action of an investigating officer should he restrict the liberty of movement of a suspected person. The fact that pressure may be placed on the courts to water down the standards for probable cause to make formal arrests in order to avoid freeing obviously guilty defendants because of relatively minor invasions of their privacy was illustrated by *Draper v. United States*.[14] A federal narcotics agent had been told by a known and reliable informer that Draper, a narcotics peddler, had gone to Chicago to obtain a supply and would return by a certain train. The agent met the train, easily recognized Draper, and without a search warrant arrested him and searched him, and seized narcotics and a hypodermic syringe found in his possession. These were later admitted as evidence in his trial. For the Court, Justice Whittaker ruled that even if the information upon which the arrest was made was "hearsay," the agent was legally entitled to consider it in determining whether he had "probable cause," within the meaning of the Fourth Amendment, to believe that Draper had committed or was committing a violation of the narcotics laws. The arrest was thus lawful, and the subsequent search and seizure, having been made incident to a lawful arrest, were likewise valid.[15]

Justice Douglas, dissenting alone, maintained that "the arrest made here on the mere word of an informer violated the spirit of the Fourth Amendment."[16] He took the occasion to berate one of the great influences upon American public opinion:

> Of course, the education we receive from mystery stories and television shows teaches that what happened in this case is efficient police work. The police are tipped off that a man carrying narcotics will step off the morning train. A man meeting the precise description does alight from the train. No warrant for his arrest has been—or, as I see it, could then be—obtained. Yet he is arrested; and the narcotics are found in his pocket and a syringe in the bag he carried. This is the familiar pattern of crime detection which has been dinned into public consciousness as the correct and efficient one. It is, however, a distorted reflection of the constitutional system under which we are supposed to live.[17]

Closely allied to search and seizure cases are those involving wiretapping. Normally the search and seizure clause protects against the seizure of physical objects useful in effecting criminal convictions, but it may also be invoked against alleged unreasonable "search" of a person's spoken words. The Communications Act of 1934[18] provided that "no person not being authorized by the sender shall intercept any communication and divulge or publish the . . . contents . . . of such intercepted communication to any person." The Supreme Court has interpreted this law to mean that evidence secured by wiretapping is inadmissible in federal trials. In *Benanti v. United States*,[19] the Eisenhower Court unanimously held that this statute forbade the use in federal courts of evidence secured by state officers under a state-approved wiretap system, even though no federal officers participated in the tapping. The *Benanti* decision was a defeat for federal law enforcement officers, because it strongly undermined the idea that evidence procured by unreasonable search and seizure by state officials would be received in federal courts and sealed off from the federal government a fertile source of what was always potent and often necessary evidence for the conviction of federal crimes.[20]

In *Silverman v. United States*,[21] government agents pushed an electronic listening device through the wall of an adjoining house until it touched the heating duct of a suspect's house. By using this "spike mike," officers listened to conversations taking place on both floors of the house. The Court held that for there to be a Fourth Amendment search, officers must have physically intruded into "a constitutionally protected area," and in this case, the physical penetration into the suspect's house violated his rights.

In *Rathbun v. United States*,[22] the Court ruled that listening in on a conversation with the consent of one of the parties to the call on a telephone extension was not wiretapping but merely a form of eavesdropping. The eavesdropper had not intercepted the message, and this was one essential element of the offense under the Communications Act of 1934. Justices Frankfurter and Douglas dissented, maintaining that "intercept" was synonymous with "listen in." To them this was "an intrusion by way of listening to the legally insulated transmission of thought between a speaker and a hearer."[23]

One Sparks, called at his home by Rathbun, who threatened to take his life, anticipated other calls and invited the police to listen in. The testimony of these officers to the content of the call formed the heart of the government's case against Rathbun for transmitting threats of personal injury in interstate commerce. The Chief Justice pointed out that the extension "had not been installed there just for this purpose but was a regular connection, previously placed and normally used."[24] The results of the *Benanti* and *Rathbun* decisions were to give some greater clarity to the Court's rule on wiretapping. The rule could then be stated: "On timely motion by a defendant who was a party to the call, a federal court will suppress the contents, and evidence derived therefrom, of any interstate or intrastate telephone communication overheard by any person, whether a private citizen or federal or state agent, if the listening in is without the permission of the other party to the call."[25]

That rule was redefined in 1986 and again in 1994 when Congress passed legislation to modernize the restrictions on electronic eavesdropping and to help police wiretappers keep pace with advancing technology.

COERCED CONFESSIONS

Fundamental in any system of ordered liberty should be repugnance toward the use of confessions coerced from an accused. American law has traditionally embodied some suspicion concerning the trustworthiness of confessions, and forced confessions have been inadmissible in federal courts. They offend both the Fifth Amendment's privilege against self-incrimination and its concept of due process of law.

One effect of the self-incrimination clause is that it forbids the use in federal courts of confessions secured under conditions of physical or mental coercion, for in such cases the defendant would obviously have been under compulsion to testify against himself. Cases of allegedly coerced confessions have frequently come up to the Supreme Court from the states. Such cases from the lower federal courts were rare because of the higher standards of federal law enforcement and because of the small number of federal criminal prosecutions for the ordinary felonies such as murder, rape, and robbery. The Fifth Amendment does not forbid the admission of evidence of a confession made while the accused was in the custody of the law, however, if such confession was made voluntarily, freely, and without compulsion of any kind.[26] The leading federal case in this area is *McNabb v. United States*,[27] in which the Court voided a conviction, not on grounds of unconstitutional self-incrimination, but because the prisoners had not been taken before the nearest judicial officer "without unnecessary delay" for hearing, commitment, or release on bail, as required by statute.[28] In that case the defendants were questioned intermittently for two days before being taken before a magistrate. During that time, incriminating statements were obtained which were used to secure their conviction. The Court stated expressly that its decision was based, not on constitutional grounds, but on its supervisory authority over the administration of justice in the federal courts. There was considerable criticism of the *McNabb* rule as placing an undue restriction upon police officials, but the Eisenhower Court reaffirmed the rule.

In *Mallory v. United States*,[29] the Court reversed the conviction of a nineteen-year-old African-American of limited intelligence who had been arrested in Washington, DC, on the charge of rape, at about two o'clock in the afternoon, and then questioned on and off until midnight, when he finally signed a written confession. It was only after he made an oral confession around 10:00 P.M. that the police made a first attempt to reach a United States Commissioner, and after this failed, Mallory agreed to be examined by a deputy coroner. Since his arrest, he had been detained in a building in the vicinity of many committing magistrates. The police did not tell the accused about his rights to counsel and to a preliminary examination and did not warn him of his right to remain silent. Said Justice Frankfurter, for a unanimous Court, "It is not the function of the police to arrest, as it were, at large and to use an interrogating process at police headquarters in order to determine whom they should charge before a committing magistrate on 'probable cause'."[30] Thus the Court broadened the *McNabb* rule to invalidate even a voluntary confession made before arraignment.

Mallory was the first time that the Court passed directly on the question of what is and what is not an unnecessary delay. The opinion clearly outlawed delay solely for the purposes of interrogation. This decision was denounced by some as an intolerable handicap to the efficient and effective enforcement of criminal law, while others hailed *Mallory* as a long overdue vindication of the civil liberties of the citizen in the face of the mounting power of the state.

The *McNabb-Mallory* rule did impose limitations upon police efficiency—but was this undesirable? Anglo-American law has traditionally viewed unlawful detentions with disfavor. Prompt production before a magistrate or other proper official is essential to the prevention of such illegal acts. It would seem especially important not to prolong the time between arrest and arraignment in that this is the period in which many police tactics of questionable validity are used to wrench evidence from a defendant. The accused was, until the mid-1960s, completely at the mercy of the police at that time.[31]

In 1958 Congress considered a bill that would have nullified the holding of the *Mallory* case by providing that confessions in federal courts should not be regarded as inadmissible merely because there had been undue delay in arraignment.[32] Although the bill was passed by the House by an overwhelming vote, it was lost in the Senate on a technical point of order.[33] Congress eventually responded to *Mallory* by making confessions admissible if the defendant is arraigned within six hours.[34]

SELF-INCRIMINATION

The provision in the Fifth Amendment that no one "shall be compelled in any criminal case to be a witness against himself" has previously been mentioned in its relation to the rights of witnesses before congressional committees and administrative agencies. The Eisenhower Court also reviewed several important cases in which self-incrimination was involved in jury proceedings and criminal trials.

In its 1954 term, the Court upheld the conviction of a District of Columbia gambler[35] who did not pay a tax required by the Gamblers' Occupational Tax Act of 1951.[36] For the majority, Justice Minton held that there was no constitutional right to gamble and that the government might tax what it has forbidden by statute. Since wagering was a crime in the District of Columbia, Lewis argued that in paying the tax he would incriminate himself. The Court held that the tax was not a penalty, while rejecting the self-incrimination argument on the ground that the privilege related only to past acts and not to future acts that may or may not be committed. All that was required here was a registration certificate in which the registrant declared that he intended to take wagers in the future. Justices Douglas, Black, and Frankfurter dissented, contending that this was an obvious type of self-incrimination since by the mere act of registering one confesses to being engaged in an illegal activity.

Under the Fifth Amendment, a defendant in a criminal trial cannot be required to take the witness stand. It is improper for opposing counsel to call attention to such failure of a defendant to take the stand in his own defense, and by federal statute a jury must be instructed that the defendant's failure to testify creates no presumption against him. In *Grunewald v. United States*,[37] the trial judge permitted the government, for the purpose of impeaching a defendant's credibility, to cross-examine him with regard to his assertion of the privilege against self-incrimination before the grand jury. In his charge to the jury the judge said that the defendant's Fifth Amendment plea could be considered only with regard to the issue of his credibility, but that no inference regarding guilt or innocence could be drawn from it. The Supreme Court ruled that the trial judge had erred since the assertion of the privilege before the grand jury was not inconsistent with this defendant's later testimony at the trial. Prior statements can be used to impeach the credibility of a defendant in a criminal trial, but only if the judge is satisfied that the prior statements were in fact inconsistent with the testimony given at the trial. The Court held that the cross-examination should have been excluded because its value on the issue of the defendant's credibility was so negligible as to be far outweighed by its possible and impermissible impact on the jury.[38] Justices Black, Douglas, Brennan, and the Chief Justice would have made a broader statement than the other five justices, because they could think of no special circumstance that would justify the use of a constitutional privilege to discredit or convict a person who had asserted it.

In *Brown v. United States*,[39] a witness was subpoenaed to testify before a federal grand jury, where he refused to answer questions on Fifth Amendment grounds. The grand jury sought the aid of a district court judge who ruled that Brown would be accorded an immunity and explicitly ordered him to answer the questions. Brown refused to do so and was sentenced to fifteen months imprisonment for criminal contempt. The Court, by a five-to-four vote, affirmed this action, holding that if a defendant voluntarily takes the stand, he may be cross-examined as any other witness, thereby risking the disclosure of incriminating information. The Chief Justice and Justices Black, Douglas, and Brennan dissented. The Court had earlier unanimously held that a custodian of union records who failed to produce them before a grand jury could not be required to explain or account under oath for their absence even if he claimed that doing so would tend to incriminate him.[40]

FEDERAL DOUBLE JEOPARDY

The Fifth Amendment provides that no person shall be subject "to be twice put in jeopardy of life or limb" for the same offense. This provision prohibits a second prosecution for the same crime, whether the accused was convicted or acquitted at the previous trial. The enforcement of this provision presents problems in determining what "jeopardy" is, when jeopardy attaches, and what constitutes "sameness" in a crime.

The Eisenhower Court encountered difficulty in attempting to resolve these questions.[41] Although all of the justices probably would have agreed with Justice Douglas that "the policy of the Bill of Rights is to make rare indeed the occasions when the citizen can for the same offense be required to run the gauntlet twice,"[42] they frequently divided in five-to-four decisions over when a gauntlet had been run.

In *Pereira v. United States*,[43] the Court ruled that convictions for violating the National Stolen Property Act and for conspiring to commit the crime did not constitute double jeopardy. On the other hand, the Court reversed the conviction of a criminal who had been indicted on two different counts of assaulting two federal officers from a single blast of his shotgun.[44] In *Heflin v. United States*,[45] the Court held that a man could not be sentenced for receiving and taking the same property. However, in *Harris v. United States*,[46] the Court upheld convictions for the separate crimes of purchasing and receiving and concealing narcotics.

An accused may waive his constitutional immunity against double jeopardy under certain circumstances. Waiver applies, for instance, if the defendant consents to an improper discharge of the jury. The most common form of waiver occurs when a defendant requests a new trial or appeals from a verdict of guilty.[47] The Eisenhower Court ruled in *Green v. United States*[48] that if a conviction is set aside on appeal, the defendant may be tried a second time for the same offense, but he cannot be subjected to the risk of being convicted on a more serious charge than in the first trial. A District of Columbia jury that had been instructed by the judge that it could find him guilty of either first- or second-degree murder convicted Green of second-degree murder. Green appealed the judge's sentence of from five to twenty years imprisonment. The appellate court reversed the conviction on the ground that the evidence did not support it.

Green was tried again under the original indictment, this time being con-victed of first-degree murder and sentenced to death.

By a five-to-four vote, the Court ruled that this was double jeop-ardy. For the majority (Black, Douglas, Warren, Brennan, and Whittaker), Justice Black argued that the decision of the jury in the first trial amounted to an acquittal on the first-degree murder charge and barred subsequent trial on that charge.[49] To hold otherwise would mean "that in order to secure the removal of an erroneous conviction of one offense, a defendant must surrender his valid defense of former jeopardy not only on that of-fense but also on a different offense for which he was not convicted and which was not involved in his appeal."[50] For the majority, it was impor-tant "that the State with all its resources and power should not be al-lowed to make repeated attempts to convict an individual for an alleged offense, thereby subjecting him to embarrassment, expense and ordeal and compelling him to live in a continuing state of anxiety and insecurity, as well as enhancing the possibility that even though innocent he may be found guilty."[51]

Justice Frankfurter, speaking for the dissenters, wrote a lengthy his-torical review of double jeopardy rulings, concluding that the majority "misconceives the purposes of the double jeopardy provision, and with-out warrant from the Constitution makes an absolute of the interests of the accused in disregard of the interests of society."[52]

The question of double jeopardy often arises where a defendant has, with one act, committed closely related offenses defined by different stat-utes of a single governmental jurisdiction. The test of identity of offenses is whether the same evidence is required to prove them. Speaking gener-ally, there is no double jeopardy if the second offense requires proof of an additional fact that the other does not. The problem attains its most exag-gerated form when the same offense is committed against more than one victim in a single transaction or event. In a leading case, *Gore v. United States*,[53] the Eisenhower Court upheld the conviction of a drug peddler who was prosecuted for three different statutory offenses deriving from a single sale, though a four-justice minority (Black, Douglas, Warren, and Brennan) contended that Congress had simply meant to give the govern-ment three avenues of prosecution, not to authorize cumulative punish-ments for a single transaction.[54]

An accused person has been placed in jeopardy when he has been tried by a court of competent jurisdiction and either acquitted or con-victed. The government may not appeal such a verdict or institute a sec-ond prosecution for the same offense. It is not necessary for a trial to have reached the stage of a verdict to bring the jeopardy rule into operation; otherwise a prosecutor would be able to halt a trial when it appeared that the jury might not convict, in order to leave the way open for a second trial. On the other hand, should the jury fail to agree on a verdict and be discharged by a judge, a second trial would be permissible, the theory being that it is merely a continuation of the first. Trial by a court which is subsequently found to lack jurisdiction cannot place the defendant in jeopardy, however, no matter how far the proceedings are carried.[55]

If two federal courts should have concurrent jurisdiction over the same criminal act, an acquittal or conviction in one court would bar a subsequent prosecution in the other. Where both federal and state governments make the same act an offense, it is not double jeopardy, however, for each government to prosecute and provide punishment.[56] In *Abbate v. United States*,[57] the middle bloc joined by Justice Clark formed the majority which ruled that a man convicted in a state court for conspiring to destroy the property of another and subsequently convicted in a federal court for conspiring to injure communications facilities controlled by the United States had not been placed twice in jeopardy for the same offense.[58]

TRIAL BY JURY AND MILITARY JUSTICE

Congress has provided the nation's military with a Uniform Code of Military Justice[59] that provides a system of courts-martial for punishment of offenses by members of the armed forces. Military justice normally operates completely outside the purview of the Supreme Court. Occasionally, however, a conviction before a military court is appealed to the regular courts by writ of habeas corpus. Such review is usually limited to the issue of jurisdiction of the court-martial, which may be challenged on the ground that the offense charged was not within its cognizance, that the court was not legally constituted, or that the punishment exceeded the limits imposed by the code. The relationship of the guarantees of the Bill of Rights to military trials is somewhat complex; but the federal courts may also examine those constitutional standards required of military justice. The concern of the Eisenhower Court was primarily with the relationship of courts-martial to the civilian courts.

When Congress adopted the Uniform Code in 1950, it wrote a provision allowing courts-martial to try former members of the armed forces after their discharge for offenses committed while in the service. This provision covered only offenses punishable under military regulations by as much as five years' imprisonment and was restricted to those instances in which the accused would otherwise escape trial in any American court. The Eisenhower Court, in *United States ex rel. Toth v. Quarles*,[60] held this provision unconstitutional. After military service in Korea, Toth was honorably discharged and went to work in a Pittsburgh steel plant. Five months later he was arrested by military authorities, charged with having committed murder while in Korea, and flown to Korea to stand trial before a court-martial. His sister instituted habeas corpus proceedings against the Secretary of the Air Force in a District of Columbia court, which ordered his return to the United States.

By a six-to-three vote, the Court held that Congress could not subject civilians to military jurisdiction and that an ex-serviceman, upon his discharge, became entitled to all the safeguards afforded other civilians under the Constitution. For the majority,[61] Justice Black pointed out the large and growing number of veterans who would be subject to the questioned provision of the code. The characteristics of military trials did not compare favorably with those of civilian courts, and the Court found that there was no sufficient justification for depriving so many Americans of their constitutional right to trial by jury and indictment by grand jury.[62]

In a much-publicized case, *Wilson v. Girard*,[63] a serviceman preferred a military trial to a trial in the civilian courts of Japan. In accordance with a Status of Forces Agreement made in pursuance of a treaty between the United States and Japan, covering offenses committed in Japan by U.S. military personnel, jurisdiction over such offenses while entrusted to American officials might be waived in any case by the United States. In this instance, Girard, while guarding military equipment, killed a Japanese woman scavenging scrap metal. On the recommendation of the State Department and with the president's approval, the military turned Girard over to Japanese authorities for trial. Girard's relatives sought habeas corpus against Secretary of Defense Wilson. A federal district judge denied the writ but granted an injunction against delivering Girard to the Japanese.

In a brief unanimous opinion, the Supreme Court reversed this action holding that there was no constitutional or statutory barrier to such agreements, and none prohibited its administration as in this case. In the view of the Court, the wisdom of the particular action in this and similar service cases was a matter of executive or congressional, rather than judicial concern. Girard was subsequently tried by a Japanese court, convicted, and given a sentence much lighter than he probably would have received from a court-martial.[64]

Several constitutional issues have arisen as the result of the role of the United States in international affairs after 1945 when members of the armed forces and their dependents in large numbers began to be stationed abroad. The question of whether military courts might assert jurisdiction over dependents accompanying American servicemen stationed abroad was involved in *Reid v. Covert* and *Kinsella v. Krueger*.[65] In these cases, wives of military personnel, living on American bases in England and Japan, had killed their husbands. After deciding in 1956 by a five-to-four vote that civilians were subject to trial by court-martial as provided in the Code of Military Justice,[66] the Court granted a rehearing and reversed itself the next term, concluding that constitutional guarantees could be denied only as to military personnel. Justice Black, speaking for the Court, maintained that the exigencies which required military rule on the battlefront are not present in areas where no conflict exists.[67] He was joined in his opinion by the Chief Justice and Justices Douglas and Brennan. Justices Frankfurter and Harlan concurred, but thought that "the question of which specific safeguards of the Constitution are appropriately to be applied in a particular context overseas can be reduced to the issue of what process is 'due' a defendant in the particular circumstances of a particular case."[68] Thus they maintained that at least in capital cases the jury trial provisions of the Constitution were applicable to overseas civilians. Justices Clark and Burton dissented, stressing the practical problems encountered in maintaining American armed forces in sixty-three foreign countries and contending that wives of servicemen should be deemed to have subjected themselves to the same jurisdiction as those they were accompanying. The Court rejected these contentions and insisted on limiting the powers of the military. The majority stood firmly on the rule that when the United States acts against civilians abroad it can not do so free of the Bill of Rights, but must give them a fair trial and all the procedural rights expressed in the Constitution.[69]

The result of the *Reid* and *Girard* cases was that the Court effectively deprived Congress and the executive of power to discipline by court-martial any member of the civilian entourage which accompanies the United States armed forces overseas in time of peace. Further, the extent of the president's power to enter into the administrative agreements important to the maintenance of U.S. military establishments on foreign soil was substantially limited.[70]

In *Lee v. Madigan*,[71] the Court reviewed a case involving a court-martial under the Articles of War, which had been the official army regulations prior to the adoption of the Uniform Code. The articles provided that "no person shall be tried by court-martial for murder or rape committed within the geographical limits of the States of the Union and the District of Columbia in time of peace." Lee was convicted by court-martial of the crime of conspiracy to commit murder in California on 10 June 1949—after actual cessation of hostilities in 1945 but before the president and Congress had proclaimed the termination of war with Germany and Japan. By a six-to-two vote, the Supreme Court held that the offense had been committed in time of peace, and hence a court-martial had no jurisdiction in the case. Justices Harlan and Clark dissented.[72]

CONCLUSIONS

In dealing with federal criminal prosecutions the Eisenhower justices were in accord in many areas. In search and seizure cases and in those concerned with military law, these justices frequently voted together. Questions of double jeopardy and self-incrimination, on the other hand, produced sharp divisions among the justices. The voting record of the members of the Court reveals that Justices Douglas and Black were the staunchest defenders of the individual against society, while Justice Clark, and formerly Burton, were at the opposite extreme. The Chief Justice showed more disagreement with his fellow activists in this area than in any other, although his record is far above the average of the Court. Justice Brennan voted similarly to Warren in most of the cases in which they were joint participants with two notable exceptions–*Abbate* and *Paoli*.[73] Justices Frankfurter and Stewart were only slightly below the average of the Court on questions of search and seizure, while Stewart and Whittaker were above the average in double jeopardy cases. Harlan was the least libertarian of the middle bloc, and in two significant instances he deserted his fellow Eisenhower appointees to vote with the Court's extreme right.[74] Whittaker defected notably from the middle group in *Giordenello*. Justice Stewart's voting record was identical with that of Whittaker and Clark in military justice cases in which they were joint participants.

In tabular form, the voting record of the justices in thirty-five important cases in this area is as in Table 7.1.

Table 7.1
Voting Records of Supreme Court Justices in 35 Selected Nonunanimous Cases Involving Federal Criminal Prosecutions, 1953–1961 Terms (in percentages)

	Search and Seizure	Double Jeopardy	Self Incrimination	Military Justice	Other	Total
No. of cases	14	6	3	8	4	35
Douglas	93	100	100	100	100	97
Black	79	100	100	100	75	92
Warren	77 (13)	83	67	100 (7)	75	82 (33)
Brennan	72 (12)	67	100 (2)	100 (6)	75	79 (30)
COURT	65	17	0	75	0	46
Stewart	57 (7)	33 (3)	0 (1)	50 (4)	0 (3)	39 (18)
Frankfurter	62 (13)	17	33	43 (7)	25	37 (33)
Whittaker	36 (11)	40 (5)	0 (2)	50 (4)	0 (3)	32 (25)
Harlan	46 (13)	17	0 (2)	38	0	30 (33)
Clark	15	0	0	50	0	17 (35)
Burton	0 (7)	0 (3)	0 (2)	0 (4)	0 (1)	0 (17)

For Claims of the Defendant

Justices Reed, Minton, and Jackson are not included in this table, which represents the
   following cases:

Table 7.1 *(continued)*

Search and seizure cases (14): For defendants' claims (9): *Rea v. U.S.* (1956); *Kremen v. U.S.* (1957); *Miller v. U.S.* (1958); *Jones v. U.S.* (1958); *Giordenello v. U.S.* (1958); *Henry v. U.S.* (1959); *Jones v. U.S.* (1960); *Elkins v. U.S.* (1960); *Rios v. U.S.* (1960).
Against defendants' claims (5): *Walder v. U.S.* (1954); *Rathbun v. U.S.* (1957); *Draper v. U.S.* (1959); *Abel v. U.S.* (1960); *Wilson v. Schnettler* (1961).
Double jeopardy (6): For defendants' claims (2): *Green v. U.S.* (1957); *Ladner v. U.S.* (1958).
Against defendants' claims (4): *Pollard v. U.S.* (1957); *Gore v. U.S.* (1958); *Harris v. U.S.* (1959); *Abbate v. U.S.* (1959).
Self-incrimination (3): Against defendants' claims (3): *Lewis v. U.S.* (1955); *Grunewald v. U.S.* (1959); *Brown v. U.S.* (1959).
Military justice (8): For defendants' claims (6): *Toth v. Quarles* (1955); *Reid v. Covert* (1957); *Lee v. Madigan* (1959); *Kinsella v. Singleton* (1960); *Grisham v. Hagan* (1960); *McElroy v. Guagliardo* (1960).
Against defendants' claims (2): *Kinsella v. Krueger* (1956); *Reid v. Covert* (1956).
Other (4): *Paoli v. U.S.* (1957); *Rosenberg v. U.S.* (1959); *Pittsburgh Plate Glass Company v. U.S.* (1959); *Pugach v. Dollinger* (1961).

NOTES

1. *McNabb v. United States,* 318 U.S. 332 at 340 (1943); see generally, David Fellman, *The Defendant's Rights.*

2. *Harris v. United States,* 331 U.S. 145 at 163 (1947) (dissenting opinion); see also Jacobs, *Justice Frankfurter,* pp. 154–61; Emmerich Handler, "Fourth Amendment, Federalism, and Mr. Justice Frankfurter," 8 *Syracuse L. Rev.* 166 (1957).

3. *United States v. Rabinowitz,* 339 U.S. 51 at 67 (1950) (dissenting opinion) .

4. *Weeks v. United States,* 232 U.S. 383 (1914); see also Yale Kamisar, "*Wolf* and *Lustig* Ten Years Later: Illegal Evidence in State and Federal Courts," 43 *Minn. L. Rev.* 1083 (1959); Comment, "Search and Seizure in the Supreme Court: Shadows on the Fourth Amendment," 28 *U. Chi. L. Rev.* 664 (1961).

5. 350 U.S. 214 (1956).

6. 54 *Mich. L. Rev.* 1177 (1956); 34 *N.C. L. Rev.* 521 (1956); but see 7 *Syracuse L. Rev.* 319 (1956).

7. 350 U.S. 214 at 220–221; see also David J. Bodenhamer, *Fair Trial: Rights of the Accused in American History* (New York: Oxford University Press, 1992), pp. 113–116.

8. 364 U.S. 206 (1960); see also *Rios v. United States,* 364 U.S. 253 (1960); *Abel v. United States,* 362 U.S. 217 (1960).

9. 353 U.S. 346 (1957). Note the amazing appendix at 349; see also 46 *Geo. L. J.* 534 (1958).

10. 357 U.S. 301 (1958).

11. 357 U.S. 493 (1958).

12. 357 U.S. 480 (1958); 27 *Geo. Wash. L. Rev.* 395 (1959).

13. *Henry v. United States,* 361 U.S. 98 (1959).

14. 358 U.S. 307 (1959).

15. See also *Walder v. United States,* 347 U.S. 62 (1954); *Chapman v. United States,* 365 U.S. 610 (1961).

16. 388 U.S. 307 at 315.

17. Ibid.

18. 48 Stat. 1064 (1934).

19. 355 U.S. 96 (1957); see also *Pugach v. Dollinger*, 365 U.S. 458 (1961).

20. Edwin J. Bradley and James E. Hogan, "Wiretapping: From *Nardone* to *Benanti* and *Rathbun*," 46 *Geo. L. J.* 418, 434 (1958); *cf.* 35 *Texas L. Rev.* 856 (1957); 19 *Ohio S. L. J.* 345 (1958); 8 *Syracuse L. Rev.* 317 (1957).

21. 365 U.S. 505 (1961).

22. 355 U.S. 107 (1957); the majority was composed of Warren, Black, Brennan, Harlan, Whittaker, Burton, and Clark.

23. 355 U.S. 107 at 113.

24. 355 U.S. 107 at 108.

25. Bradley and Hogan, p. 442; see also B. J. George, Jr. "The Potent, The Omnipresent Teacher: The Supreme Court and Wiretapping," 47 *Va. L. Rev.* 751 (1961); see also *Jones v. United States*, 362 U.S. 257 (1960).

26. Pritchett, *The American Constitution*, p. 514.

27. 318 U.S. 332 (1943).

28. 48 Stat. 1008 (1934).

29. 354 U.S. 449 (1957); but see *Coppola v. United States* 365 U.S. 762 (1961).

30. 354 U.S. 449 at 456.

31. James E. Hogan and Joseph M. Snee, "The *McNabb–Mallory* Rule: Its Rise, Rationale and Rescue," 47 *Geo. L. J.* 1, 15–16 (1958).

32. House–Senate Conference Amendment to H.R. 11477, 85th Cong., 2d Sess., 23 August 1958.

33. 104 *Cong. Record*, 18093 (daily ed. 25 August 1958).

34. 82 Stat. 210 (1968); 18 U.S.C. sec. 3501(c) (1982).

35. *Lewis v. United States*, 348 U.S. 419 (1955).

36. 26 U.S.C. sec. 3290 (1952).

37. 353 U.S. 391 (1957); the majority was composed of Frankfurter, Harlan, Whittaker, Clark, and Burton.

38. But see 71 *Harv. L. Rev.* 109 (1957); 37 *B.U. L. Rev.* 508 (1957).

39. 359 U.S. 118 (1959).

40. *Curcio v. United States*, 354 U.S. 118 (1957).

41. Schubert, *Constitutional Politics*, pp. 605–609.

42. 347 U.S. 1 (1954); see also *Reina v. United States*, 364 U.S. 507 (1960).

43. *Gori v. United States*, 367 U.S. 364 (1961) (dissenting opinion).

44. *Ladner v. United States*, 358 U.S. 169 (1958).

45. 358 U.S. 415 (1959).

46. 359 U.S. 19 (1959).

47. See generally, Fellman, *The Defendant's Rights*, p. 194.

48. 355 U.S. 184 (1957).

49. 32 *Tul. L. Rev.* 488 (1958); *cf.* 66 *Yale L. J.* 592 (1957).

50. 355 U.S. 184 at 193.

51. 355 U.S. 184 at 187–188.

52. 355 U.S. 184 at 216.

53. 357 U.S. 386 (1958).

54. *But see* 33 *Tul. L. Rev.* 397 (1959).

55. Pritchett, *The American Constitution*, p. 523.

56. See generally, Walter F. Fisher, "Double Jeopardy, Two Sovereignties

and the Intruding Constitution," 28 *U. Chi. L. Rev.* 591 (1961).

57. 359 U.S. 187 (1959).

58. 45 *Cornell L. Q.* 574 (1960); but see 44 *Minn. L. Rev.* 534 (1960); 27 *Tenn. L. Rev.* 412 (1960); see also *Forman v. United States*, 361 U.S. 416 (1960).

59. 64 Stat. 108 (1950); on courts-martial generally, see 51 *Nw. U. L. Rev.* 474 (1956).

60. 350 U.S. 11 (1955).

61. Black, Douglas, Warren, Frankfurter, Harlan, and Clark.

62. See generally, William R. Willis, Jr., "*Toth v. Quarles*—For Better or Worse?" 9 *Vand. L. Rev.* 534 (1956).

63. 354 U.S. 524 (1957). See the Security Treaty with Japan of 8 September 1951, 3 UST and OIA 3329, TIAS No. 2491.

64. 354 U.S. 1 (1957).

65. 71 *Harv. L. Rev.* 150 (1957); 32 *Sw. L. Rev.* 518 (1957).

66. *Kinsella v. Krueger*, 351 U.S. 470 (1956); *Reid v. Covert*, 351 U.S. 487; but see 31 *N.Y.U. L. Rev.* 594 (1957); 9 *Hastings L. J.* 85 (1957).

67. 354 U.S. 1 at 35.

68. 354 U.S. 1 at 75.

69. 6 *J. Pub. L.* 540 (1957); 42 *Minn. L. Rev.* 490, 825 (1958); but see 71 *Harv. L. Rev.* 712 (1957); see also Arthur E. Sutherland, "The Constitution, the Civilian, and Military Justice," 35 *St. John's L. Rev.* 215 (1961).

70. Horn, "The Warren Court and the Discretionary Power of the Executive," p. 663; for detailed analysis of the decisions of the Eisenhower Court in this area, see Ibid., pp. 658–665.

71. 358 U.S. 228 (1959); Justices Stewart, Whittaker, Brennan, Black, Douglas, and Chief Justice Warren composed the majority.

72. The Court followed the *Toth* holding on the question of whether U.S. citizens accompanying armed forces abroad in peacetime could be tried by courts-martial in the companion cases of *McElroy v. United States ex rel. Guagliardo*, 361 U.S. 281 (1960); *Wilson v. Bohlender*, 361 U.S. 281 (1960); *Grisham v. Hagan*, 361 U.S. 278 (1960); *Kinsella v. United States ex rel. Singleton*, 361 U.S. 234 (1960); see Robert D. Duke and Howard S. Vogel, "The Constitution and the Standing Army: Another Problem of Court-Martial Jurisdiction," 13 *Vand. L. Rev.* 435 (1960); 12 *Ala. L. Rev.* 343 (1960); 9 *DePaul L. Rev.* 197 (1960); 26 *Geo. Wash. L. Rev.* 913 (1960); 45 *Ia. L. Rev.* 888 (1960); 20 *La. L. Rev.* 714 (1960).

73. *Paoli v. United States*, 352 U.S. 232 (1957); 56 *Colum. L. Rev.* 1112 (1956); but see 43 *Cornell L. Q.* 128 (1957).

74. In *Rea v. United States* and *Ladner v. United States*.

8

State Procedural Rights

The adoption of the Fourteenth Amendment with its due process and equal protection clauses imposed upon the Court some responsibility over the caliber of criminal justice dispensed in the states. Over the years the Supreme Court interpreted its responsibility more narrowly for standards of criminal justice in state courts than for those in the federal courts. Until the 1960s there had been great controversy as to whether the provisions of the Fourth through the Eighth Amendments were applicable to the states. The historic position, as first stated in *Barron v. Baltimore*[1] in 1833, had been that the Bill of Rights applied to the federal government only, not to the states. The due process clause of the Fourteenth Amendment had been accepted as imposing certain limitations on state judicial procedure which would guarantee a fair hearing before an unbiased and uncoerced tribunal, but in such basic decisions as *Hurtado v. California*,[2] *Maxwell v. Dow*,[3] *Twining v. New Jersey*,[4] and *Palko v. Connecticut*,[5] the Court had held that indictment by grand jury, trial by jury, and protections against self-incrimination and double jeopardy were not such fundamental attributes of a fair trial as to be protected against state action by the due process clause. The result was that practices that would be unconstitutional in federal prosecutions were not necessarily considered as grounds for reversing state convictions.

In 1947, four of the nine justices—Black, Douglas, Murphy, and Rutledge—entertained the idea that the Fourteenth Amendment imposed upon the criminal law of the states all the restrictions contained in the Bill of Rights, but they were never successful in winning over to their views the needed fifth vote.[6] Rather than accepting the total incorporation thesis, the Court majority chose to follow the rule expressed by Justice

Cardozo in *Palko v. Connecticut*[7] that only those provisions of the first eight amendments are applicable to the states which were "implicit in the concept of ordered liberty" as declared by the Supreme Court. The Court then was to adjudge the constitutionality of state fair trial procedures by determining in each case whether the principle of justice involved was "so rooted in the traditions and conscience of our people as to be ranked as fundamental."

Such an approach, according to the exponents of this view, permitted the law and the Constitution to grow to meet new problems.[8] The critics of the *Palko* rule contended that this left due process up to some "natural law" theory of the justices. The idiosyncratic, brow-furrowing, brooding judge would ultimately decide on what he thought was a fundamental right, that is, what he preferred. In response, defenders of the fundamental rights doctrine contended that natural law in the modern world "can be pragmatic and empirical, based upon the basic needs and drives and capacities" of humans.[9]

If due process, in theory, permitted an ever-expanding interpretation of a defendant's rights, another important principle, that of American federalism, tended to counter it. As Professor William Beaney noted, the rejection by the Supreme Court of a state court's definition of the scope of federal commerce power was vastly different from a high court ruling that a state had violated due process in administering its own system of criminal justice.[10]

Obviously due process cannot be fully defined in a neat catchall rule. Perhaps Judge Learned Hand expressed it best when he stated that it embodies the English sporting sense of fair play.[11] In trial procedures, advocates of the "fundamental rights" theory contended that due process was not concerned with the making of policy but rather with the fair enforcement of it. Whereas policy questions are open to doubt and differences of opinion, questions of procedures invoke more certainty. In the words of Justice Brandeis, procedural "fundamentals do not change; centuries of thought have established standards."[12] Essentially the Anglo-American tradition of due process requires a fair hearing for a person charged with an offense and a decent opportunity to defend himself. This is one of the major foundations of the American tradition of personal liberty. It is most highly developed in the oldest form of public action, the criminal prosecution.[13] To Justice Frankfurter, the question of whether a state conviction was consistent with the requirements of due process imposed upon the Court "an exercise of judgment upon the whole course of the proceedings in order to ascertain whether they offend those canons of decency and fairness which express the notions of justice of English-speaking peoples even toward those charged with the most heinous offenses."[14] Or in the more earthy language of Justice Holmes, state administration of criminal law offends due process "if it makes you vomit."[15]

The Eisenhower Court was to formulate a third view of the appropriate relationship between the Fourteenth Amendment and the Bill of Rights, combining aspects of both the fundamental rights and the total incorporation interpretations.[16] This approach, called "selective incorporation," was to provide the theoretical basis for the Supreme Court's incorporating almost all provisions of the Bill of Rights to apply to the states during the 1960s. The Eisenhower Court also was to revitalize, after more than a decade of dormancy, the use of incorporation to protect individual rights from encroachment by the states and to actually incorporate Fourth Amendment protections—the beginning of what was to be called the "due process revolution" in the later Warren Court era of the mid- and late-1960s. The evolution of selective incorporation begins in the cases of the Eisenhower Court dealing with state criminal prosecutions.

DOUBLE JEOPARDY AND THE SAME OFFENSE DOCTRINE

Although the rejection of the total incorporation theory by the high tribunal appeared clearly settled, the Eisenhower Court during the 1958 term found it necessary to reiterate in detail its holdings in the matter. This occurred in *Bartkus v. Illinois*,[17] where the Court, by a five-to-four vote, ruled that a man acquitted by a federal court on a bank robbery charge and subsequently convicted on the same charge by a state court had not been subjected to double jeopardy. Justice Frankfurter, for the majority, found that cooperation of federal and state officials in this case did not violate the double jeopardy clause nor due process.[18] The opinion of the Court stated that it was established "conclusively that Congress and the members of the Legislatures of the ratifying States did not contemplate that the Fourteenth Amendment was a shorthand incorporation of the first eight amendments making them applicable as explicit restrictions upon the States."[19] Speaking for Justices Harlan, Whittaker, Stewart, and Clark, Frankfurter restated the *Palko* rule, contending that due process bars procedures which shock "the conscience of society ascertained as best it may be by a tribunal disciplined for the task and environed by the best safeguards for disinterestedness and detachment."[20]

The dissents in this case were important. Justice Black contended that the fact that a single act may violate the laws of two sovereigns does not diminish the harmful impact on the individual caused by successive trials. He appeared to advance the idea that at least part of the Fifth Amendment should be incorporated into the Fourteenth, and he was joined by Justice Douglas and Chief Justice Warren in this dissent. Justice Brennan, who had been in the majority in the federal double jeopardy case, *Abbate v. United States*,[21] dissented in *Bartkus* in a separate opinion on the ground that federal participation in the subsequent state trial rendered it a second federal prosecution. The dissenters found the double jeopardy prosecutions constitutionally repulsive, particularly when the federal government, after losing a case, helps a state try the person for the same offense.

The year before, Justices Black and Douglas, in another double jeopardy case, had argued that *Palko* ought to be overruled. In *Hoag v. New Jersey*,[22] a man who was alleged to have robbed five tavern patrons was tried for the robbery of three of them, and was acquitted because of the unexpected failure of four of the state's witnesses to identify the defendant. The state then tried Hoag for robbery of a fourth patron, who was the only witness at the first trial to identify the defendant. This time the jury convicted him. By a five-to-three vote the Supreme Court upheld the state's action on the ground that, while a single trial would have been "preferable practice," the Fourteenth Amendment did not lay down an inflexible rule making multiple trials unconstitutional, and the circumstances of this case did not result in "fundamental unfairness." Had this been a federal prosecution, the doctrine of collateral estoppel, which can arise only after a valid final judgment, would have prevented relitigation of issues already determined.[23] Yet collateral estoppel sometimes provides little practical help to a defendant because of the difficulty in determining what issues were in fact resolved by a prior general verdict of not guilty or guilty of a lesser included offense.[24] In federal prosecutions this was a determination of law made by the judge after examining the record in the first trial. This procedure was accepted by the New Jersey court in *Hoag*, but the trial judge was unable to determine what issues had actually been decided by the jury. In refusing to upset this ruling, the Supreme Court held collateral estoppel inapplicable as a defense. Justice Douglas, in a dissent joined by Justice Black, argued that making a man "run the gauntlet twice" violated the Fourteenth Amendment and hence *Palko* ought to be overruled. Chief Justice Warren, also dissenting, thought that the state had relitigated "the same issue on the same evidence before two different juries."[25]

A similar decision was reached by a five-to-four vote in *Ciucci v. Illinois*.[26] Here again, the defendant, without protection of collateral estoppel, was tried on four separate murder indictments. The initial prosecution for one of the murders brought conviction and a twenty-year sentence. The prosecutor, dissatisfied with this result, instituted a second trial for another of the murders, which brought a forty-five-year sentence. A third effort was then made by the state, which finally resulted in a death sentence. The Supreme Court upheld these tactics, maintaining that under Illinois law each offense was separate although they were committed at the same time. Justices Douglas, Black, and Brennan and the Chief Justice dissented contending that this was "an unseemly and oppressive use" of criminal procedure.

The Court also ruled in *Williams v. Oklahoma*[27] that the Fourteenth Amendment did not prevent a state from inflicting capital punishment upon a defendant who pleaded guilty to a kidnapping charge after he had already been sentenced to life imprisonment upon his plea of guilty to a charge of murder. Williams had kidnapped and murdered the same victim and had pleaded guilty to both charges. Justice Douglas dissented alone in this case.

The trend in these double jeopardy cases appeared to allow the national government and the states great leeway in trying persons twice for a single act. The argument that when a wrongdoer was convicted of two violations for a single act, the penalty imposed for the first was taken into account in fixing the second was not convincing. The cases reviewed in this and the previous chapter reveal that this account-taking might produce a stiffer penalty on the second attempt. In *Ciucci, Hoag, Abbate*, and *Bartkus*, the Court appeared to be saying that a person might be tried and punished more than once for the same act simply because ours is a federal system. To some observers this was a misuse of the concept of federalism by the Court and a misreading of "the traditions and conscience of our people."[28]

The underlying policy against successive trials for the same act is that an individual should not be subjected to repeated expense and anxiety. The need for protection seems especially acute in cases like *Abbate* and *Bartkus* in which the individual was faced not only with the resources of one government in successive trials, but with the combined strength of both state and federal governments, which often cooperated against the accused in each trial. There was the further possibility that, in an effort to avoid the double jeopardy protection, the second proceeding would be encouraged by the disappointed sovereign that failed to gain a conviction in the first trial. In addition, two prosecutions for the same act increased the burden on the courts.

On the other hand, these decisions might be justifiable on the ground that there are areas of conduct in which both state and federal governments have legitimate interests to protect and over which concurrent jurisdiction must exist. The weight of precedent and tradition in the United States was strongly behind this view, which appeared to be that of the Court's majority.

The double jeopardy guaranty doctrine was in a state of considerable confusion. Reform by statute would be an important corrective step. A requirement that the prosecutor try the defendant at one time for all offenses growing out of the same transaction would be a valid one.[29] The power to harass a defendant through successive prosecutions for technically separate offenses growing out of the same illegal action is not forbidden by the wording of the double jeopardy clause, but it is inconsistent with its spirit and purpose. In 1969, in *Benton v. Maryland*, the Supreme Court finally overturned *Palko* and held that the double jeopardy provision of the Fifth Amendment is fundamental to our constitutional heritage and enforceable against the states through the Fourteenth Amedment.[30]

FOURTH AMENDMENT QUESTIONS AND THE STATES

In three important cases prior to 1961 dealing with alleged illegal searches and seizures in the states, the Eisenhower Court caused something of a furor.[31] Involved also in these cases was the guaranty of the Fifth Amendment that no person "shall be compelled in any criminal case to be a witness against himself."

The Supreme Court had never made a definitive ruling on the application of the unreasonable search and seizure requirements of the Fourth Amendment to the states until 1949 in *Wolf v. Colorado*.[32] The Court held that freedom from unreasonable search and seizure is an essential element in the concept of "ordered liberty," and as such was entitled to Fourteenth Amendment protection against state action. However, the Court, at the same time, ruled that evidence secured illegally could be used in state trials, which meant that it would be extremely difficult to enforce the prohibition against unreasonable searches and seizures against the states.[33]

In its first term, the Eisenhower Court was required to interpret the *Wolf* rule in *Irvine v. California*.[34] In that case, the police entered the home of a suspected bookmaker, while he was away, and had a locksmith make a key to his door. Two days later they entered the house with the key and installed a concealed microphone, having bored a hole in the roof through which wires were strung to a neighboring garage, where officers were posted with listening apparatuses. Twice later, they reentered the house to move the microphone into better positions. At the trial, these officers were allowed to testify to conversations they had heard transmitted.

For the five-man majority, Justice Jackson said that this was trespass, and probably a burglary, but to make a distinction between *Wolf* and this case "would leave the rule so indefinite that no state court could know what it should rule in order to keep its processes on solid constitutional ground."[35] The Court adhered to the *Wolf* doctrine stating that there was no basis for denying the state's right to get a conviction by the use of such methods. Wrote Jackson: "All that was heard through the microphone was what an eavesdropper, hidden in the hall, the bedroom, or the closet, might have heard."

If Irvine had been denied a right secured to him by the Fourteenth Amendment, Justice Jackson, joined by Chief Justice Warren, contended that he could bring suit against the state officers involved for having violated the federal criminal code, which makes it an offense for a person acting under the color of law to deprive "any inhabitant of any state" of rights protected by the federal Constitution.[36] They thought that "the Clerk of this Court should be directed to forward a copy of the record in this case, together with a copy of this opinion, for attention of the Attorney General of the United States."[37]

The other seven members of the Court would not associate themselves with such a scheme. Justice Clark concurred in the interest of certainty and predictability of the law although he stated that had he been on the Court at the time of the *Wolf* decision, he would have voted to make the federal rule of exclusion applicable to state court proceedings. Justice Black, joined in dissent by Justice Douglas, maintained that the proposed action was "inconsistent with my own view of the judicial function in our government. Prosecution, or anything approaching it, should, I think, be left to government officers whose duty that is."[38] To Justice Douglas, "The search and seizure conducted in this case smack of the police state, not the free America the Bill of Rights envisaged." He urged that the Court "should be alert to see that no unconstitutional evidence is used to convict any person in Amerca."[39]

The author of the *Wolf* opinion, Justice Frankfurter, dissented, contending that the rule in that case did not apply here since there was "additional aggravating conduct which the Court finds repulsive." Although there had been no physical violence in *Irvine*, there had been "a more powerful and offensive control over the Irvines' life."[40] This control enabled the police "to hear every word that was said in the Irvine household for more than a month." Frankfurter, rejecting an inflexible view of due process, contended:

> Surely the Court does not propose to announce a new absolute, namely, that even the most reprehensible means for securing a conviction will not taint a verdict so long as the body of the accused was not touched by State officials. Considering the progress that scientific devices are making in extracting evidence without violence or bodily harm, satisfaction of due process would depend on the astuteness and subtlety with which the police engage in offensive practices and drastically invade privacy without authority of law.[41]

The basic purpose of the Fourth Amendment was to achieve a balance between two strong and frequently competing objectives of American government—society's deep concern for the individual's right of privacy and its interest in the prompt and effective apprehension of criminals. The Fourth Amendment was drawn up to allow the accommodation of the two by interposing between the effective apprehension of crime and the unwarranted disruption of one's privacy, the requirement of seeking a magistrate, before whom the law enforcement officials must appear and show cause for making the intrusion. If this is done, a warrant can be issued justifying the search and seizure with such incidental deprivation of privacy as is required in the circumstances. The major cases in this field usually involve criminals and other social misfits. When a case, involving the deep public interest of privacy on the one hand and criminal law administration on the other, places a criminal in the center of attention, it is easy for society and even the courts to lose sight of the first of these interests. This was especially true where state courts permitted the introduction of evidence in criminal cases without regard for the legality of the means by which it was obtained—a practice unwisely condoned in *Irvine* by the Supreme Court.[42]

In *Breithaupt v. Abram*,[43] the body of the accused was touched by state officials—using a hypodermic needle. A truck driven by Breithaupt in New Mexico collided with another car and three persons were killed. An almost empty pint whisky bottle was found in the glove compartment of the truck. Breithaupt, seriously injured, was taken to a hospital unconscious. When liquor was detected on his breath, and while he was still unconscious, the police directed a doctor to take a sample of his blood by the use of a hypodermic needle. Testimony regarding the blood test was admitted in evidence at the trial, and an expert gave his opinion that the amount of alcohol found in the blood was sufficient to indicate intoxication.

By a six-to-three vote the Court upheld the conviction. Justice Clark, writing for the majority, pointed out that there was nothing "brutal" or "offensive" in the taking of a sample of blood under the protective eye of a physician.[44] Since blood tests were "routine," they did not shock the conscience or offend the sense of justice. The Court also felt that the absence of conscious consent did not necessarily render the taking a violation of a constitutional right, since even the most delicate person would not consider a test so administered to be offensive. Intoxication being one of the reasons for the "increasing slaughter on our highways," the interests of society in reducing these hazards outweighed "so slight an intrusion" on the person.[45]

The Chief Justice, joined by Justices Black and Douglas, could not distinguish this case from *Rochin v. California*,[46] in which the Court had excluded evidence pumped from the stomach of the defendant. In both cases a doctor performed the operation in a hospital, using "scientific" methods to extract body fluids in such a manner as to cause no lasting ill effects. In both instances evidence that had been obtained from a man on an involuntary basis was used to convict him. Force was used on Rochin, but this was not necessary with Breithaupt since he was unconscious. In a separate dissent, Justice Douglas maintained that inserting a needle into an unconscious person in order to get evidence necessary to convict him was a repulsive police assault.

From this case, it can be seen that due process was indeed a wavering line. Decisions appeared to depend on the judges' "personal reaction to the stomach pump and blood test." In the words of Chief Justice Warren: "To base the restriction which the Due Process Clause imposes on state criminal procedures upon such reactions is to build on shifting sands." The Chief Justice proposed a definite understanding that due process forbade law enforcement officers to get evidence by "bruising the body, breaking skin, puncturing tissue or extracting body fluids, whether they contemplate doing it by force or by stealth."[47]

In the 1959 case, *Frank v. Maryland*,[48] the Court sustained the conviction of a homeowner under a local health code for resisting a health officer's mid-afternoon inspection of his dwelling without a warrant after the officer had found evidence of rodent infestation of the property. For the five-justice majority, Justice Frankfurter emphasized that the inspection had been attempted at a convenient time in the middle of the day and after the health inspector had already found outside evidence of rodent infestation. In these circumstances, the constitutional "liberty" the homeowner had asserted was "the absolute right to refuse consent for an inspection designed and pursued solely for the protection of the community's health."[49] No evidence for criminal prosecution was sought in such an inspection, the opinion pointed out. The homeowner was simply directed to do what he could have been ordered to do without inspection—remedy a situation that creates a hazard to the health of the community.[50] According to Justice Frankfurter such an "inspection without a warrant, as an adjunct to a regulatory scheme for the general welfare of the community and not as a means of enforcing the criminal law, has antecedents deep in our history." "Certainly," he added, "the nature of our society has not vitiated the need for inspection first thought necessary 158 years ago, nor has experience revealed any abuse or inroad on freedom in meeting this need by means that history and dominant opinion have sanctioned."[51] Justice Whittaker concurred on the ground that the search was not unreasonable under the Fourth Amendment.

The dissenters—Justices Douglas, Black, and Brennan and the Chief Justice—contended that the Court's opinion "greatly dilutes the right of privacy which every homeowner had the right to believe was part of our American heritage. We witness an inquest over a substantial part of the Fourth Amendment."[52] The minority thought that a search warrant could have easily been procured and should have been. They cited the practice of Great Britain that required health officers to secure a warrant before proceeding with similar inspections.

It would seem that the function of the Fourth Amendment is to protect the right of privacy as such and not primarily to protect against self-incrimination. If the guarantees of this amendment are to give way to community needs, they should do so only on a clear showing of need. According to the dissenters, there was no such showing in *Frank*. Ironically, the Court's holding in *Frank* meant that people suspected of criminal activity had a constitutional right to object to warrantless searches of their homes, while no such right existed for those not suspected of crime but who merely objected to health inspectors entering. A few years later the Warren Court placed some limits on administrative inspections, but adopted lowered standards to justify a warrant. [53]

In 1961 the Eisenhower Court, in its most important criminal procedure case, overruled *Wolf v. Colorado* and applied the exclusionary rule to the states. In *Mapp v. Ohio*, the Court completed the incorporation of Fourth Amendment protections into the due process clause of the Fourteenth Amendment and concluded that the exclusionary rule, by removing the incentive to disregard the Fourth Amendment, constituted "the only effectively available way . . . to compel respect for the constitutional guarantee."[54] Justice Clark, writing for a five-justice majority, maintained that the exclusionary rule would deter unlawful conduct by the government, provide effective protection to a person's constitutional right to privacy under the Fourth Amendment, eliminate the double standard practiced by the federal government and the states, and preserve judicial integrity by forcing the government to obey its own laws. In a separate concurrence, Justice Black advanced the novel idea that the exclusionary rule was required by a combination of the Fourth Amendment and Fifth Amendment's ban against compelled self-incrimination.

The three dissenters, Harlan, Frankfurter, and Whittaker (all of whom had dissented in *Elkins*), rejected the incorporation doctrine and refused to extend the *Weeks* exclusionary rule to the "sovereign judicial system" of the states. Justice Stewart, who had written the *Elkins* opinion, filed a separate memorandum stating that he could not join the majority because the exclusionary rule issue had not been properly presented to the Court.

Civil libertarians applauded the decision. The Washington, D.C. attorney and future Supreme Court justice, Abe Fortas, called *Mapp* "the most radical decision in recent times."[55]

Mapp was criticized for putting a straitjacket on state and local law enforcement officials (a complaint that was to be heard about most of the subsequent landmark criminal law decisions of the Warren Court). It required half of the states to change their laws and behavior and to comply with a federal rule. *Mapp* also was significant in signaling a change in direction in Supreme Court criminal law cases. For a quarter-century before *Mapp*, virtually all criminal procedure cases had been thinly disguised race cases coming from the South. After *Mapp*, the Court's decisions were concerned with nationwide rules—not just those affecting Southern practices.[56]

Furthermore, the genie of incorporation was out of the bottle that had been stoppered for over a decade. Although the advocates of total incorporation could not win the constitutional battles, they were not too disappointed in the outcome of the constitutional war. That war was to produce the Warren Court's "due process revolution" that would nationalize the Bill of Rights and put to new uses the "fundamental rights" doctrine as an aspect of "selective incorporation." By 1961 the due process revolution was under way, and the Eisenhower Court had discarded the silver platter doctrine and applied the exclusionary rule to state criminal trials—a great leap forward for a Court previously immobilized in thickets of federalism.

SELF-INCRIMINATION IN THE STATES

In the early 1960s, the Fifth Amendment's ban on self-incrimination did not carry through to the state level to prevent the drawing of unfavorable inferences from a defendant's failure to take the witness stand in a criminal prosecution.[57] Nor, according to Supreme Court decisions, did it protect a person who refused to give testimony before a state body which might lead to a federal prosecution for any state crime he might confess.[58] There were statutes that granted witnesses complete immunity from prosecution for any act regarding which the witness might be required to testify before certain regulatory agencies. Such acts, if they granted total immunity from prosecution, were constitutional. When a witness appeared before a congressional investigating committee in response to a summons served upon him and gave self-incriminating testimony, the use of this testimony against him in a federal or state prosecution was barred by act of Congress.[59] Thus in *Adams v. Maryland*,[60] the Eisenhower Court unanimously reversed the conviction in a state court of a gambling business operator that had been based on his testimony before the Senate Kefauver committee investigating crime

In *Knapp v. Schweitzer*,[61] a divided Court held that the Fifth Amendment did not protect a person who refused to give testimony before a state grand jury which might lead to a federal prosecution. Knapp had refused to answer questions in the course of a New York grand jury inquiry into labor racketeering because the state immunity law did not give him immunity from federal prosecution, and he alleged that his answers would expose him to prosecution under the Taft–Hartley Act. Speaking for the Court, Justice Frankfurter noted that Knapp's position carried dangerous implications, since it could lead to the contention that when Congress enacts a criminal statute it has as a practical matter withdrawn from the states their traditional power to investigate in aid of prosecuting conventional state crimes wherever some facts may relate to a federal offense. This was contrary to the historic distribution of powers between state and nation in our federal system.[62] For Justice Black, joined by the Chief Justice and Justice Douglas in dissent, such a procedure by which a man could be led to incriminate himself was an "intolerable state of affairs" that was not a necessary part of our federal system."[63]

Knapp's dilemma was that his agreeing to testify could bring conviction in federal court, but his refusal to testify risked state imprisonment for contempt of court. It was not until 1964 that a unanimous Court held that one jurisdiction within the federal system might not compel witnesses (who have been granted immunity) to give testimony that might incriminate them under the laws of another jurisdiction.[64]

In the 1958 term, the same voting lineup of *Knapp* affirmed a contempt conviction before a state grand jury where full immunity from state prosecution had been denied.[65] Mills and others had claimed the federal privilege against self-incrimination since their testimony would expose them to federal prosecution for violation of income tax laws.[66] In the same term, the Court affirmed the contempt conviction of a private detective who refused to answer questions for a judge in grand-jury-like proceedings on the ground that his counsel had been forced to remain outside.[67] The five-justice majority pointed out that this practice was customary under New York law. Justice Brennan joined the three dissenters of the *Mills* case in maintaining that due process had been offended.

In 1961 in *Cohen v. Hurley*, the Court, in a five-to-four decision, again affirmed that the states were not bound by the Fifth Amendment's privilege against self-incrimination.[68] In *Cohen*, a lawyer was called to testify and produce records in a judicial inquiry in a New York court. Relying primarily on the privilege against self-incrimination, he refused to answer questions about his alleged professional misconduct even though he was warned that his silence might result in "serious consequences." Solely on the ground of his refusal to cooperate in the court's inquiry, the lawyer was disbarred, and the Court held that this disciplinary action did not violate his rights under the Fourteenth Amendment.

The most significant aspect of the case, however, was Justice Brennan's dissenting opinion (joined by the Chief Justice). Brennan advanced the doctrine of selective incorporation of Bill of Rights' protections to apply to the states. Citing "fundamental rights" interpretations, Brennan said that "stopping short of the incorporation of the full sweep of the specific [protection] being absorbed" made the process "a license to the judiciary to administer a watered-down, subjective version of the individual guarantees of the Bill of Rights" when state cases came before the Court. He found this indefensible and would have held "that the full sweep of the Fifth Amendment privilege [against self-incrimination] has been absorbed in the Fourteenth Amendment. In that view the protection it affords the individual . . . against the State, has the same scope as that against the National Government." Brennan's doctrine of recognizing the incorporation of substantive and procedural rights that were "of the very essence of a scheme of ordered liberty" focused "on the total right guaranteed by the individual amendment and not merely on the element of that right before the Court or the application of that right in a particular case."[69] Thus, Brennan, the coalition builder, combined elements of both the fundamental rights and the total incorporation interpretations into a synthesized theory that might be supported by justices who were not won over to either of the old alternatives. The doctrine of selective incorporation resembled the fundamental rights' doctrine in its willingness to distinguish what is essential to due process from what is not. Further refined during succeeding terms of the Court, selective incorporation became the modus operandi of the Warren Court in its due process revolution that led to the incorporation of nine Bill of Rights' protections dealing with criminal procedure that were applied to the states between 1962 and 1969. Through this case-by-case process virtually all of the important safeguards of Amendments Four through Eight have been incorporated and applied to the states.

CONFESSIONS IN STATE CRIMINAL PROCEEDINGS

In reviewing federal convictions, the Supreme Court acts on the basis of particular provisions of the Bill of Rights, the provisions of federal statutes, the Federal Rules of Criminal Procedure, and the responsibility of the Court for "establishing and maintaining civilized standards of procedure and evidence" in the inferior federal courts. Convictions in state courts, however, are governed by different considerations.

The unconstitutionality under the Fourteenth Amendment of using physical violence or brutality to obtain confessions in the states is a firmly established principle of constitutional law.[70] The Supreme Court experienced difficulty, however, in determining what was coercion when the pressures were mental rather than physical. The Vinson Court, after 1949, evidenced a tendency to weaken the protective doctrines established by the Court during the New Deal era.[71] The Eisenhower Court, in several sharply divided decisions, indicated that there was a basic difference in the high Court's authority when reviewing federal convictions and those from the states, which lead the justices to follow a different approach in the two types of cases in answering the question of whether a confession has in fact been secured by coercion.

In its 1953 term, the Eisenhower Court invalidated a confession gained through amazing police tactics in *Leyra v. Denno*.[72] Here, a New Yorker suspected of having murdered his parents with a hammer was questioned intensively for three days. When he complained of a painful sinus condition, the police brought in a "doctor" who was a state-employed psychiatrist, highly skilled in hypnosis, to "help him." After an hour and a half, Leyra, completely exhausted from his ordeal, was beginning to accept suggestions of his guilt from the psychiatrist, who called in the police to take his confession, which he subsequently repeated to his business partner. A tape recorder set up in the next room provided the court with a record of what was said. The New York courts rejected the confession to the psychiatrist as a form of mental coercion but admitted the later confession. Justices Black, Douglas, Frankfurter, Clark, and the Chief Justice rejected all the confessions as parts of one continuous process,[73] during which "an alleged physically and emotionally exhausted suspect's ability to resist interrogation was broken to almost trance-like submission by use of the arts of a highly skilled psychiatrist."[74] Justices Minton, Reed, and Burton dissented, maintaining that these procedures were "in keeping with the fundamental essentials of justice which are due process."[75]

In *Fikes v. Alabama*,[76] the Court, by a six-to-three vote, found invalid the confession of an African-American of low mentality who had been subject to intermittent questioning. For the Court, the Chief Justice held "that the circumstances of pressure applied against the power of resistance of this petitioner, who cannot be deemed other than weak of will or mind, deprived him of due process of law."[77] Justice Frankfurter's concurrence emphasized that no single factor would justify a reversal, but rather that it was the combination of circumstances that warranted the conclusion that this course of conduct fell below standards of due process.[78] For the three dissenters, Justice Harlan stressed the absence of brutality or physical coercion, the intermittent character of the interrogation during normal hours, the fact that the defendant's mental condition was before the jury, and the fact that the absence of arraignment was not unusual in Alabama. He justified his conclusion on the premise that the corrective power of the Supreme Court over state criminal cases was narrower than its power over the lower federal courts.

Similarly in *Payne v. Arkansas*,[79] the Court rejected the conviction of a mentally dull African-American youth who had been arrested without warrant, denied a preliminary hearing before a magistrate, uninformed about his right to remain silent, held incommunicado for three days, denied food for long periods of time, and threatened with mob action. The Court ruled that this torture of the mind could affect one's will as much as physical torture, and hence a confession secured under such circumstances was obviously coerced.

In *Thomas v. Arizona*,[80] however, the Court, by a five-to-four vote, upheld a confession as "a spontaneous exclamation of a guilty conscience." Thomas was a mature man of at least normal intelligence and had some previous experiences in law enforcement proceedings. There was no evidence of a physical beating, no continuous relay questioning, no incommunicado detention, or psychiatric inducement. The Chief Justice and Justices Black, Douglas, and Brennan dissented without opinion.

The Court likewise sustained a conviction resting on a confession in *Ashdown v. Utah*,[81] where it found that the police interview had been temperate and courteous, and the emotional distress of the accused could be attributed to remorse rather than to any coercive conduct on the part of the officers. Mrs. Ashdown, suspected of having poisoned her late husband, was taken to the sheriff's office and questioned for five hours, during which time her relatives were not allowed to see her and their proposal to bring a lawyer was not granted. Only Justices Black[82] and Douglas dissented from this opinion.

From these cases it can be seen that the justices were especially sympathetic to defendants who were youthful, inexperienced, ignorant, or members of minority groups. In many of the cases, a denial of due process was found in the combination of two or more illegal features, rather than any one. Refusal to allow communication by defendants with friends or family, failure to arraign promptly, long periods of questioning, lack of advice as to their rights, and other deficiencies were frequently found in the same case. The important distinction between review of federal and state cases by the Supreme Court at that time was that any one of the illegal official actions would normally upset a federal conviction.

Building upon cases involving coerced confessions, self-incrimination, and right to counsel, the Warren Court in 1966 handed down the *Miranda* ruling that required law enforcement officials to inform persons in custody of their rights—before interrogation. Included in the warning was the right to remain silent, to be informed that anything said might be used in court, the right to consult with an attorney and to have a lawyer present during interrogation, and the right to have a lawyer appointed if the accused was indigent.[83]

RIGHT TO COUNSEL

Federal and state cases also evinced a difference in result when a defendant's right to counsel was involved. The Sixth Amendment assures such a right in federal criminal proceedings, and the Supreme Court has maintained a high standard in this respect. For the states, however, there was no such binding provision in the Fourteenth Amendment. Whether the right to counsel would be enforced by the Court against the states depended upon the facts of each case and the Court's interpretation of due process. Cases involving indigent defendants were especially vexing for the Court. Again, the line determining the essence of ordered liberty was a wavy one.

In capital cases, the Supreme Court held in *Powell v. Alabama* in 1932 that the due process clause of the Fourteenth Amendment requires the appointment of counsel for someone accused of a capital crime.[84] In 1942 in *Betts v. Brady*, however, the Court ruled that a state's refusal to appoint counsel for an indigent in a criminal proceeding did not deny due process.[85] According to the *Betts* rule, only if a defendant was young, ignorant, or inexperienced, or the case was complex, or if other "special circumstances" were present, was the state required to appoint counsel. On the other hand, the Court had ruled that the state might refuse to appoint counsel for mature criminal defendants in simple, noncapital cases. The Eisenhower Court was sharply divided in several cases involving this right in state proceedings.[86]

In its first term, the Eisenhower Court unanimously decided that when a defendant appeared for trial without a lawyer and asked the court for a continuance to get one, the trial judge violated due process by denying this request.[87] Two years later, the Court maintained that due process is not lost to a defendant even though it is not invoked for eight years.[88] In 1945 in Pennsylvania, Herman pleaded guilty to thirty charges and was sentenced to a long-term imprisonment. Eight years later, he filed a petition for a writ of habeas corpus alleging that his plea of guilty had been coerced and that he had not been represented by counsel and had not been informed of his right to counsel. Herman was twenty-one at the time of his arrest, had received only six years schooling, and had had little previous experience with criminal procedure. He alleged that he was held incommunicado for three days, during which time police had threatened him and subjected him to seventy-two hours of intermittent questioning, and that neither the judge nor the prosecutor informed him of the seriousness of the charges. The district attorney filed an answer denying all the allegations and arguing that the petitioner was tardy in making this challenge. The court accordingly dismissed Herman's petition summarily without a hearing. The Supreme Court agreed by unanimous vote that the petitioner was entitled to a hearing. Justice Black pointed to several alleged violations of due process including the coerced confession, the lack of an intelligent and understanding waiver of counsel, and the need for counsel for the fair protection of rights. He added that where a denial of a constitutional right is alleged in an appropriate proceeding, a habeas corpus petition should not be dismissed summarily merely on the denial of a state prosecuting attorney. Since there was great dispute as to the facts material to a determination of the constitutional question involved, this dispute should be decided only after a hearing. The mere fact that there had been thirty charges against him gives strong indication that a layman would be in need of the expert advice of counsel. Finally it was held that the passage of eight years before filing for habeas corpus was immaterial, since one never loses his remedy if held in flagrant violation of constitutional rights.

In re Groban,[89] decided in 1957 by a five-to-four vote, involved the right to assistance of counsel for a witness in a hearing before a state fire marshal investigating the causes of a fire. The Court held that the right to assistance from counsel was not required in such cases. For the majority, Justice Reed stated that the right did not extend to an administrative investigation which was not a criminal trial, just as there was no constitutional right to counsel before grand juries or other investigating bodies.[90] Until actual trial, the witness might protect himself with the privilege against self-incrimination. Two of the majority, Justices Frankfurter and Harlan, in a concurring opinion, suggested that a different conclusion might follow if the case involved denial of counsel where secret inquisitional powers of a district attorney were used against a criminal suspect.

For the four dissenters, again Black, Douglas, Warren, and Brennan, Justice Black strongly objected to compulsory secret examinations and insisted that the right to counsel was vital at a pretrial examination because what happens there may well assure a conviction. The privilege against self-incrimination was not enough, according to Justice Black, because the average witness did not know how to plead it, and under Ohio law, officers were not required to inform the witness on the subject.[91]

It would appear that the ruling of the Court would be correct where investigations were used to obtain information to govern future action and were not proceedings in which action was taken against anyone. The analogy to the traditional grand jury proceedings here seems overpowering. Where, however, the investigation is an inquiry into specific statutory violations that are directed at a particular individual and the evidence adduced therein may be used at the subsequent adjudication, this theory might be questioned.

Justice Reed's replacement on the Court, Justice Whittaker, cast his vote with the *Groban* dissenters to form the majority in the next term in *Moore v. Michigan*.[92] The Court found that there had been no competent and intelligent waiver of the right to counsel. The accused, a seventeen-year-old African-American with a seventh-grade education pleaded guilty to a murder charge after lengthy interrogation and after stating that he did not desire counsel. Justice Brennan, speaking for the Court, found that there had been questions of considerable technical difficulty raised during the proceedings which were obviously beyond the understanding of the accused and that he needed help with regard to the question of the degree of murder involved. The accused had been instructed to plead guilty by the sheriff because there was high tension in the community. While the trial court held as a fact that there were no threats of mob violence, this was regarded as immaterial since the accused, held in confinement, had no way of knowing what was happening in the community. The majority thus held that a rejection of a federal constitutional right because of fear could not be regarded as an intelligent waiver. For the four dissenters, Justice Burton argued that the issue was one of fact, regarding events that had occurred nineteen years ago, on which the state courts had ruled with ample evidence to support their position.

In *Cash v. Culver*,[93] the Court was again unanimous in rejecting a state denial of a writ of habeas corpus for a twenty-year-old, uneducated, inexperienced burglar suspect. Cash had been denied the right to have counsel appointed for him and had also been denied a request for continuance to give him time to get a lawyer. The Court, speaking through Justice Stewart, contended that this denied due process.

Likewise in *Spano v. New York*,[94] the Court unanimously held that the state denied due process when it questioned a foreign-born, twenty-five-year-old murder suspect for eight continuous hours before gaining a confession. Spano, who had only a junior high school education and no previous criminal record, was denied an opportunity to consult counsel. For the Court, the Chief Justice contended that Spano's will had been overborne by official pressure, fatigue, and sympathy falsely aroused. Justice Douglas wrote in a concurring opinion, in which Justices Black and Brennan joined, that denying the accused counsel prior to trial had violated due process. Justice Stewart also concurred with a separate opinion, joined by Justices Douglas and Brennan, maintaining that the confession was not admissible since counsel was not present when it was elicited. The Court's decision in *Spano* set the stage for the later Warren Court ruling in *Escobedo v. Illinois* that also invalidated a confession gained as a result of extended police questioning without the suspect's attorney being present.[95] *Escobedo* in turn was the progenitor of the Court's *Miranda* warnings.

The Eisenhower Court decided that the right to counsel during interrogation was another thing altogether. In *Crooker v. California*,[96] the Court held, by a five-to-four vote, that the fact that the police had refused to permit the accused to get in touch with his lawyer did not render the confession secured during his interrogation involuntary. Crooker confessed to murder only after he had asked for, and was denied by his official interrogators, the opportunity to phone his lawyer. According to Justice Clark, a state's denial of counsel violated due process only if the accused was deprived of counsel at the trial on the merits, or if lack of counsel in pretrial proceedings was so prejudicial as to infect the subsequent trial with fundamental unfairness.[97] In this case the imputation of coercion was negated by the defendant's age, intelligence and education, and his apparent awareness of his right to remain silent. Justices Douglas, Black, and Brennan and the Chief Justice, again dissenting together, insisted that an accused had as great a need for counsel before trial as at any other time, and that the only way to stop third-degree practices at the interrogation, "the most critical period of his ordeal,"[98] was to secure his right to have a lawyer with him. At the trial it was usually too late to prove coercion, since it was generally a matter of pitting the defendant's word against that of the law officers.

Cicenia v. LaGay,[99] decided on the same day as Crooker, also posed the issue of the scope of the right to counsel before trial, since the defendant in this case reported to the police station on the advice of his lawyer. Not only was he not permitted to see his lawyer on his request during an interrogation lasting twelve consecutive hours, but his lawyer's request to see his client, made upon and after arrival at the police station, also was denied. Justice Harlan, for the majority, invoked the principle of federalism and cited various cases of similar import to justify denial of the claim. He asserted that upholding the claim of Cicenia would mean that state police could not interrogate a suspect before giving him an opportunity to secure counsel.

The Court also ruled that the state had not denied due process because it had required the defendant to plead to the indictment without an opportunity to inspect his confession. Justice Harlan noted that many states gave the judge discretion whether or not to allow inspection before trial. Justice Brennan did not participate but was probably in sympathy with the minority view expressed in the dissents of the Chief Justice and Justices Black and Douglas.

In 1960 in Hudson v. North Carolina, the Court held that lack of counsel for an indigent in a state case deprived the accused of due process.[100] As the two dissenters, Clark and Whittaker, noted, the Court did not even mention Betts v. Brady. A year later, Whittaker, speaking for a unanimous Court, ruled that in a noncapital felony case, due process had been violated by denying counsel to an indigent, ignorant, and mentally ill African-American.[101] The Court reversed a conviction for assault because of the "complex and intricate legal questions involved" under the law of Florida, but again made no mention of Betts. Douglas, joined in a concurrence by Brennan, however, specifically called for the overruling of Betts. In 1962 in two other noncapital felony cases, a unanimous Court held that the denial of counsel violated due process. In Chewing v. Cunningham, proceedings under a multiple-offender law were so complex as to require counsel.[102] A seven-member Court (Whittaker had retired and Frankfurter had suffered a stroke and was in the hospital), in Carnley v. Cochran, held that under the "special circumstances" rule of Betts v. Brady, the defendant should have had a lawyer. In this instance, Warren, Black, and Douglas joined in a concurring opinion urging that *Betts* be overruled.[103] The Court did not overrule *Betts* with its *Carnley* decision, possibly postponing that move until a full bench was seated and perhaps preferring to take such a significant step with a case directly focused on the question of the continuing validity of the *Betts* doctrine.

Between 1958 and 1962 the Eisenhower Court made an about-face in state right-to-counsel cases. The *Crooker* and *Cicenia* cases in 1958 indicated a tendency by the Court majority toward a narrower interpretation of due process, influenced in part from the Supreme Court's reluctance to supervise the procedure of the state courts.[104] Critics of the Court's holdings that year pointed to English practice which declared inadmissible statements of an accused made to an officer after arrest and required that the police not question a person in custody about any offense with which he is or may be charged.[105] This was truly a civilized standard in comparison with frequent American pretrial practices of the 1950s which often rendered criminal trials a futile rite. The critics maintained that it was no answer to urge that police methods of that time were necessary to obtain convictions. For the most part, crimes could be proved otherwise than by confessions. The skill with which that kind of proof was obtained should have been the measure of good police work. The volume of criminal cases should not serve as an excuse for resort to tactics inconsistent with individual dignity.[106] From a judicial restraintist point of view, however, the Court stood on firm constitutional footing in maintaining that the fair conduct of state trials and pretrial interrogations were essentially state responsibilities, which should be interfered with by the federal judiciary only for actual, demonstrated unfairness.[107]

By 1960 a majority of the Court was finding that refusal of counsel in a serious criminal case constituted a denial of fundamental fairness in such cases as *Hudson* and *McNeal*. To the more libertarian justices, the value of a right to a fair trial was lessened considerably if an accused did not have counsel to advise and defend him. From their perspective, even an educated, intelligent, and experienced layman was at a serious disadvantage without counsel to aid him. He was not only lacking in knowledge of the law applicable to his case, but he was wholly ignorant of the manner in which to develop a courtroom defense against the trained prosecutors of the state. A layman might rush to confession where counsel might see advantages in a trial. Without the guiding hand of counsel at every stage of the proceedings, the accused was at a serious disadvantage—but in the eyes of Frankfurter and the restraintists this appeared to have fallen short of inclusion within "those canons of decency and fairness which express the notions of justice of English-speaking people." But by the spring of 1962, Frankfurter was in ill health and on the verge of retirement and Whittaker had resigned; the Court in *Chewning* and *Carnley* had shown that it was poised to overrule *Betts v. Brady* and to incorporate the Sixth Amendment right-to-counsel protections to the states through the Fourteenth Amendment due process clause. That was exactly what the Warren Court was to do in *Gideon v. Wainwright* in 1963.[108]

SELECTION OF JURIES

Another group of problems in state standards of justice resulted from discrimination against minority groups in the selection of jurors in various southern states. The Supreme Court had long made it clear that the systematic exclusion of African-Americans from grand or trial juries was unconstitutional.

In 1954 the Eisenhower Court for the first time extended the rule against racial discrimination in jury composition to a group other than African-Americans. In *Hernandez v. Texas*,[109] the Court unanimously ruled that persons of Mexican descent were systematically excluded from jury service in Jackson County, Texas. The state maintained that there were only two classes that fell within the protection of the Fourteenth Amendment—white and African-American. Chief Justice Warren countered this by saying "when the existence of a distinct class is demonstrated, and it is further shown that the laws, as written or as applied, single out that class for different treatment not based on some reasonable classification, the guarantees of the Constitution have been violated."[110] The Chief Justice went on to establish the fact that the community attitude indicated that there were definite classes in that area. People of Latin-American or Mexican descent had few business opportunities within the community, a restaurant sign read "No Mexicans Served," children of Mexican descent had previously been segregated in separate schools for the first four grades, and the courthouse grounds even had separate men's restrooms, one of which was marked "Hombres Aqui." For twenty-five years, no person with a Hispanic name had served on a jury in that county although 11 percent of the males over twenty-one bore such names. The argument of the county jury commissioners that their objective had been to select only those they thought best qualified fell before the requirements of equal protection.

In *Michel v. Louisiana*,[111] three African-Americans, who had been sentenced to death in Louisiana for rape, challenged in their appeals the composition of the grand juries which had indicted them on the ground that Negroes had been systematically excluded from them. But a Louisiana statute provided that objections to the grand jury had to be made before the end of the third judicial day following the adjournment of the grand jury. The Court upheld this requirement, by a six-to-three vote, ruling that on its face the statute did not raise an impossible barrier to claiming a federal right.[112] It was noted that in Louisiana a motion to quash an indictment was a short, simple document easy to prepare in a brief time, and hence the defendants had a reasonable opportunity to make their claims heard. Justices Black and Douglas and the Chief Justice dissented, arguing that these defendants had not had a reasonable opportunity to challenge the composition of the grand juries.

But the Court was again unanimous in sustaining the appeal of a Georgia African-American who had failed to conform to the state practice of challenging the grand jury before indictment.[113] Reece, a semiliterate man of low mentality, was indicted by a grand jury and the day following, counsel was appointed for him. The Court held that the right to object to a grand jury presupposed an opportunity to exercise that right, and that under these circumstances it was utterly unrealistic to say that this uncounseled defendant had an opportunity to raise his objection during the two days he was in jail before indictment. On the merits, the Court held that the petitioner had made a strong prima facie case of arbitrary exclusion of African-Americans from grand juries and that it was not enough for the state officials merely to deny discrimination.

In *Eubanks v. Louisiana*,[114] the Court unanimously reversed the murder conviction of an African-American who had been indicted by an all-white grand jury. The record showed that in the administration of Orleans parish courts, African-Americans had been systematically excluded from grand juries. Although one-third of the parish was African-American, only one black had ever been picked for grand jury duty within memory—and this had evidently resulted from the mistaken impression that the juror was white.

Without doubt, a jury from which members of any minority group has been excluded because of their race or national origin violates the right of the defendant to an impartial jury truly representative of the community.[115] As Justice Black so eloquently declared: "For racial discrimination to result in the exclusion from jury service of otherwise qualified groups, not only violates our Constitution and the laws enacted under it but is at war with our basic concepts of a democratic society and a representative government."[116]

In another equal protection case of import, *Griffin v. Illinois*, the Court ruled that a state, if it grants a right of appeal at all, might not discriminate against some criminal defendants on the ground of their poverty by denying them an appeal if they cannot afford to purchase a transcript of the trial proceedings. Said Justice Black for the four-justice plurality: "There can be no equal justice where the kind of trial a man gets depends on the amount of money he has. . . . Such a law would make the constitutional promise of a fair trial a worthless thing." [117] This was a significant extension of the rights of the accused. [118] The four dissenters maintained that equal protection of the law "does not require the States to provide equal financial means for all defendants to avail themselves of such laws." [119]

Although indigent defendants benefited from the Eisenhower Court's interpretation of the equal protection clause, indigent women did not. Since the adoption of the Fourteenth Amendment, the Supreme Court had ruled the clause did not forbid statutory gender discrimination as long as a state legislature might have a rational basis for believing that statutory distinctions promoted some aspect of the public good. Under this rational basis test, the Court had upheld bans on the practice of law by women and prohibitions on women's tending bar. [120]

In 1960 Justice Frankfurter wrote an opinion rejecting the "medieval view" that husband and wife were one person, with but a single will, and therefore legally incapable of entering into a criminal conspiracy. [121] In *Hoyt v. Florida* in 1961, however, the medieval view prevailed when the Court unanimously agreed that women could be exempted from jury duty because of their social role in serving the family in the home. [122] Gwendolyn Hoyt killed her husband with a baseball bat and was convicted of second-degree murder by an all-male jury. Hoyt argued that the conviction violated her rights to equal protection of the laws and her Sixth Amendment right to be tried by a jury of her peers. Justice Harlan, for the Court, held that the Florida statute, that automatically put men on jury lists but required women who wished to serve to volunteer, was not an arbitrary and systematic exclusion of women. Said Harlan: "Despite the enlightened emancipation of women from the restrictions and protections of bygone years, and their entry into many parts of community life formerly considered to be reserved to men, woman is still regarded as the center of home and family life." [123] It would not be until the Burger Court era in the 1970s that the Court's decisions finally countered *Hoyt*'s antiquated view of gender discrimination and equal protection.

CONCLUSION

According to the late Arthur Vanderbilt, "the right to a fair trial is the most fundamental of all rights." [124] The wide range of subjects covered in this chapter gives some indication of what is involved in a fair trial. Due process of law is basically the community's assurance that prosecutors, judges, and juries will grant the accused a fair trial within rules distilled from long centuries of legal experience. [125] Procedural safeguards are thus an important part of our system of justice, and justices are especially competent to decide procedural questions in the light of their special professional knowledge and experience.

The problem in all these cases was to find a workable balance between individual freedom, the authority of the state government, and the community's right to effective law enforcement. Complicating the problem was the question of the extent to which considerations of federalism should be an element in the balance. Table 8.1 shows that Justices Black and Douglas usually joined by the Chief Justice urged broad judicial intrusion upon state management of "local" affairs in law enforcement. In *Bartkus*, these justices sounded faint echoes of the total incorporation theory of the *Adamson* case, while urging what they believed would be greater clarity in the meaning of due process and what their critics contended would be withdrawal into the eighteenth-century Anglo-American concept of a fair trial. In addition, Black, Douglas, and Warren possessed strong sympathies for underdogs of society—racial minorities, dissidents, and the poor; and if there appeared any doubt about the fairness of a trial, they urged reversal upon the ground that due process had been violated. This libertarian bloc formed a core supporting the nationalizing of the Bill of Rights, a philosophy that would prevail in the later Warren Court.

On the other hand, Justice Frankfurter, frequently joined by the Eisenhower associate justices, sought to safeguard what they thought were minimum, or "indispensable," national and libertarian interests from local intrusion leaving the rest to the discretion of other organs of government and the political processes. The middle bloc justices appeared to base their decisions in large part on their distaste for federal intervention in problems of law enforcement and the fair conduct of state trials that they felt was essentially a state responsibility. Only for actual, demonstrated unfairness should federal interference be justified.

It is not without significance that the five middle bloc justices voted for the defendants' position in federal cases much more often than in state cases as seen in Table 8.1. Justice Frankfurter had long been noted as the expounder of the view that the Court on numerous occasions had not shown due deference to state judicial systems.[126] Surpassing Frankfurter, however, in his findings favorable to the state, was Justice Harlan who was with few exceptions a firm supporter of state criminal regulations. Justice Whittaker, who participated in fewer cases, generally was not receptive to the arguments of the Court's libertarian left, although he was won over by them in *Moore v. Michigan*. Justice Stewart also demonstrated "restraintist" tendencies in this area, but joined the activists and Brennan in *Irvin v. Dowd*[127] and concurred with Brennan and Douglas in *Spano*. The voting record of Justice Brennan again pointed out that he could not be counted as a full-fledged member of the activist bloc. In twelve important cases in which he participated where the majority upheld state criminal procedures, Brennan voted against the claim of the defendant five times (and in opposition to Douglas in all five, to Black in four, and to Warren in three).[128] His separate dissent in *Bartkus* absolved him from any interpretations of his accepting the total incorporation theory, and that opinion was followed two years later by his *Cohen* dissent that spelled out the theory of selective incorporation. It appeared that Brennan's experience as a state judge had some influence on his decisions. His libertarian philosophy was probably tempered by knowledge gained through experience that the states needed a certain amount of leeway to enforce their own notions of criminal justice.

As in the federal criminal procedure cases, Justice Clark maintained a strong preference for the views of the prosecution, although he voted for the defendant's claims (and in the majority) in *Griffin*, *Fikes*, and *Leyra* and wrote the opinion of the Court in *Mapp*.

That the middle bloc justices and the activists had quite different conceptions of the Court's functions in the federal system and the extent to which the middle justices might allow state practices to prevail was illustrated in *Knapp v. Schweitzer*.[129] According to Justice Frankfurter speaking for the Court: "If a person may, through immunized self-disclosure before a law enforcing agency of the State, facilitate to some extent his amenability to federal process or vice versa, this is a price to be paid for our federalism. Against it must be put what would be a greater price, that of sterilizing the powers of both governments by not recognizing the autonomy of each within its proper sphere."[130]

Such a view was antithetical to Justice Black who replied: "Things have now reached the point where a person can be whipsawed into incriminating himself under both state and federal law even though there is a privilege against self-incrimination in the constitution of each. I cannot agree that we must accept this intolerable state of affairs as part of our federal system of government."[131]

Although the concept of federalism as applied by the Supreme Court in the circumstances of *Knapp* may have operated to the detriment of the individual's right against self-incrimination,[132] the Court was far from saying that the states were always right in their criminal procedures. Chronic injustice by the states would bring remedies in the federal courts. It would be better that procedure in the first instance be so fair that there would be no ground for reversal on appeal. It would be far better that, if injustice does occur, it be corrected in the state's own courts. The best means of averting federal review, however, would be to establish such standards in the daily administration of criminal justice that there would be no need for such interference. Many states did not respond to this challenge, and the Eisenhower Court moved, albeit reluctantly, to impose minimum standards of fairness on state criminal process.

Table 8.1
Voting Records of Supreme Court Justices in 26 Selected Nonunanimous Cases Involving State Criminal Prosecutions, 1953–1961 Terms (in percentages)

For Claims of Defendants

	Confessions	Double Jeopardy	Self-Incrimination	Right to Counsel	Search and Seizure	Jury Selection	Other	Total
No. of cases	9	4	3	2	4	2	2	26
Douglas	100	100	100	100	100	100	100	100
Black	100	75	100	100	100	100	100	96
Warren	77	75	100	100	75	100	100	84
Brennan	83 (6)	67 (3)	33	100	67 (3)	–	100 (1)	72 (18)
COURT	45	0	0	50	25	50	100	35
Stewart	50 (2)	0 (2)	0 (2)	–	50 (2)	–	100 (1)	33 (9)
Frankfurter	45	0	0	0	25	50	50	27
Whittaker	17 (6)	0	0	100 (1)	0 (2)	–	0 (1)	20 (10)
Clark	22	0	0	0	25	0	50	15
Harlan	29 (7)	0	0	0	0 (3)	50	0	13 (23)
Burton	0 (7)	0 (2)	0 (1)	0 (2)	50 (2)	50	0 (1)	12 (17)

Justices Reed, Minton, and Jackson are not included in this table, which represents the following cases:

Confessions (9): For defendants' claims (4): *Leyra v. Denno* (1954); *Fikes v. Alabama* (1957); *Rogers v. Richmond* (1961); *Reck v. Pate* (1961).

Against defendants' claims (5): *Regan v. New York* (1955); *Ashdown v. Utah* (1958); *Thomas v. Arizona* (1958); *Crooker v. California* (1958); *Cicenia v. Legay* (1958).

Double jeopardy (4): Against defendants' claims (4): *Hoag v. New Jersey* (1958); *Ciucci v. Illinois* (1958); *Bartkus v. Illinois* (1959); *Williams v. Oklahoma* (1959).

Self-incrimination (3): Against defendants' claims (3): *Knapp v. Schweitzer* (1958); *Mills v. Louisiana* (1959); *Anonymous No.6 v. Baker* (1959).

Right to counsel (2): For defendant's claims (1): *Moore v. Michigan* (1957).
Against defendant's claims (1): *In re Groban* (1957).

Search and seizure (4): For defendant's claims (1): *Mapp v. Ohio* (1961).
Against defendants' claims (3): *Irvine v. California* (1954); *Breithaupt v. Abram* (1957); *Frank v. Maryland* (1959).

Jury selection (2): For defendant's claims (1): *Williams v. Georgia* (1955).
Against defendant's claims (1): *Michel v. Louisiana* (1955).

Other (2): For defendants' claims (2): *Griffin v. Illinois* (1957); *Irvin v. Dodd* (1959).

Our personal protections against harsh handling by officialdom of incriminating evidence originated one at a time, under the stimulus of varied impulses. Each has a good deal of independent history. Such separate development had one great advantage. It allowed much experiment in the effort to fit the worthy desires of men yearning for liberty under law to the tough facts of practical application. The case history of these multiple experiments, their successes and failures, had great value when put to use by the Court in weaving the large pattern of a reasonably harmonious system including all the sound and workable personal protections.[133]

On the other hand, it might have done harm, if instead of being so used, it was allowed to defeat harmony by segregating the rules into a number of separate molds because of their individualistic origins.[134] This result appeared to be the chief danger of the restraintist view so strongly advocated by Justice Frankfurter.

The Court's lead was constructive, on the whole, in reforming state criminal procedures. The long series of decisions handed down by the Court from 1953–1962 had their effect on the conduct of police officers and on the course of trials. This was a slow and evolutionary process requiring a good deal of litigation to overcome long years of bad practice and the natural desire of police and prosecution to win their cases. Applying the Fourteenth Amendment to state criminal procedures, the Eisenhower Court took a strong and, on the whole, a desirable line in seeking to raise the standards of local police action and state court criminal practice.[135] The pressure of the Court's opinions in the area required thought and action in every state legislature and in every court and police station. The Eisenhower Court did not still nor prevent responsible democratic action on these problems. It required it. Lawless police action had not yet been banished from American life, but the most primitive backwoods sheriff was learning that third-degree methods might backfire.[136]

Major policy considerations confronted the Court in reaching its decisions, particularly as the Court pushed procedural limitations in new directions. Present here, as in all areas, were difficult and unavoidable problems of accommodating competing interests—the most important of which was the concept of a minimum national standard of due process competing with the position and authority of the states in maintaining their systems of justice within the structure of federalism. To identify and appraise those interests, to recognize their relevancy in the context of the isolated case presented for decision, and to achieve their wise accommodation was a continuing challenge to perceptive and sober statesmanship in the exercise of judicial power.[137] In meeting this challenge through its initial use of selective incorporation, the Eisenhower Court moved toward a definition of due process possessing the merit of greater clarity while allowing continued infusion of what one can hope is an improved morality into criminal administration.

NOTES

1. 7 Pet. 243 (1833).
2. 110 U.S. 516 (1884).
3. 176 U.S. 581 (1900).
4. 211 U.S. 78 (1908).
5. 302 U.S. 319 (1937).

6. *Adamson v. California*, 332 U.S. 46 (1947); compare Charles Fairman, "Does the Fourteenth Amendment Incorporate the Bill of Rights? The Original Understanding," 2 *Stan. L. Rev.* 5 (1949) with William W. Crosskey, "Charles Fairman, 'Legislative History' and the Constitutional Limitations on State Authority," 22 *U. Chi. L. Rev.* 1 (1954).

7. 302 U.S. 319 (1937).

8. E.g., Sanford H. Kadish "Methodology and Criteria in Due Process Adjudication—A Survey and Criticism," 66 *Yale L. J.* 319, 341 (1957): "Freezing the meaning of due process . . . destroys the chief virtue of its generality: its elasticity. Future generations would become bound to the perceptions of an earlier one; the experience that develops with changing modes of governmental power, unpredicated and unpredictable, as well as the deeper insights into the nature of men in organized society that are gained in continually changing social contexts, would become irrelevant."

9. Arthur L. Harding, "Due Process," in *Fundamental Law in Criminal Prosecutions*, ed. Arthur L. Harding (Dallas, TX: Southern Methodist University Press, 1959), p. 22.

10. William M. Beaney, "The Effective Assistance of Counsel," Ibid., p. 44.

11. Quoted in Wallace Mendelson, *The Constitution and the Supreme Court* (New York: Dodd, Mead & Co., 1959), p. 229.

12. Ibid.

13. Ibid.

14. *Rochin v. California*, 342 U.S. 165 at 169 (1952) (Frankfurter, J.).

15. Quoted in William O. Douglas, *We the Judges* (Garden City, NY: Doubleday, 1956), p. 272; see also J.A.C. Grant, *Our Common Law Constitution* (Boston: Boston University Press, 1960); Alan Barth, *The Price of Liberty* (New York: Viking, 1961).

16. Ralph A. Rossum and G. Alan Tarr, *American Constitutional Law, Volume II, The Bill of Rights and Subsequent Amendments* (New York: St. Martin's/Worth, 1999), pp. 57–63.

17. 359 U.S. 121 (1959).

18. See 45 *Cornell L. Q.* 574 (1960); but see 44 *Minn. L. Rev.* 534 (1960); 28 *U. Cin. L. Rev.* 518 (1959).

19. 359 U.S. 121 at 124.

20. Ibid. at 128.

21. 359 U.S. 187 (1959); see Chapter 7 this volume, *supra*.

22. 356 U.S. 464 (1958).

23. See generally, Comment, "Collateral Estoppel in Criminal Cases," 28 *U. Chi. L. Rev.* 142 (1960).

24. See generally, 57 *Mich. L. Rev.* 409 (1959); 28 *U. Chi. L. Rev.* 142 (1960); 74 *Harv. L. Rev.* 752 (1961).

25. 356 U.S. 464 at 475.

26. 356 U.S. 571 (1958). But see 26 *U. Chi. L. Rev.* 326 (1959); *cf.* 107 *U. Pa. L. Rev.* 109 (1958); 8 *DePaul L. Rev.* 102 (1958).

27. 358 U.S. 576 (1959).

28. Fisher, "Double Jeopardy, Two Sovereignties and the Intruding Constitution," p. 591; see also Daniel K. Mayers and Fletcher L. Yarbrough, "*Bis Vexari*, New Trials and Successive Prosecutions." 74 *Harv. L. Rev.* 1 (1960); J.A.C. Grant,

"Federalism and Self-Incrimination," 4 *U.C.L.A. L. Rev.* 549 (1957); 5 *U.C.L.A. L. Rev.* 1 (1958).

29. See generally, Lawrence Newman, "Double Jeopardy and the Problem of Successive Prosecutions: A Suggested Solution," 34 *So. Calif. L. Rev.* 252 (1961). This article suggests that a joint trial by federal and state prosecutors would be appropriate in some cases.

30. 395 U.S. 784 (1969); see also Fellman, *The Defendant's Rights*, p. 202.

31. See generally, Schubert, *Constitutional Politics*, pp. 619–621.

32. 338 U.S. 25 (1949); but see *Mapp v. Ohio*, 367 U.S. 643 (1961), overruling *Wolf*; see also *Wilson v. Schnettler*, 365 U.S. 381 (1961).

33. But see J.A.C. Grant, "Tarnished Silver Platter: Federalism and Admissibility of Illegally Seized Evidence," 8 *U.C.L.A. L. Rev.* 1 (1961).

34. 347 U.S. 128 (1954).

35. 347 U.S. 128 at 134.

36. *But see* 52 *Mich. L. Rev.* 904 (1954); *cf.* 7 *Vand. L. Rev.* 405 (1954); 2 *U.C.L.A. L. Rev.* 131 (1954).

37. 347 U.S. 128 at 138.

38. 347 U.S. 128 at 142.

39. 347 U.S. 128 at 149, 152.

40. 347 U.S. 128 at 145–146.

41. 347 U.S. 128 at 146.

42. Charles A. Reynard, "The Right of Privacy," in Harding, *Fundamental Law in Criminal Prosecutions*, pp. 117–118; see also Comment, "Search and Seizure in the Supreme Court: Shadows on the 4th Amendment," 28 *U. Chi. L. Rev.* 664 (1960).

43. 352 U.S. 432 (1957).

44. 35 *Texas L. Rev.* 813 (1957); 11 *Vand. L. Rev.* 196 (1957); but see 42 *Minn. L. Rev.* 662 (1958).

45. 352 U.S. 432 at 439.

46. 342 U.S. 165 (1952).

47. 352 U.S. 432 at 442.

48. 359 U.S. 360 (1959); see also *Ohio ex rel. Eaton v. Price,* 360 U.S. 246 (1959); *Eaton v. Price*, 364 U.S. 263 (1960).

49. 359 U.S. 360 at 366.

50. See generally, D.W.M. Waters, "Rights of Entry in Administrative Officers," 27 *U. Chi. L. Rev.* 79 (1959); but see 13 *Sw. L. J.* 532 (1959); 12 *Vand. L. Rev.* 1376 (1959).

51. 359 U.S. 360 at 367, 372.

52. 359 U.S. 360 at 374.

53. *Camera v. Municipal Court*, 387 U.S. 523 (1967); *See v. City of Seattle*, 387 U.S. 541 (1967); see generally, Edward L. Barrett, Jr. "Personal Rights, Property Rights, and the Fourth Amendment," *1960 The Supreme Court Review*, p. 46; Robert F. Allnutt and Gerald J. Missinghoff, "Housing and Health Inspection: A Survey and Suggestions in Light of Recent Case Law," 28 *Geo. Wash. L. Rev.* 421 (1960); see also Kamisar, "*Wolf* and *Lustig* Ten Years Later: Illegal Evidence in State and Federal Courts," 43 *Minn. L. Rev.* 1083 (1959); Grant, "Tarnished Silver Platter," 9 *J. Pub. L. 260* (1960); 14 *U. Miami L. Rev.* 473 (1960).

54. 367 U.S. 643 (1961).

55. Schwartz, *Super Chief*, p. 412.

56. Powe, *The Warren Court*, p. 198.

57. *Twining v. New Jersey*, 211 U.S. 78 (1908); *Adamson v. California*, 332 U.S. 46 (1947).

58. *Feldman v. United States*, 322 U.S. 487 (1944); *Knapp v. Schweitzer*, 357 U.S. 371 (1958).

59. See generally, Jack Kroner, "Self-incrimination: The External Reach of the Privilege," 60 *Colum. L. Rev.* 816 (1960); Erwin W. Griswold, "The Right to Be Let Alone," 55 *Nw. U. L. Rev.* 216 (1960); Richard A. Watson, "Federalism v. Individual Rights: The Legal Squeeze of Self-Incrimination," 54 *Am. Pol. Sci. Rev.* 887 (1960).

60. 347 U.S. 179 (1954).

61. 357 U.S. 371 (1958).

62. 26 *U. Chi. L. Rev.* 164 (1958); 68 *Yale L. J.* 322 (1958); *cf.* 27 *Fordham L. Rev.* 429 (1958).

63. 357 U.S. 371 at 385.

64. *Murphy v. Waterfront Commission*, 378 U.S. 52 (1964).

65. *Mills v. Louisiana*, 360 U.S. 230 (1959).

66. But see 20 *La. L. Rev.* 584 (1960); *cf.* 34 *Tul. L. Rev.* 205 (1959).

67. *Anonymous #6 v. Baker*, 360 U.S. 287 (1959).

68. 366 U.S. 117 (1961).

69. Rossum and Tarr, *American Constitutional Law*, pp. 60–61. The selective incorporation theory was most clearly stated by Justice Brennan in *Malloy v. Hogan*, 378 U.S. 1 (1964) and in Justice Byron White's opinion for the Court in *Duncan v. Louisiana*, 391 U.S. 145 (1968). Justice Harlan remained the strongest advocate of the fundamental rights approach and was the most vociferous critic of selective incorporation.

70. See generally, 46 *Ia. L. Rev.* 388 (1961); see also *Blackburn v. Alabama*, 361 U.S. 199 (1960); *Wilde v. Wyoming*, 362 U.S. 607 (1960); *Hudson v. North Carolina*, 363 U.S. 192 (1960); *Rogers v. Richmond*, 365 U.S. 534 (1961); *Reck v. Pate*, 367 U.S. 433 (1961).

71. Pritchett, *Civil Liberties and the Vinson Court*, p. 199.

72. 347 U.S. 556 (1954).

73. 21 *Brooklyn L. Rev.*111 (1954); 28 *Temp. L. Q.* 260 (1954); *cf.* 43 *Calif. L. Rev.* 114 (1955).

74. 347 U.S. 556 at 561.

75. 347 U.S. 556 at 589.

76. 352 U.S. 191 (1957).

77. 352 U.S. 191 at 198.

78. 35 *Texas L. Rev.* 728 (1957); 26 *U. Cinn. L. Rev.* 306 (1957).

79. 356 U.S. 560 (1958).

80. 356 U.S. 390 (1958).

81. 357 U.S. 426 (1958).

82. For a detailed analysis of Justice Black's theory in this area see Donald G. Taragan, "Justice Black—Inherent Coercion: An Analytical Study of the Standards for Determining the Voluntariness of a Confession" 10 *Am. U. L. Rev.* 53 (1961).

83. *Miranda v. Arizona*, 384 U.S. 436 (1966).

84. 287 U.S. 45 (1932).

85. 316 U.S. 455 (1942).

86. Schubert, *Constitutional Politics*, pp. 624–625; see generally, William Beaney, *The Right to Counsel* (Ann Arbor: University of Michigan Press, 1955).

87. *Chandler v. Fretag*, 348 U.S. 3 (1954).

88. *Pennsylania ex rel. Herman v. Claudy*, 350 U.S. 116 (1956).

89. 352 U.S. 330 (1957).

90. 57 *Colum. L. Rev.* 887 (1957); but s*ee* 45 *Calif. L. Rev.* 773 (1957).

91. For criticism of the *Groban* decision, see Ephriam Margolin, "Right to Counsel and Compulsion to Testify," 7 *How. L. J.* 36 (1961).

92. 355 U.S. 155 (1957).

93. 358 U.S. 633 (1959).

94. 360 U.S. 315 (1959); see generally, Potter Steward, "Justice Stewart Discusses Right of Counsel," 19 *Legal Aid Brief Case* 92 (1960).

95. 378 U.S. 478 (1964).

96. 357 U.S. 433 (1958).

97. 107 *U. Pa. L. Rev.* 386 (1958); but see 38 *N.C. L. Rev.* 630 (1960).

98. 357 U.S. 433 at 444.

99. 357 U.S. 504 (1958).

100. 363 U.S. 697 (1960).

101. *McNeal v. Culver*, 365 U.S. 109 (1961).

102. 368 U.S. 443 (1962).

103. 369 U.S. 506 (1962).

104. See generally, Edmond L. Cohn, "Federal Constitutional Limitations on the Use of Coerced Confessions in the State Courts," 50 *J. Crim. L.* 265 (1959); but see Henry B. and Eugene A. Tothblatt, "Police Interrogation: The Right to Counsel and to Prompt Arraignment," 27 *Brooklyn L. Rev.* 24 (1960); *cf.* Fred E. Inbau, "Restrictions in the Law of Interrogation and Confessions," 52 *Nw. U. L. Rev.* 77 (1957); see also Abraham S. Goldstein, "The State and the Accused: Balance of Advantage in Criminal Procedure," 69 *Yale L. J.* 1149 (1960); see also *Ferguson v. Georgia*, 365 U.S. 570 (1961); *Reynolds v. Cochran*, 365 U.S. 525 (1961); *McNeal v. Culver*, 365 U.S. 109 (1961).

105. The Judges' Rules, administrative directions enunciated in *R. v. Voisin* (1918) 1 K.B. 531 at 539 (T.A.C.), discussed in T. E. St. Johnston, "The Legal Limitation of the Interrogation of Suspects and Prisoners in England and Wales," 39 *J. Crim. L.* 89 (1948); see also Jerome Hall, "Police and Law in a Democratic Society," 28 *Ind. L. J.* 133 (1953).

106. "Civil Liberties and the Supreme Court: October Term 1957," 18 *Law. Guild Rev.* 93, 132 (1958); but see the criticisms of English practice in Glanville Williams, *The Proof of Guilt* (London: Stevens & Sons, 1955), pp. 35–61.

107. On the other hand, some groups contended that all indigent defendants should be represented by counsel and that a private defender organization, subsidized by public funds, would be best equipped to do the job: Special Committee of the Association of the Bar of the City of New York and the National Legal Aid and Defender Association, *Equal Justice for the Accused* (Garden City, NY: Doubleday, 1959). Prior to the *Gideon v. Wainwright* decision, pressure was building to guarantee a right to counsel in noncapital state criminal cases.

108. 372 U.S. 335 (1963); see Anthony Lewis, *Gideon's Trumpet* (New York: Vintage, 1964), pp. 107–122.

109. 347 U.S. 475 (1954).

110. 347 U.S. 475 at 478.

111. 350 U.S. 91 (1955).

112. 54 *Mich. L. Rev.* 1173 (1956); but see 34 *N.C. L. Rev.* 367 (1956); 10 *Sw. L. J.* 200 (1956).

113. *Reece v. Georgia*, 350 U.S. 85 (1955).

114. 356 U.S. 584 (1958).

115. But see *Lea v. Louisiana*, 350 U.S. 1007 (1956), *cert. denied*; *Reeves v. Alabama*, 352 U.S. 965 (1958), where alleged discrimination in jury selection was not found.

116. *Smith v. Texas*, 311 U.S. 128 at 130 (1940).

117. *Griffin v. Illinois*, 351 U.S. 12 (1956).

118. See generally, Bertram F. Wilcox and Edward J. Bloustein, "The *Griffin* Case—Poverty and the Fourteenth Amendment," 43 *Cornell L. Q.* 1 (1957); 55 *Mich. L. Rev.* 413 (1957); 34 *Texas L. Rev.* 1083 (1956).

119. 351 U.S. 12 at 29.

120. *Bradwell v. Illinois*, 83 U.S. 130 (1873); *Goescart v. Cleary*, 335 U.S. 464 (1948).

121. *United States v. Dege*, 364 U.S. 51 (1960).

122. 368 U.S. 57 (1961).

123. 368 U.S. 57 at 62; *Hoyt* was overruled by *Taylor v. Louisiana*, 419 U.S. 522 (1975).

124. Arthur T. Vanderbilt, "The Essentials of a Sound Judicial System," 48 *Nw. U. L. Rev.* 1 (1953).

125. Fellman, *The Defendant's Rights*, pp. 3–4.

126. For a critical analysis of this view, see Louis H. Pollack, "Mr. Justice Frankfurter: Judgment and the Fourteenth Amendment," 67 *Yale L. J.* 304, 315 (1957).

127. 359 U.S. 394 (1959).

128. In *Breithaupt, Ashdown, Knapp, Mills,* and *Williams v. Oklahoma.*

129. Justice Brennan wrote a separate concurring opinion in *Knapp*, which along with his separate dissenting opinion in *Bartkus* best illustrates his basic disagreement with the activists over due process in the late 1950s.

130. 357 U.S. 371 at 380.

131. Ibid. at 385.

132. Watson, "Federalism v. Individual Rights," p. 887.

133. See Bodenhamer, *Fair Trial*, pp. 137-138; Charles Fairman, "Compulsory Self-Incrimination," in Harding, *Fundamental Law in Criminal Prosecutions,* pp. 59, 81; see also Kurland, "The Supreme Court and the Attrition of State Power," 10 *Stan. L. Rev.* 274 (1958).

134. Jacobs, *Justice Frankfurter,* pp. 207–209; Alfred H. Kelly, "Where Constitutional Liberty Came From," in *Foundations of Freedom in the American Constitution,* ed. Alfred H. Kelly (New York: Harper & Bros., 1956), pp. 25–33; Grant, *Our Common Law Constitution*; see also John R. Green, "The Bill of Rights, the Fourteenth Amendment and the Supreme Court," in *Essays in Constitutional Law,* ed. Robert G. McCloskey (New York: Knopf, 1957), chapter 12.

135. See Eugene V. Rostow, "The Court and Its Critics," 4 *S. Tex. L. J.* 160, 173 (1959): "In the . . . area . . . of state criminal law administration . . . I believe

the Supreme Court has done some of its finest work in this century"; Contra, John P. Frank, "The Historic Role of the Supreme Court," 48 *Ky. L. J.* 26, 45 (1959): "In the field of the State administration of criminal justice . . . I have real doubts as to whether (the Court) is accomplishing much more than tinkering with the result in an occasional case."

136. Rostow, "The Democratic Character of Judicial Review," 66 *Harv. L. Rev.* 193, 210 (1952).

137. Paul G. Kauper, *Frontiers of Constitutional Liberty* (Ann Arbor: University of Michigan Law School, 1956), p. 166; see also Stanley H. Friedelbaum, "The Warren Court and American Federalism—A Preliminary Appraisal," 28 *U. Chi. L. Rev.* 53 (1960); Richard Arens and Harold D. Lasswell, *In Defense of Public Order* (New York: Columbia University Press, 1961).

9

The Equal Protection Revolution

Brown v. Board of Education was widely assumed to be the most significant decision of the Supreme Court during the Chief Justiceship of Earl Warren. But the Chief Justice thought that the malapportionment case, *Baker v. Carr*,[1] was "the most important case of my tenure on the Court."[2] *Baker* and its progeny led to the "one person, one vote" rule for legislative reapportionment and corrected a shortcoming of American democracy with which Warren, the former governor, was very familiar—the dominance of legislative bodies by rural interests. These cases transformed the political landscape of the country by shifting power from rural areas to urban and suburban districts that were more representative of the demographics of America in the 1960s. In addition, the *Baker* decision marked the start of an "equal protection revolution" that was to have a profound impact on society.

In earlier decisions the Court had held that federal courts had no jurisdiction in legislative reapportionment cases. In 1946 in *Colegrove v. Green*, Justice Frankfurter for a four-justice plurality, found that apportionment was a "political question" and that it was "hostile to a democratic system to involve the judiciary in the politics of the people."[3] Frankfurter admonished his brethren that "courts ought not to enter this political thicket." For fair apportionment, according to the Court, "the ultimate remedy lies with the people." Unfortunately for the people who were urban voters, rural legislators had little interest in fair apportionment and in willingly giving up their power. As a result many states had not changed their apportionment schemes for decades, and urban areas often were underrepresented in state legislatures.

The Eisenhower Court actually had entered the political thicket in 1960 in the *Gomillion v. Lightfoot* racial gerrymander case. Justice Whittaker's concurring opinion would have decided that case on equal protection grounds. Two years later, in *Baker,* the Court took on malapportionment of the Tennessee legislature that had last been apportioned in 1901 despite massive population shifts since then. Disgruntled voters from Memphis and other cities felt they were grossly underrepresented in the legislature because their votes had only a fraction of the weight of those from lesser populated areas of the state. Tennessee did not have initiative and referendum; constitutional conventions could be called only by the legislature, and state courts provided no relief. Thus, the only remedy for the voting majority was to seek help in federal courts. A federal district court threw the case out relying on the precedent of *Colegrove.* In a six-to-two decision (Whittaker had retired), Justice Brennan, for the Court, held that on equal protection grounds the Supreme Court had jurisdiction in reapportionment cases and that plaintiffs could obtain appropriate relief in the courts and had standing to challenge state apportionment statutes. Brennan also expounded on "the political question doctrine" in order to define its scope and to indicate that it was not applicable in apportionment cases. The particular remedy for Tennessee's malapportionment, described by Justice Clark as a "crazy quilt without rational basis," was left to the federal district court.

Justice Frankfurter dissenting, in the last opinion he would write before retiring from the Court, claimed that the remedy for malapportionment should come from "an aroused popular conscience that sears the conscience of the people's representatives." Frankfurter alleged that the Court's decision was a "massive repudiation of the experience of our whole past in asserting destructively novel judicial power demands." He contended that the Court was being asked to "choose among competing bases of representation—ultimately, really, among competing theories of political philosophy" and that was not an appropriate issue for the justices.

Justice Harlan also dissented and alleged that there was nothing in the U.S. Constitution requiring that state legislatures give equal electoral weight to all voters. Harlan worried that "the majority has wholly failed to reckon with what the future may hold in store" when federal courts attempt to determine the constitutional merits of a state's apportionment policy.

The *Baker* decision was a classic example of the struggle between two schools of judicial liberalism. The Eisenhower Court majority represented the school that sought out social injustice and inequalities and tried to set them right. Opposed to that school was the Holmes–Frankfurter tradition of judicial self-restraint that tried to limit the Court's reforming

powers. By 1962 the restraintists were in retreat, and the activism of the
Eisenhower Court "was not a rein but a spur to democracy."[4]

Baker, unlike several of the other landmark decisions of the
Eisenhower Court was generally popular. A few critics, principally from
the South, added apportionment to their list of "assaults on the constitutional system" by the Court. But the new administration of President John
Kennedy spoke out enthusiastically for the "historic" Baker decision—a
response from the chief executive in sharp contrast to Eisenhower's silence or ambivalent stands on earlier Court actions. Very soon, thirty-six
states were involved in malapportionment lawsuits, and the Warren Court
furthered the reapportionment revolution in its later decisions. Baker was
"the beginning of the end of America's rotten boroughs."[5]

In retrospect, Chief Justice Warren thought the Court's action appropriate, if not overdue, and maintained that "many of our [the nation's]
problems would have been solved a long time ago if everyone had the
right to vote, and his vote counted the same as everybody else's. Most of
these problems could have been solved through the political process rather
than through the courts. But as it was, the Court had to decide."[6] In its
reapportionment cases the Eisenhower Court revitalized the equal protection clause and began to explore the broader implications of its use.
Ultimately, this was to lead to a new substantive equal protection by which
later Courts would provide heightened judicial scrutiny to cases involving discrimination on the basis of gender, age, illegitimacy, alienage, and
indigency, as well as affirmative action.

DODGING THE RIGHT TO PRIVACY

The Supreme Court, in its opinions, often reflects what Justice Holmes
referred to as the "felt necessities" of each period in American history.
The activism of the Eisenhower Court, reflecting the values of a changing
American society, revolutionized many areas of constitutional law such
as reapportionment, race relations, criminal procedures, associational
rights, and separation of church and state. On the other hand, the Court's
judicial restraint produced decisions affirming society's status quo. For
example, the Court's paternalistic attitude toward women reflected the
male chauvinist attitudes of a pre-Feminine Mystique generation. In addition, the restraintist justices avoided making decisions in areas of law for
which American society perhaps was not yet ready. The question of miscegenation was thought to be too incendiary for the Court to rule on in
1956. But by 1967 miscegenation cases that formerly had been refused
review because they were "devoid of a properly presented federal question" merited close scrutiny by the Court which unanimously struck down
laws prohibiting "interracial marriages."[7]

In 1961 the Eisenhower Court dodged the opportunity to pass on the right to privacy—a topic that as interpreted by the judiciary a decade later was to rive the nation. In *Poe v. Ullman*, the Court dismissed a challenge to a Connecticut law that prohibited the use of contraceptives and the giving of medical advice on their use.[8] Justice Frankfurter, for the five-justice majority, held that the case lacked ripeness because the plaintiff had not been prosecuted. Two of the dissenters were bolder in arguing that the statute invaded "the right of privacy"—a new idea in Supreme Court cases dealing with family and marriage. Justice Douglas, the most-married and most-divorced member of the Court, found that the Connecticut law improperly "touches the relationship between man and wife and reaches into the intimacies of the marriage relationship." Douglas' dissent enunciated a "total incorporation plus" interpretation of due process: "Though I believe that 'due process' as used in the Fourteenth Amendment includes all of the first eight Amendments, I do not think it is restricted and confined to them." Due process might encompass other rights in addition to those explicitly listed in the Bill of Rights.

Justice Harlan's dissent also relied on an expanded due process: "It is not the particular enumeration of rights in the first eight Amendments which spells out the reach of Fourteenth Amendment due process, but rather . . . those concepts which are considered to embrace those rights 'which are . . . *fundamental*; which belong . . . to the citizens of all free governments'." For Harlan, due process was "a discrete concept which subsists as an independent guaranty of liberty and procedural fairness, more general and inclusive than the specific prohibitions." Through the course of the Court's decisions, due process "represented the balance which our Nation, built upon postulates of respect for the liberty of the individual, has struck between that liberty and the demands of organized society." Harlan concluded the Connecticut law "making it a criminal offense for *married* couples to use contraceptives is an intolerable and unjustifiable invasion of privacy in the conduct of the most intimate concerns of an individual's personal life."

Douglas and Harlan embraced the right of privacy four years before a majority of the Court did. In 1965 in *Griswold v. Connecticut*, the Supreme Court finally decided the constitutionality of the Connecticut statute and found it violated the constitutionally protected right to "privacy" of married persons.[9] Writing for the Court, Justice Douglas promulgated a right of privacy, based on zones of privacy derived from the First, Third, Fourth, Fifth, and Ninth Amendments. In his concurring opinion, Justice Harlan found the law unconstitutional for violating basic values implicit in the concept of ordered liberty and protected by the due process clause of the Fourteenth Amendment. The right of privacy later became the basis for the abortion case, *Roe v. Wade*.[10]

THE EQUAL OPPORTUNITY REVOLUTION

In addition to the "due process revolution" and the "equal protection revolution," the Eisenhower court revolutionized the right of poor people to redress grievances before the Supreme Court. Appeals to the Supreme Court from litigants who cannot afford to pay court costs are known as *in forma pauperis*. Since the 1923 term of the Court, indigents have been allowed to file *in forma pauperis* (in the manner of a pauper) appeals without being required to pay the required fees or submit the various legal arguments and documents typically required of appellants. The number of *in forma pauperis* cases accepted by the Court was small (e.g., 59 in 1935), and after World War II, they were placed in the Miscellaneous Docket "made up mostly of cases brought by persons who are too poor to have their court papers printed or to pay the usual fee . . . for docketing a case in the Supreme Court."[11] By the 1953 term, as seen in Table 9.1, the number of such cases had increased to 542 out of 1,211 total paid and *in forma pauperis* certiorari petitions. During the 1954 term, Chief Justice Warren began the practice of transferring *in forma pauperis* petitions from the Miscellaneous Docket to the Appellate Docket that consists of cases that have been appealed from a lower state or federal court and includes certiorari petitions.[12]

In *Griffin v. Illinois* in 1956, the Eisenhower Court ruled that indigency should not bar a defendant from filing a criminal appeal.[13] Justice Black's plurality opinion hinted that state classifications based on indigency were suspect and should be subject to the same strict scrutiny as cases of racial discrimination. By 1957, the Court was granting certiorari in much higher numbers to *in forma pauperis* cases, and in 1959 the number reached 55, the largest ever granted up until that time.[14] After the Eisenhower Court's signals that it was more sensitive to appeals by poor criminal defendants, the number of *in forma pauperis* certiorari petitions received soared to 1,330 (out of 2,182 total cases) during the 1961 terms—an increase of 59 percent during the Eisenhower Court era. In addition, indigent petitioners frequently won before the Supreme court—in contrast to declining numbers of petitioner victories in the Burger and Rehnquist courts.[15] The *in forma pauperis* revolution of the Eusenhower Court set the stage for the later Warren Court's landmark decision in *Gideon v. Wainwright* in 1963. Table 9.1 shows that following *Gideon*, the number of total certiorari cases and the number of *in forma pauperis* petitions increased substantially while the Court's acceptance of them decreased fairly steadily.[16]

Table 9.1
Grant Rates for Paid and *In Forma Pauperis* Certiorari Petitions from Select
Terms, 1926–1992

Term	Total Total No.	Paid Cases		I.F.P. Cases	
		Total No.	Percent Granted (No.)	Total No.	Percent Granted (No.)
1926	586	586	20 (117)	0	0 (0)
1935	901	842	17 (142)	59	14 (8)
1941	1,010	832	18 (150)	178	9 (16)
1951	1,093	668	14 (94)	425	5 (19)
1953	1,211	669	12 (78)	542	2 (10)
1955	1,487	842	15 (123)	645	3 (16)
1957	1,587	840	13 (110)	747	5 (34)
1959	1,771	838	15 (122)	933	6 (55)
1961	2,182	852	12 (103)	1,330	3 (38)
1963	2,279	972	12 (118)	1,307	5 (69)
1965	2,774	1,164	12 (124)	1,610	3 (43)
1967	3,067	1,269	13 (166)	1,798	5 (84)
1969	3,653	1,425	8 (108)	2,228	2 (38)
1971	4,515	2,070	12 (238)	2,445	3 (61)*
1973	5,065	2,480	9 (229)	2,585	2 (30)
1975	4,747	2,352	10 (244)	2,395	1 (28)
1980	5,120	2,749	6 (167)	2,371	1 (17)
1985	5,148	2,571	7 (166)	2,577	1 (20)
1986	5,111	2,547	6 (152)	2,564	2 (15)
1988	5,643	2,587	5 (130)	3,056	2 (17)
1990	6,302	2,351	5 (114)	3,951	0.7 (27)
1992	7,233	2,441	3 (83)	4,792	0.3 (14)

*The Disproportionately high percentage of *i.f.p.* cases granted review in 1971 reflects an
   unusual proportion of capital cases held over from earlier terms for joint consideration.
   See Doris Marie Provine, *Case Selection in the United States Supreme Court* (Chicago:
   University of Chicago Press, 1980), p. 18.

Source: Lee Epstein, Jeffrey A. Segal, Harold J. Spaeth, and Thomas J. Walker, *The Supreme
   Court Compendium: Data Decisions & Developments* (Washington, DC: Congressional
   Quarterly, 1994), pp. 66–71; compiled in William A. Adsit, "A History and Outlook of
   the Supreme Court and Indigent Access to the Courts," Paper delivered at the 2001
   Annual Meeting of the Oklahoma Political Science Association, Stillwater, OK, 15–16
   November 2001.

NOTES

1. 369 U.S. 186 (1962). *Baker* was the eleventh case in which the Eisenhower
Court overruled a previous decision. Powe, *The Warren Court*, p. 201.

2. Earl Warren, *Memoirs of Earl Warren* (New York: Doubleday, 1977), p.
306.

3. 328 U.S. 549 (1946).

4. Max Lerner, *Nine Scorpions in a Bottle*, Richard Cummings, ed. (New York: Arcade Publishing, 1994), pp. 217–219; Benjamin F. Wright, "The Rights of Majorities and Minorities in the 1961 Term of the Supreme Court," 57 *Am. Pol. Sci. Rev.* 98 (1963).

5. Clark, Justice Brennan, p. 164; the principal apportionment cases following *Baker* were, e.g., *Gray v. Sanders*, 372 U.S. 368 (1963); *Wesberry v. Sanders*, 376 U.S. 1 (1964); *Reynolds v. Sims*, 377 U.S. 533 (1964).

6. Jack H. Pollock, *Earl Warren*, p. 209.

7. *Loving v. Virginia*, 388 U.S. 1 (1967).

8. 367 U.S. 497 (1961).

9. 381 U.S. 479 (1965).

10. 410 U.S. 113 (1973).

11. Lewis, *Gideon's Trumpet*, p. 4.

12. John p. Comer, *The Forging of the Federal Indigent Code* (San Antonio: Principia Press, 1966), p. 111.

13. 351 U.S. 12 (1956).

14. Less Epstein, jeffrey A. Segal, Harold J. Spaeth, and Thomas J. Walker, *The Supreme Court Compendium: Data Decisions & Developments* (Washington, DC: Congressional Quarterly, 1994), pp. 66–77.

15. William A. Adsit, "A History and Outlook of the Supreme Court and Indigent Access to the Courts," Paper delivered at the 2001 Annual Meeting of the Oklahoma Political Science Association, Stillwater, OK, 15–16 November 2001.

16. Ibid.

10

The Chief Justice and the Pre-Warren Justices

The seven preceding chapters, in discussing the important civil liberties decisions of the Eisenhower Court, have given some indication of where the justices disagreed and their reasons for doing so. The tables at the end of these chapters have pointed out the alignment of the justices in each area, while the tables of Chapter 2 contained general quantitative information covering not only the civil liberties cases but also all nonunanimous decisions of the Court. To understand better the alignment of the justices on civil liberties, we must turn to a more specific examination of the values of the justices.

THE NATURE OF JUDICIAL DECISION MAKING

Every law that comes before the Supreme Court for interpretation represents conflicting principles that require a value choice by the judges. The same thing is of course true in the other forms of political (official) action carried on by the legislative and executive branches.[1]

In general, few Americans are so naive as to seriously believe that the Supreme Court has the simple task expounded by Justice Roberts of laying "the article of the Constitution which is invoked beside the statute which is challenged and to decide whether the latter squares with the former."[2] This idea of mechanical jurisprudence referred to as the "slot machine," "phonograph," or "stork" methods, overlooks the fact that selection from among the courses of decision open to the Court is a process in which personal choice plays a deciding role.[3] When the interpretation of a law becomes a contest of conflicting values, and when courts are called upon to make decisions among them, the results are bound to be difficult. This is the price that any society that allows for a free play of ideas and of group associations must expect to pay.

Supreme Court justices work within a judicial framework, which furnishes institutional ground rules with which their own preferences must compete. Judicial rules and traditions play a large part in the operating conditions under which judges make their choice. The rule of "stare decisis" may be discarded by a judge, but only after he has satisfied himself that he has met the obligations of consistency and respect for settled principles which his responsibility to the Court imposes upon him.[4] The private views of a judge as an individual are an important part of his or her public views, but again these decisions are limited within an institutional setting.[5]

In civil liberties cases the justices are not asked whether they favor civil liberties. In the words of Justice Douglas: "Any American court is supposed to be pro-First Amendment, pro-Fourth Amendment, pro-Fifth Amendment, pro-Fourteenth Amendment, and so on. For it is the Constitution the judges are sworn to defend. But it is somewhat shocking to hear that an American judge is supposed to be pro or against anyone who stands before him for justice."[6] What the Court must decide is how it can, consistent with its role as the highest tribunal in the federal system, dispose of a proceeding, the basic facts in which have been found and the form of which has been given by lower judicial bodies. Under these circumstances, justices will be greatly influenced in their decision making by the direction and intensity of their libertarian sympathies by which they rank the relative claims of liberty and order in our society and by their conception of their role as judges and the role of the judiciary as an institution.

Ranking of justices on an attitude scale in an absolute fashion is impossible, but they can be ranked relative to each other, and particularly by reference to their deviation from the Court's majority position at any one time. Table 10.1 is a "box score"[7] made up on the votes of the Eisenhower Court justices in 155 of the principal nonunanimous civil liberties decisions from the 1953 through 1961 terms of the Court.[8] Cases involving First Amendment claims and criminal procedures are divided according to whether they were federal or state prosecutions.

Table 10.1

Voting Records of Supreme Court Justices in Certain Nonunanimous Civil Liberties Cases, 1953–1961 Terms

	For Rights of Minorities	For Alien Claims	For Criminal Defendants' Claims		For Free Speech Claims		Total
			State	Federal	State	Federal	
No. of cases	5*	28*	26	35	28	33*	155*

In Percentages

Douglas	80	97	100	97	100	100	98
Black	80	97	96	92	86	100 (33)	94 (155)
Warren	100	73	84	79 (30)	76 (25)	91	81 (148)
Brennan	100	67 (21)	72 (18)	82 (33)	79 (24)	87 (24)	79 (125)
COURT	100	44	35	46	39	59	47
Frankfurter	40	45	27	37 (33)	26 (27)	44	37 (153)
Stewart	100	0 (7)	33 (9)	39 (18)	28 (14)	31 (13)	35 (66)
Harlan	40	20 (19)	13 (23)	30 (33)	26 (27)	40 (33)	28 (140)
Whittaker	25 (4)	21 (20)	20 (10)	32 (25)	14 (21)	29 (21)	24 (101)
Burton	–	13 (23)	12 (17)	0 (17)	29 (14)	47 (19)	20 (90)
Clark	60	7	15	17	14	16 (33)	15 (155)
Minton	–	0 (8)	0 (7)	0 (4)	0 (4)	18 (11)	6 (34)
Reed	–	0 (8)	0 (9)	0 (6)	0 (4)	10 (10)	3 (37)

* – For the purposes of analysis, *Kent v. Dulles* (1958) and *Shelton v. Tucker* (1960) have been considered in two separate categories as the holdings in those cases affected both categories. *Kent* is included under alien claims and federal free speech claims. *Shelton* is included under rights of minorities and state free speech claims. So, although the total number of decisions is considered in this table to be 155, the actual number is 153 cases with the two above repeated cases.

Note the massive point spread between the pre-Eisenhower justices and Warren as compared with a more limited point spread in the middle bloc (composed of Justices Brennan, Frankfurter, Harlan, Whittaker, and Stewart).

Justice Jackson participated in such a small number of cases included in this table that figures on his voting record are omitted. The numbers in parenthesis indicate the number of cases in which a justice participated if he took part in fewer than the total number. The cases included in Table 9.1, classified according to the seven headings used in the table, are as follows:

Rights of minorities (5): For minority claims (5): *Baker v. Carr* (1962); *Hannah v. Larche* (1960); *Boynton v. VA* (1960); *Burton v. Wilmington Parking Authority* (1961); *Shelton v. Tucker* (1960).

Alien cases (28): For alien, expatriate, and denaturalized citizens' claims (10): *Barber v. Gonzales* (1954); *Shaughnessy v. Pedreiro* (1955); *U.S. v. Zucca* (1956); *Rowoldt v. Perfetto* (1957); *U.S. v. Witkovich* (1957); *Nowak v. U.S.* (1958); *Maisenberg v. U.S.* (1958); *Kent v. Dulles* (1958); *Trop v. Dulles* (1958); *Nishikawa v. Dulles* (1958).

Against alien, expatriate, and denaturalized citizens' claims (18): *Longshoreman's Union v. Boyd* (1954); *Galven v. Press* (1954); *Marcello v. Bonds* (1955); *Shaughnessy v. Accardi* (1955); *Jay v. Boyd* (1956); *Hintopoulos v. Shaughnessy* (1957); *Rabang v. Boyd* (1957); *Lehman v. Carson* (1957); *Mulcahey v. Catalanotte* (1957); *Rodgers v. Quan* (1958); *Leng May Ma v. Barber* (1958); *U.S. v. Cores* (1958); *Brown v. U.S.* (1958); *Perez v. Brownell* (1958); *Tak Shan Fong v. U.S.* (1959); *Fleming v. Nestor* (1960); *Niukkanen v. McAlexander* (1960); *Kim v. Rosenberg* (1960).

Table 10.1 *(continued)*

State criminal defendants (26): For defendants' claims (9): *Leyra v. Denno* (1954); *Williams v. Georgia* (1955); *Fikes v. Alabama* (1957); *Moore v. Michigan* (1957); *Griffin v. Illinois* (1957); *Irvin v. Dodd* (1959); *Rogers v. Richmond* (1961); *Reck v. Pate* (1961); *Mapp v. Ohio* (1961). Against defendants' claims (17): *Irvine v. California* (1954); *Regan v. New York* (1955); *Michel v. Louisiana* (1955); *In re Groban* (1957); *Breithaupt v. Abram* (1957); *Ashdown v. Utah* (1958); *Thomas v. Arizona* (1958); *Crooker v. California* (1958); *Cicenia v. Legay* (1958); *Hoag v. New Jersey* (1958); *Ciucci v. Illinois* (1958); *Bartkus v. Illinois* (1959); *Williams v. Oklahoma* (1959); *Knapp v. Schweitzer* (1958); *Mills v. Louisiana* (1959); *Anonymous No. 6 v. Baker* (1959); *Frank v. Maryland* (1959).

Federal criminal defendants (35): For defendants' claims (17): *Toth v. Quarles* (1955); *Rea v. U.S.* (1956); *Kremen v. U.S.* (1957); *Reid v. Covert* (1957); *Green v. U.S.* (1957); *Ladner v. U.S.* (1958); *Miller v. U.S.* (1958); *Jones v. U.S.* (1958); *Giordenello v. U.S.* (1958); *Henry v. U.S.* (1959); *Lee v. Madigan* (1959); *Jones v. U.S.* (1960); *Elkins v. U.S.* (1960); *Kinsella v. Singleton* (1960); *Grisham v. Hagan* (1960); *Rios v. U.S.* (1960); *McElroy v. Guagliardo* (1960). Against defendants' claims (18): *Walder v. U.S.* (1954); *Lewis v. U.S.* (1955); *Kinsella v. Krueger* (1956); *Reid v. Covert* (1956); *Rathbun v. U.S.* (1957); *Pollard v. U.S.* (1957); *Paoli v. U.S.* (1957); *Gore v. U.S.* (1958); *Harris v. U.S.* (1959); *Abbate v. U.S.* (1959); *Draper v. U.S.* (1959); *Grunewald v. U.S.* (1959); *Brown v. U.S.* (1959); *Rosenberg v. U.S.* (1959); *Pittsburgh Plate Glass Company v. U.S.* (1959); *Abel v. U.S.* (1960); *Wilson v. Schnettler* (1961); *Pugach v. Dollinger* (1961).

State free speech (28): For defendants' claims (11): *Pennsylvania v. Nelson* (1956); *Slochower v. Board of Education* (1956); *Konigsberg v. State Bar* (1957); *Sweezy v. New Hampshire* (1957); *Speiser v. Randall* (1958); *First Unitarian Church v. Los Angeles* (1958); *Staub v. City of Baxley* (1958); *Farmer's Union v. WDAY* (1959); *Talley v. California* (1960); *Shelton v. Tucker* (1960); *Engle v. Vitale* (1961). Against defendants' claims (17): *Barsky v. Board of Regents* (1954); *Black v. Cutter Laboratories* (1956); *Kingsley Books v. Brown* (1957); *International Brotherhood of Teamsters v. Vogt* (1957); *Youngdahl v. Rainfair* (1957); *Beilan v. Board of Education* (1958); *Lerner v. Casey* (1958); *Uphaus v. Wyman* (1959); *Nelson v. County of Los Angeles* (1960); *Nostrand v. Little* (1960); *Konigsberg v. State Bar* (1961); *In re Anastaplo* (1961); *Times Film Corporation v. Chicago* (1961); *McGowan v. Maryland* (1961); *Two Guys from Harrison-Allentown v. McGinley* (1961); *Braunfield v. Brown* (1961); *Gallagher v. Crown Kosher Super Market* (1961).

Federal free speech (33): For defendants' claims (19): *Quinn v. U.S.* (1955); *Emspak v. U.S.* (1955); *Bart v. U.S.* (1955); *Peters v. Hobby* (1955); *Communist Party v. Subversive Activities Control Board* (1956); *Cole v. Young* (1956); *Mesarosh v. U.S.* (1956); *Yates v. U.S.* (1957); *Jencks v. U.S.* (1957); *Watkins v. U.S.* (1957); *Harmon v. Brucker* (1958); *Sacher v. U.S.* (1958); *Dayton v. Dulles* (1958); *Kent v. Dulles* (1958); *Greene v. McElroy* (1959); *Vitarelli v. Seaton* (1959); *Campbell v. U.S.* (1961); *Clancy v. U.S.* (1961); *Deutch v. U.S.* (1961). Against defendants' claims (14): *U.S. v. Harriss* (1954); *Ullmann v. U.S.* (1956); *Yates v. U.S.* (1957); *Roth v. U.S.* (1957); *Green v. U.S.* (1958); *International Association of Machinists v. Gonzales* (1958); *Barenblatt v. U.S.* (1959); *Gonzales v. U.S.* (1960); *McPhaul v. U.S.* (1960); *Wilkinson v. U.S.* (1961); *Braden v. U.S.* (1961); *Communist Party v. Subversive Activities Control Board* (1961); *Scales v. U.S.* (1961); *Cafeteria Workers v. McElroy* (1961).

The warning of Professor John Frank should be added here: "A major vice of the statistical method is that the reader is dangerously likely to accept the capsulated knowledge in the omniscient columns of figures without realizing how dubious was the compiler's judgment on which the figures were based. The statistics are no better than that scholarly comprehension of their compiler, and he must be cautious indeed. His questions should be reserved in footnotes, and the most dubious cases should be set aside altogether." John P. Frank, "Book Review," 34 *Iowa L. Rev.* 144 at 146 (1948).

Table 10.1 *(continued)*

For criticism of statistical studies of the Supreme Court, See generally, Franklin M. Fisher, "The Mathematical Analysis of Supreme Court Decisions: The Use and Abuse of Quantitative Methods," 52 *Am. Pol. Sci. Rev.* 321 (1958); John P. Roche, "Political Science and Science Fiction," 52 *Am. Pol. Sci. Rev.* 1026 (1958).

Table 10.1 gives for each category the percentage of cases which the Court as a whole, and each individual justice, decided favorably to the particular civil liberties claim involved. This "pro-individual, antigovernment" formula is a questionable one as an adequate measure for testing the actual liberalism of a justice. These votes were cast in a judicial environment and represent the resolution of situations where many legitimate values may have been competing for attention. What the table does establish is the degree to which each member of the Court found it desirable as a judge to prefer libertarian values rather than others present in those cases.

Table 10.1 shows that four members of the Eisenhower Court—Warren, Black, Douglas, and Brennan voted for libertarian claims substantially more often than the Court majority. The extremely high rate of support for libertarian claims registered by these justices indicates that they held strongly libertarian views and they believed their judicial role permitted them to express those views in their opinions. Yet there was frequently disagreement between Justice Brennan and the other three expressed in separate dissents or concurring opinions even when all four justices agreed on the outcome of a given case. For this and other reasons to be noted later, Justice Brennan could not be counted as a firm member of the Court's libertarian left, and analysis of his voting record will be reserved for the following chapter. There are also nuances in the philosophies of Black, Douglas, and the Chief Justice that will be noted. Without assuming an identity of views on their part, however, these three justices could be characterized as "libertarian activists."

There is, of course, no such thing as an undiluted "activist." The views of these justices were not unequivocally absolutist regardless of their many comments in dicta to the contrary. Also, it was obvious that they were "activist" at a given time in dealing with certain subjects. For instance, Justice Black was an activist favoring restriction of state action interfering with First Amendment rights, but he was less of an activist in protecting economic rights of the states or in approving state criminal procedures. The "restraintist" attitude of Justice Black in the *Lady Chatterley* case has previously been noted. Indeed, so much has been written about the judicial activism of Justices Black and Douglas that only a brief review of their philosophy and a few examples of its application during the Eisenhower Court years are needed here.[9]

SIGNS OF ACTIVISM

Ranking at the top of the hierarchy of values of the more libertarian Justices Black and Douglas was the idea of an open, pluralistic society vital-
ized by the free expression and exchange of ideas. In this view, the First
Amendment freedoms—those explicitly stated and the implied freedoms
of belief and association—are in a preferred position because of their essential nature to a free society. Any legislative action infringing those freedoms must be justified by overwhelmingly conclusive considerations. In
the words of Justice Black, First Amendment freedoms "are absolutely
indispensable for the preservation of a free society in which government
is based upon the consent of an informed citizenry and is dedicated to the
protection of the rights of all, even the most despised minorities."[10] Such
a viewpoint led these justices to dissent from the opinion of the Court
holding obscene speech to be outside of the First Amendment protection.

Justice Douglas defended this theory in absolutist terms: "The First
Amendment, its prohibition in terms absolute . . . puts free speech in the
preferred position."[11] The Fourteenth Amendment was likewise the protector of an open society to Douglas, who believed that it guaranteed a
person "the right to believe what one chooses, the right to differ from his
neighbor, the right to pick and choose the political philosophy that he
likes best, the right to associate with whomever he chooses, the right to
join the groups he prefers, the privilege of selecting his own path to salva-
tion."[12] Black and Douglas, then, gave a broad interpretation to the First
and Fourteenth Amendments, confident that Americans had the "capacity to sort out the true from the false in theology, economics, politics, or
any other field."[13]

Yet both of those justices admitted that there were some conditions
under which speech could be controlled. Justice Douglas conceded in *Roth*
that "freedom of expression can be suppressed if, and to the extent that, it
is so closely brigaded with illegal action as to be an inseparable part of
it."[14]

The failure of the activists to find such conditions in cases dealing
with picketing rights divided them from the rest of the Court.[15] Beginning
in 1940, organized labor had strong allies in the more libertarian justices
of the highest tribunal. In the late 1950s, however, the former "underdog"
labor appeared to be of age and its ardent defenders were dwindling in
number. Dissenting in *Vogt*, Justice Douglas reiterated that picketing might
involve more than speech,[16] but in language reminiscent of the Roosevelt
Court, he bewailed the Court's "retreat" from the *Thornhill* doctrine which
he felt became a "route" ending in a formal "surrender." In picketing cases,
according to Douglas, "the Court has now come full circle."[17]

In *United States v. UAW*,[18] the activists dissented from the majority
opinion which failed to find a constitutional question in the case and re-

manded it to the lower court. The UAW was charged with having used union dues to sponsor commercial television broadcasts designed to influence the electorate to select certain candidates for Congress in violation of a federal statute. Justice Douglas's dissent argued that the act "as construed and applied" was "a broadside assault on the freedom of political expression guaranteed by the First Amendment." According to the activists there was a principle involved that transcended the immediate case: "The principle at stake is not peculiar to unions. It is applicable as well to associations of manufacturers, retail and wholesale trade groups, consumers' leagues, farmers' unions, religious groups and every other association representing a segment of American life and taking a part in our political campaigns and discussions. It is as important an issue as has come before the Court for it reaches the very vitals of our system of government."[19]

Justice Douglas, in *Perez*, indicated that the preferred position doctrine might be expanded to include areas outside the First Amendment: "Citizenship, like freedom of speech, press, and religion, occupies a preferred position in our written Constitution because it is a grant absolute in terms."[20]

Closely associated with the opinions of the libertarian activists is a high degree of sympathetic reaction to the claims of litigants whose civil liberties have allegedly been violated. In cases involving denaturalization, expatriation, or deportation, the activists set forth in detail the personal circumstances of the people involved, including the length of time they have been in this country, their occupations, military service, community ties, and sometimes their health.[21] In *Konigsberg* and *Schware*, the personal histories of aspiring lawyers as presented by Justice Black were an integral part of the opinion of the Court.

The libertarian three seemed to have a sense of personal involvement when the rights of "unpopular citizens" were in question. The discussion of the preceding chapters should have made clear the extent of libertarian support of the "underdogs" of society such as aliens, racial and political minorities, and defendants in criminal trials. Justice Douglas expressed the libertarian activist values regarding unpopular citizens in *Michel v. Louisiana*: "I would give every accused, regardless of his record, conduct, reputation or beliefs, the full benefit of the constitutional guarantees of due process."[22] The Court's left also consistently championed procedural regularity for "subversives," although many of those defendants were neither social nor economic underdogs.

The libertarian activists used matters of form and procedure to meet their needs in a given case. In cases involving the Court's review of criminal prosecutions, the libertarian typically insisted upon strict adherence to the procedural safeguards surrounding the administration of justice. Justices Black and Douglas frequently echoed their broad pronouncements of the "total incorporation" theory, especially where Fourth and Fifth Amendment protections were abridged by a state. In such cases they were usually joined by the Chief Justice and sometimes Justice Brennan. Thus in *Frank v. Maryland*, all three libertarians insisted, in dissent, that a search warrant was necessary to justify the inspection of a private dwelling even though there was evidence of a rat infestation on the premises. Where procedure was a restraint on interference with liberties, it was welcomed as seen in the activists' stand in cases dealing with "subversives" and those involving military justice. But in some cases Black and Douglas wanted to deal with the constitutional issues, and concurred only in the result. In *Yates* and *Nishikawa* these two justices would have found the Smith Act and part of the Nationality Act of 1940 unconstitutional. All three activists were in the *Trop* and *Reid* majorities that declared congressional acts unconstitutional, and they urged similar action in dissent in *Perez*. In *Speiser*, they concurred in both the judgment and the opinion of the Court, but they also filed separate statements reiterating their disapproval of the *Dennis* decision and declaring that freedom of belief and utterance are absolute.

On the other hand, the silence of Congress could be construed to achieve a libertarian victory. This technique was used by Justice Douglas for the Court in *Kent v. Dulles*, where he stated: "The right to travel is part of the 'liberty' of which the citizen cannot be deprived without due process of law under the Fifth Amendment. . . . Freedom of movement is basic in our scheme of values."[23] When opportunity is present, Congress could be endowed with benevolent intentions by the activists—or even field-filling capabilities as in *Nelson*.

Where stare decisis blocked the way of a libertarian result, the activists had a simple remedy—reject it. This was exactly what was urged by Justice Douglas in *Ullmann* and by Justice Black in his eloquent dissent in *Green v. United States*:

> Ordinarily it is sound policy to adhere to prior decisions but this practice has quite properly never been a blind, inflexible rule. Courts are not omniscient. Like every other human agency, they too can profit from trial and error, from experience and reflection. As others have demonstrated, the principle commonly referred to as *stare decisis* has never been thought to extend so far as to prevent the courts from correcting their own errors. Accordingly, this Court has time and time again from the very beginning reconsidered the merits of its earlier decisions even though they claimed great longevity and repeated reaffirmation. . . . Indeed, the Court has a special responsibility where questions of constitutional law are involved to review its decisions from time to time and where compelling reasons present themselves to refuse to follow erroneous precedents; otherwise its mistakes in interpreting the Constitution are extremely difficult to alleviate and needlessly so.[24]

Black and Douglas also sought an end to the long-established rule of not applying ex post facto provisions to alien proceedings.[25]

Police techniques used against suspected lawbreakers could likewise be accepted or rejected by the Court's left. In *Rathbun,* Black and Warren accepted listening on a telephone extension as common practice, while in *Breithaupt,* the activists in dissent could not so find for a blood test. Justice Douglas's dissent with Justice Frankfurter in *Rathbun* again emphasized the fact that the activists were not always in agreement.

According to a study by Harold Spaeth, "Douglas [was] more attitudinally extreme than Black (extremity of viewpoint, in relation to attitudes held by other members of the Court, being equated with frequency of dissent)."[26] Or put another way, Black's less extreme dissenting behavior was a manifestation of attitudes less extreme than those of Douglas. This was illustrated by Douglas's solo dissents in *Draper* and *Williams v. Oklahoma.* Justice Douglas also showed stronger antipathy toward long drawn out litigation in the state courts accounting for other disagreements with Black.[27] In *Martin v. Creasy,* Douglas maintained in dissent (without the support of Justice Black) that

> the federal courts, created by the First Congress are today a haven where rights can sometimes be adjudicated even more dispassionately than in state tribunals. At least Congress in its wisdom has provided since 1875 (18 Stat. 470) that the lower federal courts should be the guardian of federal rights. . . . This is not intermeddling in state affairs nor creating needless friction. It is an authoritative pronouncement at the beginning of a controversy, which saves countless days in the slow, painful, and costly litigation of separate individual lawsuits in state . . . proceedings.[28]

Black and Douglas also had pronounced differences in areas other than civil liberties—notably on questions of federal taxation.

During the Eisenhower Court era, Black was the catalyst for the Court's advances in protecting civil liberties, and his zeal made the Bill of Rights central to the work of the Court. Douglas, an original judicial mind, made his most significant contribution during this era by articulating the constitutional value of liberty in memorable rhetoric.[29]

THE ACTIVISM OF CHIEF JUSTICE WARREN

Chief Justice Warren showed substantial agreement with most of the activist pronouncements of Justices Black and Douglas. Warren's philosophy of libertarian activism appears to have developed over a period of time, however, for during his first two terms on the Court, he was frequently in disagreement with Black and Douglas in civil liberties cases. A less libertarian viewpoint might be expected of the Chief Justice in light of his previous experience with the law, which was limited to the enforcement side. As a county attorney and state attorney general, he established a reputation of being tough on lawbreakers. During World War II, as California's attorney general, Warren defended the constitutionality of evacuating Japanese-Americans from the West Coast on the ground that in time of war the military authorities have the right to determine who could remain in a strategic zone.[30] Warren's atypically Republican governorship, on the other hand, was noted for its liberalism, and his public speeches gave some indication that he possessed libertarian viewpoints on several civil liberties issues.[31]

As Chief Justice, Warren probably moved with caution in learning the intricacies of his new position. During his first two terms, Warren relied heavily upon Justice Frankfurter as a guide, and he sought Frankfurter's advice on a number of on- and off-the-Court matters. Frankfurter, of course, was making a concerted effort to win the new Chief to his point of view—a tactic that he used on many of the new appointees to the Court during his long service. Warren apparently was initially pleased by the attention paid him by a senior justice, and the two men worked well in tandem. Together they secured unanimous decisions in both *Brown I* and *Brown II*, and Frankfurter advised Warren on other cases. In his personal correspondence and in remarks to friends, Frankfurter spoke highly of Warren and had high hopes for him as Chief Justice—so long as the associate justice's charm offensive seemed to be working. From the beginning Warren also enjoyed a friendly relationship with Justice Clark, whom he had known for many years. Warren voted with Frankfurter and Clark more than 70 percent of the time in the 1953 and 1954 terms.

This background may explain some of Warren's early votes in cases involving criminal procedures. In 1954 and 1955, while reaching a libertarian result in *Toth, Leyra,* and *Williams v. Georgia*, Warren voted with the majority and against the defendant's claims in *Walder, Irvine, Lewis,* and *Regan*.

By the end of the 1954 term, Warren appears to have settled comfortably into his role as Chief. He had shouldered his share of the work, writing as many or more opinions for the Court as any of his colleagues during his first two terms. Warren also had developed his own judicial philosophy in civil liberties cases. He perhaps was less inclined to rely on the advice of others, and the number of his votes with Clark and Frankfurter declined. Instead, the Chief Justice began voting regularly with Black and Douglas and parted company with them in only a few instances (notably in *Roth, Alberts, Ashdown, Harriss,* and *Paoli*). Frankfurter's enthusiasm for the Chief began to wane after the end of the 1956 term, and he increasingly criticized Warren in communications with his friends—calling Warren's work "dishonest nonsense."[32] There were often personality conflicts between the two, and their relationship became extremely bitter.

During sitting conferences, hard words passed between Warren and Frankfurter on several occasions. Once Frankfurter's anger flared, and he purportedly told Warren, "You're the worst Chief Justice this country has ever had."[33] Not surprisingly, the Chief Justice advised his law clerks to stay away from Frankfurter's chambers and observe noble silence around his clerks.

Several public manifestations of off-the-record dissidence occurred in the Supreme Court chambers and involved Warren and Frankfurter. On three occasions, Warren publicly took offense at Frankfurter's oral version of a dissenting opinion and answered back. The first occurred when the *Trop* decision was announced on 31 March 1958. Anthony Lewis referred to the justices' remarks as "bitter, even waspish," when Frankfurter challenged the accuracy of cases cited in the Chief Justice's opinion.[34] At the end of that same term, the Chief Justice retorted hotly to a lengthy dissent by Frankfurter. On 30 June 1958, Warren announced an unsigned opinion turning down a challenge to California's method for determining the sanity of prisoners scheduled for execution.[35] Frankfurter delivered a sharply worded dissent which took him several minutes to read. Chief Justice Warren, visibly disturbed, offered a rebuttal beginning: "Neither the judgment of this Court nor that of California is quite as savage as this dissent would indicate."[36] Frankfurter also drew an irate reply from the Chief Justice under similar circumstances during the 1960 term.[37] That time the exchange was even more unusual because Chief Justice Warren had written no opinion in the case involving a "same offense" double jeopardy question. Justice Frankfurter assailed the majority opinion of Justice Stewart stating: "I know what the Court has said but I don't understand the meaning of it." Several times Frankfurter suggested that the majority view simply made no sense. The Chief Justice felt compelled to rejoin that "since so much has been said here that was not in any written opinion" he wanted to add a word as to why he joined the majority. Having done so, he turned to Frankfurter who sat immediately to his left and murmured an invitation to respond if the latter wished to. To this Frankfurter replied: "The Chief Justice urges me to comment on what he said, but of course I won't. I have another case."[38]

Such intemperate remarks in the courtroom would have been better left unsaid or at least reserved for the privacy of the secret conference. The heated exchanges between Frankfurter and Warren incisively destroyed the notion that the Chief Justice, with his public image as a solemn, fatherly, and majestic-looking Chief,[39] had restored harmony to a badly divided Court.[40] Warren doubtlessly was challenged in trying to reign in his prickly, verbose, didactic colleague while maintaining his own sense of dignity.

The Chief's fellow justices, excluding Frankfurter, liked and respected Warren during the Eisenhower years, and he made good use of his tact, humor, and persuasion in leading the Court by being its most influential member. He was a splendid political leader known for his "openness, optimism, and idealism without ideology."[41]

In dealing with alleged subversives, Warren insisted that defendants receive procedural regularity. In this area, his votes were identical with those of Black and Douglas, with two notable exceptions. In *Barsky v. Board of Regents of New York*, Warren was with the majority that upheld the state's six-month suspension of a medical doctor solely on the basis of his conviction for contempt of Congress, and in *Ullmann*, he concurred in Frankfurter's opinion upholding the Immunity Act of 1954.

In most of his criminal law decisions, Warren's conception of fairness was the key factor. In oral argument, he would frequently inquire of counsel, "But was it fair?" Legal rules or precedents rarely stood in the way of the Chief's effort to remedy a situation where he thought an individual had been treated unfairly. For Warren, justice consisted of seeing that the right side, the good side, prevailed in a particular case.

Although not going to the same extremes as Black and Douglas in his opinions, Chief Justice Warren placed strong reliance on the First Amendment's protection of beliefs, expressions, and associations—especially in *Watkins*, *Sweezy*, *Barenblatt*, and *Uphaus*. He also saw the dangers of conformity that would follow the suppression of those freedoms. Professor Schwartz suggested that Warren perhaps had been won over to the preferred position view by his joining Justice Black in his *Barenblatt* dissent,[42] but this could be disputed in light of the Chief Justice's rejection of the absolutist position of Black and Douglas in *Roth* and *Alberts* where the Chief's strong animus towards "smut-peddlers" or those involved in vice came into play.

In cases involving alleged violations of the rights of African-Americans, Warren and Douglas urged the Court to grant certiorari more often and showed displeasure with the lengthy litigation sometime required in state courts before the cases reached federal jurisdiction.[43] Warren's opinions protecting the rights of minority groups are classic examples of sociological jurisprudence applied to contemporary problems. The notion of equality was a great theme in Warren's jurisprudence—equality of races, of citizens, rich and poor, and of prosecutor and defendant.[44]

Warren on occasion solicitously endowed Congress with presumptive good intentions and invested its silence with concern for procedural regularity similar to that felt by the Court. As the Chief Justice said: "Where the legislature has failed to make its intention manifest, courts should proceed cautiously, remaining sensitive to the interests of defendant and society alike. All relevant criteria must be considered and the most useful aid will often be common sense."[45]

Because of his endorsement of Justice Black's dissent in *Bartkus*, Warren was accused of accepting the total incorporation theory of Black and Douglas.[46] Careful reading of this opinion, however, casts doubt on this theory—as did Warren's votes cast in opposition to both Black and Douglas in *Ashdown, Harriss,* and *Paoli.*

In summary, the judicial activists were justices who were philosophically or perhaps emotionally concerned with the outcome or consequences of any decision of the Court. Because of their involvement, they felt a genuine sense of personal responsibility for such consequences. The standards, techniques, and methods of the American legal system were of less concern to the activists who tended to feel that achievement of the libertarian goals that they evaluated as "right" was of first importance. The activists, then, were goal-oriented reformers who might be called "pragmatists" since they tested the utility of a particular positive law proposition by its consequences in action when applied.

Of course, these judicial reactions were not unique or characteristic of only three members of the Court. Only very irresponsible or unrealistic justices would not be concerned about the consequences of their decisions and would not test their reasoning by the type of results it produced. It should be emphasized again that the differences between the justices classified as libertarian activists and other members of the Court were differences of degree.

The activists served a useful purpose on the Court in defending the rights of the individual in such an important forum. Their strong appeals for libertarian claims doubtlessly had some effect on public opinion. On the Eisenhower Court, the advocates of judicial activism were in the majority more often than at any time since the deaths of Murphy and Rutledge in 1947. In their majority opinions and biting and scornful dissents, Black, Douglas, and Warren expressed a diligence to maintain civil liberties which gave intellectual leadership and stimulus to those citizens who believed, at a minimum, that when the Constitution of the United States provided a Bill of Rights, very few abridgments were to be tolerated.[47]

The main criticism of the activist approach was that it tended to overemphasize one set of values. According to Professor McCloskey, "With all respect, it is suggested that the civil liberties position adopted by Justices Black and Douglas smacks strongly of the judicial absolutism of the pre-1937 era."[48] A Supreme Court justice has a duty to balance competing claims of liberty and authority in society. If a justice automatically takes the libertarian side on every issue, he or she is not functioning in a balancing capacity. As Justice Jackson put it: "Perhaps the most delicate, difficult and shifting of all balances which the Court is expected to maintain is that between liberty and authority. It is not so easy as some people believe to determine what serves liberty best by way of restriction of authority."[49]

The activists were accused of "label thinking,"[50] because they held a strong presumption that certain types of restrictions were unconstitutional and limited the judicial task to determining whether a restriction in a given case fit into one of the proscribed categories. If so, it was automatically void. Perhaps the best example of this practice was in the censorship cases. For Justices Black and Douglas, practically any form of censorship of any media was unconstitutional. Critics stated that it would seem preferable that the determining factor in a judgment of unconstitutionality should be, not the label of the restraint, but rather the seriousness of the threat to freedom and the justification offered for the limitation. The activist reply to this would be that what was called "labeling" was actually an honest weighing of the ends to be achieved by restraints on the justices' scales of democratic values. On this scale, civil liberties weighed heaviest with First Amendment rights probably outweighing all the rest.[51]

It was the failure of the popularly elected "political" branches to live up to the constitutional mandates guaranteeing minority rights against majority rule which furnished the activists with what they considered their special duty—to restore, by vigilant use of the judicial veto, those constitutional rights of which the people had been improperly deprived. To do this, in the eyes of the libertarian three, was the Court's most challenging task and finest achievement.

JUSTICE CLARK AND THE VINSON COURT MAJORITY

At the opposite extreme from the activist justices was Justice Clark, the one remaining Truman appointee to the Court, who was also the only survivor of the latter-day Vinson Court majority (Vinson, Reed, Minton, Burton, and Clark) which was criticized for its less-libertarian attitude toward civil liberties. As a young assistant in the Justice department, Clark had known Warren when he was attorney general of California. On the Court, Clark enjoyed a friendly relationship with Warren, and during the 1953 term he agreed with him more than any other justice. As the Eisenhower appointees replaced these less-libertarian justices, Clark found himself often in dissent from the opinions of the Court. For a time he was joined in dissent by Minton and Reed (and less frequently, Burton) who were also incongruous with the new tendencies of the Eisenhower Court. After the retirement of Minton and Reed, Justice Clark was frequently the sole dissenter in security cases; and in ruling on federal criminal prosecutions, he was, in many instances, in agreement with only Justice Burton. In security program cases, Clark made an interesting switch. After voting with the majority in finding for Dr. Peters, he dissented with Minton and Reed in *Cole* and after their retirement, Clark continued his opposition to the Court's findings of violations of administrative procedures in *Harmon* and *Greene*. In ruling on the privilege against self-incrimination before congressional committees, Justice Clark was with the majority in *Quinn,* *Emspak,* and *Bart* (a record more libertarian in this area than that of Justice Harlan who dissented with Minton and Reed in the latter two cases). Clark voted with the majority in *Nelson* but wrote the opinion of the Court in *Uphaus* that limited *Nelson* and demonstrated that the states could still legislate against some types of subversion. He was also in the majority that ordered a new trial for Mesarosh (over the objections of dissenters Frankfurter, Harlan, and Burton). His vote produced a libertarian result in the five-to-four *Slochower* decision, although he was later with the five-justice majority in *Beilan* and *Lerner* that ruled against the claims of dismissed state and local employees. In sum, Clark held a strong commitment to federalism and separation of powers in Communist cases.

His experience as attorney general probably was significant in shaping his judicial attitudes, though hardly explanatory of them.[52] In cases dealing with federal and state criminal proceedings, Clark tended to affirm practically any action which the governments deemed necessary. Yet there were occasions when state police methods were too extreme even for Clark. In *Leyra* and *Fikes v. Alabama,* he voted with the majority in ruling against the state. In *Griffin,* where poverty was a bar to the right of appeal in state courts, Justice Clark was with the majority that ruled that equal protection had been denied. Similarly in a few federal cases he deviated from his usual pattern. In *Rea v. United States,* he provided the fifth vote needed by the libertarian majority to hold that a federal agent could be enjoined from testifying in a state court proceeding with respect to evidence obtained by him in the course of an unlawful search that had been suppressed in a prior federal prosecution under the federal rule barring illegal evidence. In *Toth,* he joined the majority in finding a provision of the Uniform Code of Military Justice unconstitutional. Clark also showed little sympathy for aliens in deportation cases and supported the government's claims in decisions involving expatriation and denaturalization.

Justice Clark exhibited libertarian attitudes in three very important areas—cases involving the rights of minority groups, non-seditious First Amendment cases, and most significantly, in search and seizure cases. As attorney general, Clark was a staunch supporter of President Truman's strong civil rights stand, and on the Court, he was a member of the majority in desegregation cases. In 1952 he was the author of the *Burstyn* opinion that brought movies under the protection of freedom of the press, and his concurring opinion in the *Lady Chatterly's Lover* decision reaffirmed his caution in dealing with movie censorship. In addition, Clark's vote with the Chief Justice and Justices Black, Douglas, and Brennan formed the libertarian majority in the *WDAY* case. He likewise joined the majority in the school prayer case, *Engel v. Vitale.* He wrote his most significant opinion in the controversial landmark case, *Mapp v. Ohio*, which applied the federal exclusionary rule to state criminal procedure.

With the exceptions noted, Justice Clark usually was a member of the bloc reaching the less-libertarian result in cases when the Court was sharply divided. In following an independent course, he exhibited little accord with the activist or restraintist philosophies of his surviving fellow justices of the Vinson era. He probably wished "a pox on both houses" but during the Eisenhower years usually ended up voting with Justice Frankfurter when the two schools disagreed. Although overshadowed by his more brilliant brethren, Clark, according to Bernard Schwartz, "developed into a more competent judge than any of the other Truman appointees. In fact, Clark has been the most underrated justice in recent Supreme Court history."[53]

The justices who retired from the Eisenhower Court—Minton, Reed, and Burton—deserve brief mention although they exerted their greatest influence on the Court prior to the appointment of Warren. These justices were all participants in the unanimous school segregation decision, but their legal philosophies were, for the most part, less libertarian than those of their successors, and the changed attitude of the Court became pronounced only after the retirement of Minton. Until that time the four survivors of the Vinson majority were sometimes able to win over one or more additional votes and thus remained a strong force on the high tribunal.

Justice Burton, a Truman appointee, served five terms on the Eisenhower Court. He was a studious and cautious justice who displayed great respect for precedent. His voting statistics indicate that he could not be classified as a strong libertarian. He possessed the distinguishing characteristics of the McCarthy-era, less-libertarian justice—the judicial belief that almost all was fair for government in fighting crime and Cold War internal subversion. Burton had a consistent record of voting against defendants' claims in the split decisions in Table 10.1 involving federal criminal prosecutions. In state cases, his antilibertarian record was spoiled only by his finding of denials of due process in *William v. Georgia* and *Irvine*. He was also generally tough on defendants in deportation, denaturalization, and expatriation cases. In dealing with political offenders, Burton was, next to Clark, the chief supporter of the government's program against suspected subversives, although he was with the majority in two of the controversial 1957 decisions—*Yates* and *Jencks*. He also was willing to grant subversives the use of the privilege against self-incrimination before congressional committees and voted against state loyalty oaths. He contended that the dismissal of Dr. Peters was legitimate but then found that administrative procedures had been violated in *Cole* and *Harmon*. Burton cast a key vote in the *Konigsberg* majority, joining the activists and Brennan in finding a denial of due process in state bar proceedings.

Justices Reed and Minton, the other survivors of the Vinson-era majority on the Eisenhower Court for more than two terms, exhibited little agreement with the more libertarian philosophy of the Court after the additions of Warren and Harlan. Their voting records for defendants' claims were revealing: Justice Minton could find that constitutional rights had been denied only Quinn and Peters, while Justice Reed voted favorably only for Mesarosh. As these justices approached retirement they found themselves more and more often in dissent from the opinions of the new libertarian majority composed of Black, Douglas, Frankfurter, and the two Eisenhower appointees. Minton's frustration with the changing judicial order surfaced during the *Griffin* case conference when he is reported to have complained, "Here we go again" interfering with state criminal procedure.[54]

JUSTICE FRANKFURTER: JUDICIAL RESTRAINT

Between the Black–Douglas–Warren and the Clark extremes, the other members of the Court were ranged with Justice Frankfurter occupying the center position. Around this center the Eisenhower Court majority developed, with Frankfurter being a key figure in leading the Court from an era of passivity to one of greater activity in protecting civil liberties. His philosophy of judicial restraint appears to have been an important influence on the legal philosophies of the Eisenhower associate justices, including Brennan during his early terms on the Court. Requisite to an understanding of the jurisprudence of the Eisenhower Court majority, then, is a familiarity with the philosophy of judicial restraint.

On the Eisenhower Court, Frankfurter was, by far, the strongest proponent of judicial restraint, but by no means the least libertarian justice. Differing from the judicial activist, the libertarian judicial restraintist was not an advocate or crusader, and he did not hold as strong a view of the Court as an instrument of social and political change. His restraint sprang partly from self-imposed habits of discipline and partly from his respect for the standards of the legal system. The restraintist regarded the Court as a balancer of conflicting interests, powers, and policies at work in a society of diversified groups, organizations, and associations already made excessively complex by too much advocacy. He was not unconcerned with values and goals but he felt these were the aims of politics, and he tended to view a nonelected yet powerful judicial body as incompetent for a major political role. In the words of Justice Frankfurter: "To assume that a lawyer who becomes a judge takes on the bench merely his views on social and economic questions leaves out of account his rooted notions regarding the scope and limits of a judge's authority. The outlook of a lawyer fit to be a Justice regarding the role of a judge cuts across all his personal preferences for this or that social arrangement."[55] The restraintist accepted the consequence that justices could not contribute to the solution of some social problems and could offer only partial solutions, perhaps inadequate and belated, for others.

In deciding whether the Court was commissioned to protect some of the people from what judges might feel were the aberrations of democracy, or whether the Court, in the absence of the clearest violation of constitutional liberties, should trust the people themselves to move toward tolerance and wisdom under their own power, the restraintist tended to place more emphasis on the latter choice. The advocates of self-denial, with their belief in the limits of the judicial process, indicated that they felt the activists manipulated the law in accordance with their own ideals. The activists, with their skepticism about judicial objectivity, could not resist feeling that self-denial was a cover for conservatism.

Historically, it was a liberal minority that stressed the necessity for judicial self-restraint, as opposed to the conservative practice of broad judicial review in economic matters in the early twentieth century. This liberal doctrine of judicial restraint was used by the Roosevelt Court to protect progressive social legislation from invalidation, but it was less well adapted for use by crusading liberal justices faced with legislative attacks on basic civil liberties. The Roosevelt Court split apart on the issue of restraint and the division continued on the Eisenhower Court. The attempts of Justice Frankfurter to apply those principles of restraint accounted for what some of his critics considered antilibertarian results.

JUDICIAL RESTRAINT AND THE SEPARATION OF POWERS

From the restraintist view, the Supreme Court is but one of the instruments of political and social accommodation and adjustment in a complicated governmental system. The standards, then, for determining the appropriateness of judicial action should be based on the position of the judiciary vis-à-vis the other two branches in our system of separation of powers. In the restraintist system of ordered liberty, the proper allocation of competencies among the institutions of our legal order was of prime import. The justices should thus be greatly concerned with fixing the boundaries of judicial power beyond which the Court should not roam. These considerations of judicial prudence were reinforced by Frankfurter's strong restraintist belief that the courts were the least representative or democratically responsible of the three branches.[56] In the words of Justice Frankfurter: "The Court is entitled to rule that legislating is for Congress and that the judicial branch should not be saddled with functions which are not within its sphere of competence."[57] Or as Frankfurter wrote in a letter to Black: "Legislatures make law wholesale, judges retail. In other words they cannot decide things by invoking a new major premise out of whole cloth, they must make the law that they do make out of the existing materials and with due deference to the presumptions of the legal system of which they have been made a part."[58]

Thus, in *Galvan v. Press*, Justice Frankfurter appeared to bemoan the fact that the Court affirmed the deportation of an alien who did not understand the purpose of the Communist Party when he joined, but his personal feelings yielded to the power of Congress to control aliens: "That the formulation of these policies is entrusted exclusively to Congress has become about as firmly imbedded in the legislative and judicial tissues of our body politic as any aspect of our government."[59] Frankfurter was more ready than his brethren to accept the dangers of administrative finality simply because Congress had chosen to accept them. In his view, the Court had no special function to protect the people against legislative encroachments on personal freedoms.

In a letter to Brennan, Frankfurter rehearsed his personal disapproval of state antisubversive activities while upholding the contempt conviction of Uphaus appearing before the attorney general of New Hampshire: "There isn't a man on the Court, who personally disapproves more than I do of the activities of all the un-American Committees, of all the Smith prosecutions, of all the Attorney General's list, etc., etc."[60]

Justice Frankfurter, according to Professor Summers, in interpreting laws "read into statutes considerations which may never have occurred to the legislature. . . . What Frankfurter says is that these values or policies are so basic, so integral a part of our social and legal pattern, that Congress cannot deny or destroy them without thinking. The Court will protect these values at least until Congress has given them the deliberate consideration that is evidenced by explicit statutory words. The Court does not block Congress; it only checks its thoughtlessness."[61]

In *Gore v. United States*, Justice Frankfurter sternly warned the Court that it could not "enter the field of penology and apportion punishments," this being the function of others as determined by the people.[62] Likewise, Justice Frankfurter, for the Court, found that even President Eisenhower had to be kept within his proper sphere of power. In the historic case *Humphrey's Executor v. United States*[63] in 1935, the Supreme Court ruled that removal of officials from certain independent agencies, such as the Federal Trade Commission, could be limited to causes defined by Congress. In *Wiener v. United States*,[64] Justice Frankfurter's opinion contended that failure of Congress to provide for removal for cause in no way diminished the essential principle of *Humphrey's* decision—that the function of the agency was determinative. Thus President Eisenhower was held powerless to remove a member of the War Claims Commission for political reasons similar to those offered in the *Humphrey* affair by President Roosevelt because the "nature of the function" of the Commission, as expressed in the 1948 act under which it was established, revealed a congressional intention that its members should be free of such presidential control:

> Judging the matter in all the nakedness in which it is presented, namely, the claim that the President could remove a member of an adjudicatory body like the War Claims Commission merely because he wanted his own appointees on such a Commission, we are compelled to conclude that no such power is given to the President directly by the Constitution, and none is impliedly conferred upon him by statute simply because Congress said nothing about it. The philosophy of *Humphrey's Executor*, in its explicit language as well as its implications, precludes such a claim.[65]

Thus Frankfurter, the apostle of self-restraint, was guided by an "adjudicatory function" criterion in finding that Congress did not intend to grant the power of removal without cause rather than bowing in deference to the president.[66]

This great respect for past pronouncements was another aspect of the restraintist view that had a strong bearing on civil liberties problems. This was indicated in Frankfurter's concurrence in *Orson v. United States*, a case dealing with an unusually severe summary punishment for contempt, where he said: "Law is a social organism, and evolution operates in the sociological domain no less than in the biological."[67] He then listed a roll call of fifty-three justices, who had during the Court's history accepted the power to punish summarily.

Frankfurter concluded with a reprimand to the dissenters, Chief Justice Warren and Justices Black and Douglas, scolding them for their disapproval of such a well-established practice:

> To say that everybody on the Court has been wrong for 150 years and that that which has been deemed part of the bone and sinew of the law should now be extirpated is quite another thing. Decision-making is not a mechanical process, but neither is this Court an originating lawmaker. . . . It is not for this Court to fashion a wholly novel constitutional doctrine that would require such participation whatever Congress may think on the matter, and in the teeth of an unbroken legislative and judicial history from the foundation of the Nation.[68]

Frankfurter's other disquisitions on legal history, as exemplified in his *Frank* opinion and his lengthy appendices of precedent cases as seen in *Bartkus*, were almost overwhelming.

Frankfurter's final illustration of the restraintist doctrine in separation of powers was found in his last dissent on the Court in *Baker v. Carr*: "The Framers carefully and with deliberate forethought refused . . . to enthrone the judiciary. In this situation [voters questioning a state's lack of apportioning legislative seats] . . . appeal must be to an informed, civically militant electorate. In a democratic society like ours, relief must come through an aroused popular conscience that sears the conscience of the people's representatives."[69]

One of the main restraintist safeguards against excessively personal judicial judgments was deciding no more than was necessary in any given case—and if possible to decide on a nonconstitutional ground. Justice Frankfurter vigorously invoked rules that enabled the Court to avoid passing on constitutional issues. Realizing the delicacy of determining issues essentially political which come to the Court only thinly disguised in legal garb, Frankfurter felt that it was his duty not to decide constitutional issues unless inescapable. Most of the cases in the field of antisubversive activities, as noted previously, were determined that way. In *Trop*, where the majority found an act of Congress unconstitutional, Justice Frankfurter dissented strongly. In *Reid*, Frankfurter, joined by Harlan, concurred in striking a portion of the Uniform Code of Military Justice as unconstitutional—but limited their concurrence to capital cases. Also, in *Jay v. Boyd*, Frankfurter's dissent did not mention due process or constitutional rights, but maintained instead that Congress had invested the attorney general and not his subordinates with the dispensing power.

Frankfurter manifested great concern about the technicalities of jurisdiction and was reluctant to adjudicate unless he felt reasonably certain that every technical matter involved in a case had been resolved to his satisfaction. This concern was sometimes carried to such extremes by Justice Frankfurter as to merit the appellation of "legal crocheting."[70] Such restraintist doctrine demanded that the Court refuse to accept cases that for any reason were not fully ready for review by the highest tribunal. For this reason Justice Frankfurter dissented on technical grounds in *Staub v. Baxley*, maintaining that the union organizer's appeal should have been dismissed since the Georgia courts had not been given full opportunity to rule on all the questions involved. In *Poe v. Ullman*, Frankfurter wrote for the Court dismissing the challenge to Connecticut's anti-contraceptive law: "The fact that Connecticut has not chosen to press the enforcement of this statute deprives these controversies of the immediacy which is an indispensable condition of constitutional adjudication. This Court cannot be umpire to debates concerning harmless, empty shadows."[71] By thus disposing of *Poe* on the ground of ripeness, Frankfurter may have inspired Justice Douglas to find something more than harmless, empty shadows in the penumbras of *Griswold v. Connecticut* four years later.

In sum, Justice Frankfurter was a walking, always talking, personification of the rules developed by his friend, Justice Louis Brandeis, in *Ashwander v. TVA*, used by the Court to limit its exercise of judicial review.[72] He was a zealous referee blowing the whistle at what he thought were frequent judicial infractions by his colleagues. Umpires are seldom popular, and Frankfurter came to be called, among other things, "the Supreme Court Emily Post."[73]

FEDERALISM AND SELF-RESTRAINT

Judicial responsibility for maintaining the constitutional allocation of functions between the federal and state courts was another part of the restraintist creed.[74] This motivation could be seen clearly at work in Frankfurter's review of criminal convictions coming up from the state courts. The activists urged the Court to rule in such a way as to produce a just result for the individual, while the advocates of self-restraint maintained that the Court could remedy injustices only if its actions allowed a wide measure of autonomy for state systems of justice and substantial presumptions of regularity in state procedures.[75] Thus, restraintists refused to strike down state law enforcement practices which they passionately disapproved. Justice Frankfurter's opinions dealing with federal criminal procedure indicated that he had a strong respect for the integrity of the individual. But this strong libertarian sympathy often yielded to other considerations when federalism was involved in criminal procedures in the states. Thus he and several of the Eisenhower associate justices[76] exhibited a willingness to play a limited role even as to issues about which they felt strongly on the theory that the judicial function should be exercised in as "rational" a manner as human capacity could attain. This rational approach involved careful balancing of conflicting claims.

This was illustrated by the words of Justice Frankfurter, joined by Justice Harlan, in *Sweezy*, where his conclusion to concur in the majority result was based on his balancing of conflicting principles—the right of a citizen to political freedom and the right of the state to self-protection:

> Striking the balance implies the exercise of judgment. This is the inescapable judicial task in giving substantive content, legally enforced, to the Due Process Clause, and it is a task ultimately committed to this Court. It must not be an exercise of whim or will. It must be an overriding judgment founded on something much deeper and more justifiable than personal preference. As far as it lies within human limitations, it must be an impersonal judgment. It must rest on the fundamental presuppositions rooted in history to which widespread acceptance may fairly be attributed. Such a judgment must be arrived at in a spirit of humility when it counters the judgment of the State's highest court.[77]

And to this he added a stern warning: "It would make the deepest inroads upon our federal system for this Court now to hold that it can determine the appropriate distribution of powers and their delegation within the [then] forty-eight states."[78]

Again, in his dissent in *Konigsberg*, Justice Frankfurter expressed a similar attitude of respect for state courts. The majority had held that the California bar examiners' conclusions were contrary to the evidence in the case and should be reversed. But Justice Frankfurter thought that the Court erred in not giving greater weight to the presumption of regularity in state procedures: "Insistence on establishment of the Court's jurisdiction is too often treated, with slighting intent, as a 'technicality.' In truth, due regard for the requirements of the conditions that alone give this Court power to review the judgment of the highest court of a State is a matter of deep importance to the working of our federalism."[79]

Although several of the Eisenhower associate justices wrote opinions expressing similar views, it was Justice Frankfurter who was still the most eloquent exponent of the division of power within American federalism. In the self-incrimination case, *Knapp v. Schweitzer*, Justice Frankfurter held for the majority that a witness before a state grand jury could not refuse to testify because the state immunity law would not protect him from federal prosecution for what he would be required to answer. His words deserve quotation:

> To yield to the contention of the petitioner would not only disregard the uniform course of decision by this Court for over a hundred years in recognizing the legal autonomy of state and federal governments. . . . While corruptions and generally low standards in local government may not today be as endemic as Lord Bryce reported them to be in *The American Commonwealth* (1888), not even the most cheerful view of the improvements that have since taken place can afford justification for blunting the power of the States to ferret out, and thereby guard against such corruption by restrictions that would reverse our whole constitutional history. . . . This Court with all its shifting membership has repeatedly found occasion to say that whatever inconveniences and embarrassments may be involved, they are the price we pay for our federalism, for having our people amenable to—as well as served and protected by—two governments.[80]

One final illustration of the restraintist doctrine of federalism is found in *Beilan*, where Frankfurter indicated where ultimate political responsibility lies in the states: "I am of course wholly unconcerned with what I may think of the wisdom or folly of the state authorities. . . . The Fourteenth Amendment does not check foolishness or unwisdom. . . . The good sense and right standards of public administration in (the) States must be relied upon for that, and ultimately the electorate."[81]

THE RESTRAINTIST-ACTIVIST CONFLICT

The activists and restraintists disagreed on the granting of review by writ of certiorari, with the former tending to be more liberal in voting for such grants.[82] Frankfurter, on the other hand, limited granting of certiorari to "cases involving principles the settlement of which is of importance to the public."[83] Thus, he sometimes complained that certiorari was "improvidently granted."[84] Likewise, Frankfurter was reluctant to use precious judicial time on minor matters that, in his opinion, could be or had already been more profitably canvassed elsewhere.

The restraintists rejected "doctrines" or "certainty formulas" such as the preferred position doctrine or the total incorporation theory urged by some of the activists. Thus in free speech cases the question was whether the state or Congress had struck a reasonable balance between the other needs of society and freedom of the individual. This approach theorized that competing interests and principles embody relative values rather than absolute commands. In the words of Justice Frankfurter in *Ullmann*: "As no constitutional guarantee enjoys preference, so none should suffer subordination or deletion."[85]

Sharp differences of opinion between Frankfurter and the activists, expressed in the formal reports, were only a surface indication of an even greater underlying dissonance. Most reports of discord on the Court are usually nothing more than rumors, although the Black–Jackson feud of the late 1940s culminated in unfortunate public pronouncements of a type that can but lower the standing of the judiciary in the eyes of the populace.[86] For a number of years, there were hints of an animosity between Frankfurter and Black, and these accounts reached their zenith during the 1958 term when it was rumored that Justice Frankfurter, despite his age and physical infirmity, felt that he could not wisely retire so long as Justice Black remained active.[87]

Frankfurter also apparently disliked his other longtime colleague from the Roosevelt Court, Justice Douglas. According to James Simon, Frankfurter called Douglas "one of the two completely evil men" he had ever known. When Douglas once told Frankfurter that he and Black viewed him as a nut to be cracked, the justice from Vienna was not amused.[88] The ex-professor Frankfurter remained "notoriously a professor, lecturing and heckling attorneys and Court colleagues alike."[89] In conference debate over *Lambert v. California* in 1957, Frankfurter and Douglas had an especially acrimonious moment. Douglas eventually became so annoyed with Frankfurter that in 1960 he wrote a memorandum in which he concluded that he would no longer participate in conferences where Frankfurter sat. On the advice of Warren, he did not send it.[90] Fred Rodell called Frankfurter the Court's most "controversial and unhappy member,"[91] and except for Justice James McReynolds, it was "difficult to recollect a member of the Court who had worse personal relations with his colleagues."[92]

But Frankfurter had one close friend on the Eisenhower Court— Justice Harlan, and after he retired from the Court, Frankfurter made two valedictory gestures that give insight into how he saw the end of his career as a justice. In 1963 he gave Harlan a paperback copy of his 1927 book, *The Case of Sacco and Vanzetti*, inscribed: "For JMH, As a token of esteem both a judge and man, who . . . afforded me strong and reliable comfort and support during our happy years of judicial companionship in our effort to vindicate the national profession . . . that our standards in the administration of criminal justice are highly civilized on the basis of legal reasoning unaided by doctrinaire dogmas, however couched in appealing rhetoric."[93] On 28 May 1963, Frankfurter wrote Harlan confessing, "Most of my years on the Court have been years not of gladness but of sadness and not primarily because of the outrageous decisions that have been rendered in our time but because of the atmosphere of disregard for law and to a large extent of the legal profession that now dominates the present Court."[94] Frankfurter did not retire a happy warrior.

THE DANGER OF RESTRAINT RUN WILD

From what has been said of the philosophy of restraint, it is apparent that a genuine follower of this creed during the Eisenhower era should have had a general reluctance to invalidate state action, whether constitutionality of statutes or criminal prosecutions were at issue (although it might be argued that there was much less reason for self-restraint in passing on questions of correct judicial procedure, a task for which the Court was peculiarly qualified). But at the national level, principles of restraint should operate mainly to protect legislation from declarations of unconstitutionality and to show proper respect for administrative jurisdiction. Thus a restraintist could indicate libertarian values more easily in interpreting federal statutes and checking federal criminal procedures.

An inspection of Table 10.2 reveals that Justice Frankfurter practiced what he preached. In dealing with state criminal convictions and in passing on the constitutionality of various types of state restrictions on freedom of speech, Frankfurter often failed to reach libertarian results. But in federal proceedings involving aliens, in enforcing procedural protections in federal criminal prosecutions, and in the various federal free speech cases arising mostly out of the prosecutions of Communists, Frankfurter consistently favored the libertarian result.

This is made clear by dividing the 153 cases covered in Table 10.1 into two categories according to their origin in federal or state proceedings, as is done in Table 10.2. This analysis shows that for the Court, as a whole, support for libertarian claims in federal cases was higher than in state cases. For the activists, including Brennan and for Clark and Burton, there was no significant difference in reaction between the two categories of cases. The rest of the Eisenhower associate justices (except Stewart) were stronger in support of libertarian claims in federal cases. Harlan and Whittaker had approximately a ten-point spread, while Justice Stewart recorded a fourteen-point spread in favor of libertarian claims in state cases. Frankfurter's record of 42 percent favorable votes in federal cases, contrasted with his 28 percent figure in state cases, seems a definite indication that he found a barrier of restraint in dealing with state proceedings which was not operative in the federal area.[95]

Table 10.2
Voting Records of Supreme Court Justices in Federal and State Civil Liberties Cases, 1953–1961 Terms (in percentages)

	Support for Libertarian Claims	
	State Cases	Federal Cases
Douglas	98	98
Black	90	96 (96)
Warren	82 (56)	82 (92)
Brennan	79 (47)	80 (78)
Stewart	43 (28)	29 (38)
COURT	42	50
Frankfurter	28 (58)	42 (95)
Harlan	22 (55)	32 (85)
Whittaker	17 (35)	28 (66)
Burton	20 (31)	20 (59)
Clark	18	14 (96)
Minton	0 (11)	9 (23)
Reed	0 (13)	4 (24)

Although their discord attracted more publicity, the restraintist Frankfurter and the activists of the Eisenhower Court came together in agreement in many of the important decisions in the 1953–1961 terms. What both restraintists and activists appeared to share was a humanitarian respect for the integrity of the individual, a belief that libertarian values were of tremendous importance, an insistence that the Court use its legitimate power to compel adherence to procedural safeguards, and a demand for close scrutiny of the cases where there was any possibility of infringing on human liberty.[96] The restraintists, however, emphasized more than the activists the importance of the autonomy of the states and the primacy of popularly-elected representatives as the chief policy-makers.

That fundamental disagreement could exist among justices of high intelligence and unquestioned patriotism emphasized the complexity of civil liberties issues during those days of burgeoning national power and Cold War. One of the dangers of the restraintist view of the Court was that it could be interpreted to imply that judicial review was inherently undemocratic in character. Perhaps overlooked in this view was the basic idea of the American Constitution—that government is limited and that the majority is not always right. Judicial review is not opposed to the principles of "free government"; it is, rather, important to its implementation. There is no reason, then, why the Court should cast doubt on its own ability to participate in the vital process of interpreting the Constitution. There are altogether too many ready and willing to take up the cry and urge disrespect for law in general.[97]

The Supreme Court has a significant role to play in American society—one that should not be passed off to legislatures or lower courts. Justice Frankfurter, in *Black v. Cutter Laboratories*, exhibited a conscientious effort to carry the restraintist idea to a logical extreme, which resulted in the Supreme Court's ignoring the clear import of the decision of the California Supreme Court. In the words of one astute observer, the Court "read excerpts out of context, discovered separate state grounds for the decision and held that it would therefore not decide the constitutional issue."[98]

The doctrine of restraint sought external standards to control the Court—standards commanding obedience because they were based on fundamental principles of a democratic society. The problem was, how do justices find these standards external to their own value systems? And how fundamental were standards that Supreme Court justices disagree about so strongly as to divide the Court by a five-to-four vote? The true restraintist reply to this would be that where values conflict, disputes should be resolved by reliance on the political processes. But this answer, in many instances, causes the Court to avoid statutory interpretation—one of the Court's major responsibilities. In addition, rules for avoiding constitutional issues become absolutes to be followed with equal strictness in all situations. The Court's function of determining the constitutionality of an act must be, according to the restraintist view, the same for laws limiting hours as for laws limiting speech,[99] a formula which on its face denied any amendment a preferred position. To allow variations would be to undercut the principle on which judicial restraint was based and open the door to judicial willfulness.

In Justice Frankfurter's view, all reasonable doubts should be resolved in favor of the integrity of sister organs of government or the states. He thus adhered to one of the strongest of our constitutional traditions, the dispersion of power. As Professor Mendelson has stated: "He is wary of judicial attempts to impose justice on the community; to deprive it of the wisdom that comes from self-inflicted wounds and the strength that grows with the burden of responsibility. It is his deepest conviction that no five men, or nine, are wise enough or good enough to wield such power over the lives of millions."[100]

According to the Frankfurter view, the function of the Court must vary according to the danger of irresponsible majority rule. If judicial review was to fulfill its purpose, the Court had to assess at each point the dangers that democratic processes would go astray and then adjust its level of review to meet that danger. The critical danger points were not permanently fixed but had to shift from one period of history to another. There may be no enduring standards for the Court that are equally valid for all time. Such a view is both the strength and weakness of the Frankfurter position. Carried to the extreme exemplified by the Vinson Court in the early 1950s, the doctrine of restraint amounted to judicial abdication. To shrink the functions of the highest tribunal by appealing to principles which have only a half-measure of reality may impede instead of further government's ability to meet the felt needs of society. Judicial humility does not demand abdication but suggests that judges meet the responsibilities which the system of their day requires.[101]

NOTES

1. Julius Paul, "The Supreme Court: Mirror of the American Conscience," 19 *Am. J. Econ. Sociology* 1 (1959).

2. *United States v. Butler*, 297 U.S. 1 at 62 (1936).

3. See generally, Peltason, *Federal Courts in the Political Process*; Rosenblum, *Law as a Political Instrument*.

4. See generally, Rostow, "The Supreme Court and the People's Will," 33 *Notre Dame Law.* 573 (1958).

5. Pritchett, *Civil Liberties and the Vinson Court*, pp. 191–192.

6. William O. Douglas, "On Misconception of the Judicial Function and Responsibility of the Bar," 59 *Colum. L. Rev.* 227 (1959).

7. Compare, Pritchett, *Civil Liberties and the Vinson Court*, p. 190.

8. The decisions included in this table fall into the categories covered by Chapters 3–9, whether or not they were discussed in those chapters.

9. Justice Black was usually referred to as the leader of the activist bloc, and most of the writing about judicial activism on the Court has centered on his philosophy as expressed in his opinions. Justice Douglas wrote numerous books expressing his views, while comparatively little was written about the judicial philosophy of Chief Justice Warren during his first nine terms on the Court. Since that time, Warren's jurisprudence has been well analyzed. See, e.g., Cray, *Chief Justice*; Schwartz, "Earl Warren," in Schwartz, ed., *The Warren Court: A Retrospective*; Edward G. White, "Earl Warren's Influence on the Warren Court," in Tushnet, ed., *The Warren Court in Historical and Political Perspective*.

10. *Speiser v. Randall*, 357 U.S. 513 at 530; see also Hugo L. Black, "The Bill of Rights," 35 *N.Y.U. L. Rev.* 865 (1960).

11. *Roth v. United States*, 354 U.S. 476 at 514.

12. *Beilan v. Board of Education*, 357 U.S. 399 at 412–413.

13. 354 U.S. 476 at 514.

14. Ibid. *Cf. Barenblatt v. United States*, 360 U.S. 109 at 141 (Black, J.) (dissenting opinion).

15. *International Brotherhood of Teamsters v. Vogt*, 354 U.S. 284 (1957); *Youngdahl v. Rainfair*, 355 U.S. 131 (1957); *United States v. UAW*, 352 U.S. 567 (1957).

16. Quoting *Bakery Drivers Local v. Wohl*, 315 U.S. 769, 776–777 (1942) (Douglas, J., concurring.)

17. 354 U.S. 284 at 295. But *cf. Hunt v. Crumboch*, 325 U.S. 821 at 830 (1945) (Jackson, J., dissenting): "With this decision, the labor movement has come full circle."

18. 352 U.S. 567 (1957).

19. 352 U.S. 567 at 593; see also Sam Kagel and Virginia B. Smith, "Chief Justice Warren and Labor Law," 49 *Calif. L. Rev.* 126 (1961).

20. 356 U.S. 44 at 84 (dissenting opinion); see also Schubert, *Constitutional Politics*, pp. 199–202.

21. See, e.g., *Galvan v. Press*, 347 U.S. 522, 532–533 (1954); where Black in dissent described the defendant as "a good, law-abiding man, a steady worker and a devoted husband and father loyal to this country"; *Jay v. Boyd*, 351 U.S. 345, 364 (1956) (Black, J., dissenting).

22. 350 U.S. 91 at 106.

23. 357 U.S. 116–117.

24. 356 U.S. 165 at 194.

25. *Lehman v. United States ex rel. Carson*, 353 U.S. 685, 690 (1957) (Black, J., dissenting); *Mulcahey v. Catalonotte*, 353 U.S. 692 (1957).

26. Harold J. Spaeth, "An Approach to the Study of Attitudinal Differences as an Aspect of Judicial Behavior," 5 *Mw. J. of Pol. Sci.* 165, 171 (1961).

27. *Harrison v. NAACP*, 360 U.S. 167, 179 (1959) (Douglas, J., dissenting); *Martin v. Creasy*, 360 U.S. 219 (1959); but see Justice Black's dissent (joined by Douglas and Warren) in *Clay v. Sun Insurance Office*, 363 U.S. 207, 213 (1960); *cf.* Douglas's dissent, Ibid. at 227.

28. 360 U.S. 219 at 228 (1959); for Black–Douglas differences on questions of taxation, see Spaeth, "An Approach to the Study," p. 175.

29. Schwartz, "Hugo L. Black," in Schwartz, ed., *The Warren Court: A Retrospective*, pp. 195–203; James F. Simon, "William O. Douglas," Ibid., pp. 211–223.

30. Stone, *Earl Warren, A Great American Story*, pp. 112–114; compare this with the account in Robert E. Burks, *Olson's New Deal for California* (Berkeley and Los Angeles: University of California Press, 1953), pp. 194–206.

31. See generally, Gordon E. Baker and Bernard Teitelbaum, "An End to Cross-filing," 48 *National Civic Review* 286 (1959); see also "Governor Warren: The Great Paradox," 4 *Fortnight* 11 (1948).

32. Harry N. Hirsh, *The Enigma of Felix Frankfurter* (New York: Basic Books, 1981), p. 190.

33. Pollack, *Earl Warren*, pp. 197–99; Anthony Lewis, "Earl Warren," in Richard H. Sayler and Barry B. Boyer, eds., *The Warren Court: A Critical Analysis* (New York: Chelsea House, 1969), pp. 2–3; Philip J. Cooper, *Battles on the Bench: Conflict Inside the Supreme Court* (Lawrence: University Press of Kansas, 1995),

pp. 26–95; *New York Times*, 21 March 1961, p. 18. For details about the Warren–Frankfurter relationship, see White, *Earl Warren*, pp. 173–190.

34. Anthony Lewis, "High Court Backs Contempt Ruling in Non-Jury Trial," *New York Times*, 1 April 1958, pp. 1, 22.

35. *Caritativo v. California*, 357 U.S. 549 (1958).

36. *New York Times*, 21 March 1961, p. 1; see also Osborne, "One Supreme Court," p. 93; *The Economist*, 13 May 1961, pp. 674–679.

37. *Milanovich v. United States*, 365 U.S. 551 (1961).

38. *New York Times*, 21 March 1961, p. 1.

39. For a vivid description of the Chief Justice presiding on the bench, see Bernard Taper, "Gomillion Versus Lightfoot," *New Yorker*, 17 June 1961, pp. 39, 42, 68. Note how Warren's "booming voice" made it seem "somewhat as if Mount Rushmore had spoken."

40. Schwartz, "The Warren Court, An Opinion," *New York Times*, 30 June 1957, VI (Magazine), p. 10.

41. Lewis, "Earl Warren," p. 3.

42. Schwartz, "The Supreme Court–October 1958 Term," 58 *Mich. L. Rev.* 165 (1959); Schwartz, "Earl Warren," p. 269–270.

43. See Chapter 6, *supra*.

44. See Ira M. Heyman, "The Chief Justice, Racial Segregation, and the Friendly Critics," 49 *Calif. L. Rev.* 104 (1961); Schwartz, "Earl Warren," p. 270.

45. *Gore v. United States*, 357 U.S. 386 at 394.

46. Schwartz, "The Supreme Court–October 1958 Term," p. 207.

47. Frank, "The Historic Role of the Supreme Court," p. 46; but see Edward McWhinney, "The Great Debate: Activism, and Self-Restraint and Current Dilemmas in Judicial Policy-Making," 33 *N.Y.U. L. Rev.* 775, 791–792 (1958).

48. McCloskey, "Tools, Stumbling Blocks, and Stepping Stones," p. 1029.

49. Robert H. Jackson, *The Supreme Court in the American System of Government* (Cambridge, MA: Harvard University Press, 1955), p. 75.

50. Pritchett, *Civil Liberties and the Vinson Court*, p. 249.

51. Fred Rodell, "Judicial Activists, Judicial Self-Deniers, Judicial Review and the First Amendment—Or, How to Hide the Melody of What You Mean Behind the Words of What You Say," 47 *Geo. L. J.* 483 (1959); for other studies of the values of the activists, see e.g., "Mr. Justice Black—A Symposium," 65 *Yale L. J.* 449 (1956); Daniel M. Berman, "Mr. Justice Black: the Record After Twenty Years," 25 *Mo. L. Rev.* 155 (1960); Murray A. Gordon, "Justice Hugo Black—First Amendment Fundamentalist," 20 *Law G. Rev.* 1 (1960); Charlotte Williams, *Hugo L. Black: A Study in Judicial Process* (Baltimore: Johns Hopkins University Press, 1961); Black, "The Bill of Rights"; Marian D. Irish, "Mr. Justice Douglas and Judicial Restraint," 6 *U. Fla. L. Rev.* 537 (1953); Douglas, "The Supreme Court and Its Case Load," 45 *Cornell L. Q.* 401 (1960); Douglas, *America Challenged* (New York: Avon, 1960); "Earl Warren Anniversary Issue," 49 *Calif. L. Rev.* 1 (1961); James R. Bell, "The Executive Office of the California Governor Under Earl Warren, 1943–1953," (unpublished Ph.D. dissertation, Dept. of Political Science, University of California, Berkeley, 1956); Richard F. Pedersen, "Governor Earl Warren, As Seen Through His Speeches," (unpublished Master's thesis, Dept. of Political Science, Stanford University, 1947); Warren, "The Law and the Future," in Henry M. Christman, ed., *The Public Papers of Chief Justice Earl Warren* (New York: Simon and Schuster, 1959).

52. Justice Clark demonstrated antipathy toward procedural requirements invoked by the majority on behalf of individual claimants. His dissent in *Speiser* indicated a willingness to extend the scope and application of *Adler, Garner,* and *Dennis*—cases in which the Court broadly sanctioned the abridgement of First Amendment liberties on security grounds. See Jacobs, *Justice Frankfurter*, pp. 148–149. Other former attorneys general who have served on the Court in recent years were more libertarian in their civil liberties outlook—notably Stone, Jackson, and Murphy.

53. Schwartz, *Super Chief*, p. 58; Osborne, "One Supreme Court," p. 92; but note Clark's agreement with the Chief Justice during the 1953 and 1954 terms, Tables 2.3 and 2.4.

54. Berry, *Stability, Security, and Continuity*, p. 186.

55. Felix Frankfurter, "Some Observations on the Nature of the Judicial Process of Supreme Court Litigation," 98 *Proceedings, Am. Philosophical Society* 233, 238 (1954).

56. Paul A. Freund, "Mr. Justice Frankfurter," 26 *U. Chi. L. Rev.* 205, 209 (1959).

57. *Textile Workers Union v. Lincoln Mills*, 353 U.S. 448 at 465–466 (1957).

58. Harlan Papers, Seeley G. Mudd Library, Box 484, Princeton University, Princeton, NJ.

59. 347 U.S. 522 at 531.

60. Warren Papers, Library of Congress, Manuscripts Division, Washington, DC, I: 17, No. 34.

61. Clyde W. Summers, "Frankfurter, Labor Law and the Justice's Function," 67 *Yale L. J.* 266, 285 (1957).

62. 357 U.S. 386 at 393.

63. 295 U.S. 602 (1935).

64. 357 U.S. 349 (1958).

65. 357 U.S. 349 at 356.

66. Horn, "The Warren Court and the Discretionary Power of the Executive," p. 645.

67. 356 U.S. 165 at 189.

68. 356 U.S. 165 at 193.

69. 369 U.S. 186 at 270 (1962).

70. Walton Hamilton, "Book Review," 56 *Yale L. J.* 1458, 1460 (1947); see also Rodell, *Nine Men*, p. 271; *but see* Jacobs, *Justice Frankfurter*, pp. 113–14; Mendelson, *Justices Black and Frankfurter*, pp. 129–31.

71. 367 U.S. 497 (1961).

72. 297 U.S. 288 (1936).

73. Rodell, *Nine Men*, p. 271.

74. See generally, Louis H. Pollack, "Mr. Justice Frankfurter: Judgment and the Fourteenth Amendment," 67 *Yale L. J.* 304 (1957).

75. Pritchett, *Civil Liberties and the Vinson Court*, pp. 213–214.

76. Justice Brennan was the least likely of the four to assent to this view.

77. 354 U.S. 234 at 266–267.

78. Ibid., 256.

79. 353 U.S. 252 at 274.

80. 357 U.S. at 378–379.

81. 357 U.S. 399 at 411.

82. Schubert, *Quantitative Analysis of Judicial Behavior*, p. 235; see also Fowler V. Harper and Alan S. Rosenthal, "What the Supreme Court Did Not Do in the 1949 Term—An Appraisal of Certiorari," 99 *U. Pa. L. Rev.* 293 (1950); articles by Harper and various of his students, on the next three terms, appeared successively in Vols. 100–102; see also Harper and Rosenthal, "The Court, the Bar, and Certiorari," 108 *U. Pa. L. Rev.* 1160 (1959).

83. Except in Federal Employers' Liability Act and Jones Act cases; see Mendelson, *Justices Black and Frankfurter*, pp. 22–30.

84. See *Ferguson v. Moore-McCormack Lines*, 352 U.S. 521 at 524–529 (1957) (dissenting opinion); see also Schubert, *Quantitative Analysis*, pp. 45–50.

85. 350 U.S. 422 at 428.

86. See Gerhart, *America's Advocate*, pp. 235–277.

87. Loren P. Beth, "The Supreme Court and the Future of Judicial Review," 76 *Political Sci. Q.* 11, 18 (1961); but see *The Economist*, 13 May 1961, p. 674, 679.

88. Simon, *Independent Journey*, p. 217.

89. Rodell, *Nine Men*, p. 269.

90. Cooper, *Battles on the Bench*, p. 110.

91. Rodell, *Nine Men*, p. 271.

92. Michael E. Parrish, "Felix Frankfurter," in Melvin I. Urofsky, ed., *The Supreme Court Justices: A Biographical Dictionary* (New York: Garland, 1994), p. 177.

93. Harlan Papers, Seeley G. Mudd Library, Princeton University, Box 534, Princeton, NJ.

94. Ibid.

95. Compare with Pritchett, *Civil Liberties and the Vinson Court*, p. 225.

96. Ibid., p. 238.

97. See generally, Charles L. Black, Jr., *The People and the Court* (New York: MacMillan, 1960); see also Arthur L. Harding, ed., *The Rule of Law* (Dallas, TX: Southern Methodist University Press, 1961).

98. Summers, "Frankfurter, Labor Law and the Justice's Function," p. 275.

99. But see the dissenting opinion of Justice Douglas in *Kingsley Books v. Brown*, 354 U.S. 436 at 447: "Free speech is not to be regulated like diseased cattle and impure butter." Frankfurter probably would have questioned whether speech was ever regulated in such a way.

100. Mendelson, *Justices Black and Frankfurter*, p. 131.

101. See Horn, *Groups and the Constitution*, p. 32; for additional comments on the judicial restraint of Justice Frankfurter, see Jacobs, *Justice Frankfurter*, pp. 210–217; Mendelson, *Justices Black and Frankfurter*, pp. 124–131; Mendelson, "Mr. Justice Frankfurter and the Process of Judicial Review," 103 *U. Pa. L. Rev.* 295 (1954); "Symposium—Mr. Justice Frankfurter," 67 *Yale L. J.* 179 (1957); Helen S. Thomas, *Felix Frankfurter, Scholar on the Bench* (Baltimore: Johns Hopkins University Press, 1961); Ray D. Henson, "Study in Style: Mr. Justice Frankfurter," 6 *Vill. L. Rev.* 377 (1961); "Judicial Restraint," *The Economist*, 11 Oct. 1958, p. 142; Beth, "The Supreme Court and the Future of Judicial Review," p. 18: "Frankfurter not only seems to think such objectivity is achievable, but at times he is suspiciously close to saying that he has achieved it."

11

The Eisenhower Associate Justices

Following the appointment of Chief Justice Warren, all the Eisenhower appointees to the Court were former judges, and each gave indication of holding more libertarian values in many fields than did his predecessor of the Vinson Court. While the Eisenhower associate justices were not always in agreement, they evidenced common judicial tendencies which, on the whole, brought the Court from the less libertarian record of the Vinson Court to a more libertarian position in civil liberties cases. According to the statistics presented in Chapter 3, the Eisenhower justices were in a middle-of-the-road position between the extreme left of Justices Black and Douglas and the extreme right of Justice Clark. In this middle ground, Justice Frankfurter held a central position. It is these middle ground justices who, when united, dominated the Eisenhower Court. Whereas Professor Pritchett could speak of a continental divide in the Roosevelt Court running between Rutledge and Reed,[1] the Eisenhower Court during most of its terms appeared to lack such a feature, having rather a middle high ground which slanted down to the more libertarian left and to the less libertarian right. In split decisions it was somewhat unusual for the two extremes to unite. More often, the middle coalition would attract one of these wings to bolster its majority.[2]

Table 11.1 indicates participation in the majority in the 153 important civil liberties cases included in Table 10.1. These statistics show that in the areas covered, Justices Stewart, Harlan, Frankfurter, and Whittaker were most frequently in the majority while Justices Black and Douglas were the leading dissenters. Between the two groups are Justices Brennan and Clark (and formerly Burton) and the Chief Justice.

Table 11.1
Participation in the Majority in 153 Nonunanimous Civil Liberties Cases,*
1953–1961 Terms

	Number of cases participated in	Percentage in the majority
COURT	153	
Stewart	62	87
Frankfurter	151	79
Harlan	141	79
Whittaker	103	78
Clark	152	70
Burton	90	69
Brennan	118	66
Warren	150	63
Black	152	52
Douglas	153	46

*For a list of the cases included, see Table 10.1, *supra*.

Further indications of who wielded power in civil liberties decisions is provided by Table 11.2 which divides Table 11.1 into two term increments. In all three instances, a sharply divided Court decided more than half of the cases by votes of 5–4, 6–3, or 5–3.

In the eighteen cases represented, which were decided during its first two terms, the Eisenhower Court was dominated by a majority composed of the Chief Justice and Justice Clark (who were almost always on the winning side) and Justices Frankfurter, Burton, Harlan, and Minton. Justice Reed had already passed from his position of prominence in the Vinson Court majority in civil liberties cases, while Douglas, and especially Black, remained primarily voices of dissent.

In the controversial 1955 and 1956 terms, a new majority emerged with the two new appointees, Whittaker and Brennan, assuming important roles, and Justices Frankfurter and Harlan attaining more predominance. The Chief Justice was in the majority less than previously. Justices Burton and Clark dropped out of the usual majority (the latter making a substantial decline) and had percentages in the majority similar to those formerly attained by Harlan and Minton. Justices Black and Douglas continued to be the leading dissenters, although both maintained records of over 50 percent majority participation—indicating that the activists were exerting a stronger, but far from dominant, influence at this time. Indicative of this was the participation of Black and Douglas in the majorities in more than half of the 6–3 and 5–3 decisions and in half of the 5–4 splits. In six of the 5–4 decisions, the Chief Justice and Brennan joined them with the fifth vote being provided three times by Frankfurter, twice by Whittaker, and once by Clark. Five of Brennan's dissents in this period were cast with Black and Douglas in 5–4 decisions.

Table 11.2
Participation in the Majority in Certain Nonunanimous Civil Liberties Cases
by Term Increments for 1953–1954, 1955–1956, 1957–1958, and 1959–1961

Terms	1953–54	1955–56	1957–58	1959–61
No. of cases	18	37	56	42
5–4 Decisions	1	8	28	21
6–3 Decisions	6	10	9	6
5–3 Decisions	4	6	3	1

Percentage in Majority		Percentage in Majority		Percentage in Majority		Percentage in Majority	
Warren	100	Whittaker	100	Stewart	90	Stewart	86
Clark	94	Frankfurter	84	Frankfurter	86	Clark	74
Frankfurter	72	Brennan	81	Harlan	83	Harlan	74
Burton	72	Harlan	81	Whittaker	81	Whittaker	70
Harlan	67	Warren	73	Brennan	67	Frankfurter	68
Minton	67	Clark	68	Clark	61	Black	60
Reed	56	Burton	67	Warren	46	Warren	59
Douglas	50	Black	57	Black	46	Brennan	57
Black	44	Douglas	54	Douglas	40	Douglas	43
				Burton	69		

The 1957 and 1958 terms witnessed a decline in the influence of the libertarian activists while Justice Stewart joined Frankfurter, Harlan, and Whittaker (who remained in the majority from the previous two terms) in forming frequently winning coalitions. The middle-of-the-road position of this group is emphasized by the fact that Justice Brennan of the left and Justice Clark of the right had almost equal records of majority participation, although Brennan and Clark seldom agreed. Burton retired from the court with a relatively high percentage participation in the majority due largely to the Court's less libertarian trend in cases involving state criminal procedures and deportation. Justice Brennan's nineteen dissents, all cast in 5–4 decisions with Black, Douglas, and Warren, lowered his percentage substantially although he was well above the record of the activists.[3] Justice Clark maintained his low sixties mark and remained in the same place in the relative standings. The Chief Justice continued his downward spiral to a record equal to that of Black. Warren's thirty-one dissenting votes were all registered in close decisions in the company of Black and Douglas (joined by Brennan in nineteen of these). Black and Douglas hit their nadir and were in the majority in only five of the twenty-eight 5–4 decisions and three of the 6–3 splits.

The 1959 through 1961 terms showed Frankfurter's influence declining while Black's increased. A new libertarian bloc of Black, Warren, Brennan, and Douglas emerges, while Clark's majority participation rises to match Harlan's and surpasses that of Whittaker and Frankfurter. Stewart continued to be the justice most often in the majority.

These tables clearly trace the change in the judicial attitude of Chief Justice Warren who in two term intervals declined from a top position identical with Justice Clark, to a middle ground place adjacent to Harlan, to a minority spot with the activists from whom he had originally been farthest removed, and finally came to rest in the 1959–1961 terms on an upswing with the libertarian bloc.[4] The increasing influence of Justice Frankfurter and, to a lesser degree, Harlan, in the first six years of the Eisenhower Court is also demonstrated. Joined by Stewart and Whittaker, these justices formed the middle ground core that usually dominated civil liberty case majorities through the 1958 term. When ruling against defendants in cases involving alleged subversives, deportation, or state or federal criminal procedure, Justice Clark almost always joined them. When this majority included Brennan, however, the Court would more than likely reach a libertarian result and would probably win over all or at least part of the activists. In most of the cases in Table 11.1 in which Justice Brennan was in the majority with two or more of the middle bloc justices, all three of the Court's left were also in the majority while Justice Clark dissented. Where Brennan and only one other middle bloc justice were together in a majority, it always included all of the activists. In ten cases in which Brennan was in a majority without at least one activist, Clark was also a majority participant. The polarization in civil liberties cases between Clark and the left-of-middle justices is demonstrated in Table 11.3, which shows joint participation in the 154 civil liberties cases of the preceding tables. Justice Brennan had a record of 77 percent or more affiliation with the activists, in contrast to his lower percentages with Clark and formerly Burton. Through the 1958 term, Brennan maintained at least 50 percent participation with each of the other middle bloc justices, but that number declined, especially with Whittaker during the 1959–1961 terms. The participation of Chief Justice Warren with Frankfurter in 45 percent of the cases is the best record of an activist with any of the other middle bloc justices.

The index of inter-agreement shows that the core of the middle bloc, Frankfurter, Harlan, Whittaker, and Stewart, had a slightly lower percentage average than the activists. Adding Brennan to this group lowers the percentage by 13 points, but even so, the middle bloc maintained a very respectable 66 percent average inter-agreement. If Clark instead of Brennan was the fifth justice, the percentage is 76, but this is distorted somewhat by Clark's more libertarian voting record in the 1953 and 1954 terms.[5] A comparison of Table 11.3 with Tables 2.8, 2.9, and 2.10, *supra*, reveals that

Table 11.3
**Agreement Among Supreme Court Justices in Certain Nonunanimous Civil
Liberties Cases 1953–1961 Terms* (in percentages)**

	Douglas	Black	Warren	Brennan	Frankfurter	Stewart	Harlan	Burton	Whittaker	Clark
Douglas		92	81	77	37	32	27	20	18	16
Black	92		85	82	42	40	35	21	29	22
Warren	81	85		86	45	40	37	36	31	34
Brennan	77	82	86		49	52	46	43	41	31
Frankfurter	37	42	45	49		75	86	62	81	67
Stewart	32	40	40	52	75		71	–	77	68
Harlan	27	35	37	46	86	71		75	83	70
Burton	20	21	36	43	62	–	75		86	73
Whittaker	18	29	31	41	81	77	83	86		79
Clark	16	22	34	31	67	68	70	73	79	

Index of Inter-agreement

Douglas–Black–Warren	86 (very high)
Douglas–Black–Warren–Brennan	84 (very high)
Frankfurter–Harlan–Whittaker–Stewart	79 (high)
Frankfurter–Harlan–Whittaker–Burton	79 (high)
Frankfurter–Harlan–Whittaker–Stewart–Clark	76 (high)
Brennan–Frankfurter–Harlan–Whittaker–Stewart	66 (mod.)

*Agreements in nonunanimous opinions between every pair of justices, whether on the
majority or the minority side. For a list of cases included in the analysis, see Table 10.1,
supra.

most of Clark's agreement with the Court's left in nonunanimous opinions was in areas other than civil liberties. More important, however, is
the statistical reaffirmation, by Tables 11.1 through 11.3, of the strength of
the middle bloc in civil liberty cases through the 1958 term. Thereafter,
there were more pronounced left-wing and right-wing blocs. Having
shown this, it is appropriate to pursue in depth the judicial philosophies
of the Eisenhower associate justices.

JUSTICE BRENNAN

The link between the activists of the Court and the middle ground majority was Justice Brennan. This justice, although sometimes categorized with
Black, Douglas, and Warren, with whom he frequently agreed,[6] must fall
outside the activist bloc on the basis of his voting record and his indi-

vidual concurring and dissenting opinions in several important cases. Nor did he settle in the restraintist camp, although Frankfurter made the usual attempt to recruit Brennan during his first terms on the Court. Instead he was a pragmatist who cultivated his own result-oriented jurisprudence-based consensus. At the time of his appointment, Justice Brennan was described as a "moderate liberal" and a "middle-of-the-road" judge.[7] His votes and opinions in his early years on the Supreme Court, however, indicated that he might more appropriately be called a moderate libertarian, who held a position just to the left of center on the Eisenhower Court.

Although it may have been coincidental, relations between Chief Justice Warren and Justice Frankfurter began to deteriorate within a year of Brennan's appointment to the Court. Frankfurter followed his usual practice of trying to lure a new justice to his point of view, writing and conferring with Brennan frequently regarding upcoming cases and occasionally providing negative comments about Black and Douglas. For example, during his first term on the Court, Frankfurter sent Brennan a handwritten note, following the conference on *Jencks v. United States*, that berated Black and Douglas through a remark of Justice Holmes: "Because we have differing views we ought not to behave as though we were two cocks fighting on a dung hill."[8] The honeymoon was short-lived, however, because Brennan, along with several of the other justices, took homage to Frankfurter's filing a separate concurrence in *Cooper v. Aaron* at the start of the 1958 term.[9] Shortly thereafter, "the Little Judge," as Frankfurter was affectionately called by his law clerks, was talking about Brennan being an independent thinker but perhaps too independent. David Halberstam contends that the source of Brennan's difficulties with Frankfurter might stem from his not having taken Frankfurter's course in constitutional law while a student at Harvard—doubtlessly a major error in judgment from the preeminent professor's view.[10] At any rate, the break between Brennan and Frankfurter became irreparable as a result of Frankfurter's behavior following the Court's decision in *Irvin v. Dowd* in 1959 when Frankfurter influenced friends in the academic world to attack Brennan. Frankfurter wrote a stinging dissent in the case and enlisted surrogates to go after Brennan. Harvard law professor Henry Hart made such an attack on Brennan in the 1959 edition of the *Harvard Law Review*. In correspondence to friends, Frankfurter referred to Brennan's work as "shoddy." In response, Brennan made public comments about Frankfurter's writing disparaging remarks about justices who did not agree with him.[11] After the *Irvin* incident, Brennan never again joined Frankfurter in a dissent.

The breakdown in the relationship of Frankfurter, first with Warren, and later with Brennan, coincided with a bonding between Brennan and the Chief Justice. Brennan became Warren's closest colleague and his trusted lieutenant. Socially, Warren, Harlan, and Douglas and their wives became Brennan's good friends, the latter being quite an accomplishment since according to Professor Yarbrough, Douglas seemed genuinely close to none of his colleagues.[12] Brennan also thought highly of Justice Black and his work on the Court.[13]

The pragmatic Brennan soon developed a skill in winning over at least one moderate associate justice to the side of the activists to form a majority. In the same way that Louis Leakey had an innate ability to find the bones of human ancestors in Olduvai Gorge, Brennan could locate a fifth vote for his cause in the Court's marble palace. He became a master at drawing conservative justices to an opinion more narrowly drafted than the activists would have preferred by writing his brethren personal letters setting forth his views about cases and using direct, personal diplomacy.

Justice Brennan's career as judge and justice is somewhat unique in that he was a Democrat who received all the appointments to the bench from Republican executives.[14] New Jersey's Republican governor Driscoll appointed Brennan to a judgeship in the law division of that state's Superior Court in January 1949. In the next year he moved up to the appellate division of the New Jersey Superior Court, and in March 1952, Governor Driscoll appointed Brennan to the New Jersey Supreme Court. His opinions in the state courts gave some clues about his judicial philosophy and how he would respond to similar questions on the high tribunal.

Justice Brennan had a strong respect for First Amendment freedoms of speech and press, although he rejected the preferred position of Black and Douglas. In *Speiser,* he introduced the "chilling effects" doctrine that focused attention on the wider consequences of laws that suppressed speech. Brennan noted, "the operation and effect of the method by which speech is sought to be restrained must be subjected to close analysis and critical judgment in light of the particular circumstances to which it is applied."[15] Thus statutes could be challenged even when the particular application at issue might survive a First Amendment balancing test, since such statute's mere presence on the books would tend to prevent others from exercising their First Amendment rights to the fullest extent. Brennan drew a line between protected and unprotected speech, rather than a line between speech and action—a new approach for the Court.

As a state judge, Brennan ruled that prior restraint could not be applied to a burlesque show in *Adams Theatre Co. v. Kennan.*[16] He stated: "The performance of a play or show, whether burlesque or other kind of theatre, is a form of speech and prima facie expression protected by the State and Federal Constitutions, and thus only in exceptional cases subject to previous restraint by means of withholding of a theatre license or otherwise."[17] But in *United Advertising Corp. v. Borough of Raritan,*[18] he distinguished First Amendment guarantees as inapplicable to purely commercial advertising. He concurred with the majority in *City of Absecon v.*

Vettese,[19] however, where the New Jersey Supreme Court held that: "The free press is a bulwark of our democratic way of life and courts must be ever vigilant to curb insidious as well as candid attempts to restrict its vital public functions."[20]

Applying similar criteria in his opinions on the Supreme Court, Justice Brennan wrote the majority opinions in *Roth* and *Alberts* upholding federal and state criminal obscenity laws. He gave no indication of what "contemporary community standards" might encompass, leaving himself open to the possible charge of relativism in moral matters. More importantly, Brennan's opinion in *Roth* opened the door to free expression because it reigned in the censors, despite the fact that the decision upheld Roth's conviction and declared obscenity beyond the scope of First Amendment protection. In *Kingsley Books*, Brennan thought the absence of a provision for trial by jury in the New York statute was a mistake and wrote a separate dissent, again rejecting the absolutist language of Justices Black and Douglas, who also dissented. In his dissent in *Barr v. Matteo*,[21] a libel case involving federal administrative officers, Brennan expressed his concerns about an actual malice test—a concept that he would develop further five years later in *New York Times v. Sullivan*.[22]

Justice Brennan was a staunch defender of the right of alleged subversives to procedural regularity. In the few instances in this area where the Court was sharply divided, Brennan usually voted with the activists. In *Green v. United States*, however, he rejected the dissenting opinion of Black, Douglas, and Warren, which contended that the time had come for establishing a rule that trial by jury be required in federal criminal contempt proceedings.[23] Brennan maintained that the evidence was insufficient to establish guilt of criminal contempt. In *Barenblatt*, Brennan could not accept the preferred position language of the activists' dissent but wrote a separate dissenting opinion contending that the investigatory committee had no purpose except exposure for the sake of exposure. In *Uphaus*, he wrote a dissent in which he was joined by the three activists in contending that the New Hampshire investigation lacked a rational connection with a discernable legislative purpose.[24] Justices Black and Douglas would have gone further and in a separate dissenting opinion argued that First and Fourteenth Amendment rights had been abridged. Again in *Beilan* and *Lerner*, Brennan chose a narrower course and found that the employees had been discharged for disloyalty and, there being no evidence in that respect before the state authorities, had been denied due process. The dissent of Black and Douglas, however, contended that constitutional freedoms of belief and association had been violated. Brennan deserted the Court's left, and joined the majority in upholding the contested sentence for contempt of court in *Yates*. Perhaps his experience as a trial judge makes Brennan more sensitive than the activists to the use of the contempt power in upholding the authority of trial courts.

Brennan's votes in the *Watkins–Barenblatt* and *Sweezy–Uphaus* cases reflected his concern about abuses of legislative investigatory powers which he had expressed in two speeches made prior to his appointment to the Court.[25] According to the late Senator Joseph McCarthy, he referred to congressional investigations of communism as Salem witch hunts and inquisitions and accused some committee members of barbarism. During the hearing on his nomination before the Senate Judiciary Committee, Brennan received a grueling questioning on this matter by Senator McCarthy, who concluded: "I believe that Justice Brennan has demonstrated an underlying hostility to Congressional attempts to expose the Communist conspiracy."[26] McCarthy was subsequently the only senator to vote against Brennan's confirmation.

On the New Jersey courts, Brennan was keenly sensitive to procedural violations in trial court procedures as demonstrated in *Palestroni v. Jacobs*,[27] where the trial judge innocently furnished a dictionary to jurors who were in deliberation at their request without prior notice to the defendant or his counsel. Brennan held that this was prejudicial error, stating: "The irregularity of the privy communication of the judge with the jury must be deprecated in the strongest terms. . . . Such communication borders perilously close in every case on an infringement upon the litigant's basic right to due process and in particular circumstances, may in fact invade that right."[28] This concern for possible violations of due process by the states carried over to Brennan's Supreme Court decisions.

In *Knapp v. Schweitzer*, Brennan voted with the six-justice majority which held that a person given immunity under state law cannot refuse to answer questions put to him by a state grand jury on the ground that it might expose him to prosecution under a federal law. In a separate opinion Brennan stated that the only question decided was that a witness who was granted immunity by a state against state prosecution may be compelled to testify in a state proceeding and cannot successfully assert the privilege against self-incrimination under the Fifth Amendment.

In *Abbate*, Brennan spoke for the Court in finding that action aimed at destruction of communication facilities was punishable by both state and federal laws. In addition, however, Brennan appended an independent expression of his own concurring views. Brennan dissented in *Bartkus v. Illinois*, where he thought that the Fifth Amendment was violated by a state trial so dominated by federal officers as to be in actuality a second federal prosecution (in an opinion separate from the dissent of the activists who contended that federal–state cooperation in the second trial violated due process as well as the double jeopardy clause of the Fifth Amendment).

As a state judge, Brennan indicated that the privilege against self-incrimination, while an important procedural safeguard, was subject to control by the bench and was not to be treated as an absolute right. In

State v. Frary,[29] he contended that ultimately courts must decide when the privilege may be invoked:

> It has endured as a wise and necessary protection of the individual against arbitrary power; the price of occasional failures of justice under its protection is paid in the larger interest of the general personal security. . . . It is a fallacy, however, to regard the right of a witness to remain mute when a criminating fact is inquired about as a fixed barrier to the search of the judicial process for truth. The barrier is up as to any question only when the witness himself chooses to put it up, but the court, and not the witness, is the ultimate arbiter whether the witness is entitled to the protection of the privilege.[30]

Prior to his vote with the majority in *Breithaupt*, upholding the use of a blood sample taken from an unconscious drunk as evidence in a state trial, Judge Brennan had, in another context, upheld the state's right to use blood tests. In *Cortese v. Cortese*,[31] a case involving a paternity suit, the mother refused to permit a blood test to be taken either of herself or of her child on the grounds that this was an invasion of the right of personal property and that the statute providing for such blood tests was unconstitutional. Brennan rejected these objections and reversed the trial court which had held for the mother, maintaining: "The citizen holds his citizenship subject to the duty to furnish to the courts, from time to time and within reasonable limits, such assistance as the courts may demand of him in their effort to ascertain truth in controversies before them."[32] In *Breithaupt*, Justice Brennan was willing to extend these reasonable limits in search of the truth beyond what the Chief Justice and Justices Black and Douglas thought constitutional. Indeed, Brennan's allowance for flexibility in state court proceedings was an area of sharp contrast between his judicial philosophy and that of the activists.

The right of a defendant to inspect records used in his trial as annunciated by Brennan in his broadly worded majority opinion in *Jencks* had likewise been the subject of his earlier state court decisions. In *State v. Tune*,[33] he contended that the right of access is extremely important in criminal cases: "It shocks my sense of justice that in these circumstances counsel for an accused facing a possible death sentence should be denied inspection of his confession which, were this a civil case could not be denied. . . . To shackle counsel so that they cannot effectively seek out the truth and afford the accused the representation which is not his privilege but his absolute right seriously imperils our bedrock presumption of innocence."[34] In *Casey v. MacPhails*,[35] however, Brennan indicated that there are two qualifications of this right:

> The general principle of the right of any citizen and taxpayer to inspect and have access to public records when such inspection and access can be had without undue interference with the conduct of

the public business is qualified not only by the right in the judicial discretion of the trial judge to deny the inspection or access when the motive is improper but also is qualified by any enactments of the legislature which may bear upon his right of use of the information.[36]

A more sympathetic reaction to the claim of labor in picketing cases might be expected of Brennan since his father had been active in organized labor and had once been a business manager of a union.[37] In an address before the Essex County Bar Association in 1946, however, Brennan recognized the changes in labor that had come about since the prewar era and made a prophetic statement: "No reflective American can doubt that the time has arrived when we must have some remedial legislation which recognizes the changes of the last ten years in labor's influence in our national life. Its present day great strength and power and the evidences we see toward abuse of that power, cry out for some measure of control."[38] This idea of control was reflected in his opinion in *International Ass'n of Machinists v. Bergen Ave. Bus Owners' Ass'n*,[39] where he stated: "The sanctions of seizure and compulsory arbitration and the attendant prohibitions of stoppages and strikes are involved only when the paramount public interest is threatened by an actual or imminent interference."[40] On the Supreme Court, in *NLRB v. Truck Drivers Local Union*,[41] Brennan upheld members of an employers' bargaining association and found that they had not committed an unfair labor practice, during negotiations for a new contract with the union, when they temporarily locked out their employees as a defense against a union strike aimed at one of their members. Justice Brennan, speaking for the majority, reversed the Court of Appeals decision that had found the employers guilty of an unfair labor practice on the ground that a lockout could be justified only if there were facts showing unusual economic hardship. Brennan made it plain that the Court was deciding a narrow question—whether a temporary lockout is lawful as a defense to a union strike tactic that threatened the destruction of the employer's interest in bargaining on a group basis. The Court ruled that the preservation of the integrity of the multiemployer bargaining unit was a purpose for which employers might lawfully resort to the lockout as an economic weapon.

In general, Justice Brennan was sympathetic to the claims of aliens and defendants in denaturalization and expatriation proceedings. In the *Brown* denaturalization case, Brennan voted with the activists in dissent but stated his own reasons in a separate opinion. While the opinion of the Chief Justice contended that waiver of the privilege against self-incrimination should not be extended to civil cases, Brennan held that the lower court had ruled incorrectly on the waiver. His votes in the expatriation cases were based on his view that expatriation for desertion from the military did not have the "requisite rational relation" to the war power that voting in a foreign election had to the power to regulate the conduct of foreign relations. Brennan's separate concurring opinion in *Trop* weakened the effect of the Chief Justice's strongly worded opinion of the Court declaring an act of Congress unconstitutional.

Although Brennan was not on the Court at the time the *Brown* desegregation case was decided, he was a firm supporter of the use of sociological knowledge by the judiciary.[42] Warren assigned Brennan to draft the ringing declaration of the Court's supreme authority in *Cooper v. Aaron*, and although other justices contributed to the final opinion, it is Brennan's rhetoric that gives force to the per curiam pronouncement. Justice Brennan, along with Justice Douglas and the Chief Justice, showed impatience with the Court's requiring interpretation by state courts of statutes involving the rights of African-Americans before federal courts could decide upon their constitutionality.[43] These same three justices on occasion dissented from the Court's denial of certiorari in equal protection cases.

To Warren, Brennan's single most important contribution was his opinion in *Baker v. Carr* that put to rest the "bugaboo" of the political question doctrine and ruled that legislative malapportionment cases were justiciable under the equal protection clause.[44] In the case's continuing conference, Brennan, the consummate coalition builder on the Court, knew the overriding importance of winning five votes. The libertarians and the restraintists were evenly split: Frankfurter, Harlan, Whittaker, and Clark contended that the case presented a nonjusticiable political question; Warren, Black, Douglas, and Brennan held a diametrically opposite view. Stewart, the swing justice, thought the question justiciable but did not want to address the merits of the case. Brennan craftily drafted an opinion that won Stewart's vote while dissuading the libertarians from writing concurrences addressing the question that would have threatened the majority's loss of Stewart. Eventually, Clark was won over to Brennan's opinion, and Whittaker retired before the decision was handed down, leaving only Frankfurter and Harlan in dissent.[45]

From his voting record and opinions on the Court, Justice Brennan emerged as a new type of libertarian who rejected the wide-ranging language of the activists in many cases but who was not bound by so strict restraintist requirements as was Justice Frankfurter. In this in-between position, Brennan rejected the preferred position doctrine and total incorporation theory of the activists and seldom joined them in urging the Court to pass on constitutional issues. Instead, Brennan frequently voted for the same result as the three justices to his left, but stated more limited reasons for doing so. In a manner similar to Justice Frankfurter, he was more likely to base his opinions on statutory construction rather than constitutional interpretation. On the other hand, Brennan did not hesitate to use his powers as a justice to overrule what he considered abridgements of fundamental freedoms. His record of voting to invalidate state actions, although not as high as the activists, was far above that of Justice Frankfurter. In ruling on federal criminal cases, however, Brennan's percentage support for defendants' claims was almost as high as Warren's.[46] Brennan's advocacy of "selective incorporation" as a middle position between total incorporation and interpreting the Fourteenth Amendment as entirely independent of the Bill of Rights was a major contribution in placing the protection of individual rights at the forefront of the Court's jurisprudence.

JUSTICE HARLAN

The first associate justice appointed to the Court by President Eisenhower was John Marshall Harlan, who served on the Second Circuit Court of Appeals from March 1954 until October 1954—the shortest length of prior judicial service of any of the justices appointed subsequent to Chief Justice Warren. Eisenhower and Attorney General Brownell were looking for a justice with prior trial experience as well as experience on the bench, and Harlan came highly recommended on both counts. As a token of his esteem for his first associate justice appointee, the president invited Harlan and his wife to sit with him on the reviewing stand during his second inauguration parade in January 1957.

Perhaps Harlan's most important opinion on the lower court was in *United States v. Flynn*[47] in which a unanimous court affirmed the convictions of thirteen so-called "second-string" Communists charged with violations of the Smith Act. Harlan's reasoning followed closely the lead of the Supreme Court in the *Dennis* case. On the Supreme Court, however, Harlan wrote a number of opinions curbing excessive governmental zeal in denying the rights of accused subversives. Most of these opinions were decided on nonconstitutional grounds but rested on First Amendment principles. He was the author of the carefully-worded *Yates* opinion which made procedural requirements more stringent for convictions under the Smith Act. He voted for employees' claims in the loyalty-security program cases and participated in the majority in *Jencks*, *Nelson*, and the loyalty oath cases. In contrast to these votes, he dissented with Minton and Reed in *Emspak* and *Bart* and disagreed with the majority in the passport cases. Harlan was the only member of the Court who voted against all three state employees involved in security cases—Slochower, Beilan, and Lerner. In *Mesarosh* and *Konigsberg*, the two important cases involving alleged subversives in which Justice Frankfurter dissented, he was joined by Justice Harlan. As mentioned previously, Justices Harlan and Frankfurter were in the majority in the *Watkins–Barenblatt* and *Sweezy–Uphaus* series of cases.

In several of his opinions in this area, Justice Harlan spoke in cautious language, keeping the findings of the Court within narrow limits. In

Yates he maintained: "We need not . . . decide the issue before us in terms of constitutional compulsion, for our first duty is to construe this statute."[48] In *Barenblatt*, he carefully distinguished the opinion of the Court from the earlier *Watkins* decision, emphasizing not the limitations but the extent of congressional powers in ruling that the particular investigation involved related to a valid legislative purpose. The Federal Loyalty-Security Program opinions were likewise couched in terms of strict adherence to the various administrative agencies' own rules with Justice Harlan writing for the Court in several instances.

Harlan was not a strong judicial friend of aliens. In *Jay,* he voted with the majority to allow "faceless informers" to testify in deportation hearings. Although he was in the majority upholding the claims of Witkovitz and Pedreiro, he was one of four dissenters in *Rowoldt* who contended "that in order to reach its result the Court has had to take impermissible liberties with the statute and the record upon which this case is based."[49] On the Court of Appeals, Judge Harlan had refused to set aside an order for deportation of an alien of the People's Republic of China, but gave him a further opportunity to choose deportation to Taiwan.[50] Also on the lower court, in *United States ex rel. Accardi v. Shaughnessy,*[51] he dissented from the majority's reversal of the district court, which had found that the Attorney General had not unconsciously influenced the Board of Immigration Appeals by issuing a list of "unsavory characters" that included Accardi's name. The Supreme Court ultimately accepted Harlan's view that before the district court, Accardi was entitled only to a hearing on whether the Board reached its own decision or had it dictated by the attorney general. Also noteworthy were Justice Harlan's votes to uphold the government's action in all three expatriation cases in the 1957 term.

On the Court of Appeals, Harlan heard few cases involving criminal procedures and showed little sympathy for the defendants' claims.[52] In state cases on the Supreme Court, Harlan, perhaps influenced by considerations of federalism, usually sustained the criminal procedures involved. In *Griffin* and *Fikes,* where the Court achieved libertarian results, Justice Harlan dissented with remnants of the Vinson Court majority. In *Fikes,* Harlan warned his colleagues "that due regard for the division between state and federal functions in the administration of criminal justice requires that we let Alabama's judgment stand."[53]

In federal criminal cases, Justice Harlan voted for defendants' claims more often. He dissented with Burton, Minton, and Reed in the *Rea* search and seizure case and was in the minority in *Mapp,* although he voted with the majority against the government in other important cases in this area. In double jeopardy and self-incrimination cases, Harlan consistently ruled against the defendant. In *Reid,* Harlan and Frankfurter concurred in striking a portion of the Uniform Code of Military Justice as unconstitutional— but limited their concurrence to capital cases.

In First Amendment cases, Harlan voted for defendants' claims in two important instances. In *Roth*, he joined Black and Douglas in dissent but in a separate opinion contended that Congress has no substantive power over sexual morality and that federal censorship should be discouraged. Yet he concurred with the majority in *Alberts*, which upheld California's censorship law, noting: "It has often been said that one of the greatest strengths of our federal system is that we have, in the forty-eight States, forty-eight experimental social laboratories"[54]—a statement with which the activists would heartily agree in economic cases where no First Amendment rights were involved. In *Staub v. Baxley*, Justice Harlan agreed with the majority that declared a city ordinance requiring labor organizers to register and pay a high fee was an unconstitutional prior restraint on speech. In religious freedom cases, he joined the majority in prohibiting state-sponsored prayer in public schools and in invalidating a requirement that state officials declare a belief in a deity.

In *NAACP v. Alabama*, Justice Harlan wrote the forceful opinion of the Court protecting associational freedom and rejecting the state's contention that the U.S. Supreme Court did not have jurisdiction in the case for lack of a federal question. But in the same case, the NAACP attacked an Alabama restraining order preventing it from soliciting support in that state. Since that matter had never received a hearing on the merits, that question was not properly before the Court. Said Justice Harlan: "The proper method of raising questions in the state appellate courts pertinent to the underlying suit for an injunction appears to be by appeal, after a hearing on the merits and final judgment by the lower state court. Only from the disposition of such an appeal can review be sought here."[55] This statement was indicative of Harlan's embracing the principles but not always the pace of the Court's civil rights decisions. In the *Brown II* opinion, Harlan is credited with contributing the most forceful sentence: "It should go without saying that the vitality of these constitutional principles cannot be allowed to yield simply because of disagreement with them."[56]

In voting on civil liberty issues, Justice Harlan was most closely allied with Justice Frankfurter.[57] Harlan and Frankfurter were acquaintances before Harlan's appointment, and the two became close friends and frequent allies during their years together on the Court. The two justices shared a strong respect for the efforts of state courts to solve their own judicial problems. In *Konigsberg*, for instance, Justice Frankfurter dissented, contending that the state bar admittance procedures should not be easily overruled. Justice Harlan harbored the same feelings and thought "what the Court has really done . . . is simply to impose on California, its own notions of public policy and judgment. For me, today's decision represents an unacceptable intrusion into a matter of state concern."[58]

Harlan's dissent in *Mapp* opposing application of the Bill of Rights and the exclusionary rule to the states reflected his core values of federalism and a limited judicial function:

> In overruling the *Wolf* case the Court . . . has forgotten the sense of judicial restraint which, with due regard for *stare decisis*, is one element that should enter into deciding whether a past decision of this Court should be overruled. . . . The preservation of a proper balance between state and federal responsibility in the administration of criminal justice demands patience on the part of those who might like to see things move faster among the States in this respect. Problems of criminal law enforcement vary widely from State to State.[59]

Likewise, in his dissent, joined by Frankfurter in the malapportionment case *Baker v. Carr*, Harlan chided his brethren for delving into an issue that plainly depended on state action:

> I can find nothing in the Equal Protection Clause or elsewhere in the Federal Constitution which expressly or impliedly supports the view that state legislatures must be so structured as to reflect with approximate equality the voice of every voter. Not only is that proposition refuted by history . . . but it strikes deep into the heart of our federal system. Its acceptance would require us to turn our backs on the regard which this Court has always shown for the judgment of state legislatures and courts on matters of basically local concern.[60]

From Harlan's perspective the Court needed to move with caution in bringing about social change. He had a fundamental disagreement with Brennan and the activist bloc about the role of the Court in that regard. But he did not always agree with Frankfurter either.

Harlan parted company with Frankfurter in *Poe v. Ullman*, and in dissent enunciated a living due process theory in interpreting the Fourteenth Amendment's due process clause. In reviewing Connecticut's anticontraceptive statute, Harlan harked back to Cardozo's "fundamental rights" doctrine in applying a balancing test to a state's action. Harlan balanced liberty of the individual against the demands of organized society and found Connecticut's statute wanting. Within the nation's tradition, Harlan found that liberty could not be limited by precise terms of specific guarantees provided in the Constitution (such as those advocated by proponents of the total incorporation theory). For Harlan, liberty was "a rational continuum which, broadly speaking, included a freedom from all substantial arbitrary impositions and purposeless restraints." Within the ambit of due process protection was the "private realm of family life," including "the most intimate details of the marital relation."[61] Thus Harlan publicly embraced a constitutional right of privacy four years before a majority of his brethren did. Harlan's dissent in *Poe* reopened debate about the doctrine of substantive due process, but, more importantly, it became the foundation for many of the Court's subsequent findings of a right to privacy. The *Poe* dissent was a classical example of Harlan's "liberal opinions" that were later to be admired by Justice Stewart.[62]

Harlan generally enjoyed good relations with virtually all members of the Court, allies and opponents alike. He was especially close to Frankfurter and Stewart and friendly with Whittaker and Clark. Even Black, with whom he frequently disagreed, said, "John Harlan is one of the few people who convince me that there is such a thing as a good Republican." [63]

On two occasions, however, Harlan became embroiled in Court feuds that inaugurated new October terms. The first decision handed down by the Court in the 1959 term was a railroad injury case in which the Court summarily restored a $25,000 jury reward that had been reversed by the Ohio Supreme Court. As usual, Justice Frankfurter dissented, contending that certiorari had been improvidently granted in such a Federal Employer's Liability Acts case. But Justice Harlan, in an opinion concurred in by Justice Whittaker, chided the majority for taking time from more important cases. He stated: "The opening of a new term that confronts the court with the usual volume of important and exacting business impels me to reiterate the view that cases involving only factual issues and which are of no general importance have no legitimate demands upon our energies, already taxed to the utmost."[64]

Harlan further accused the majority of silently deciding that in railroad injury cases "anything a jury says goes." If so, he added, "the time has come when the Court should frankly say so."[65] This charge drew a strong reply from Justice Douglas, who spoke for the other members of the majority—Black, Warren, Brennan, and Clark—and maintained that the Court should be vigilant to safeguard the right of jury trial in federal courts. Douglas also summarized the liability act cases taken to the Supreme Court in the preceding ten years with his figures indicating that the Court had granted thirty-two petitions for review, all brought by injured employees, while rejecting forty petitions from employees and thirty-seven from employers. Thus the Court had averaged only three such cases a year—a none-too-burdensome total.

When a similar exchange by opinion opened the 1960 term, it appeared that the high tribunal might be establishing an annual tradition of beginning each term with an argument over whether the Court was wasting its time on trivial cases. This time Justice Brennan spoke for the majority, which again included Black, Douglas, Warren, and Clark, and which again ruled in favor of an injured employee in a routine negligence case.[66] Justice Frankfurter would have dismissed the entire proceeding, while Justices Stewart and Whittaker subscribed to the dissenting opinion of Justice Harlan, which maintained that: "At the opening of a term which finds the court's docket crowded with more important and difficult litigation than in many years, it is not without irony that we should be witnessing among the first matters to be heard a routine negligence case involving only issues of fact. . . . Such cases, distressing and important as they are for unsuccessful plaintiffs, do not belong in this court."[67] Unlike Frankfurter, who refused to consider the merits of such cases at all, Justice Harlan went on to say that the worker should lose anyway. This indicated that Justice Harlan, the "lawyer's judge," did not, like Justice Black, have his heart "still visible scarcely below the surface of his opinions."[68]

Perhaps opinions such as these along with his dissents based on restraintist considerations which even Justice Frankfurter was unable to find in several incidences, explain why Professor Paschal contended that one sensed in Harlan "puzzlement and wonder at a strange, new landscape."[69] Whether or not this was the case, Justice Harlan's opinions denoted values that were, on the whole, middle-of-the-road and traditional (similar to those of Justice Jackson whom he replaced),[70] while at the same time libertarian. In almost every area of the Eisenhower Court's work, there were cases in which Harlan was part of a libertarian consensus and in which he spoke for the Court. He was admired as one of the most thoughtful and perceptive of the justices. In remaining true to his principal judicial values of federalism, separation of powers, majoritarian democracy, precedent, and proceduralism—the "passive virtues"—Harlan, as an anchor of the moderate bloc, embodied the temper of the Eisenhower era.

JUSTICE WHITTAKER

Prior to his appointment to the Supreme Court, Justice Whittaker had served as a judge of the district court in Missouri, where according to Justice Douglas, he was happiest as a jurist,[71] and later, the Eighth Circuit Court of Appeals. Whittaker's appointment involved geographical considerations: the Midwest was underrepresented on the Court at that time. He was recommended by Rob Roberts of the *Kansas City Star* and by leaders of the Missouri bar.[72] Like the other Eisenhower associate justices, his opinions on the inferior courts provided some clues about his judicial philosophy on the high tribunal. His view of subversives in public employment was revealed in *Davis v. University of Kansas City*,[73] where Whittaker upheld the dismissal of a professor who refused to answer university officials when they asked whether he was or ever had been a member of the Communist Party. According to Whittaker:

> Plaintiff had a lawful right, under the Fifth Amendment to the Constitution, to refuse to answer, and no inference of criminality can be drawn from his failure to answer. But he did not have a Constitutional right to remain a public school teacher. And the refusal of a teacher—in a most intimate position to mould the minds of the

youth of the country—to answer to the responsible officials of the school whether he is a member of a found and declared conspiracy by a godless group to overthrow our government by force, constitutes an "adequate case" for the dismissal of such a teacher. The public will not stand, and they ought not to stand for such reticence or refusal to answer by the teachers in their schools. And the University officials would have been derelict in their duties . . . had they not dismissed him.[74]

In light of this opinion his vote with the majority in *Beilan* and *Lerner* was to be expected. Whittaker's dissent with Clark in *Sacher*, likewise forecast his subsequent votes in *Barenblatt, Sweezy, Wilkinson,* and *Braden.* He was with the majority in the Federal Loyalty-Security Program cases but was one of the four passport case dissenters.

In the expatriation cases, Whittaker contended that Congress might expatriate a citizen for an act which it may reasonably find to be fraught with danger of embroiling our government in an international dispute or of embarrassing it in the conduct of foreign affairs. He found neither of these conditions present in *Trop* or *Perez.* On the district court Whittaker ruled against an alien who sought suspension of a deportation order on the ground that a statute empowered the attorney general to suspend such orders if the alien had been present continuously for the ten preceding years.[75] Whittaker found that a one-hour trip to Canada had broken a requisite ten-year period. On the Supreme Court his record of voting both for and against the claims of aliens and defendants in denaturalization proceedings indicated that he carefully balanced competing claims in the frequently odd and unique circumstances involved in these cases.[76]

In cases involving criminal proceedings, Whittaker showed readiness to accept findings of state and lower federal courts, although there were notable exceptions. In the 1958 term, he cast the decisive fifth vote with the Court's left in *Moore v. Michigan,* setting aside a murder conviction because of a denial of right to counsel. The following year, however, it was Whittaker whose fifth vote created the majority affirming such a conviction in *Crooker v. California.* These types of cases were especially dependent on the particular facts involved and indicated that Whittaker determined violations of due process on a case-by-case method. On the Court of Appeals, Whittaker held that the Post Office Department had no right to open a first-class parcel which it suspected contained narcotics.[77] In federal search and seizure cases on the Supreme Court, Whittaker was with the majority in the *Miller* and *Jones* cases, but he joined Burton and Clark in dissent in *Giordenello.* The impact of considerations of federalism on the justice from Missouri was seen in two double jeopardy cases. In *Green v. United States,* he voted with the left, upholding the defendant's claims, while in *Hoag v. New Jersey,* he refused to upset the state court findings.

Whittaker's most notable opinion for the Court was *Staub v. Baxley* invalidating a city ordinance requiring labor organizers to register. In his dissent, however, in *Lambert v. California*,[78] where First Amendment rights were not involved, Whittaker would have upheld an ordinance requiring felons to register. Whittaker was with the majority in civil rights cases and he demonstrated his concern for carefully worded opinions in a memorandum suggesting form and word changes on every page of Justice Brennan's draft in *Cooper v. Aaron*.[79]

Justice Whittaker did not clearly state his views of the balancing process in an opinion. Yet his votes in certain cases indicated that he followed a balancing theory of his own: compare his vote in *Moore v. Michigan* with that in *Crooker v. California*; compare his search and seizure votes in *Miller* and *Jones* with *Giordenello*.

From this review of cases, it is difficult to classify Justice Whittaker. In a large number of five-to-four decisions he joined the majority. In forty-one crucial decisions, Whittaker cast the deciding vote, most often in the judicial company of Justices Frankfurter, Harlan, and Stewart, and usually denying protection of civil liberties. Some of his lower court opinions expressed restraintist values akin to those of Frankfurter. In a criminal case on the Court of Appeals he reminded the defendants, who urged consideration of other matters, that the court's "function is limited to a determination of whether the trial was conducted fairly, in accordance with the law, and free from substantial or prejudicial error."[80] In a district court case involving a chicken raiser who mortgaged his chickens to a finance company, Whittaker in typical restraintist language lamented: "While I have great sympathy for him, and I think rather naturally, would like to find a way to protect him even against his own folly . . . I have been unable to find a basis in the law that gives any right to him against this defendant."[81]

Justice Whittaker had to his discredit one of the most intemperate opinions written by an Eisenhower Court justice. In a routine Federal Employer's Liability Acts negligence case,[82] he read a concurring opinion which poked fun at the dissent of Justice Douglas who spoke for the four-justice minority.[83] According to Whittaker: "The only way a railroad could protect its watchmen against injury by such outsiders as drunken drivers would be to provide them with military tanks and make sure they stay in them." Whittaker added with a smile: "I am not even sure that this be certain protection, for someone might shoot him, an act not very different, it seems to me, from the drunken driver's conduct. How this can be thought to square with any known concept of 'negligence' can be divined only in heaven."[84]

At this Justice Douglas reddened and prefaced his dissent by stating: "The case is rather an important one. It cannot be dismissed by this attempted humor." Douglas obviously had Whittaker in mind as he continued: "Those of us who have read the record, as I am sure only a few of us have . . . would understand that the case tested the constitutional and statutory right to trial by juries rather than judges." Douglas concluded his extemporaneous remarks by saying that the gravity of the issue belies the "rather smart-alecky things that have been said."[85] Whittaker's facetiousness in this case aligned him with Frankfurter and Harlan in the camp of those who have publicly clashed with the activists (although Justice Black remained aloof from these outbursts).

When Whittaker resigned from the Court, Justice Harlan paid homage to him as "a prodigious worker who was satisfied with nothing less than full mastery of every record and brief."[86] Unfortunately, in mastering the work of the Court, Whittaker frequently was indecisive. According to Justice Stewart, Whittaker was a "very conscientious man and a fine man, but he just didn't have the power of decision."[87] In conference, Whittaker apparently would agree with whoever was speaking. After the conference, Whittaker would agonize over decisions, swinging back and forth in key cases—making opinion writing difficult for his colleagues. This was exactly what he did in the important expatriation cases, *Trop v. Dulles* and *Perez v. Brownell* in 1958, and what he was doing in *Baker v. Carr* when he retired before making up his mind. The tensions generated by the *Baker* case post-conference activities drove Whittaker to the hospital suffering from exhaustion, and he ended up not participating in the ruling. One week later, Whittaker resigned from the Court. At that time Justice Douglas, who stated that he and Whittaker had become close friends, found him in "very poor physical condition, very worried and very depressed. . . . He found the details of the court work here very, very wearisome. . . . He was an extremely thorough and painstaking man who just never, never stopped working on a case."[88]

In the eyes of critics, Whittaker was neither a judicial thinker nor a legal technician, and his opinions were considered "pedestrian." He simply was unable to keep up with the Court's demanding workload. After retiring, Whittaker became a high-salaried legal advisor for General Motors and attacked the Court's decisions and even some of the justices in widely reported remarks, notably in a 1964 speech before the American Bar Association.

JUSTICE STEWART

Justice Stewart's voting record classified him as a middle bloc justice, and he frequently agreed with Justices Frankfurter, Harlan, and Whittaker in civil liberty cases. One must note his libertarian pronouncements, however, in several of his opinions—this in contrast to the work of Justice Burton whom he replaced. He wrote the opinion of the Court in *Cash v.*

Culver and a concurring opinion in *Spano* indicating that he looked askance at state denials of counsel. On the Court of Appeals, Stewart had found that a denial of right to counsel that had occurred sixteen years previously was a violation of due process.[89]

Like Frankfurter, he appeared to have a high regard for the importance of federalism in state criminal prosecutions, for as a judge he warned that federal courts must be chary of interfering "in an area of possible friction between state and federal jurisdictions."[90] Stewart was with the activists and Brennan in *Irvin v. Dowd*,[91] however, to form a five-justice majority that reversed an Indiana Supreme Court decision in a criminal case. He joined the majority upholding state action in most instances, and in *Abbate* and *Bartkus* he found that successive trials by different sovereignties did not violate the Fifth or the Fourteenth Amendments. Stewart also expressed his belief that all proper remedies in the state courts should be exhausted before the federal judiciary reviewed a case or granted relief.

In federal criminal prosecutions he voted to uphold the claims of Lee and Ladner, but he was the author of the majority opinion in the five-to-four *Brown* case requiring testimony from a witness who invoked Fifth Amendment privileges. Stewart also joined Frankfurter, Harlan, Whittaker, and Clark to form majorities in the two 1959 cases clarifying the *Jencks* rule.

On the lower courts, Justice Stewart indicated that he probably followed a careful balancing plan in reaching a decision. In facing an aftermath of the *Brown* desegregation case, Stewart refused to order immediate desegregation for Hillsboro, Ohio, contending that it would be more prudent to wait until the beginning of the next school year.[92] The fact that he held libertarian values in this area, however, was reflected by the Senate vote (70–17) confirming his appointment. The seventeen votes of southern senators cast against him were, up until that time, the most recorded in opposition to any Supreme Court nominee since 1930, when Hoover's nomination of John J. Parker was refused.[93]

Stewart also interpreted and applied the doctrine of the *Yates* case in *Wellman v. United States*.[94] When that case was first before the Court of Appeals, Judge Stewart subscribed to the opinion of the court affirming the convictions of several Communists. After the *Yates* decision, the case was remanded to the circuit court where a new trial but not acquittal was ordered since the court could not say that there was no evidence of incitement to violent action. In a separate concurrence Judge Stewart stated that a new trial was justified but thought that "the effort to discern the germ of illegal advocacy in a handful of equivocal statements culled from the present record" would be unrewarding. He felt that "standing alone, these statements . . . hardly amount to the incitement to action of the kind defined in *Yates*."[95]

During his first term on the Supreme Court, Stewart voted with the majority in *Barenblatt* and *Uphaus* indicating that he was in basic agreement with the Frankfurter–Harlan balancing theory. In *Greene v. McElroy*, however, he did not join the concurring opinion of Justices Frankfurter, Harlan, and Whittaker but chose to endorse the majority opinion of the Chief Justice.[96]

Stewart did not participate in any important deportation cases during his first several terms on the Court, but on the lower bench he indicated that he might be more sympathetic to the claims of aliens than Burton had been. Although the Supreme Court reversed his decision, Stewart maintained in *Lehmann v. United States ex rel. Carson*[97] that the retroactive provisions of the Immigration and Nationality Act of 1952 caused inequities.

Justice Stewart's opinion of the Court in the *Kingsley Pictures* case demonstrated his high regard for First Amendment protection of the dissemination of ideas. On the Court of Appeals, however, he contended that there were limitations on the scope of this protection. In *Garland v. Torre*,[98] movie star Judy Garland sued the Columbia Broadcasting System for defamatory statements about her, allegedly made by one of its executives as reported by newspaper columnist, Marie Torre. In the taking of a pretrial deposition, Torre refused to identify her source, for which she was convicted of contempt. Judge Stewart wrote the opinion of the court upholding her conviction and rejecting the claim that the First Amendment protected her. He stated: "Freedom of the press, hard-won over the centuries by men of courage, is basic to a free society. But basic too are courts of justice, armed with the power to discover truth. The concept that it is the duty of a witness to testify in a court of law has roots fully as deep in our history as does the guarantee of a free press."[99] Freedom of the press, said Stewart, "must give place under the Constitution to a paramount public interest in the fair administration of justice." Such statements were far removed from the preferred position doctrine of the activists and implied a balancing formula that produced results on a case-by-case determination. In speaking of his disapproval of barriers to the judicial search for truth, Stewart expressed views similar to those of Justice Brennan during his state court service. On the Supreme Court, Stewart wrote significant freedom of association opinions in *Bates v. Little Rock* and *Shelton v. Tucker*.

In the sixty-two cases in Table 11.1 in which he participated, Justice Stewart was in the majority in all but eight. During his four terms on the Eisenhower Court, Stewart demonstrated that he possessed libertarian views that he subordinated to considerations of restraint in some instances. Thus, in most cases where the Court was sharply divided, Stewart agreed with Frankfurter, Harlan, and Whittaker. Yet in several notable exceptions he sided with Brennan and the activists. Stewart agreed with Brennan

52 percent of the time in important civil liberties cases, a higher percentage than that of Brennan and Frankfurter over a longer time. Stewart, thus, was a swing-man between the Court's left and right in civil liberties cases, a moderate holding a position between Brennan and Frankfurter; and because of his restraintist tendencies he was a frequent author of libertarian opinions.

Justice Stewart also avoided entanglement in the occasional polemics involving the other Eisenhower justices and Frankfurter and Douglas. This may attest to his position between the activists and the other middle bloc justices. Perhaps also as a younger man, he was just not so crotchety.

THE VALUES OF THE MIDDLE BLOC

A perusal of the judicial records of the Eisenhower associate justices reveals that they shared several common qualities.[100] Perhaps the most important of these were those qualities gained from experience on the bench where attempting to answer hard questions was the daily diet. All four Eisenhower associates had, prior to their appointments to the high tribunal, faced the complexities involved in litigation both as attorneys and as judges of appellate courts where judicial decisions were made in conferences with fellow judges. Here they became acquainted with the procedural and interpretive niceties that are close to the essence of a judge's craft. It is difficult to evaluate the results of such prior judicial experience, but being a judge for even a short period of time would appear to foster certain habits of mind differing from those of other public officials. Perhaps judicial experience "educates and reinforces those moral qualities—disinterestedness and deep humility—which are indeed preconditions for the wise exercise of the judicial function on the Supreme Bench."[101] These qualities, which appeared to be characteristic of the Eisenhower associate justices, might help explain why they frequently agreed with the restraintist doctrine of Justice Frankfurter, who, of all the justices remaining from the pre-Warren Courts, was in closest accord with the philosophy of the former judges. In this connection, it is noteworthy that none of the Eisenhower associate justices had been in "politics" as had all the other members of the Court except Frankfurter (i.e., none of the middle bloc had held high elective or nonjudicial appointive office prior to his appointment to the Court). It is clear, too, that the Eisenhower justices shared the conviction that libertarian values were important and exhibited a humanitarian sympathy that the Vinson majority frequently failed to achieve.

Still another primary value of the Eisenhower justices was their belief in the importance of removing many barriers to the search of the judicial process for truth. In this regard, courts were considered the ultimate arbiters whether witnesses were entitled to invoke procedural protections to keep from testifying. That the Eisenhower justices disagreed about the rights of witnesses before legislative investigatory bodies has been amply demonstrated.[102] But in a case such as *Mills v. Louisiana* involving grand jury witnesses, the middle bloc justices upheld a contempt conviction of a witness, who, after being offered immunity from state prosecution, claimed the privilege against self-incrimination and refused to testify on the ground that he would be exposed to federal prosecution.[103] These justices also were willing to allow the judiciary a certain amount of freedom to determine what was necessary in the search for truth. The Eisenhower associate justices in *Breithaupt* approved the taking of a blood sample from an unconscious man to aid a state court in its effort to ascertain what had happened in the controversy before it. Courts were further invested with broad authority to insure proper respect for the judiciary as seen in the *Yates* contempt case in which the middle justices affirmed a contempt conviction imposed as punishment in vindication of the authority of the court.

It has been noted that the middle-of-the-road justices who played such a prominent role in the decisions of the Eisenhower Court were neither libertarian zealots of the activist variety nor were they of the "less libertarian" persuasion of Clark and his associates of the Vinson majority. Instead these justices emerged as new type libertarians, who, in balancing delicate issues on a case-by-case basis, followed a cautious, restraintist path usually limited to non-substantive scrutiny of the questions involved. In following a balancing theory the middle bloc moved toward a jurisprudence free from the defects of excessive judicial abstention or absolutism, and at the same time founded upon a recognition of the importance of political and civil freedoms to a democratic society.[104]

Although the Court had from time to time decided civil liberties cases by balancing conflicting interests since *Cantwell v. Connecticut*,[105] a formal balance of interest doctrine was never enunciated until Justice Frankfurter so eloquently provided one in his concurring opinion in *Sweezy*. Here the Court had to balance "the right of a citizen to political privacy . . . and the right of the State to self-protection." According to Frankfurter: "Ours is the narrowly circumscribed but exceedingly difficult task of making the final judicial accommodation between the competing weighty claims that underlie all such questions of due process."[106] Striking the balance, then, required the exercise of judgment, which, Frankfurter added, "is the inescapable judicial task." First the interest of the state was weighed against an invasion of academic freedom: "When weighed against the grave harm resulting from governmental intrusion, into the intellectual life of a university, such justification for compelling a witness to discuss the contents of his lecture appears gravely inadequate. Particularly is this so where the witness has sworn that neither in the lecture nor at any other time did he ever advocate overthrowing the Government by force or violence."[107] Intrusions on political freedom of the individual likewise failed to meet the balancing test, which required that "for a citizen to be made to forego even a part of so basic a liberty as his political autonomy, the subordinating interest of the State must be compelling."[108] But Justice Frankfurter contended:

> The inviolability of privacy belonging to a citizen's political loyalties has so overwhelming an importance to the well-being of our kind of society that it cannot be constitutionally encroached upon on the basis of so meager a countervailing interest of the State as may be argumentatively found in the remote, shadowy threat to the security of New Hampshire allegedly presented in the origins and contributing elements of the Progressive Party and in the petitioner's relations to these.[109]

A similar balancing method was used by the Court in *NAACP v. Alabama* where it was held that the state could not compel the organization to reveal its membership list without trespassing upon Fourteenth Amendment freedoms. In this case Justice Harlan spoke for the Court and in balancing the compelling interest of the state with freedom of association noted the "vital relationship between freedom to associate and privacy in one's association." Harlan stressed that the right of privacy was not constitutionally protected for its own sake but because it was often an essential condition to the exercise of freedom of speech and association. The Court concluded that Alabama could not demonstrate "so cogent and compelling interest" as to justify "the deterrent effect on the free enjoyment of the right to association which disclosure of membership lists is likely to have."[110] In the 1959 term, Justice Stewart was to write a similar opinion in a case involving demands for membership lists by municipalities.[111]

In *Barenblatt*, Justice Harlan again spoke for the Court and in applying the balancing formula found that governmental interest in investigating communism overbalanced those of the individual's political privacy. Since the investigation related to a valid legislative purpose and since there was no evidence that the committee was indulging indiscriminately in a dragnet procedure, Harlan concluded that the governmental interest in self-preservation overbalanced those of the individual. Justice Black, speaking for the Chief Justice and Justice Douglas, dissented, protesting the use of the balancing doctrine in First Amendment cases on principle. He maintained that the Court, after stating the test, ignored it completely. As might be expected, the expounders of the preferred position doctrine contended that such a balance mistook the factors to be weighed. According to Black, Barenblatt's private interest to remain silent was really the interest of a free people "to join organizations, advocate causes and make political 'mistakes' without later being subjected to governmental penalties for having dared to think for themselves."[112] These interests of society rather than Barenblatt's own right to silence, according to Black, should be balanced against the demands of the government—if a balancing process must be employed in First Amendment cases. In this thought, Justice Black echoed a theory of Dean Roscoe Pound who warned that in weighing conflicting interests, care must be taken to compare them on the same plane. According to Pound: "If we put one as an individual interest and the other as a social interest . . . our way of stating the question may leave nothing to decide."[113] Black's dissent in *Barenblatt*, then, appears to state the conflict in more meaningful terms than the opinion of the majority. Instead of balancing an individual interest against a social interest, the Court should rather balance two social interests. During the latter years of the Eisenhower Court, the justices did not again declare in reviewing a contempt conviction that "the balancing between the individual and the governmental interests . . . must be struck in favor of the latter." Individual interests prevailed instead, although usually the Court did not base its decisions on the First Amendment.

Less convincing than the opinion of the Court in *Barenblatt*, however, was Justice Clark's attempt in *Uphaus* to determine "whether the public interests overbalance (the) conflicting private ones." Here associational privacy was downgraded to a mere "private interest" while the interest of the state was exalted as the "interest of self-preservation, 'the ultimate value of any society'." There appears to be no evidence in Clark's opinion that the state was required to demonstrate that the security of New Hampshire was even remotely threatened by the summer camp of Dr. Uphaus. Justice Brennan's dissent maintained that the Court failed to recognize the close relationship between freedom of association and privacy that was involved in the case. The Court had completely misconstrued the balance of interest doctrine, according to Brennan, who concluded "there has been no valid legislative interest of the State actually defined and shown in the investigation as it operated, so that there is really nothing against which the appellant's rights of association and expression can be balanced."[114] Brennan indicated, however, that weights may vary in different types of cases: "Of course, the considerations entering into the weighing of the interests concerned are different where the problem is one of state exposure in the area of assembly and expression from where the problem is that of evaluating a state criminal or regulatory statute in these areas."[115]

In this connection, the justices, at least in the language they used, unnecessarily often failed to heed the warning of Dean Pound to view conflicting interest on a comparable plane—to the detriment of our law. Justices Black and Douglas, maintaining their position of doctrinaire absolutism, noted that they would decide the case on the ground that Uphaus was denied his rights under the First and Fourteenth Amendments but

joined Brennan's dissent because he made clear that the investigating committee had violated the bill of attainder clause of the Constitution.[116]

Critics of the Court's use of the balance of interest test as a standard
for adjudicating civil liberty cases contended that members of the Court
should have refrained from reading into the doctrine their own precon-
ceptions. A more correct test should leave the Court unencumbered by
the myth that the interest of the state was somehow based upon the will
of the majority which must be right as well as the myth that "the commands of the First Amendment were self-evident" and must be given
added weight.[117] Actually, Chief Justice Warren posed the problem central
to the balancing doctrine in his *Watkins* opinion before wandering far afield
in obiter dicta:

> The critical element is the existence of, and the weight to be ascribed
> to, the interest of the Congress in demanding disclosures from an
> unwilling witness. We cannot assume, however, that every
> Congressional investigation is justified by a public need that
> overbalances any private rights affected. To do so would be to
> abdicate the responsibility placed by the Constitution upon the
> judiciary to insure that Congress does not unjustifiably encroach upon
> an individual's right to privacy nor abridge his liberty of speech,
> press, religion or assembly.[118]

The activists, of course, applied a heavy weight to the protection of the
individual where First Amendment freedoms were involved regardless
of the circumstances of the case. The majority in *Sweezy* took such an absolutist position where Warren stated: "We do not now conceive of any
circumstance wherein a state interest would justify infringement of rights
in these fields."[119] By maintaining that extra weight should be given to the
freedom of the individual in First Amendment cases, the activists missed
an excellent opportunity to exert greater influence on the decisions of the
Court. They, in effect, turned their backs on the "rules of the game" as
formulated by the Court; and as admirable as the ideals and purposes of
the preferred position doctrine were, it appeared that the Chief Justice,
and especially Justices Black and Douglas, might have achieved more libertarian victories by being less absolutist in outlook and applying their
best efforts to participation in an honest balance of interest test in civil
liberties cases, pressing the point that the burden of proof rested with
those defending a restriction of a constitutional right.[120]

In such a test, values should be argued in relation to actual facts of
the case and not in terms of eternal principles or labels unrelated to the
time or circumstance. For balancing of interests, based upon the facts and
circumstances of a case, is ultimately the task of the judiciary, which must
determine whether a conflict actually exists and if so which interest should
prevail. The Eisenhower Court's formula wisely placed the burden on the
state to demonstrate that the exercise of the rights involved was a serious

threat to important and legitimate interests of the state. To the extent that the balance of interest doctrine developed by the middle bloc justices of the Eisenhower Court met these requirements, a major contribution to the jurisprudence of the Supreme Court was made. This test, discreetly applied, would have been a useful guide, far more helpful than the dichotomy presented by the restraintist and activist philosophies of the 1950s in reaching decisions affecting civil liberties. The balancing formula devised by the Eisenhower Court followed a line of thought that Professor Pritchett contended was a proper one for the judiciary:

> A Supreme Court justice must be able, and willing, to balance some of the most delicate, intangible, yet superlatively important, issues that can arise in a democratic society. He must be a creature of the times and sensitive to the same currents of opinion as move legislators, to the end that the standards of reasonableness by which he judges legislative action will not be detached from reality. But he must at the same time be sensitive to the system of expectations which has made the Supreme Court the American conscience, with the responsibility not merely of preaching to legislatures but of passing judgment on their actions in the light of the great libertarian principles of the Bill of Rights.[121]

The further development of the balance of interest doctrine defined by the Eisenhower Court and refined by Pound and Pritchett would be a welcomed addition to civil liberty case adjudication.

NOTES

1. Pritchett, *The Roosevelt Court*, p. 260.

2. Where the activists and the middle bloc were able to agree on the result in a particular case, they all too frequently articulated their differences in approach in separate concurrences. See, e.g., *Vitarelli v. Seaton*, 359 U.S. 535 (1959); *Greene v. McElroy*, 360 U.S. 474 (1959); *Kingsley International Pictures v. New York*, 360 U.S. 684 (1959).

3. In civil liberties cases, Brennan appeared to be the most gregarious dissenter, having cast almost all of his minority votes in Table 11.1 with at least three other justices. This is in sharp contrast to Justice Clark who was most often a solo dissenter or in a two-justice minority.

4. Determining the reasons for these changes has presented a formidable challenge to biographers of the Chief Justice.

5. See Schubert, *Constitutional Politics*, pp. 157–158.

6. Schwartz, "The Supreme Court—October 1958 Term," p. 207; Schubert, *Constitutional Politics*, pp. 157–158; Pritchett, *Congress Versus the Supreme Court, 1957–1960*, p. 12; but see Jacobs, *Justice Frankfurter*, p. 149; McCloskey, "Tools, Stumbling Blocks, and Stepping Stones," p. 1054; Arthur Krock, *New York Times*, 3 April 1958, p. 30.

7. *New York Times*, 30 September 1956, p. 76.

8. Warren Papers, Library of Congress, Manuscripts Division, Washington, DC, Box I: 2, No. 23.

9. Cooper, *Battles on the Bench*, p. 136.

10. David Halberstam, "The Common Man as Uncommon Man," in Bernard Schwartz and E. Joshua Rosenkranz, *Reason and Passion: Justice Brennan's Enduring Influence* (New York: W.W. Norton, 1997), p. 24.

11. Cooper, *Battles on the Bench*, pp. 26, 81–82, and 136; Harry N. Hirsh, *The Enigma of Felix Frankfurter*, p. 190; Eisler, *A Justice for All*, pp. 162–164; see H. M. Hart, "The Supreme Court 1958 Term, Foreword: The Time Chart of the Justices," 73 *Harv. L. Rev.* 84 (1959).

12. Yarbrough, *John Marshall Harlan*, p. 139.

13. Clark, *Justice Brennan*, pp. 101–103.

14. See McQuade and Kardos, "Mr. Justice Brennan and His Legal Philosophy," pp. 323–324.

15. 357 U.S. 513 at 520.

16. 12 N.J. 267, 96 A.2d 519 (1953).

17. Ibid. at 520.

18. 11 N.J. 144, 93 A.2d 362 (1952).

19. 13 N.J. 581, 100 A.2d 750 (1953).

20. Ibid. at 366.

21. *Barr v. Matteo*, 360 U.S. 564 (1959).

22. 376 U.S. 254 (1964).

23. See Jacobs, *Justice Frankfurter*, pp. 178–181; the Court divided five-to-four in the passport cases, *Green, Barenblatt, Uphaus, Slochower, Beilan*, and *Lerner*.

24. Pritchett, *Congress Versus the Supreme Court, 1957–1960*, pp. 55–56, gives an excellent analysis of Brennan's *Uphaus* dissent.

25. McQuade and Kardos,"Mr. Justice Brennan and His Legal Philosophy," p. 326.

26. *Hearings on Nomination of William J. Brennan, Jr., Before the Senate Committee on the Judiciary*, 85th Congress, 1st Session (1957), p. 5.

27. 10 N.J. Super. 619, 65 A.2d 657 (1949).

28. Ibid. at 184.

29. 19 N.J. 431, 117 A.2d 499 (1955).

30. Ibid. at 501–502.

31. 10 N.J. Super. 152, 76 A.2d 717 (1950).

32. Ibid. at 720–721.

33. 13 N.J. 203, 98 A.2d 881 (1953).

34. Ibid. at 896–897.

35. 2 N.J. Super. 619, 65 A.2d 657 (1949).

36. Ibid. at 660.

37. McQuade and Kardos, "Mr. Justice Brennan and His Legal Philosophy," pp. 321–322; see also Jack Alexander, "Mr. Justice from New Jersey," *Saturday Evening Post*, 28 September 1957, p. 25.

38. 69 *N.J. L. J.* 146 (1946).

39. 3 N.J. Super. 558, 67 A.2d 362 (1949).

40. Ibid. at 365.

41. 353 U.S. 87 (1957).

42. *New York Times*, 27 November 1957, p. 17; see Chapter 6, *supra*.

43. See Chapter 6, *supra*.

44. Clark, *Justice Brennan*, p. 164.

45. David M. O'Brien, *Storm Center: The Supreme Court in American Politics* (New York: W.W. Norton, 1996), pp. 315–317.

46. See Table 7.1; Table 10.1, *supra*.

47. 216 F.2d 354 (2d Cir. 1954).

48. 354 U.S. 298 at 319.

49. 355 U.S. 115 at 121.

50. *United States ex rel. Leong Choy Moon v. Shaughnessy*, 218 F.2d 316 (2d Cir. 1954).

51. 219 F.2d 77, 90 (2d Cir. 1955).

52. E.g., *United States v. Wiesner*, 216 F.2d 739 (2d Cir. 1954).

53. 325 U.S. 191 at 201.

54. 354 U.S. 476 at 505.

55. 357 U.S. 449 at 466–467.

56. Yarbrough, *John Marshall Harlan*, p. 235.

57. See S. Sidney Ulmer, "The Analysis of Behavior Patterns on the United States Supreme Court," 22 *J. of Politics* 629 (1960).

58. 353 U.S. 252 at 274.

59. 367 U.S. 643 at 682.

60. 369 U.S. 186 at 339.

61. 367 U.S. 497 at 540.

62. Norm Dorsen, "John Marshall Harlan," in Schwartz, *The Warren Court: A Retrospective*, p. 241.

63. Quoted in Yarbrough, *John Marshall Harlan*, pp. xii, 139; Harlan Papers, Seeley G. Mudd Library, Box 610 Princeton University, Princeton, NJ.

64. *New York Times*, 20 October 1959, p. 28; *Harris v. Penn. R.R.*, 361 U.S. 15 at 25–26. (1959).

65. Ibid. at 26.

66. *Michalic v. Cleveland Tankers*, 364 U.S. 325 (1960).

67. Ibid. at 332–333.

68. Kadish, "Methodology and Criteria in Due Process Adjudication—A Survey and Criticism," p. 339.

69. Paschal, "Mr. Justice Stewart on the Court of Appeals," p. 340.

70. For an analysis of the values of Justice Jackson, see Hockett, *New Deal Justice*.

71. Whittaker served as a district court judge from July 1954 until June 1956; and as a circuit court judge from June 1956 until his appointment to the Supreme Court in March 1957; see "Transcriptions of Conversations Between Justice William O. Douglas and Professor Walter E. Murphy, Tape Recorded during 1961–1963," Princeton University Library, 1981, pp. 153–154.

72. Brownell, *Advising Ike*, pp. 180–181.

73. 129 F. Supp. 716 (W.D. Mo. 1955).

74. Ibid. at 718.

75. *United States v. Sweet*, 133 F. Supp. 3 (W.D. Mo. 155); *cf. Bonetti v. Rogers*, 156 U.S. 691 (1958).

76. Notably for, in *Heikkinen v. United States*, 755 U.S. 273, 277 (1958); and against, in *Lehmann v. Carson*, 353 U.S. 685 (1957) and *Leng May Ma v. Barber*, 357 U.S. 185 (1958).

77. *Oliver v. United States*, 239 F.2d 818 (8th Cir. 1957).

78. 355 U.S. 225 (1957); for Whittaker's memorandum to Brennan, see Warren Papers, Box I: 14, No.1 *Aaron v. Cooper*, Library of Congress, Manuscripts Division, Washington, DC.

79. Warren Papers, Library of Congress, Manuscripts Division, Washington, DC, Box I: 14, No. 1.

80. *Kleven v. United States*, 240 F.2d 270 at 275 (8th Cir. 1957).

81. *Farm Bureau Cooperative Mills and Supply v. Blue Star Foods*, 137 F. Supp. 486, 488, 491 (W.D. Mo. 1956).

82. *Inman v. Baltimore & Ohio R.R.*, 361 U.S. 138 (1959).

83. Douglas, Black, Warren, and Brennan.

84. 361 U.S. 138 at 142; perhaps the most successful use of humor in an opinion was Justice Jackson's dissent in *Ballard v. United States*, 322 U.S. 78, 92 (1944).

85. *New York Times*, 15 December 1959, p. 25.

86. Quoted in Yarbrough, *John Marshall Harlan*, p. 344.

87. Quoted in Schwartz, *A Book of Legal Lists* (New York: Oxford University Press, 1997), p. 31.

88. "Transcriptions of Conversations Between Justice William O. Douglas and Professor Walter E. Murphy, Tape Recorded during 1961–1963," Princeton University Library, 1981, pp. 153–154; Albert P. Blaustein, *The First One Hundred Justices: Statistical Studies on the Supreme Court of the United States* (Hamden, CT: Archon Books, 1978), p. 48.

89. *Henderson v. Bannan*, 256 F.2d 363 (6th Cir. 1958); see Potter Stewart, "Justice Stewart Discusses Right of Counsel," 19 L. A. B. C. 92 (1960).

90. *Williams v. Dalton*, 231 F.2d 646 (6th Cir. 1956).

91. See also *Irwin v. Dowd*, 366 U.S. 717 (1961).

92. *Clemons v. Board of Education*, 228 F.2d 853, 859 (6th Cir. 1956) (concurring opinion).

93. Berman, "Mr. Justice Stewart: A Preliminary Appraisal," p. 413.

94. 227 F.2d 757 (1955); 354 U.S. 931 (1957); 253 F.2d 601 (1957).

95. Ibid. at 608–609.

96. But see *Vitarelli v. Seaton*, 359 U.S. 535 (1959) (separate opinion) where Stewart along with Clark and Whittaker subscribed to the opinion of Justice Frankfurter; see also *In re Sawyer*, 360 U.S. 622 (1959).

97. *United States ex rel. Carson v. Kershner*, 228 F.2d 142 (6th Cir. 1955) *rev'd sub nom. Lehmann v. United States ex rel. Carson*, 353 U.S. 685 (1957).

98. 259 F.2d 545 (6th Cir. 1958).

99. 259 F.2d 545 at 548.

100. The values of some of the Eisenhower justices are described in Brennan, "State Court Decisions and the Supreme Court," 34 *Fla. B. J.* 269 (1960); Harlan, "Some Aspects of the Judicial Process," 33 *Aust. L. J.* 108 (1959).

101. Frankfurter, "The Supreme Court in the Mirror of Justices," 105 *U. Pa. L. Rev.* 785, 787 (1957); see also William H. Hastie, "Judicial Method in Due Process Inquiry," *Government Under Law*, ed., Arthur E. Sutherland (Cambridge, MA: Harvard University Press, 1956), p. 194.

102. See Chapter 3, *supra*.

103. *Knapp v. Schweitzer*, decided before the appointment of Justice Stewart, was a similar case uniting the middle bloc as then constituted in the majority.

104. See generally, Peter Bachrach, "The Supreme Court, Civil Liberties, and the Balance of Interest Doctrine," 15 *W. Polit. Q.* 391 (1961).

105. 310 U.S. 296 (1940).

106. 354 U.S. 234 at 256.

107. Ibid. at 261.

108. Ibid. at 265.

109. Ibid.

110. 357 U.S. 449 at 466.

111. *Bates v. Little Rock*, 361 U.S. 516 (1960). Note the similarity of Stewart's balancing statement with that of Harlan in the Alabama case at 524.

112. 360 U.S. 109 at 144.

113. Pound, "A Survey of Social Interests," 57 *Harv. L. Rev.* 1, 2 (1943); for analysis of Pound's theories in this area, see Stone, *The Province and Function of Law*, pp. 487–494; see also Ibid., pp. 355–766.

114. 360 U.S. 72 at 106.

115. Ibid. at 85.

116. Ibid. at 108.

117. 354 U.S. 178 at 198–199.

118. Ibid.

119. 354 U.S. 234 at 251.

120. Bachrach, pp. 397–399.

121. Pritchett, *Civil Liberties and the Vinson Court*, p. 253. See also Jacobs, *Justice Frankfurter*, pp. 214–217; Mendelson, *Justices Black and Frankfurter*, pp. 54–58; Bickel, "The Supreme Court 1960 Term, Foreword: The Passive Virtues," 75 *Harv. L. Rev.* 40 (1961).

12

The Eisenhower Court and Civil Liberties: An Evaluation

The era of the Eisenhower Court was marked by monumental changes in American society. The population shifted from the old, rural, small-town, regionalized America to a more modern, cosmopolitan, urban, and suburban industrialized nation. The powerful in the old order were reluctant to relinquish control to new groups seeking a share of political power. The result was frequent clashes between representatives of the old and the new orders in the arena of politics. The old order establishment retained relevant police powers principally in state and local governments and often used them to reinforce old patterns of repression.[1] When many newly rising elites were stymied in their efforts to secure representation and participation in democratic processes and were denied equal rights and due process in the courts, they sought help at the national level. There again, they met recalcitrant politicians in the executive and legislative branches who blocked their efforts to secure equal rights. It was in the federal judiciary, and specifically in the Supreme Court, that political, racial, and cultural minorities received encouragement and sometimes redress for their grievances. The Court used the Bill of Rights and the Fourteenth Amendment to extend basic liberties to those seeking to become politically empowered. Rather than deferring to the popularly elected branches when they were denying citizens simple fairness, the Court took an active role in securing rights for individuals and groups. For its troubles, the Court was branded as "activist" and almost "curbed" by its old guard critics. But the Court survived significant attacks by a conservative Congress, followed shortly thereafter by the electorate choosing a more liberal Congress and defeating several anti-Court senators. Thus the people indicated that they might be ready for the legal, social and ethical revolution that characterized the Eisenhower Court era, and in interpreting the Constitution, the Court did not appear to be ahead of the country and the values of the people. The major accomplishments of the Eisenhower Court were the advancement of equality and the beginning of the process of the nationalization of civil liberties standards—both helping to secure for excluded groups the right to participate in the larger American society.

The constitutional doctrines fashioned by the Eisenhower Court generally were discussed in terms of fanatical denunciation. The old order was passing, inevitably giving way to the new, but it was not going silent into the night. In the eyes of fervent anticommunists, Southern segregationists, book and film censors, states-righters, strong religious accommodationists, and their assorted fellow travelers, the activist Eisenhower Court was a danger to the republic and to their ways of life. In light of the analysis of the preceding chapters, most of the hysteria was baseless. A careful examination of the decisions of the Eisenhower Court indicates that the Court mainly reinforced new societal relationships and dealt with civil liberties that required a generous spirit and devotion to the principles of an open society[2]—unpopular attributes to the Court's critics. The justices were more sympathetic to claims of individual liberty while being simultaneously more equalitarian than their predecessors and more willing to intervene in contentious controversies.[3] Critics saw the writing on the wall for their old order and raised a cacophony about the Court that all too often was ruling against them. The Court meanwhile was providing rulings, frequently based on the narrowest possible grounds, which attracted support from people with diverse backgrounds and commitments. The Eisenhower Court had withstood the sharpest blows its enemies could deliver and continued its policy of enlightened restraint, protecting liberty against encroachments of government when and to the extent possible under the circumstances of a given case.

Some journalists and academic analysts did not recognize how much the Eisenhower Court had accomplished. Perhaps they were dazzled by the more activist and libertarian accomplishments of the later Warren Court. Perhaps they did not know what they should have been looking for in appraising the Court of that era. Some contended that the Court had not affected major constitutional changes except in the field of school segregation during its first nine terms of Warren's Chief Justiceship and that its long-term influence on the course of American constitutional development might prove to be slight.[4] They underestimated what had been accomplished. The Eisenhower Court had stature. A rehearsal of its major accomplishments in protecting civil liberties and civil rights would include:

1. In dealing with the issue of subversion, the area that drew the most vocal criticism from several segments of American society, the Court made some inroads on governmental antisubversive activity, while contenting itself with

sharp scrutiny of procedural requirements and of the legislative authority for oppressive governmental actions. The opinions of the justices as noted in Chapters 3 and 4 were characterized by a tendency to confront the smaller questions rather than the larger in each case, although on several occasions far-ranging obiter dicta confused the strict holding. The net effect, however, was to cast the Court's weight on the side of moderating antisubversive practices. What the Court did was to require legislative and executive authorities to reexamine some of their own policies that might have been in error.[5] Insofar as such error was almost wholly irrational, as in *Sweezy*, the Court assumed the burden of correcting it by balancing the interests involved as suggested in Frankfurter's opinion. *Barenblatt* demonstrated, however, that such correction did not cripple the legislative investigatory power. In ruling on congressional investigations, the Court moved cautiously on a case-by-case basis giving a strong presumption of validity to legislative purposes. For in the words of Justice Brennan: "the problem is one in its nature calling for traditional case-by-case development of principles in the various permutations of circumstances where the conflict may appear."[6] The Court followed the cautious Brennan approach and in reviewing contempt convictions did not again find that governmental interests "outbalanced" individual interests.

When procedural imperatives of the Constitution were violated as in *Jencks*, the Court properly intervened, although, again the high tribunal along with Congress indicated that the instant decision was of limited applicability. When antisubversive activities rested on a loose interpretation of a statute, as in *Yates* and some of the deportation cases, the Court adopted a more restrictive interpretation and gave Congress a chance to look again at its intent. Court interpretation of the silence of Congress was the key factor in the passport cases and the Loyalty-Security Program cases. Indeed, in many of the cases in this area, the justices attributed to Congress benevolent ideas that could be traced with greater logic to the Bill of Rights. The Court also was creative in passport cases, where Justice Douglas declared the right to travel a protected liberty under the Fifth Amendment's due process clause—a right that should be dear to peripatetic Americans.

In its gradual dismantling of McCarthyism in law, the Court usually scrutinized legislative and executive mandates without reaching constitutional questions. In 1959–1961 terms, the Court majority used extreme caution in this area.[7] Criticized for its accommodation of Cold War repression, the Court upheld several dubious prosecutions even as it announced liberalizing technical doctrines that ultimately made further prosecutions impractical.[8] In balancing competing interests in these cases the majority appeared to give heavy emphasis to the nation's interest in self-preservation. Justice Clark's words in the *Uphaus* opinion were representative of the consensus of opinion. On the other hand, "the surgery Justice Harlan performed on the Smith Act's membership clause, like that inflicted in *Yates* on its advocacy provisions made successful prosecution under the act exceedingly difficult."[9] After the *Scales* decision in 1961, Smith Act prosecutions ceased altogether, and the Subversive Activities Control Act was headed for oblivion after being exhaustively reviewed by Frankfurter in 1961.

2. The Court likewise avoided substantive issues in rulings affecting state anti-subversion activities. If *Nelson* was misleading, *Uphaus* furnished a needed corrective. Further, the libertarian pronouncements of *Slochower* were balanced by the decisions in *Lerner* and *Beilan*. Even the most alarming case in this area, *Konigsberg*, was subsequently proved to be of limited compass by other reviews. Frankfurter articulated the "compelling state interest" doctrine in *Sweezy* and also wrote the Court's finest defense of academic freedom in that case.

3. In other First Amendment cases, the Court was required to rule on the censorship of books and motion pictures by applying its *Roth* test of obscenity. Considering the wording of the test, it was conceivable that some censorship by state or local authorities might be upheld. Even so, Brennan's opinion in *Roth* had radically liberalized standards to be applied in obscenity cases. In his dissent in *Roth*, Justice Douglas resurrected the preferred position doctrine. Among the Eisenhower appointees, however, only Chief Justice Warren was an occasional convert to that free speech doctrine of Black and Douglas. Brennan also introduced the concept of "chilling effects" that focused attention on the wider consequences of laws that suppressed speech. Stewart originated two significant speech-protecting doctrines: "overbreadth" that recognized that any regulation of speech must be carefully drafted so as not to threaten expression that should be protected and "less restrictive alternatives" that would limit any abridgement of speech if the government purpose that it promoted could effectively be served by some other measure posing less danger to free speech.

In *Engel*, the Regents' Prayer case, the remnants of the Eisenhower Court set off a storm by holding that "in this country it is no part of the business of government to compose official prayers for any group of the American people to recite as a part of a religious program carried on by government." The Court's stand on the establishment clause created controversies that continue to the present.

4. The expatriation case in which the Eisenhower Court actually struck down an act of Congress received little notice from the critics of the Court. Only a bare majority, which could not agree on the same theory, voted to limit legislative power to divest citizenship—this in contrast to the large majorities in the "Red Monday" decisions that bore the brunt of the attack on the Court. In his *Trop* opinion, Chief Justice Warren provided a standard for determining the meaning of the Eighth Amendment from the "evolving standards of decency that mark the progress of a maturing society"—rhetoric frequently cited by the Court in determining what is a cruel and unusual punishment.

5. In judgments in cases that involved civil rights questions unassociated with communism and related menaces, the Court followed a line, whose beginnings go back at least as far as the Roosevelt Court, that was characterized by an alert consideration for the rights of the individual.[10] An important new contribution to American constitutional development here was the formal recognition of the right of association. In *NAACP v. Alabama*, the Court modified the long-standing practice of deferring to state regulation of organizations by expanding the constitutional right of association. Decisions protecting civil rights' organizations encouraged the Court to overturn precedents

that had given the federal government, during the previous decade, a virtual blank check to destroy radical organizations.[11] The Eisenhower justices produced a new and expansive body of constitutional jurisprudence on the rights of freedom of expression and association that gradually transformed the Court's interpretation of the First Amendment.

6. The Eisenhower Court showed "a growing awareness of the depth of police misconduct and need for a judicial remedy."[12] Such awareness was needed, for in the 1950s, states virtually had a free hand in the administration of justice. Trials often proceeded without counsel or juries. Convictions were allowed to stand even though they turned on illegally seized evidence or on statements extracted from the accused under coercive circumstances.[13] The Court's criminal justice decisions focused attention on the culture of police departments across the country and began a process of making some needed corrections.

   Although the Court initially continued to be divided in its case-by-case determination of due process, it made significant contributions to criminal law—especially in its elimination of poverty as a bar to appeal in certain circumstances. By calling attention to poverty as a bar to fair trial, the Court unveiled the racial contours of criminal law in many states. More importantly, the Court started what was to become "the due process revolution" by applying the exclusionary rule to the states in *Mapp*. By explicitly overruling its earlier decision in *Wolf*, the Court took a major step away from Frankfurter's fundamental rights interpretation of the due process clause. At the same time, the total incorporation theory of Black and Douglas had no adherents among the Eisenhower associate justices. This set the stage for Justice Brennan's advocacy of "selective incorporation" as a middle position between the competing theories in 1961. In subsequent terms, the Court was to selectively incorporate almost all of the guarantees of the Bill of Rights that were fundamental to our justice system to be applied against the states through the Fourteenth Amendment due process clause. The Eisenhower Court's criminal cases provided evidence that the justices were beginning to view protection of rights of unpopular minorities as integral to democracy itself. It was only a short step then for the Court to apply the same rules of fair trials to the federal and state governments.

7. After declaring that separate educational facilities are inherently unequal in *Brown I* and requiring states to desegregate their public schools with all deliberate speed in *Brown II*, events in Arkansas forced the Court, in *Cooper v. Aaron*, to declare its determination not to sacrifice constitutional rights to the threat of violence. The Court struck down attempts by the states or municipalities to continue discrimination in public schools or other public facilities or to deny civil rights to African-Americans or other minority groups, although it granted certiorari with great caution in such cases. The Court also continued its policy of restraint in requiring interpretation of discriminatory statutes by state courts before allowing federal court review. Reactions to *Brown* were of historic proportions. They led Southern whites to "massive resistance" against desegregation and at the same time inspired the Civil Rights Movement.

8. Another judicial revolution, "the equal protection revolution," had its origins in the Eisenhower Court. After its vigorous reinterpretation of the equal protection clause in *Brown*, the Court opened the gates to adjudication of cases involving inequalities other than racial classifications in *Baker v. Carr*. The Court accepted jurisdiction in disputes over the apportionment of legislative seats and pointed out that in the context of mid-twentieth-century American society, malapportionment of legislatures was indefensible. The nation increasingly had become urban, and the idea that city dwellers, labor, and racial minorities should be underrepresented in policy-making bodies was repugnant to the concept of fairness. The *Baker* decision was based on the notion of "democracy-reinforcement," the protection of political outsiders from political insiders—an idea formulated by Justice Stone in the *Carolene Products* case footnote.[14] *Baker* was significant in its own right, but it also was the predecessor of a new body of law encompassing substantive equal protection of among others, affirmative action, alienage, illegitimacy, age, mental retardation, gender-based classifications, and indigency.

9. Finally, it should be noted that the Eisenhower Court was primed to address the question of marital privacy when the Connecticut anti-contraceptive statute case was properly before it. The dissents of Justices Douglas and Harlan, finding the law unconstitutional in *Poe v. Ullman* in 1961, indicated that there were effective but differing approaches to a right of privacy. When the Connecticut statute again was contested four years later in *Griswold*, in a case that met requirements of standing, the Court found that various constitutional guarantees created zones of privacy. In 1973 the Burger Court interpreted *Griswold* as a substantive due process case and extended its holding in *Roe v. Wade* to encompass the right to abortion.

THE "CAREER" OF THE EISENHOWER COURT

In many civil liberty cases the Court's approach was to acknowledge the legitimacy of the government's interest but conclude that the government had not done it appropriately in the case at bar. The Court left open the possibility that the government could rethink its program or action and correct its errors. Thus the Court could approve the government's ends but find fault with its means.[15] The justices were alert to the existence of reasonable disagreement among public policy-makers and took a discerning, cautious, balancing approach while deciding cases on narrow grounds. This strategy allowed everyone except the libertarian absolutists to take some consolation from most of the opinions.

Between 1953 through 1962 most decisions were compromises between different wings of the Court. No bloc of justices was an automatic winner. Although Warren was recognized as the most important presence on the Court, there was no dominant intellectual center. The Eisenhower Court was an "organic," "holistic" group with a roster of impressive, strong-willed members. Excluding Whittaker, who had a short tenure on the Court, all of the justices contributed to the "product" of the Court, the significant cases of the era. Brennan, the consummate coalition builder, broke the intellectual deadlock between the Frankfurter and Black–Douglas blocs inherited from the Vinson Court and used his influence to further centrist libertarian values. The Frankfurter and Black poles still repelled each other but were magnetic enough to attract support from other justices. Harlan, frequently accompanied by Stewart, provided principled leadership for more conservative values. Clark, despite his generally pro-government stance would sometimes join the Court's libertarians in advancing civil liberties claims. Judicial activism and judicial restraint both were significant at different times in the Court's jurisprudence.

In many areas of the law, the justices articulated significant themes such as equality or participation but did not develop those themes in detail. Alert to the existence of reasonable disagreement among public policymakers and aware of their own limitations, the justices sometimes left the hardest and most contested issues for continuing democratic and judicial debate.[16]

The record of the Eisenhower Court in civil liberties cases did not warrant the furor and above all the proposed impeachment of members of the Court during the late 1950s. Lack of knowledge, misunderstanding, and oversimplification of complicated cases all contributed to a distorted public image of the Court. In reality the Court was performing its highest duty in requiring procedural regularity for defendants. Even so, the 85th Congress in 1958 came within a hair's breadth of curbing the Court. The close escape of the Eisenhower Court illustrates a fact of American political life succinctly pointed out by Professor John Roche. Because of the fragmentation of political power that is normal in this country, there are few issues on which cohesive majorities exist. Within our complex social and institutional framework, the Court has considerable room to maneuver. If, for example, the Court rules either for or against an executive agency in a controversial decision, it will be supported, either way, by a substantial bloc of congressmen. Under these circumstances, there is little possibility that Congress will exact any vengeance on the Court for its actions regardless of which way it decided the case. A disciplined majority would have been necessary to restrict the Court, and on most issues such a majority did not exist.[17] On the other hand, opposition to the Eisenhower Court seemed great because there was no large "prestige" group in American society which stood to gain directly from libertarian decisions—especially those involving suspected subversives. Much of the Court's strength was dependent upon the degree to which public opinion sustained it, and such support had to go beyond the membership of the NAACP, Americans for Democratic Action, and the American Civil Liberties Union.[18] Supporters of the Jenner–Butler omnibus bill almost achieved a conjoint majority by mustering the varied opposition to the

Court. It was not surprising that during the 1958–1960 terms, the Court demonstrated increased judicial self-restraint so as to dull much of the criticism. The Court was following what Professor Roche calls its usual pattern of applying self-restraint in order to maintain its power.

At a time before the idea of consciousness-raising was au courant, the Eisenhower Court was raising public consciousness about the boundaries of political struggle, as well as parameters of legitimate criticism of government actions.[19] The Court, as part of a system of democratic deliberation, fostered discussion and demands for government accountability. In demonstrating its concern and support for the weak and powerless, the Court reformulated American political theory. Democracy became a primary value in American constitutional discourse, and discrete and insular minorities were protected as never before. While extending basic liberties to political, racial, and cultural minorities, the Eisenhower Court was involved in cautiously redefining the relationship between judicial review and democracy, and specifically starting an *in forma pauperis* revolution.[20] The Eisenhower Court thus prepared the path for the later Warren Court that in the 1962–1968 terms would be celebrated for its due process and equal protection revolutions. The triumph of the Warren Court, however, was made possible by the earlier struggles of the Eisenhower era.

During the later Warren Court, the justices made the Court an instrument for dealing with changes by judicial policy-making, and thus for shaping the Constitution with no articulated principle of limits.[21] The Court elaborated and deepened the themes that had been articulated by the Eisenhower Court. A majority of the justices demonstrated a willingness to use judicial power to shape social policy in key areas of individual rights. The Warren Court was committed to basic fairness and to reaching the right outcome, sometimes without much concern for consistent legal principles. Another legacy of the later Court was an increase in the independence of the supreme tribunal, in part as a result of alliances with interest groups that had become more powerful during the 1960s.[22]

As Max Lerner has pointed out, each Supreme Court has a "career"— "the trajectory of a shifting community of judges as they ponder the cases, maneuver for position, and choose between alternative ways of interpreting the Constitution. Yet each Court takes on a character of its own as its members compete to leave their imprint on constitutional history." [23] As we have seen, the career of the Eisenhower Court was quite different from that of the later, more activist Warren Court. In some ways the Eisenhower Court reflected the values of the moderate Republican administration of its era. Like Dwight Eisenhower as described by Fred Greenstein, the justices put energy into curbing outcomes they wanted to avoid, such as having their appellate jurisdiction removed in certain cases. They quietly dealt with likely sources of controversy by adopting a crisis-minimizing demeanor in volatile situations. In short, the Eisenhower Court used what Professor Greenstein calls the "hidden-hand strategy" to conceal its activities. The justices were masterly in the careful use of language instead of the "instrumental use of language."[24] They created smoke screens for their actions. The Court often took small rather than large steps and avoided making clear rules and final resolutions.

This limited role of the Eisenhower Court was disappointing to those who thought that the decisions of 1957 heralded a new era of activism by the high tribunal. But it is submitted that this limited role is the proper one for the Supreme Court and one that may ultimately provide even more expanded protection of civil liberties than that of an activist court cut short.

The Supreme Court has served the American judicial tradition most usefully when it has operated within its area of real expertise in insisting upon standards of highest regard for regularity and fairness while respecting the judgment of the other branches. This has been especially true in reviewing those matters of high political decision that are the peculiar responsibility of the legislative and executive authorities.[25] By following this formula, the Eisenhower Court established a record that must be regarded as one of marked improvement in the field of civil liberties. In the words of Professor McCloskey: "This may not be quite all a Court could have done. But it is a lot to do nonetheless."[26]

NOTES

1. Frederick P. Lewis, *Context of Judicial Activism: The Endurance of the Warren Court Legacy in a Conservative Age* (Lanham, MD: Rowman & Littlefield, 1999), pp. 112–122; Pollack, *Earl Warren*, p. 338.

2. Lerner, *Nine Scorpions in a Bottle*, p. 205.

3. Powe, *The Warren Court*, p. xv.

4. See, e.g., Berman, "Constitutional Issues and the Warren Court," p. 500.

5. Pritchett, *Congress Versus the Supreme Court*, pp. 128–133

6. 360 U.S. 72 at 77.

7. For some suggested explanations for the Court's caution in this area, see Pritchett, *Congress Versus the Supreme Court*, pp. 12-13.

8. Lewis, *Context of Judicial Activism*, p. 36.

9. Yarbrough, *John Marshall Harlan*, p. 197.

10. Pritchett, *The Roosevelt Court*; *Civil Liberties and the Vinson Court*; Beth, "The Supreme Court and the Future of Judicial Review"; McCloskey, "Tools, Stumbling Blocks, and Stepping Stones."

11. Horwitz, *The Warren Court*, p. 35.

12. *Monroe v. Pape*, 365 U.S. 167 (1961).

13. Clark, *Justice Brennan*, p. 62.

14. Sunstein, *One Case at a Time*, p. 7.

15. Powe, *The Warren Court*, p. 117.

16. Sunstein, *One Case at a Time*, p. xiii; Tushnet, *The Warren Court*, p. 31.

17. Roche, "Judicial Self-Restraint," 49 *Am. Pol. Sci. Rev.* 762 (1955).

18. Beth, "The Supreme Court and the Future of Judicial Review," p. 13.

19. Horwitz, *The Warren Court*, p. 37.

20. Ibid., pp. xi–xii.

21. Lerner, *Nine Scorpions in a Bottle*, p. 205.

22. Sue Davis, "The Chief Justice and Judicial Decision-Making," in Cornell W. Clayton and Howard Gillman, eds., *Supreme Court Decision-Making: New Institutionalist Approaches* (Chicago: University of Chicago Press, 1999) p. 149; Tushnet, *The Warren Court*, p. 31.

23. Lerner, *Nine Scorpions in a Bottle*, p. 179.

24. Greenstein, *The Hidden-Hand Presidency*, p. 232.

25. See also McCloskey, *The American Supreme Court*, p. 220: "The Court's greatest successes have been achieved when it operated near the margins rather than in the center of political controversy, when it has nudged and gently tugged the nation, instead of trying to rule it."

26. McCloskey, "The Supreme Court Finds a Role," p. 760.

Bibliography

BOOKS

Abernathy, Glen. *The Right of Assembly and Association*. Columbia: University of South Carolina Press, 1961.

Abraham, Henry J. *Courts & Judges*. New York: Oxford University Press, 1959.

Acheson, Patricia C. *The Supreme Court: America's Judicial Heritage*. New York: Dodd-Mead, 1961.

Ambrose, Stephen E. *Eisenhower (Volume Two): The President*. New York: Simon & Schuster, 1984.

Arens, Richard and Lasswell, Harold D. *In Defense of Public Order*. New York: Columbia University Press, 1961.

Auerbach, Frank L. *Immigration Laws of the United States*. Indianapolis, IN: Bobbs-Merrill, 1961.

Barnard, Chester I. *The Functions of the Executive*. Cambridge, MA: Harvard University Press, 1956.

Barth, Alan. *Government by Investigation*. New York: Viking Press, 1955.

———. *The Price of Liberty*. New York: Viking Press, 1961.

Beaney, William. *The Right to Counsel*. Ann Arbor: University of Michigan Press, 1955.

Berns, Walter. *Freedom, Virtue and the First Amendment*. Baton Rouge: Louisiana State University Press, 1957.

Berry, Mary Frances. *Stability, Security, and Continuity: Mr. Justice Burton and Decision-Making in the Supreme Court, 1945–1958*. Westport, CT: Greenwood Press, 1978.

Bickel, Alexander M. *Politics and the Warren Court*. New York: Harper & Row, 1965.

Black, Charles L., Jr. *The People and the Court*. New York: MacMillan Co., 1960.

Black, Hugo and Black, Elizabeth. *Mr. Justice and Mrs. Black: Memoirs*. New York: Random House, 1986.

Blaustein, Albert P. *The First One Hundred Justices: Statistical Studies on the Supreme Court of the United States.* Hamden, CT: Archon Books, 1978.

Blaustein, Albert P. and Ferguson, Clarence. *Desegregation and the Law.* New Brunswick, NJ: Rutgers University Press, 1957.

Bloch, Charles J. *States' Rights, the Law of the Land.* Atlanta, GA: Harrison Co., 1958.

Bodenhamer, David J. *Fair Trial: Rights of the Accused in American History.* New York: Oxford University Press, 1992.

Bontecou, Eleanor. *The Federal Loyalty-Security Program.* Ithaca, NY: Cornell University Press, 1953.

Brown, Ralph S., Jr. *Loyalty and Security Employment Tests in the United States.* New Haven, CT: Yale University Press, 1958.

Brownell, Herbert and Burke, John P. *Advising Ike: The Memoirs of Attorney General Herbert Brownell.* Lawrence: University Press of Kansas, 1993.

Burks, Robert E. *Olson's New Deal for California.* Berkeley and Los Angeles: University of California Press, 1953.

Cardozo, Benjamin N. *The Nature of the Judicial Process.* New Haven, CT: Yale University Press, 1933.

Carr, Robert K. *The Constitution and Congressional Investigating Committees: Individual Liberty and Congressional Power.* New York: Carrie Chapman Catt Memorial Fund, 1954.

———. *The House Committee on Un-American Activities*, 1945–1950. Ithaca, NY: Cornell University Press, 1952.

Chafee, Zechariah, Jr. *Free Speech in the United States.* Cambridge, MA: Harvard University Press, 1941.

Chamberlain, Lawrence H. *Loyalty and Legislative Action: A Survey of Activity by the New York State Legislature, 1919–1949.* Ithaca, NY: Cornell University Press, 1951.

Chase, Harold W. *Federal Judges: The Appointing Process.* Minneapolis: University of Minnesota Press, 1972.

———. *Security and Liberty: The Problem of Native Communists*, 1947–1955. New York: Doubleday & Co., 1955.

Christman, Henry M., ed. *The Public Papers of Chief Justice Earl Warren.* New York: Simon & Schuster, 1959.

Clark, Hunter R. *Justice Brennan: The Great Conciliator.* Secaucus, NJ: Carol Publishing Group, 1995.

Clayton, Cornell W. and Gillman, Howard, eds. *Supreme Court Decision-Making: New Institutionalist Approaches.* Chicago: University of Chicago Press, 1999.

Comer, John P. *The Forging of the Federal Indigent Code.* San Antonio: Principia Press, 1966.

Commanger, Henry Steele, ed. *Immigration and American History.* Minneapolis: University of Minnesota Press, 1961.

Cook, Thomas I. *Democratic Rights versus Communist Activity.* New York: Doubleday & Co., 1954.

Cooper, Philip J. *Battles on the Bench: Conflict Inside the Supreme Court.* Lawrence: University Press of Kansas, 1995.

Corwin, Edward S., ed. *The Constitution of the United States of America: Analysis and Interpretation.* Washington, DC: Government Printing Office, 1953.

————. *Total War and the Constitution*. New York: Knopf, 1947.

Countryman, Vern, ed. *Douglas of the Supreme Court*. New York: Doubleday & Co., 1959.

Cray, Ed. *Chief Justice: A Biography of Earl Warren*. New York: Simon & Schuster, 1997.

Cushman, Robert E. *Civil Liberties in the United States: A Guide to Current Problems and Experience*. Ithaca, NY: Cornell University Press, 1956.

Douglas, William O. *America Challenged*. New York: Avon, 1960.

————. *We the Judges*. Garden City, NY: Doubleday & Co, 1956.

Dowell, Eldridge F. *A History of Criminal Syndicalism Legislation in the United States*. Baltimore: Johns Hopkins Press, 1939.

Downs, Robert B., ed. *The First Freedom*. Chicago: American Liberty Association, 1960.

Drinker, Henry S. *Some Observations on the Four Freedoms of the First Amendment*. Boston: Boston University Press, 1957.

Dumbauld, Edward. *The Bill of Rights and What It Means Today*. Norman: University of Oklahoma Press, 1957.

Eisler, Kim Isaac. *A Justice for All: William J. Brennan, Jr., and the Decisions that Transformed America*. New York: Simon & Schuster, 1993.

Emery, Walter B. *Broadcasting and Government: Responsibilities and Regulations*. East Lansing: Michigan State University Press. 1961.

Epstein, Lee, Segal, Jeffrey A., Spaeth, Harold J. and Walker, Thomas J. *The Supreme Court Compendium: Data Decisions & Developments*. Washington, DC: Congressional Quarterly, 1994.

Fassett, John D. *New Deal Justice: The Life of Stanley Reed of Kentucky*. New York: Vantage, 1994.

Fellman, David. *The Defendant's Rights*. New York: Rhinehart, 1958.

Fletcher, John L. *The Segregation Case and the Supreme Court*. Boston: Boston University Studies in Political Science, No.1, 1958.

Frank, John P. *Marble Palace: The Supreme Court in American Life*. New York: Knopf, 1958.

————. *Mr. Justice Black: The Man and His Opinions*. New York: Knopf, 1949.

Fried, Albert, ed. *McCarthyism: The Great American Red Scare, A Documentary History*. New York: Oxford University Press, 1997.

Friedman, Leon and Israel, Fred L., eds. *The Justices of the United States Supreme Court, 1789–1969, Volume IV*. Broomall, PA: Chelsea House, 1995.

Gelhorn, Walter. *American Rights*. New York: MacMillan Co., 1960.

————, ed. *The States and Subversion*. Ithaca, NY: Cornell University Press, 1952.

Gerhart, Eugene C. *America's Advocate: Robert H. Jackson*. New York: Bobbs-Merrill, 1958.

Goldman, Roger L. *Justice William J. Brennan, Jr., Freedom First*. New York: Carroll & Graf Publishers, 1994.

Gordon, Charles and Rosenfield, Harry N. *Immigration Law and Procedure*. Albany, NY: Banks, 1959.

Gordon, Rosalie M. *Nine Men Against America: The Supreme Court and Its Attack on American Liberties*. New York: Devin-Adair, 1958.

Grant, J.A.C. *Our Common Law Constitution*. Boston: Boston University Press, 1960.

Greenberg, Jack. *Race Relations and American Law*. New York: Columbia University Press, 1959.

Greenstein, Fred I. *The Hidden-Hand Presidency: Eisenhower as Leader.* New York: Basic Books, 1982.

Griffin, John H. *Black Like Me.* New York: Houghton Mifflin, 1961.

Griswold, Ervin W. *The 5th Amendment Today.* Cambridge, MA: Harvard University Press, 1955.

Gugin, Linda C. *Sherman Minton: New Deal Senator, Cold War Justice.* Indianapolis: Indiana Historical Society, 1997.

Halberstam, David. *The Fifties.* New York: Villard Books, 1993.

Hand, Learned. *The Bill of Rights.* Cambridge, MA: Harvard University Press, 1958.

Harding, Arthur L. *Fundamental Law in Criminal Prosecutions.* Dallas, TX: Southern Methodist University Press, 1959.

———, ed. *The Rule of Law.* Dallas, TX: Southern Methodist University Press, 1961.

Hart, Henry M., Jr. and Wechsler, Herbert. *The Federal Courts and the Federal System.* Brooklyn, NY: The Foundation Press, 1953.

Hirsh, Harry N. *The Enigma of Felix Frankfurter.* New York: Basic Books, 1981.

Hockett, Jeffrey D. *New Deal Justice: The Constitutional Jurisprudence of Hugo L. Black, Felix Frankfurter, and Robert H. Jackson.* Lanham, MD: Rowman & Littlefield, 1996.

Hofstadter, Samuel H. *The Fifth Amendment and the Immunity Act of 1954.* New York: Fund for the Republic, n.d.

Hook, Sidney. *Common Sense and the Fifth Amendment.* New York: Criterion Books, 1957.

Horn, Robert A. *Groups and the Constitution.* Stanford, CA: Stanford University Press, 1956.

Horwitz, Morton J. *The Warren Court and the Pursuit of Justice: A Critical Issue.* New York: Hill and Wang, 1998.

Jackson, Robert H. *The Struggle for Judicial Supremacy.* New York: Knopf, 1941.

———. *The Supreme Court in the American System of Government.* Cambridge, MA: Harvard University Press, 1955.

Jacobs, Clyde E. *Justice Frankfurter and Civil Liberties.* Berkeley and Los Angeles: University of California Press, 1961.

Javits, Jacob K. *Discrimination—U.S.A.* New York: Harcourt, Brace & Co., 1960.

Kauper, Paul G. *Frontiers of Constitutional Liberty.* Ann Arbor: University of Michigan Law School, 1956.

Kelly, Alfred H., ed. *Foundations of Freedom in the American Constitution.* New York: Harper & Bros., 1956.

Kelly, Alfred H. and Harbison, Winfred A. *The American Constitution.* New York: W. W. Norton & Co., 1955.

Kennan, George F. *Realities of American Foreign Policy.* Princeton, NJ: Princeton University Press, 1954.

Kilpatrick, James J. *The Smut Peddler.* New York: Doubleday & Co., 1960.

Konvitz, Milton R. *The Alien and the Asiatic in American Law.* Ithaca, NY: Cornell University Press, 1946.

———. *Civil Rights in Immigration.* Ithaca, NY: Cornell University Press, 1953.

———. *Fundamental Liberties of a Free People.* Ithaca, NY: Cornell University Press, 1957.

Konvitz, Milton R. and Leskes, Theodore. *A Century of Civil Rights*. New York: Columbia University Press, 1961.

Kluger, Richard. *Simple Justice*. New York: Knopf, 1976.

Kurland, Philip B. *Mr. Justice Frankfurter and the Constitution*. Chicago: University of Chicago Press, 1971.

————, ed. *1960 The Supreme Court Review*. Chicago: Chicago University Press, 1960.

Lerner, Max. *Nine Scorpions in a Bottle*. Richard Cummings, ed. New York: Arcade Publishing, 1994.

Levy, Leonard W. *Legacy of Suppression*. Cambridge, MA: Belknap Press of Harvard University Press, 1960.

————. *The Supreme Court Under Earl Warren*. New York: Quadrangle Books, 1972.

Lewis, Anthony. *Gideon's Trumpet*. New York: Vintage, 1964.

Lewis, Frederick P. *Context of Judicial Activism: The Endurance of the Warren Court Legacy in a Conservative Age*. Lanham, MD: Rowman & Littlefield, 1999.

Longaker, Richard P. *The Presidency and Individual Liberties*. Ithaca, NY: Cornell University Press, 1961.

Lowenstein, Edith, ed. *The Alien and the Immigration Law*. New York: Oceana Publications, 1956.

McCloskey, Robert G., ed. *The American Supreme Court*. Chicago: University of Chicago Press, 1960.

————. *Essays in Constitutional Law*. New York: Knopf, 1957.

Marion, David E. *The Jurisprudence of Justice William J. Brennan, Jr.: The Law and Politics of "Libertarian Dignity."* Lanham, MD: Rowman & Littlefield, 1997.

Mason, Alpheus T. *Harlan Fiske Stone: Pillar of the Law*. New York: Viking Press, 1956.

————. *The Supreme Court from Taft to Warren*. Baton Rouge: Louisiana State University Press, 1958.

———— and Beaney, William M. *The Supreme Court in a Free Society*. Englewood Cliffs, NJ: Prentice-Hall, 1959.

———— and Leach, Richard H. *In Quest of Freedom*. Englewood Cliffs. NJ: Prentice-Hall, 1957.

Mendelson, Wallace. *The Constitution and the Supreme Court*. New York: Dodd, Mead & Co., 1959.

————. *Justices Black and Frankfurter: Conflict in the Court*. Chicago: University of Chicago Press, 1961.

Michelman, Frank I. *Brennan and Democracy*. Princeton, NJ: Princeton University Press, 1999.

Miller, Arthur S. *Racial Discrimination and Private Education*. Chapel Hill: University of North Carolina Press, 1957.

Miller, John C. *Crisis in Freedom: The Alien and Sedition Acts*. Boston: Little, Brown, 1951.

Miller, Richard L. *Whittaker: Struggles of a Supreme Court Justice*. Westport, CT: Greenwood Press, 2001.

Murphy, Walter F. and Pritchett, C. Herman, eds. *Courts, Judges, and Politics*. New York: Random House, 1961.

Murray, Robert K. *Red Scare: A Study in National Hysteria*, 1919–1920. Minneapolis: University of Minnesota Press, 1955.

Myrdal, Gunnar. *An American Dilemma*. New York: Harper & Bros., 1944.

Newman, Roger K. *Hugo Black: A Biography*. New York: Fordham University Press, 1994.

Nieman, Donald G. *Promises to Keep: African-Americans and the Constitutional Order, 1776 to the Present*. New York: Oxford University Press, 1991.

O'Brien, David M. *Storm Center: The Supreme Court in American Politics*. New York: W.W. Norton, 1996.

O'Brien, F. William. *Justice Reed and the First Amendment: The Religion Clause*. Washington, DC: Georgetown University Press, 1958.

Palmer, Jan. *The Vinson Court Era*. New York: AMS Press, 1990.

Patterson, James T. *Brown v. Board of Education: A Civil Rights Milestone and Its Troubled Legacy*. New York: Oxford University Press, 2001.

Peltason, Jack W. *Federal Courts in the Political Process*. Garden City, NY: Doubleday Short Studies in Political Science, 1955.

———. *Fifty-eight Lonely Men: Southern Federal Judges and School Desegregation*. New York: Harcourt, Brace, & World, 1961.

Pollack, Jack H. *Earl Warren: The Judge Who Changed America*. Englewood Cliffs, NJ: Prentice-Hall, 1979.

Powe, Lucas A., Jr. *The Warren Court and American Politics*. Cambridge, MA: Belknap Press, 2000.

Pritchett, C. Herman. *The American Constitution*. New York: McGraw-Hill Co., 1959.

———. *Civil Liberties and the Vinson Court*. Chicago: University of Chicago Press, 1954.

———. *Congress Versus the Supreme Court, 1957–1960*. Minneapolis: University of Minnesota Press, 1961.

———. *The Political Offender and the Warren Court*. Boston: Boston University Press, 1958.

———. *The Roosevelt Court: A Study in Judicial Politics and Values, 1937-1947*. New York: MacMillan Co., 1948.

Provine, Doris Marie. *Case Selection in the United States Supreme Court*. Chicago: University of Chicago Press, 1980.

Renstrom, Peter G. *The Stone Court: Justices, Rulings, and Legacy*. Santa Barbara, CA: ABC–CLIO, 2001.

Rodell, Fred. *Nine Men*. New York: Random House, 1955.

Rogge, O. John. *The First and the Fifth, With Some Excursions into Others*. New York: T. Nelson, 1960.

Rosenblum, Victor G. *Law as a Political Instrument*. Garden City, NY: Doubleday Short Studies in Political Science, 1955.

Rossum, Ralph A. and Tarr, G. Alan. *American Constitutional Law, Volume II, The Bill of Rights and Subsequent Amendments*. New York: St. Martin's/Worth, 1999.

Rudko, Frances H. *Truman's Court: A Study in Judicial Restraint*. Westport, CT: Greenwood Press, 1988.

Sabin, Arthur J. *In Calmer Times: The Supreme Court and Red Monday*. Philadelphia: University of Pennsylvania Press, 1999.

St. John-Stevas, Norman. *Obscenity and the Law*. London: Secker & Warburg, 1956.

Sayler, Richard H. and Boyer, Barry B., eds. *The Warren Court: A Critical Analysis*. New York: Chelsea House, 1969.

Schubert, Glendon A. *Constitutional Politics*. New York: Holt, Rhinehart & Winston, 1960.

―――, ed. *Dispassionate Justice: A Synthesis of the Judicial Opinions of Robert H. Jackson*. New York: Bobbs-Merrill, 1969.

―――. *The Presidency in the Courts*. Minneapolis: University of Minnesota Press, 1957.

―――. *The Public Interest*. Glencoe, IL: The Free Press, 1961.

―――. *Quantitative Analysis of Judicial Behavior*. Glencoe, IL: The Free Press and the Michigan State University Bureau of Social and Political Research, 1959.

Schwartz, Bernard. *A Book of Legal Lists*. New York: Oxford University Press, 1997.

―――. *Super Chief: Earl Warren and His Supreme Court: A Judicial Biography*. New York: New York University Press, 1983.

―――. *The Supreme Court: Constitutional Revolution in Retrospect*. New York: Ronald Press, 1957.

―――, ed. *The Warren Court: A Retrospective*. New York: Oxford University Press, 1996.

Schwartz, Bernard and Rosenkranz, E. Joshua, eds. *Reason and Passion: Justice Brennan's Enduring Influence*. New York: W.W. Norton, 1997.

Simon, James F. *The Antagonists: Hugo Black, Felix Frankfurter and Civil Liberties in Modern America*. New York: Simon & Schuster, 1989.

―――. *Independent Journey: The Life of William O. Douglas*. New York: Harper and Row, 1980.

Smith, Huston., ed. *The Search for America*. Englewood Cliffs, NJ: Prentice-Hall, 1959.

Smith, James M. *Freedom's Fetters*. Ithaca, NY: Cornell University Press, 1956.

Smith, J. Malcom and Cotter, Cornelius P. *Powers of the President during Crisis*. Washington, DC: Public Affairs Press, 1960.

Special Committee of the Association of the Bar of the City of New York and the National Legal Aid and Defender Association. *Equal Justice for the Accused*. Garden City, NY: Doubleday & Co., 1959.

Spicer, George W. *The Supreme Court and Fundamental Freedoms*. New York: Appleton-Century-Crofts, 1959.

Steamer, Robert J. *Chief Justice: Leadership and the Supreme Court*. Columbia: University of South Carolina Press, 1986.

Stone, Irving. *Earl Warren, A Great American Story*. New York: Prentice-Hall, 1948.

Stone, Julius. *The Province and Function of Law*. Cambridge, MA: Harvard University Press, 1950.

Stouffer, Samuel A. *Communism, Conformity, and Civil Liberties: A Cross-Section of the Nation Speaks Its Mind*. New York: Doubleday & Co., 1955.

Sunstein, Cass R. *One Case at a Time: Judicial Minimalism on the Supreme Court*. Cambridge, MA: Harvard University Press, 1999.

Sutherland, Arthur E., ed. *Government Under Law*. Cambridge, MA: Harvard University Press, 1956.

Swisher, Carl B. *The Supreme Court in Its Modern Role*. New York: New York University Press, 1958.

Taylor, Albion G. *Labor and the Supreme Court*. Ann Arbor, MI: Braun-Brumfield, 1961.

Taylor, Telford. *Grand Inquest: The Story of Congressional Investigations*. New York: Simon & Schuster, 1955.

Thomas, Helen S. *Felix Frankfurter, Scholar on the Bench*. Baltimore: Johns Hopkins University Press, 1961.

Tompkins, Dorothy (Campbell). *The Supreme Court of the United States: A Bibliography*. Berkeley: Bureau of Public Administration, University of California, 1959.

Tushnet, Mark, ed. *The Warren Court in Historical and Political Perspective*. Charlottesville: University Press of Virginia, 1993.

Urofsky, Melvin I., ed. *Division and Discord: The Supreme Court under Stone and Vinson, 1941–1953*. Columbia: University of South Carolina Press, 1997.

————. *The Douglas Letters*. Bethesda, MD: Adler & Adler, 1987.

————. *Felix Frankfurter: Judicial Restraint and Individual Liberties*. Boston: Twayne, 1991.

————, ed. *The Supreme Court Justices: A Biographical Dictionary*. New York: Garland, 1994.

————. *The Warren Court; Justices: Rulings, and Legacy*. Santa Barbara, CA: ABC–CLIO, 2001.

Vose, Clement E. *Caucasians: Only: the Supreme Court, the NAACP, and the Restrictive Covenant Cases*. Berkeley: University of California Press, 1959.

Warren, Earl. *Memoirs of Earl Warren*. New York: Doubleday, 1977.

Weaver, John D. *Warren: The Man, the Court, the Era*. Boston: Little, Brown, 1967.

Westin, Alan F., ed. *The Supreme Court: Views from Inside*. New York: W.W. Norton & Co., 1961.

White, G. Edward. *Earl Warren, A Public Life*. New York: Oxford University Press, 1982.

Wilcox, Thomas. *States' Rights vs. the Supreme Court*. Boston: Forum Publishing Co., 1960.

Williams, Charlotte. *Hugo L. Black: A Study in Judicial Process*. Baltimore: Johns Hopkins University Press, 1961.

Williams, Glanville. *The Proof of Guilt*. London: Stevens & Sons, 1955.

Wright, Benjamin F. *The Growth of American Constitutional Law*. Boston: Houghton Mifflin, 1942.

Yarbrough, Tinsley E. *John Marshall Harlan: Great Dissenter of the Warren Court*. New York: Oxford University Press, 1992.

————. *Mr. Justice Black and His Critics*. Durham, NC: Duke University Press, 1988.

Ziegler, Benjamin M. *Desegregation and the Supreme Court*. Boston: DC Heath, 1958.

ARTICLES AND PERIODICALS

Abzug, Bella S. "Legislative Proposals in the South Against Integration," *Lawyers Guild Review* 16 (1956): 45.

Alnutt, Robert F. and Missinghoff, Gerald J. "Housing and Health Inspection: A Survey and Suggestions in Light of Recent Case Law," *George Washington Law Review* 28 (1960): 421.

Alpert, Leo M. "Judicial Censorship of Obscene Literature," *Harvard Law Review* 52 (1937): 40.

Auerbach, Carl A. "Communist Control Act of 1954: A Proposed Legal-Political Theory of Free Speech," *University of Chicago Law Review* 23 (1956): 173.

Bachrach, Peter. "The Supreme Court, Civil Liberties, and the Balance of Interest Doctrine," *Western Political Quarterly* 15 (1961): 391.

Baker, Gordon E. and Teitelbaum, Bernard. "An End to Cross-filing." *National Civic Review* 48 (1959): 286.

Ball, Fred S. "The Tyranny of Ideas," *Alabama Lawyer* 20 (1959): 418.

Ball, William B. "Judicial Review in Deportation and Exclusion Cases," *Interpreter Releases*, 10 June 1957.

Ballantine, Arthur A. "John M. Harlan for the Supreme Court," *Iowa Law Review* 40 (1955): 391.

Barnett, Helaine M. and Levine, Kenneth. "Mr. Justice Stewart," *New York University Law Review* 40 (1965): 526.

Barrett, Edward L., Jr. "Personal Rights, Property Rights, and the Fourth Amendment," *1960 The Supreme Court Review.*

Berman, Daniel M. "Constitutional Issues and the Warren Court," *American Political Science Review* 53 (1959): 500.

———. "Hugo Black and the Negro," *American University Law Review* 10 (1961): 35.

———. "Hugo Black: The Early Years," *Catholic University Law Review* 8 (1959): 103.

———. "Mr. Justice Black: The Record after Twenty Years," *Missouri Law Review* 25 (1960): 155.

———. "Mr. Justice Stewart: A Preliminary Appraisal," *University of Cincinnati Law Review* 28 (1959): 401.

———. "Mr. Justice Whittaker: A Preliminary Appraisal." *Missouri Law Review* 24 (1959): 1.

Beth, Loren P. "Judge into Justice: Should Supreme Court Appointees Have Judicial Experience?" *South Atlantic Quarterly* 58 (1959): 521.

———. "The Supreme Court and the Future of Judicial Review," *Political Science Quarterly* 76 (1961): 11, 18.

Bickel, Alexander M. "Original Understanding and the Segregation Decision," *Harvard Law Review* 69 (1955): 1.

———. "The Supreme Court 1960 Term, Foreword: The Passive Virtues," *Harvard Law Review* 75 (1961): 40.

——— and Wellington, Harry H. "Legislative Purpose and the Judicial Process: The Lincoln Mills Case," *Harvard Law Review* 71 (1957): 1.

Bigel, Alan I. "The First Amendment and National Security: The Court Responds to Governmental Harassment of Alleged Communist Sympathizers," *Ohio Northern University Law Review* 19 (1993): 885.

Black, Charles L., Jr. "Lawfulness of the Segregation Decisions," *Yale Law Journal* 69 (1960): 421.

Black, Hugo L. "The Bill of Rights," *New York University Law Review* 35 (1960): 865.

Boudin, Leonard B. "Involuntary Loss of American Nationality," *Harvard Law Review* 73 (1960): 1510.

Braden, George D. "Mr. Justice Minton and the Truman Bloc," *Indiana Law Journal* 26 (1951): 153.

Bradley, Edwin J. and Hogan, James E. "Wiretapping: From Nardone to Benati and Rathbun," *Georgetown Law Journal* 46 (1958): 418.

Brandwen, Maxwell. "Reflections on *Ullmann v. United States*," *Columbia Law Review* 58 (1957): 500.

Brennan, William J., Jr. "The Bill of Rights and the States," *New York University Law Review* 36 (1961): 761.

———. "Chief Justice Warren," *Harvard Law Review* 88 (1974): 5.

———. "State Court Decisions and the Supreme Court," *Florida Bar Journal* 34 (1960): 269.

Carl, B. M. "Problema de la Segregacion Racial en los Estados Unidos," *Revista de Derecho* (Chile) 26 (1958): 469.

Chase, Harold W. "Improving Congressional Investigations: A No Progress Report," *Temple Law Quarterly* 30 (1957): 126.

———. "The Warren Court and Congress," *Minnesota Law Review* 44 (1960): 595.

Christensen, Barbara B. "Mr. Justice Whittaker: The Man on the Right," *Santa Clara Law Review* 19 (1979): 1039.

Clark, Elias. "Charitable Trusts, the Fourteenth Amendment and the Will of Stephen Girard," *Yale Law Journal* 66 (1959): 979.

Cohn, Edmond L. "Federal Constitutional Limitations on the Use of Coerced Confessions in the State Courts," *Journal of Criminal Law* 50 (1959): 265.

Cook, Eugene and Potter, William I. "School Segregation Cases: Opposing the Opinion of the Supreme Court," *American Bar Association Journal* 42 (1956): 313.

Cooke, Alistair. "Congress Stunned by Supreme Court's Rulings," *Manchester Guardian* 76 (21 June 1957): 7.

Corwin, Edward S. "Bowing Out 'Clear and Present Danger'," *Notre Dame Lawyer* 27 (1952): 329.

Cotter, Cornelius P. and Smith, J. Malcom. "Freedom and Authority in the Amphibial State," *Midwest Journal of Political Science* 1 (1957): 40.

Cranton, Roger C. "Supreme Court and State Power to Deal with Subversion and Loyalty," *Minnesota Law Review* 43 (1959): 1025.

Crosskey, William W. "Charles Fairman, 'Legislative History' and the Constitutional Limitations on State Authority," *University of Chicago Law Review* 22 (1954): 1.

Daykin, Walter L. "The Operation of the Taft–Hartley Act's Non-Communist Provisions," *Iowa Law Review* 36 (1957): 607.

DeGrazia, Edward. "Obscenity and the Mail: A Study of Administrative Restraint," *Law and Contemporary Problems* 20 (1955): 531.

Dilliard, Irving. "Hugo Black and the Importance of Freedom," *American University Law Review* 10 (1961): 7.

Dimock, Edward J. "The Public Defender: A Step Towards a Police State," *American Bar Association Journal* 42 (1956): 219.

Douglas, William O. "The Black Silence of Fear," *New York Times Magazine* 40 (13 January 1952): 38.

———. "On Misconception of the Judicial Function and Responsibility of the Bar," *Columbia Law Review* 59 (1959): 227.

——. "The Supreme Court and Its Case Load," *Cornell Law Quarterly* 45 (1960): 401.

Duke, Robert D. and Vogel, Howard S. "The Constitution and the Standing Army: Another Problem of Court-Martial Jurisdiction," *Vanderbilt Law Review* 13 (1960): 435.

Durr, Clifford J. "Hugo Black, Southerner," *American University Law Review* 10 (1961): 27.

Dutton, C. B. "Mr. Justice Tom Clark," *Indiana Law Journal* 26 (1951): 169.

Elliott, Sheldon D. "Court-Curbing Proposals in Congress," *Notre Dame Lawyer* 33 (1958): 597.

Everett, Robinson O. "Military Jurisdiction Over Civilians," *Duke Law Journal* 9 (1960): 366.

Fairman, Charles. "Attack on the Segregation Cases," *Harvard Law Review* 70 (1956): 83.

——. "Does the Fourteenth Amendment Incorporate the Bill of Rights? The Original Understanding," *Stanford Law Review* 2 (1949): 5.

Farmer, Guy and Williamson, Charles G., Jr. "Picketing and the Injunctive Power of State Courts—From Thornhill to Vogt," *University of Detroit Law Journal* 35 (1958): 431.

Fellman, David. "Constitutional Law in 1955–1960," *American Political Science Review* 49–54 (March 1955–1961) (annual review of the work of the Supreme Court).

Fisher, Franklin M. "The Mathematical Analysis of Supreme Court Decisions: The Use and Abuse of Quantitative Methods," *American Political Science Review* 52 (1958): 321.

Fisher, Walter F. "Double Jeopardy, Two Sovereignties and the Intruding Constitution," *University of Chicago Law Review* 28 (1961): 591.

Forkosch, Morris D. "Analysis and Re-evaluation of Picketing in Labor Relations," *Fordham Law Review* 26 (1957): 391.

Fortas, Abe. "Chief Justice Warren: The Enigma of Leadership," *Yale Law Journal* 84 (1975): 405.

Frank, John P. "Book Review," *Iowa Law Review* 34 (1948): 144.

——. "Court and Constitution: The Passive Period," *Vanderbilt Law Review* 4 (1951): 400.

——. "Fred Vinson and the Chief-Justiceship," *University of Chicago Law Review* 21 (1954): 212.

——. "The Historic Role of the Supreme Court," *Kentucky Law Journal* 48 (1959): 26.

—— and Munro, Robert F. "The Original Understanding of 'Equal Protection of the Laws'," *Columbia Law Review* 50 (1950): 131.

Frankfurter, Felix. "Some Observations on the Nature of the Judicial Process of Supreme Court Litigation," *Proceedings, American Philosophical Society* 98 (1954): 233.

——. "The Supreme Court in the Mirror of Justices," *University of Pennsylvania Law Review* 105 (1957): 785.

Freund, Paul A. "Mr. Justice Frankfurter," *University of Chicago Law Review* 26 (1959): 205.

——. "Storm Over the American Supreme Court," *Modern Law Review* 21 (1958): 345.

Friedelbaum, Stanley H. "The Warren Court and American Federalism—A Preliminary Appraisal," *University of Chicago Law Review* 28 (1960): 53.

Friedman, Edward L. "Mr. Justice Harlan," *Notre Dame Lawyer* 30 (1955): 349.

Funston, Richard. "The Supreme Court and Critical Elections," *American Political Science Review* 69 (1975): 810.

Galloway, Russell W., Jr. "The Early Years of the Warren Court: Emergence of Judicial Liberalism (1953–1957)," *Santa Clara Law Review* 18 (1978): 609.

——. "The Second Period of the Warren Court: The Liberal Trend Abates (1957–1961)," *Santa Clara Law Review* 19 (1979): 947.

——. "The Supreme Court Since 1937," *Santa Clara Law Review* 24 (1984): 565.

——. "The Warren Court: The Third Period of Liberal Dominance (1962–1969)," *Santa Clara Law Review* 20 (1980): 773.

Garfinkel, Herbert, "Social Science Evidence and the School Segregation Cases," *Journal of Politics* 21 (1959): 37.

George, B. J., Jr. "The Potent, the Omnipresent Teacher: The Supreme Court and Wiretapping," *Virginia Law Review* 47 (1961): 751.

Goldstein, Abraham S. "The State and the Accused: Balance of Advantage in Criminal Procedure," *Yale Law Journal* 69 (1960): 1149.

Goostree, Robert E. "Denationalization Cases of 1958," *American University Law Review* 8 (1959): 87.

Gordon, Murray A. "Justice Hugo Black—First Amendment Fundamentalist," *Lawyers Guild Review* 20 (1960): 1.

Gorfinkel, John A. and Mack, Julian W. "*Dennis v. United States* and the Clear and Present Danger Rule," *California Law Review* 39 (1951): 475.

Grant, J.A.C. "Federalism and Self-Incrimination," *UCLA Law Review* 4 (1957): 549.

——. "Tarnished Silver Platter: Federalism and Admissibility of Illegally Seized Evidence," *UCLA Law Review* 8 (1961): 1.

Griswold, Erwin W. "The Right to Be Let Alone," *Northwestern Law Review* 55 (1960): 216.

Groves, H. E. "Problems of Integration Following the School Desegregation Cases in the United States," *Journal of the Indian Law Institute* 2 (1960): 507.

Hall, Jerome. "Police and Law in a Democratic Society," *Indiana Law Journal* 28 (1953): 133.

Hamilton, Walton. "Book Review," *Yale Law Journal* 56 (1947): 1458.

Handler, Emmerlich. "Fourth Amendment, Federalism, and Mr. Justice Frankfurter," *Syracuse Law Review* 28 (1957): 166.

Harlan, John M. "Some Aspects of the Judicial Process," *Australian Law Journal* 33 (1959): 108.

Harper, Fowler V. and Rosenthal, Alan S. "The Court, the Bar, and Certiorari," *University of Pennsylvania Law Review* 108 (1959): 1160.

——. "What the Supreme Court Did Not Do in the 1949 Term—An Appraisal of Certiorari," *University of Pennsylvania Law Review* 99 (1950): 293.

Harris, Robert J. "The Constitution, Education, and Segregation." *Temple Law Quarterly* 29 (1956): 409.

Hart, H. M. "The Supreme Court 1958 Term, Foreword: The Time Chart of the Justices," *Harvard Law Review* 73 (1959): 84.

Henson, Ray D. "Study in Style: Mr. Justice Frankfurter," *Villanova Law Review* 26 (1961): 377.

Heyman, Ira M. "The Chief Justice, Racial Segregation, and the Friendly Critics," *California Law Review* 49 (1961): l04.

Hogan, James E. and Snee, Joseph M. "The McNabb–Mallory Rule: Its Rise, Rationale and Rescue," *Georgetown Law Journal* 47 (1958): 1.

Holloway, Harry. "The Negro and the Vote: The Case of Texas," *Journal of Politics* 23 (1961): 526.

Horn, Robert A. "Book Review," *University of Chicago Law Review* 18 (1951): 683.

———. "Protection of Internal Security," *Public Administration Review* 16 (1956): 40.

———. "A Quantitative Study of Judicial Review," *Political Research: Organization and Design* 1 (1957): 27.

———. "The Warren Court and the Discretionary Power of the Executive," *Minnesota Law Review* 44 (1960): 639.

Horsky, Charles A. "Law Day: Some Reflections on Current Proposals to Curtail the Supreme Court," *Minnesota Law Review* 42 (1958): 1105.

Hotes, William J. and Hotes, Catherine H. "Freedom of Association," *Cleveland-Marshall Law Review* 10 (1961) 104.

Hunt, Alan R. "State Control of Sedition: The Smith Act as the Supreme Law of the Land," *Minnesota Law Review* 41 (1957): 287.

Inbau, Fred E. "Restrictions in the Law of Interrogation and Confessions," *Northwestern Law Review* 52 (1957): 77.

Irish, Marian D. "Mr. Justice Douglas and Judicial Restraint," *University of Florida Law Review* 6 (1953): 537.

Isaacson, William J. "Organizational Picketing: What Is the Law?—Ought the Law to Be Changed?" *Buffalo Law Review* 8 (1959): 345.

Jenkins, Thomas M. "Judicial Discretion in Desegregation: The Hawkins Case," *Howard Law Journal* 4 (1958): 193.

"Judicial Restraint," *Economist* 189 (11 October 1958): 142.

"Justice Harold Hitz Burton, United States Supreme Court," *Kappa Beta Pi Quarterly* 40 (1956): 35.

Kadish, Sanford H. "Methodology and Criteria in Due Process Adjudication—A Survey and Criticism," *Yale Law Journal* 46 (1957): 319.

Kagel, Sam and Smith, Virginia B. "Chief Justice Warren and Labor Law," *California Law Review* 49 (1961): 126.

Kalven, Harry, Jr. "Book Review," *University of Chicago Law Review* 24 (1957): 769.

———. "Mr. Alexander Meiklejohn and the Barenblatt Opinion," *University of Chicago Law Review* 27 (1960): 3l5.

Kamisar, Yale. "*Wolf* and *Lustig* Ten Years Later: Illegal Evidence in State and Federal Courts," *Minnesota Law Review* 43 (1959): 1083.

Kelly, Alfred H. "Fourteenth Amendment Reconsidered: The Segregation Question," *Michigan Law Review* 54 (1956): 1049.

Kennan, George F. "Where Do You Stand?" *New York Times Magazine* (27 May 1951): 53.

Kort, Fred. "Predicting Supreme Court Decisions Mathematically: A Quantitative Analysis of the Right to Counsel Cases," *American Political Science Review* 51 (1957): 1.

Kramnowicki, Jan Z. "Confrontation by Witnesses in Government Employee Security Proceedings," *Notre Dame Lawyer* 30 (1958): 180.

Kroner, Jack. "Self-Incrimination: The External Reach of the Privilege," *Columbia Law Review* 60 (1960): 816.

Kurland, Philip B. "On Misunderstanding the Supreme Court," *University of Chicago Law School Record* 9 (1960): 13.

———. "The Supreme Court and Its Judicial Critics," *Utah Law Review* 6 (1959): 457.

———. "The Supreme Court and Its Literate Critics," *Yale Review* 47 (1958): 596.

———. "The Supreme Court and the Attrition of State Power," *Stanford Law Review* 10 (1958): 274.

Latham, Earl. "Perspectives on the Warren Court," *Nation* 186 (18 January 1958): 46.

Lewis, Anthony. "High Drama in the High Court," *New York Times Magazine* (26 October 1958): 10.

———. "Minor Cases Irk 2 on High Court," *New York Times* (20 October 1959): 28.

———. "The Supreme Court and Its Critics," *Minnesota Law Review* 45 (1961): 305.

———. "Top Court Hears a Familiar Issue," *New York Times* (8 November 1960): 27.

Lockhart, William B. and McClure, Robert C. "Censorship or Obscenity: The Developing Constitutional Standards," *Minnesota Law Review* 45 (1960): 5.

Losos, Joseph O. "Relativism and the Legal Process," *Southwestern Social Science Quarterly* 42 (1961): 8.

———. "The Supreme Court and Its Critics: Is the Court Moving Left?" *Review of Politics* 21 (1959): 495.

Maloney, Walter H., Jr. "Involuntary Loss of American Citizenship," *St. Louis University Law Review* 3 (1956): 168.

Margolin, Ephriam. "Right to Counsel and Compulsion to Testify," *Howard Law Journal* 7 (1961): 36.

Maslow, Will. "Recasting Our Deportation Law: Proposals for Reform," *Columbia Law Review* 56 (1956): 309.

Mavrinac, Albert A. "From *Lochner* to *Brown vs. Topeka*: The Court and Conflicting Concepts of Political Process," *American Political Science Review* 52 (1958): 641.

Mayers, Daniel K. and Yarbrough, Fletcher L. "*Bis Vexari*, New Trials and Successive Prosecutions," *Harvard Law Review* 74 (1960): 1.

McAulay, Lloyd and Brewster, Carroll. "In re Application of the Association for the Preservation of Freedom of Choice," *Howard Law Journal* 6 (1960): 169.

McCloskey, Robert G. "Deeds without Doctrines: Civil Rights in the 1960 Term of the Supreme Court," *American Political Science Review* 56 (1962): 71.

———. "The Supreme Court Finds a Role: Civil Liberties in the 1955 Term," *Virginia Law Review* 42 (1956): 735.

———. "Tools, Stumbling Blocks, and Stepping Stones: Civil Liberties in the 1957 Term of the Supreme Court," *Virginia Law Review* 44 (1958): 1029.

———. "Useful Toil or the Paths of Glory? Civil Liberties in the 1956 Term of the Supreme Court," *Virginia Law Review* 43 (1957): 803.

McKay, Robert B. "The Supreme Court and Its Lawyer Critics," *Fordham Law Review* 28 (1960): 615.

McQuade, Francis P. and Kardos, Alexander T. "Mr. Justice Brennan and His Legal Philosophy," *Notre Dame Lawyer* 33 (1958): 321.

McTernan, John T. "Schware, Konigsberg, and Independence of the Bar: The Return to Reason," *Lawyers Guild Review* 17 (1957): 149.

McWhinney, Edward. "The Great Debate: Activism, and Self-Restraint and Current Dilemmas in Judicial Policy-Making," *New York University Law Review* 33 (1958): 775.

Meiklejohn, Alexander. "The Balancing of Self-Preservation Against Political Freedom," *California Law Review* 49 (1961): 4.

———. "The Barenblatt Opinion," *University of Chicago Law Review* 27 (1960): 329.

Mendelson, Wallace. "Clandestine Speech and the First Amendment," *Michigan Law Review* 51 (1953): 553.

———. "Clear and Present Danger—From Schenck to Dennis," *Columbia Law Review* 52 (1952): 313.

———. "Mr. Justice Black and the Rule of Law," *Midwest Journal of Political Science* 4 (1960): 250.

———. "Mr. Justice Frankfurter and the Process of Judicial Review," *University of Pennsylvania Law Review* 103 (1954): 295.

———. "Mr. Justice Frankfurter—Law and Choice," *Vanderbilt Law Review* 10 (1957): 333.

Murphy, Walter F. "Desegregation in Public Education—A Generation of Future Litigation," *Maryland Law Review* 15 (1955): 221.

———. "Mr. Justice Jackson, Free Speech, and the Judicial Function," *Vanderbilt Law Review* 12 (1959): 1019.

Nathanson, Nathaniel L. "The Communists Trial and the Clear and Present Danger Test," *Harvard Law Review* 63 (1950): 1167.

Newland, Chester A. "Innovation in Judicial Technique," *Southwestern Social Science Quarterly* 42 (1961): 22.

———. "Legal Periodicals and the U.S. Supreme Court," *Midwest Journal of Politics* 3 (1959): 58.

Newman, Lawrence. "Double Jeopardy and the Problem of Successive Prosecutions: A Suggested Solution," *Southern California Law Review* 34 (1961): 252.

Note. "The Constitutional Right to Anonymity: Free Speech, Disclosure and the Devil," *Yale Law Journal* 70 (1961): 1084.

Note. "Constitutional Shadows and Security Clearances—The Right to Confrontation," *Georgetown Law Journal* 48 (1960): 576.

Note. "Entertainment: Public Pressures and the Law," *Harvard Law Review* 71 (1957): 326.

Note. "Ex Post Facto Clause and Deportations," *Wyoming Law Journal* 11 (1956): 32.

Note. "Extralegal Censorship of Literature," *New York University Law Review* 33 (1958): 989.

Note. "The Jencks Legislation: Problem in Prospect," *Yale Law Journal* 67 (1958): 674.

Note. "Punishment: Its Meaning in Relation to Separation of Power and Substantive Constitutional Restrictions and Its Use in the *Lovett, Trop, Perez,* and *Speiser* Cases," *Indiana Law Journal* 34 (1959): 231.

Note. "Rights of Aliens in Deportation Proceedings," *Indiana Law Journal* 31 (1956): 218.

Note. "Rights of Communist Aliens Subject to Deportation," *Notre Dame Lawyer* 30 (1955): 438.

O'Brian, John Lord. "New Encroachments on Individual Freedom," *Harvard Law Review* 66 (1952): 1.

O'Brien, William S. J. "Mr. Justice Reed and Democratic Pluralism," *Georgetown Law Journal* 45 (1957): 364.

Osborne, John. "One Supreme Court," *Life* 44 (16 June 1958): 92.

Paschal, J. Francis. "Mr. Justice Stewart on the Court of Appeals," *Duke Law Journal* 8 (1959): 325.

Paul, Julius. "The Supreme Court: Mirror of the American Conscience," *American Journal of Economics and Sociology* 19 (1959): 1.

Pollack, Louis E. "Mr. Justice Frankfurter: Judgment and the Fourteenth Amendment," *Yale Law Journal* 67 (1957): 304.

―――. "Racial Discrimination and Judicial Integrity: A Reply to Professor Wechsler," *University of Pennsylvania Law Review* 108 (1959): 1.

―――. "The Supreme Court Under Fire," *Journal of Public Law* 6 (1957): 428.

Pollit, Daniel H. "Pleading the Fifth Amendment Before a Congressional Committee: A Study and Explanation," *Notre Dame Lawyer* 32 (1956): 43.

Pound, Roscoe. "The Supreme Court and Responsible Government: 1864–1930," *Nebraska Law Review* 40 (1960): 16.

―――. "A Survey of Social Interests," *Harvard Law Review* 57 (1943): 1.

Prickett, Morgan D. "Stanley Forman Reed: Perspectives on a Judicial Epitaph," *Hastings Constitutional Law Quarterly* 8 (1981): 343.

Pritchett, C. Herman, "Divisions of Opinion among Justices of the U.S. Supreme Court, 1939–1941," *American Political Science Review* 35 (1941): 890.

―――. "The Supreme Court Today: Constitutional Interpretation and Judicial Self-Restraint," *South Dakota Law Review* 2 (1958): 51.

"Racial Desegregation and Integration," *The Annals of the American Academy of Political and Social Science* 304 (1956): 1.

Rankin, J. Lee. "The Supreme Court, the Depression, and the New Deal: 1930–1941," *Nebraska Law Review* 40 (1960): 35.

Rauh, Joseph L. "Nonconfrontation in Security Cases: The Greene Decision," *Virginia Law Review* 45 (1959): 1175.

―――. "The Truth About Congress and the Court," *Progressive* 22 (1958): 30.

Robison, Joseph B. "Protection of Associations from Compulsory Disclosure of Membership," *Columbia Law Review* 58 (1958): 614.

Roche, John P. "Education, Segregation, and the Supreme Court—A Political Analysis," *University of Pennsylvania Law Review* 99 (1951): 949.

―――. "Judicial Self-Restraint," *American Political Science Review* 49 (1955): 762.

———. "Political Science and Science Fiction," *American Political Science Review* 52 (1958): 1026.

Rodell, Fred. "Judicial Activists, Judicial Self-Deniers, Judicial Review and the First Amendment—Or, How to Hide the Melody of What You Mean Behind the Words of What You Say," *Georgetown Law Journal* 47 (1959): 483.

———."Justice Douglas: An Anniversary Fragment for a Friend," *University of Chicago Law Review* 26 (1958): 2.

Rogge, O. John. "Compelling the Testimony of Political Deviants," (pts. 1–2), *Michigan Law Review* 55 (1956–1957): 163, 375.

———. "State Power Over Sedition, Obscenity, and Picketing," *New York University Law Review* 34 (1959): 817.

Rostow, Eugene V. "Book Review," *Yale Law Journal* 56 (1947): 1472.

———. "The Court and Its Critics," *South Texas Law Journal* 4 (1959): 160.

———. "The Democratic Character of Judicial Review," *Harvard Law Review* 66 (1952): 193.

———. "The Supreme Court and the People's Will," *Notre Dame Lawyer* 33 (1958): 573.

Sacks, Albert M. "Mr. Justice Frankfurter," *University of Chicago Law Review* 101 (1959): 217.

St. Johnston, T. E. "The Legal Limitation of the Interrogation of Suspects and Prisoners in England and Wales," *Journal of Criminal Law* 39 (1948): 89.

Samoff, Bernard L. "Picketing and the First Amendment: 'Full Circle' and 'Formal Surrender'," *Labor Law Journal* 9 (1948): 889.

Schmidhauser, John. "The Justices of the Supreme Court: A Collective Portrait," *Midwest Journal of Political Science* 3 (1959): 1.

Schmidhauser, John and Gold, David. "Scaling Supreme Court Decisions in Relation to Social Background," *Political Research: Organization and Design* 1 (1958): 6.

Schubert, Glendon A. "The 1960 Term of the Supreme Court: A Psychological Analysis," *American Political Science Review* 56 (1962): 90.

———. "The Study of Judicial Decision-Making as an Aspect of Political Behavior," *American Political Science Review* 52 (1958): 1007.

Schwartz, Bernard. "Administrative Law," *New York University Law Review* 33 (1958): 154.

———. "Is Criticism of the High Court Valid?" *New York Times Magazine* (25 August 1957): 14.

———. "The Supreme Court—October 1957 Term," *Michigan Law Review* 57 (1958): 315.

———. "The Supreme Court—October 1958 Term," *Michigan Law Review* 58 (1959): 165.

———. "The Supreme Court—October 1959 Term," *Michigan Law Review* 59 (1960): 403.

———. "The Warren Court, An Opinion," *New York Times Magazine* (30 June 1957): 10.

Seymour, Whitney N. "Mr. Justice Harlan," *American Bar Association Journal* 41 (1955): 434.

Snyder, Eloise C. "Political Power and the Ability to Win Supreme Court Decisions," *Social Forces* 39 (1960): 36.

————. "The Supreme Court as a Small Group," *Social Forces* 36 (1958): 232.

————. "Uncertainty and the Supreme Court's Decisions," *American Journal of Sociology* 65 (1959): 241.

Spaeth, Harold J. "An Approach to the Study of Attitudinal Differences as an Aspect of Judicial Behavior," *Midwest Journal of Political Science* 5 (1961): 165.

Steamer, Robert J. "Statesmanship or Craftsmanship: Current Conflict Over the Supreme Court," *Western Political Quarterly* 11 (1958): 265.

Stein, Herman. "Enjoinable Organizational Picketing: A Phantasy on the Constitutional Doctrine of *International Teamsters v. Vogt*," *Temple Law Quarterly* 31 (1957): 12.

Stewart, Potter. "Justice Stewart Discusses Right of Counsel," *Legal Aid Brief Case* 19 (1960): 92.

Summers, Clyde W. "Frankfurter, Labor Law and the Justice's Function," *Yale Law Journal* 67 (1957): 266.

"The Supreme Court: October Term 195_," *Lawyers Guild Review* 15–20 (1955–1959) (Titles of this annual review of the work of the Supreme Court vary; in 1961 the journal became *Law in Transition*).

"The Supreme Court. 195_ Term," *Harvard Law Review* 68–74 (1953–1962) (annual review of the work of the Supreme Court appearing in the November issue).

Sutherland, Arthur E. "American Judiciary and Racial Desegregation," *Modern Law Review* 20 (1957): 201.

————. "The Constitution, the Civilian, and Military Justice," *St. John's Law Review* 35 (1961): 215.

Tanenhaus, Joseph. "Supreme Court Attitudes Toward Federal Administrative Agencies," *Journal of Politics* 22 (1960): 502.

Taper, Bernard. "Gomillion Versus Lightfoot," *New Yorker* (17 June 1961): 39.

Taragan, Donald G. "Justice Black—Inherent Coercion: An Analytical Study of the Standards for Determining the Voluntariness of a Confession," *American University Law Review* 10 (1961): 53.

Tothblatt, Henry B. and Eugene A. "Police Interrogation: The Right to Counsel and to Prompt Arraignment," *Brooklyn Law Review* 27 (1960): 24.

Ulmer, S. Sidney. "The Analysis of Behavior Patterns on the United States Supreme Court," *Journal of Politics* 13 (1960): 502.

————. "Judicial Review as Political Behavior: A Temporary Check on Congress," *Administrative Science Quarterly* 4 (1960): 426.

————. "Label Thinking and the Supreme Court: A Methodological Note," *Political Research: Organization and Design* 1 (1958): 25.

————. "Polar Classification of Supreme Court Justices," *South Carolina Law Quarterly* 12 (1960): 407.

————. "Supreme Court Behavior and Civil Rights," *Western Political Quarterly* 13 (1960): 288.

Van Alstyne, William W. "Discrimination in State University Housing Programs—Policy and Constitutional Considerations," *Stanford Law Review* 13 (1960): 60.

Vance, Anthony C. "Freedom of Association and Freedom of Choice in New York State," *Cornell Law Quarterly* 46 (1961): 290.

Vanderbilt, Arthur T. "The Essentials of a Sound Judicial System," *Northwestern University Law Review* 48 (1953): 11.

Vestal, Allan D. "Freedom of Movement," *Iowa Law Review* 41 (1955): 7.

Volz, Marlin M. "Charles Evans Whittaker—A Biographical Sketch," *Texas Law Review* 40 (1962): 742.

———. "Mr. Justice Whittaker," *Notre Dame Lawyer* 33 (1958): 159.

Wallace, Harry L. "Mr. Justice Minton—Hoosier Justice on the Supreme Court," (pts. 1–2), *Indiana Law Journal* 34 (l959): 145, 378.

Warren, Earl. "The Law and the Future," *Fortune* 52 (1955): 107.

Waters, D.W.M. "Rights of Entry in Administrative Officers," *University of Chicago Law Review* 27 (1959): 79.

Watson, Richard A. "Federalism v. Individual Rights: The Legal Squeeze of Self-Incrimination," *American Political Science Review* 54 (1960): 887.

Wechsler, Herbert. "Toward Neutral Principles of Constitutional Law," *Harvard Law Review* 73 (1959): 1.

Wells, Lloyd M. "Interposition and the Supreme Court," *Southwest Review* 41 (1956): 305.

Westin, Alan F. "The Supreme Court and Group Conflict: Thoughts on Seeing Burke Put Through the Mill," *American Political Science Review* 52 (1958): 665.

White, J. Patrick. "The Warren Court Under Attack," *Maryland Law Review* 19 (1959): 181.

Wilcox, Bertram F. and Bloustein, Edward J. "The Griffin Case—Poverty and the Fourteenth Amendment," *Cornell Law Quarterly* 43 (1957): 1.

Willis, William R., Jr. "*Toth v. Quarles*—For Better or Worse?" *Vanderbilt Law Review* 9 (1956): 534.

Wright, Benjamin F. "The Rights of Majorities and Minorities in the 1961 Term of the Supreme Court," *American Political Science Review* 57 (1963): 98.

Zeller, Belle. "The Federal Regulation of Lobbying Act," *American Political Science Review* 42 (1948): 329.

PUBLIC DOCUMENTS

U.S. *Annual Report of the Administrative Office of the United States Courts*, 1953–1962.

U.S. Commission on Civil Rights. *The National Conference and the Reports of the State Advisory Committees to the United States Commission on Civil Rights*. 1959.

U.S. *Congressional Record*. 1953–1962.

U.S. Department of Defense. *Uniform Code of Military Justice*. 1950.

U.S. House of Representatives. Committee on the Judiciary. Special Subcommittee to Study Decisions of the Supreme Court of the United States. *Report*. 85th Cong., 2d Sess., 1957.

U.S. Report of the President's Committee on Civil Rights. *To Secure These Rights*. Washington, DC: Government Printing Office, 1947.

U.S. Report of the President's Commission on Immigration and Naturalization. *Whom We Shall Welcome*. Washington, DC: Government Printing Office, 1952.

U.S. Reports, 1953–1962.

U.S. Senate. Committee on the Judiciary. *Hearings on Nomination of John Marshall Harlan*. 84th Cong., 1st Sess., 1955.

U.S. Senate. Committee on the Judiciary. *Hearings on Nomination of William J. Brennan, Jr*. 85th Cong., 1st Sess., 1957.

U.S. Senate. Committee on the Judiciary. *Hearings on Nomination of Charles E. Whittaker*. 85th Cong., 1st Sess., 1957.

U.S. Senate. Committee on the Judiciary. *Hearings on Nomination of Potter Stewart*. 86th Cong., 1st Sess., 1959.

U.S. Senate. Committee on the Judiciary. Investigation of Limitation of Supreme Court Jurisdiction and Strengthening of Anti-subversive Laws. *Report*. 85th Cong., 2nd Sess., 1958.

U.S. Senate. Committee on the Judiciary. Subcommittee to Investigate the Administration of the Internal Security Act and Other Internal Security Laws and the Limitations of Appellate Jurisdiction of the United States Supreme Court. *Report*. 85th Cong., 1st and 2d Sess., 1957–1958.

U.S. Senate. Committee on the Judiciary. Staff Report. *The Right to Travel*. 85th Cong. 2d Sess., 1958.

U.S. *Statutes at Large*.

REPORTS

American Civil Liberties Union. *Annual Report* (titles vary), New York: American Civil Liberties Union, 1953–1962.

American Jewish Congress. Commission on Law and Social Action. *The Civil Rights and Civil Liberties Decisions of the United States Supreme Court for the 1957–1958 Term*. New York: American Jewish Congress, 1958.

Conference of Chief Justices. Committee on Federal-State Relationships as Affected by Judicial Decisions. *Report 7* (1958).

Southern Regional Council. *Schools in the South: Answers for Action*. Atlanta. 1954.

UNPUBLISHED MATERIAL

Adsit, William A. "A History and Outline of the Supreme Court and Indigent Access to the Courts." Paper Delivered at the 2001 Annual Meeting of the Oklahoma Political Science Association. Stillwater, OK, 15–16 November 2001.

Bell, James R. "The Executive Office of the California Governor Under Earl Warren, 1943–1953." Unpublished Ph.D. dissertation, Department of Political Science, University of California, Berkeley, 1956.

Danelski, David J. and Danelski, Jeanne C. "Leadership in the Warren Court." Paper Delivered at the 1986 Annual Meeting of the American Political Science Association, Washington, D.C., 28–31 August 1986.

Harvey, Richard B. "The Political Approach of Earl Warren, Governor of California." Unpublished Ph.D. dissertation, Department of Political Science, University of California, Los Angeles, 1959.

Jans, Ralph T. "Negro Civil Rights and the Supreme Court 1865–1949." Unpublished Ph.D. dissertation, Department of Political Science, University of Chicago, 1950.

MacCallum, Gerald Cushing. "Judicial Review by the United States Supreme Court: An Analysis of Some Controversies in Accounts of a Judicial Activity." Unpublished Ph.D. dissertation, Department of Philosophy, University of California, Berkeley, 1961.

Neustadt, Robert Gardner. "The Commentators and the Supreme Court's Quest for Constitutionality." Unpublished Master's thesis, Department of Political Science, University of California, Berkeley, 1959.

Pedersen, Richard F. "Governor Earl Warren, as Seen Through His Speeches." Unpublished Master's thesis, Department of Political Science, Stanford University, 1947.

Snyder, Eloise C. "A Quantitative Analysis of Supreme Court Opinions from 1921 to 1935: A Study of the Responses of an Institution Engaged in Resolving Social Conflict." Unpublished Ph.D. dissertation, Department of Sociology, Pennsylvania State University, 1956.

Tester, Dwight Leland. "The Supreme Court and Obscene Literature: *Roth v. United States*." Unpublished Master's thesis, Department of Journalism, University of California, Berkeley, 1959.

Vestal, Theodore M. "Mr. Justice Jackson and Freedom of Association." Unpublished Master's thesis, Department of Political Science, Stanford University, 1958.

Case Index

General Index

About the Author

THEODORE M. VESTAL is Professor of Political Science at Oklahoma State University. Among Professor Vestal's earlier publications are *International Education* (Praeger, 1994) and *Ethiopia* (Praeger, 1999).